God's Country or Devil's

NUMBER FIFTY-FOUR
THE CORRIE HERRING HOOKS SERIES

God's Country
OR *Devil's Playground*

THE BEST NATURE WRITING
FROM THE BIG BEND OF TEXAS

EDITED BY BARNEY NELSON

UNIVERSITY OF TEXAS PRESS AUSTIN

First edition, 2002

Requests for permission to reproduce material from this work should be sent
to Permissions, University of Texas Press, Box 7819, Austin, TX 78713-7819.

Every effort has been made to trace any copyright owners.
The University of Texas Press will be happy to hear from any who proved
impossible to contact.

⊗ The paper used in this book meets the minimum requirements
of ANSI/NISO Z39.48-1992 (R1997) (Permanence of Paper).

Library of Congress Cataloging-in-Publication Data
God's country or devil's playground : an anthology of nature writing from
the Big Bend of Texas / edited by Barney Nelson.
        p.   cm. — (The Corrie Herring Hooks series; no. 54)
Includes bibliographical references (p.   ).
ISBN 0-292-75577-5 (cloth : alk. paper) — ISBN 0-292-75580-5 (pbk.: alk. paper)
1. Natural history—Texas—Big Bend Region.   2. Big Bend Region (Tex.)—Fiction.
I. Nelson, Barney, 1947–   II. Series.
QH105.T4 G64   2002
508.764'93—dc21

                                                           2002000354

TO CHERYLL GLOTFELTY

Contents

Acknowledgments

ANY BOOK IS ALWAYS AN ACCUMULATION OF FAVORS, other people's expertise, and tremendous amounts of support. I am indebted to the Sul Ross State University Research Enhancement Committee for two grants, which gave me the financial support to begin and then finish this project.

I wish to thank The Archives of the Big Bend, especially Melleta Bell, Gaylan Corbin, and Troy Solis for their patience, expertise, and encouragement. Mr. Solis also read the entire manuscript and gave valuable advice on border etiquette. Other valuable readers who gave advice on various parts of the manuscript include local rancher Roddy Schoenfeldt, Bill Ivey, former owner of the Lajitas Trading Post, Travis Tucker, Roy McBride, Walter Isle, Steven Wolverton, and Gary Paul Nabhan.

I thank Michael Dearing, who salvaged most of the text when—every writer's nightmare—my computer crashed without a backup copy.

I thank John Klingemann, who under repeated nagging and begging, finally produced, along with Dr. Rubén Osorio Juniga, a new translation of the Antonio de Espejo journey through their native land. I wanted Hispanic translators who knew the place as well as the language. They provided both.

During the search for permissions and copyright holders, I became indebted to hundreds of people. Some went the extra mile, like Carl E. Cassidy, M.D., who visited his safe deposit box in order to retrieve papers containing the possible addresses and heirs for one author. Ro Wauer, who waived his reproduction fees and persuaded Texas A&M Press to do the same, also went the extra mile. Others whose memory, family history, or collection of contacts were invaluable include Eleanor Wilson, Shirley Neville, Jane White, Rube Evans, Mary Ann Murray, Vaughn Cockran, Patty Roach, Shirley Neville, Vern Elliot, George Ward at the Texas State Historical Association, Mike and Jean Hardy at Front Street Books in Alpine and Marathon, and Sam Richardson, editor of the *Lajitas Sun*.

For help with final details, I am indebted to Dr. Jesús Tafoya for Spanish accents and spelling (which I often did not use) and to Donna Green for typing an index (which I decided not to use).

Finally, I thank my family: my daughter and son-in-law, Carla and Chris Spencer, my grandson, Riley, and my adopted family, the owners and employees of Big Bend Saddlery in Alpine. I deeply appreciate all their support through the years.

Monolingual in Two Languages

RENO, NEVADA, HAD BEEN CLOUDY AND RAINY FOR weeks, and my mood matched the weather. Home to me is south of New Mexico and west of the Pecos: Far West Texas, Big Bend country, Chihuahuan Desert, borderland, a place where the sun always shines. I didn't know how homesick I'd become until I received a package sent by friends who lived on a ranch just north of Big Bend National Park. As soon as I tore open the box, out poured desert wind and hot sun. Cody and Diana Crider had sent pieces of plants from home. Cody is one of the best cowboy colt breakers I've ever known, and his Mexico-born wife, Diana, crawls into black bear dens to study their cubs. Affectionately, I call him "the Code of the West" and her "the Bear Lady." They knew the desert plants would make me homesick. As I pulled each thorny piece out of the box, wave after wave of emotion and memories swept through me.

The piece of lechuguilla (*Agave lecheguilla*) brought out the most emotion because, like the West Texas March winds, I never guessed I would miss it. When I was growing up, my brother once decided that he was going to be a baseball pitcher. His pitching career was short-lived, however, because in order to practice he needed me for a catcher, and the first pitch he threw toppled me backward into the sharp points of an agave. I've had an extreme dislike for the agave family ever since—big ones, little ones, medium-sized ones. My prejudices grew worse after I began living on the Texas-Mexico border in the Big Bend. Agave family members constantly stabbed me, crippled my horses, and left ugly scratches across my expensive leather. Distilled into tequila, they often persuaded me to make foolish decisions and impaired my normally astute judgment. I've cussed the family most of my life, yet standing there in that post office parking lot, I was so glad to see their little dried-up cousin lechuguilla that I broke down and cried—and being a West Texan I don't cry often.

This gray-green, ragged agave, the lechuguilla, grows only about eight inches tall, reproducing by offshoots. Trying to be a fat-leaved succulent, its sharply pointed fibrous leaves look somewhat sucked out, stringy, homely, and usually curve in one direction as if wind-blown. But the curves seldom match the prevailing west-to-east desert wind or even the plant next door. When they bloom, they send up tall, lancelike flower stalks that always make me imagine a tiny army of little Don Quixotes and Sancho Panzas marching down the mountainside and through the rocks, tilting at windmills—or in this country, probably greasing them.

After the lechuguilla, the next piece I was able to shake loose and separate from the fairly tangled mass of thorns in the box was a small piece of Corona de Cristo (*Koeberlina spinosa*). This thorny shrub produces leaves and even red berries, but I'd seldom seen them. As usual, this piece—a familiar, bare, sharply pointed, almost bright green woody stick covered with thorns—had neither. Since I'd been struggling for two years to learn Spanish at the ripe old age of fifty—after being a monolingual all my life—I now made an educated guess that the name must mean Christ's crown in Spanish. I'd never thought about it before, but, yes, a person could make a very wicked crown from a few sprigs of this plant. It did look exactly like the thorny crown often painted around Christ's head by artists, blood dripping from the wounds where nature's callous thorns had pierced his divine skin—by now a familiar symbolic image.

Mary Austin, a turn-of-the-twentieth-century desert author I'd admired for years, once lived in the Mojave Desert and had written a book about Jesus being from a small desert town. She felt the desert had influenced his vision and believed deserts were natural birthplaces for religion. Well, where I come from, the desert seems to be a natural birthplace for smuggling, banditry, murder, and mayhem. Being an uppity woman, Mary had called herself a prophet and predicted that the world's next great culture would spring from the desert Southwest. But she probably didn't plan on it being a drug culture. I chuckled to myself as I imagined a drug lord as Lord. I guess everything she predicted has come true, but I don't think it's quite what she had in mind. Images and ideas kept making sparks off the sharp tips of the Corona de Cristo in my hand. Out horseback, I'd often seen small creatures hiding among those wicked thorns: jackrabbits, cottontails, mice, even snakes. How ironic that snakes would hide in the crown of Christ for safety—or maybe not. In my desert, Lucifer is just a harmless little purple-throated hummingbird who nests only in lechuguilla stalks.

Reaching back into the box and pricking my finger on a sharp leaf, I shook loose a piece of algerita (*Berberis trifoliolata*). I had always had a love-hate relationship with this plant. The yellow flowers are usually the first to bloom in February. I would often be so starved for a table bouquet that I would brave the sharp, Arthurian-sword-shaped leaves in order to pick a small bouquet. Once and only once was I ambitious—and foolish—enough to make jelly from the tiny red fruits. The berries being impossible to pick, I would spread a bedsheet under a big algerita bush and whack it with a hoe handle. Spiders, worms, bugs, dead leaves, small twigs, grass awns, and a few berries would shower onto the sheet. The berries came off in bundles of three, if I remember correctly, and each tiny stem had to be carefully removed by hand. Even the dried blossom ends were not properly shed and had to be rubbed off. So I would guess that a half-cup of berries took about an hour to gather and prepare. Enough for one batch of jelly took me an entire summer! When company arrived, I would proudly set a tiny jar on the table. The amber-red, grainy ambrosia tasted like a tangy strawberry-plum-watermelon cross, and I always expected compliments. Instead, I would watch horrified as cowboy friends would dip a big spoon into the tiny jar, smear my precious hard work lavishly on a biscuit, and go right on with their stories—as though jelly is jelly!

Algerita stems are woody and tough. I tipped up the branch in my hand. No one would suspect, looking at the gray bark, that hidden inside was a brilliant yellow wood. I once dug up a root on a large bush to find a thick enough piece of yellow wood for a knife handle. A friend was trying to make his living making hand-forged anvil knives at the time, and he liked to experiment with desert woods. Knife handles seemed a good, respectful way to use desert wood without using too much. The algerita turned out to be my favorite, and polished into a fine-grained, sunshine yellow streaked with olive.

Gingerly I pulled out a piece of cardenche that was sticking through the box in two places. I wondered how many postal workers had mysteriously been stabbed while the box was en route. Cardenche (*Opuntia imbricata*) forms dense, treelike thickets and has spines sometimes covered with paper sheaths, like pale yellow wrappers protecting long brown needles as if to keep them sharp. The wrappers were missing on these thorns, and the sharp needles looked especially wicked in cold, foggy Nevada. I might make jelly from algerita or prickly pear, but never from cardenche. They had my utmost respect, and I kept my distance. Rumor was that if you rode too near, they actually jumped and attacked, and I sometimes believed it. Once a joint of it was stuck into your boot, you would somehow stick yourself in at least three fingers, your leg, your arm, your horse's leg, and your saddle before finally removing it with a couple of sticks. The pain in those pricked places would last for days. This piece was already stuck to one of my fingers as well as the box. I chuckled.

At home, I would only get close enough to photograph cardenche's flowers and yellow fruit. My daughter has a framed art print hanging on her wall that she bought when she was a little girl with her first cowboy wages. A healthy Hereford calf is standing sideways, looking out at the viewer, its big brown eyes fringed with soft white eyelashes. The calf is framed by a huge clump of beautiful fuchsia-bloomed cardenche. In a photograph or a painting, I could love cardenche. But the only time I ever loved the real plant (before I pulled it out of the box that day) was after it was dead. Once its wicked flesh rots and blows away, only the beautiful gray, hollow bones full of holes—cardenche skeletons—remain. Cactus in my mythic country seems to die of gunshot wounds.

Stuck to the piece of cardenche was a smaller piece of tasajillo (*Opuntia leptocaulis*), maybe even more deadly and fierce than the bigger stabber. A sneak, it likes to hide in a clump of brush and pierce without warning. Do not ride into this stuff. Do not walk through or even near it, especially if you are a female (it has another name I can't say in public). It is supposed to be good quail food. I could never imagine a fat little quail risking its tender breast to squeeze between the sometimes three-inch thorns in order to reach small red fruits clinging to the pencil-stems, until one of my drinking buddies explained that the berries seem to act as some kind of intoxicant for quail, and they act drunk after eating them. Then I understood.

Next I pulled out a waxy, grayish green, skinny little crooked finger of candelilla which reminded me of some rancher friends that I missed very much who also buy and sell the wax. North of the Rio Grande, candelilla wax is legally imported from Mexico, but south of the border, the wax is usually smuggled into the United States because the wax makers, who work tremendously hard in blistering temperatures and whose camps are far from a bank of cerote (wax), are enticed to sell to better paying buyers north of the border instead of taking it back to the socialistic company store and paying the export tax. They simply cross the border with their wax-laden donkeys or old broken-down trucks. I don't blame them.

Sometimes the lines between right and wrong, good and bad, legal and illegal blur, and sometimes I sympathize with the wrong side. These plants reminded me that law and order straddle a complicated border in my country. In one of his novels, *Fire on the Mountain,* Edward Abbey writes about a place called Thieves' Mountain. He says the Spanish first stole it from the Anasazi, then the Apaches stole it from the Spanish, then Anglo ranchers stole it from the Apaches, and finally the U.S. government stole it from everyone. Amazingly, it was just a barren pile of hot desert rocks dotted with cactus—not worth dying for, couldn't make a living on it, but everybody seemed to want it bad enough to die for it. Although Abbey's book is fiction, he captures the strange border-crossing value system of the desert Southwest.

According to the wax makers, if candelilla is cut off above the roots for harvesting, the roots will bleed to death and the plants will need to be replanted in order to maintain a future supply. But if the plants are pulled up by the roots, then the plants will grow back thicker. Harvesting candelilla by the squat-and-jerk method is backbreaking work, but the gatherers, whose livelihoods depend on the plants as well as their backs, squat and jerk. Some botanists say the workers are wrong, that pulling up the plant by its roots destroys it. ¿Quién sabe?

Anyway, there is very little work done in Big Bend National Park today. It's a playground, a place to get away from it all and relax. I love to go there too, but not often. My trips into the park always end in some kind of disaster: twelve hours on horseback without water, feet that swell in the heat until I'm forced to cut slashes in $300 boots, sunburn, hives from swimming in the river water, or a case of poison ivy on my butt after squatting to pee in a shady canyon.

A good example of one of my disastrous trips is the time my daughter woke up one Friday morning about ten years ago wanting to spend some quality time with Mom before moving back into her college dorm room at Sul Ross State University. I suggested shampooing the carpet, but she suggested packing an ice chest, driving to the park, and eating lunch across the river at Boquillas. I had a million things to do, but nineteen-year-olds rarely want to spend a day with their moms, so I dropped everything and headed south.

We forgot plastic music, so along about Elephant Mountain, where the Alpine radio "Voice of No Choice" waves fade out, the long road became very quiet. My thoughts wandered over the desert mountains as I compared our national park to others I had visited. In Yellowstone, traffic is bumper to bumper and crawls along at a snail's pace—stopping at each entertainment spot (geyser, mud pot, grazing bison) just long enough for three hundred instamatic cameras to click once, simultaneously—and then crawls on. There is no entertainment in Big Bend—the Chisos don't erupt or bubble, mountain lions don't pose for tourists—and we hadn't met a single car.

My daughter and I speculated about what a New York tourist would think of our park. Can you imagine leaving the big towns behind at the interstate and heading out into smaller and smaller towns farther and farther apart, then finally leaving the tiny towns of Alpine, Marathon, or Marfa—none of which is large enough for a real traffic light—for a hundred-mile drive into more and more remote country? Even phone lines and electric lines disappear as the road gets narrower. At night, it's like driving into a black hole. We know who lives beyond the cattle guards and who takes care of the windmills, but the average New Yorker would think they had been dropped on the moon. We laughed at the helplessness of the New York tourist in Big Bend.

About the time we were laughing the loudest, I heard water spewing and my truck's heat gauge jumped from cool to red hot in seconds. There we were, broken down on the empty road, sun beating down, about seven miles north of Panther Junction. I looked at the sandals on our feet, our shorts, and our sleeveless shirts and thought wistfully about our cowboy hats hanging like prayer flags on a shrine of mule deer antlers at home. Uh oh.

We sat there for several long minutes wondering what to do as the pickup cab slowly turned into an oven. Just before heat stroke set in, we spotted a fancy black dually headed our way and stuck out our thumbs. The occupants turned out to be friendly Hispanic tourists from San Antonio, and they gave us a ride to the little Chevron station at Panther Junction. As a knowledgeable local, I started to give the tourists some advice about traveling in the Big Bend, but after noticing their long-sleeved shirts, hats, hiking boots, and water jugs—I decided to keep quiet.

To make a long, very expensive story short, my daughter and I spent the day on a little wooden bench on the shady side of the tiny Panther Junction gas station. The attached tiny store sold boxes of chalk and Scotch tape, so we thought about playing hopscotch or tearing paper into little pieces and taping them back together. My daughter decided she was spending "quantity time" with her mother instead of quality time. I tried calling all the friends I thought I had in the park, but they were either already gone for the weekend or not quite as interested in my dilemma as I thought they should be. Even the phone at the station evidently stopped working on Friday afternoon. No possibility of pickup repair until Monday, and then only maybe. A New Yorker would have had a coronary.

Locals cheered us with "It could be worse" stories. One station employee said he had once been poking around in the Solitario, had three flats, and it was three days before a horseback cowboy out of Mexico, looking for lost goats, found him. All he had with him to drink or eat was beer. At least I was driving an old Ford, they said. It could be worse—did I know how far a Mercedes parts house and repairman were from Panther Junction? It could be worse—the station could have sold only gas, no cold drinks and ice cream. It could be worse—we did have shade.

Finally, heading north at sunset in a wrecking truck that had come a hundred expensive miles to tow us back another hundred expensive miles,

I again looked out across the endless mountains of Big Bend. We could have flown to Yellowstone cheaper, but somehow I felt we'd had the kind of real wilderness experience that people are missing today when they take guided tours to the top of Alaska's Denali or pack into the Tetons. Those wilderness experiences make the pilgrims feel competent. They hate to go home, hate to go back to the traffic, their jobs, and the rush of city life. Instead of going home refreshed, they go home dragging their feet, wishing they owned a cabin in the pines. In contrast, the Chihuahuan Desert always makes me feel quite incompetent. I couldn't wait to get back to running water, air conditioning, cushioned chairs, the auto parts store, and my trusty Marfa mechanic, Ruben Hernandez. I certainly needed to get back to my job and paycheck.

I also felt that I could have had the same experience if the people who had been moved out of the park still lived there: the Johnsons, the Holguins, the Langfords, the Garcías, the Millers, the Solíses. They had been gentle curanderos, traders, drought-hardened ranchers, cotton farmers, small-time silver miners; maybe a few had been liquor smugglers during the Roaring Twenties. Many of them, of course, bought, harvested, hauled, or made wax from candelilla. The going rate in 1920 for a ton of wax was $2.50. The workers who boiled the plants to extract the wax made $1.00 a day. Nobody was getting rich, so they all got along pretty good. But with the coming of a national park, things changed. The people and their picturesque homes—made of adobe, cactus woods, and sometimes even thatched layers of boiled candelilla—were bulldozed off the map and replaced with official cement block NPS homes and offices. With the coming of the national park in 1944 concessionaires instead of Chata Sada prepared food for travelers—a great loss to both the Sadas and the travelers.

I had never quite gotten used to the essays I would get from both my Anglo and Hispanic students whose families still mourned for land and homes and neighbors that had fallen within park boundaries. Recently, I had attached a copy of Dan Flores' environmental justice essay, "Environmentalism and Multiculturalism," to a student's paper. The student had written about his father's land along Arroyo de Lobos, and how some men were trying to force his father to sell it in order to put in a sludge dump. Like his family, people who had once lived in Big Bend National Park had been forced to sell their lands and move in order to make a playground that is seldom used. Ironically, I couldn't decide which was worse: playground or dump.

With difficulty I pulled myself back from my black thoughts to the box of plants and the piece of candelilla in my hand. Poor people still live along the Rio Grande, and some still smuggle wax into Texas from Mexico. I don't think anyone has yet invented a mechanized way that can economically or aesthetically compete with four to six hungry people, drifting across the desert with a boiling vat, a few handmade tools, and a couple of donkeys. The soft, high-quality wax was once used to waterproof tents; to make wax amulets and figurines, candles, shoe polish, chewing gum, and phonograph records; and to make waxes for cars, floors, and tanned leather. Today perhaps most of it finds its way into women's cosmetics. Again I marveled at the irony. Those ugly little witch-like fingers of candelilla eventually touch the lips of the most beautiful women in the world. Judging by its Latin name, *Euphorbia antisyphilitica,* it must have also once been used as either a cure or a prevention—or maybe it was even thought to be a cause—of syphilis. Lipstick, candles, music, shoe polish, leather, and car wax do tend to help spread venereal disease. Beauty always has had a dark side.

Along one side of the box lay a long strip of sacahuista (*Nolina erumpens*). By now sensitized to all the self-protectiveness that seemed to be a characteristic of every plant from home, I laughed. Only in the desert would Mother Nature line a grass blade with tiny teeth.

Curled on the very bottom of the box was sotol (*Dasylirion leiophyllum*) —I call it the pampas grass of the Chihuahuan Desert. A coarse grass with razor-sharp edges, it is eaten by cattle, I've heard, when they're desperate—but I guess I've never seen them that desperate. I once found sotol woven into bits of mat or sandals or something in a cave. According to my old friend Barton Warnock, sotol produces male and female plants and comes from the lily family. Even the symbolic lily makes quite a change when it becomes desertified.

Carefully placing all the plant pieces back into the box brought on a second wave of emotion as I ticked off the names again: lechuguilla, Corona de Cristo, algerita, cardenche, tasajillo, candelilla, sacahuista, and sotol. I stood there in that Nevada post office parking lot with tears welling up when I realized that I didn't know any English names for plants from home. Very white, with a grandfather on the Mayflower and descending from ancestors who spoke English, French, German, Dutch, Welsh, and Gaelic, I'd lost all those languages but one. Although I thought I was too dumb and old ever to learn Spanish, I suddenly realized that by osmosis it had become at least partly my own native tongue. I was a monolingual in two languages!

I also remembered thinking how totally the melting pot had mixed us up when I read that the Mayflower Society had elected a Hispanic, Mildred Ramos, to their top national office in 1992. The races and languages have quietly blended into one another, not only in my border country, but across the nation. In a recent book, John McPhee describes the way geologists have proved that even Plymouth Rock originally came from Africa. Like the Americas, the Chihuahuan Desert is beautiful because of its variety. Leslie Silko says the Native American culture is founded on a belief in the power of blending cultures.

Living along the border fosters a pride in this mixed-upness. Instead of valuing the purebloods, I'm interested in dissolving the borders and boundaries by exploring the ways plants, birds, animals, geology, and even rivers ignore them. The desert, the races, and the languages straddle the border. Instead of being separated by the Rio Grande, people seem to come together here. I've eaten tortillas with steak and french fries, shrimp enchiladas, and jalapeños on pizza. I've danced to "El Rancho Grande," the schottische, and George Strait at the same dance and with the same partner. My friends are blonde ladies who guide pack trips into Mexico, Hispanics who speak no Spanish, and mixed-blood people who drink both Coors and Tecate. In the Big Bend our university dance group has Hispanic students doing Polynesian dances and African American students doing Mexican folk dances. People from either side of the border might have a dentist in Ojinaga and a doctor in Midland. Even skin color gets very confusing. "White" ladies sometimes bare the darkest skin. Some claim that even our local ranch horses are bilingual. We are quite a mixed-up place, and we like it that way.

So, standing there in that Nevada parking lot, carefully closing my box of desert plants, I suddenly knew why I'd been lying awake at night listening to the Mexican radio station some nearby farmworkers had been playing. Their music made me remember a cowboy poem about the radio being the only cure when rural people come down with a case of the high-lonesomes. The farmworkers lived in a small trailer on down the Truckee River past my apartment on the ag-experiment station. They spoke no English. About once a month the police would show up at their place to break up a fight. One weekend while I was gone, one of them was found alongside the road about ten yards from my door—robbed, gagged, tied, with his head and shoulders stuffed inside a gunnysack—unhurt but mad. Strangely, I went to them for help instead of to my white, English-speaking male neighbor on the snowy morning my old, second-hand Ford Bronco would not start. I walked into their all-male, Spanish-only camp with no hesitation and said with no shame, "Por favor—truca—muy malo." I knew they'd understand me and wouldn't laugh at my illiterate Spanish. I knew they would try to help me, and I knew they could fix whatever ailed my vehicle. The white neighbor who lived next door was a stranger, probably not a mechanic. These guys, although I'd never met them, seemed safer—more like family. Once they had me rolling, I offered them money that I didn't have, knowing they would refuse, and they did.

"Mil gracias."

"De nada."

I had considered myself a handicapped monolingual until that moment in the Nevada post office parking lot when I realized how deeply the border country had embedded itself in my life. Adaptation to place is a process that happens to a person over time and is usually subconscious. You just wake up one day, maybe in some parking lot, and realize that under certain conditions you don't even speak English. You're a mixed-up Chihuahuan Desert rat with a nest of sticks, thorns, snakes, and all.

I soon returned to the Big Bend.

So this collection is a tribute to that place I call home.

People tend to draw their own boundaries for the Big Bend. Some consider just the very tip of the Rio Grande's bend, now Big Bend National Park, to be the place. For the purposes of this collection, however, I embrace all of what used to be called "the Big Empty," the whole Big Bend: the watersheds, the Chihuahuan Desert, the trade routes, the smuggler's and Comanche trails, and both sides of the river. Big Benders live scattered throughout this area. So I draw a big circle beginning with the Jornada del Muerto near El Paso where the river begins to cross mountain ranges, down through the Franklins, the Quitmans, and the Chinatis to its junction with the Río Conchos. There is something very symbolic about a river headed southwest out of the Rocky Mountains that changes its mind and turns southeast to rendezvous with a river headed north out of Mexico's Sierra Madre. Then my boundary cuts through the deep canyons—Santa Elena, Mariscal, Boquillas, and through the Sierra del Carmens to join forces with the Pecos. Everyone knows that things are different west of the Pecos, so my boundary does not cross it. Following the Pecos north, I include Horse Head Crossing and the Rustler Hills, then west again to El Capitan, across the salt flats and the Diablo Plateau. This draws a big circle around the old Big Empty.

This collection also comes from a broad range of sources. Some are very literary excerpts from novels and essays published by New York presses, some have never been published nor read by the public, some are historical, some are scientific, and some come from diaries, master's theses, or newspapers. I've tried to include all of the many voices that make up the Big Bend people: explorers, trappers, cowboys, ranch wives, curanderos, college presidents, scientists, locals, tourists, historians, avisadores, waitresses, and those who bring the mail. In fact these voices prove that the Big Empty was never really empty at all.

As I did the reading for this collection, I continually found that people either felt the area was a utopia (God's country), a great place to visit (playground), or a dangerous place that people should stay away from (full of devils). So, to me, the title bridges these extremes and incorporates several levels of meaning. The word "country" is most often used by ranchers, cowboys, and other local residents: "I'm leasing some country from Mac." "This is Big Bend country." "This is grass country." "This is good country." "This is big outfit country." "That is Moe Morrow's country." "This is lion country." Those who love it call it "God's country."

On the other hand, others often refer to it as a hell or a desert wasteland or a place where the mountains often look like what the Devil had left over after he built Hell. It is so hot even the Devil wouldn't want to live here. And this division between Heaven and Hell is also prevalent in the culture. Big Benders are almost equally split between those who are fourth-generation Baptists or Catholics, fourth-generation law officers, and fourth-generation smugglers—and sometimes I'm not sure which group I like best. From another perspective, many of our visitors view this as a place to play and forget the laws and morals they left at home while attending chili cookoffs or visiting across the border. So locals sometimes consider visitors "devils," although we need their money. Throughout the collection, I try to give complex, nonjudgmental views and emphasize the oxymorons, paradoxes, and ironies inherent in the language and myths of the place and people. Because I want to encourage the reader to look at the pieces through a literary rather than an historical lens, I have grouped the collection into thematic chapters rather than following a linear time frame. Each chapter includes a brief introduction to the theme of that section, in which I encourage readers to take a deeper look at desert nature writing. The selections span various kinds of nature writing, from fiction to backcountry living to rambles to field notes.

The most difficult decision I faced as editor was what to do about language—spelling, Spanish accents, italics, colloquial terms, regional names for plants and animals. Is it algerita, aigrita, agerita, or algarita? Some local residents object to Spanish accents on their own Hispanic surnames, saying they prefer the "English version" since they are U.S. citizens. If I use italics for foreign words, then what do I do about "lechuguilla," which is the English name for the plant, just as "tortilla" is the English name for a type of bread and "presidio" is the English name for a local border town? Modernizing "cañon" to "canyon" seems to take some of the flavor away from a piece written at the turn of the previous century. Does one of the authors misspell the name of a local mountain range, or is he trying to disguise the location? Should I accept the word of one expert over another? For instance, Aldo Leopold spells the name of the parrot he finds in the Sierra Madre guacamaja. My Spanish expert corrected that to guacamaya—which my Spanish/English dictionary says means macaw, and gives papagayo, loro, and cotorra for parrot. Was Aldo Leopold wrong, or did he give us a name used by locals in the parrots' home territory? Bestowers of common names are often quite independent thinkers, especially in the Big Bend. In Alpine, for instance, if you want crisp corn tortilla chips smothered in beans, hamburger, cheese, and guacamole, you'd order campechanas. But just twenty-five miles east, in Marfa, you'd order botanas. Someone braver than I will have to correct these local cooks. My answer to this language dilemma has been to stay true to the original document. We Tex-Mex borderistos tend to either butcher or creatively enhance both languages, depending on one's attitude toward proper English and Spanish grammar.

By the time readers have reached the last page, I hope they will have gained a sense of place rather than feeling like they have taken a vicarious, voyeuristic trip through an exotic land peopled with bandits, endangered species, and tourist trappers.

God's Country or Devil's Playground

ONE

Paradise Found and Lost

IMAGINING THE PRECOLUMBIAN NORTH AMERICAN continent as a wilderness paradise has recently been severely challenged as a form of colonialism and racism, since the entire continent had been home to millions of hard-working and intelligent indigenous people before Europeans arrived. Ethnobotanist Gary Paul Nabhan, in his excellent essay "Cultural Parallax in Viewing the North American Habitats," recounts the many ways four to twelve million people "speaking two hundred languages variously burned, pruned, hunted, hacked, cleared, irrigated, and planted in an astonishing diversity of habitats for centuries."[1] We are discovering that many "wild" desert plants, such as agaves, had actually been transported, planted, cultivated, and harvested by indigenous farmers for generations. Everything from willows (planted for basketry) to creek boulders (placed as "water tamers") was a part of complicated land management practices.

The authors collected in this chapter represent the desert as a wilderness paradise in various interesting ways. Robert T. Hill might be called the John Wesley Powell of the Rio Grande. Writing in 1901 as head of the Texas geological survey team, Hill's description of the canyons threaded by the Rio Grande is still the most eloquent. The colorful rock formations have never produced a more articulate spokesperson. This essay and the next one by Antonio de Espejo are classic examples of exploration and entrada narratives. Curiously, the "first English white man" usually travels, like Hill, downriver in a boat, riding the rapids like a bucking bronco. The "first Spanish white man," on the other hand, usually travels upriver on horseback looking for souls to save and finds the natives innocent even when they shoot his horses.

Childlike noble savages are stereotypical of much early adventure writing. The noble savage became a stock character during the nineteenth century in a popular style of writing known as romanticism. Romantics embraced the idea that wild nature would bring out the human's best character traits and a natural nobility. Romantics believed that civilization corrupted the human race and that a return to the simple, idyllic, and peaceful life of the wilderness savage would eliminate tendencies toward greed, thievery, murder, and all of the sins associated with life in the city.

The hidden agenda of romanticism and the entrada narratives was often colonization—the desire to turn "unowned" and "uninhabited" wilderness places and "innocent" people into utopian homes or playgrounds, complete with servants and slaves, for wealthy Europeans. Most explorers were trying to impress those in power back home with their discoveries: fortunes to be made in amazingly fertile lands free for the taking and numerous passive pagan souls ripe for conversion, taxation, and slavery. Thus the modern naturalist is often shocked at the destruction of these teeming Gardens of Eden, when in reality the early explorers had exaggerated the cornucopia for promotional reasons. Modern authors often warn against the tendency of scholars to build on previous work when, as quite often happens, the early research or translation is full of errors.[2] As knowledgeable readers wend their way through this collection, they will discover numerous cases of misidentification or misrepresentation of plants, places, and people. One interesting example of this turned up when I asked John Klingemann and Dr. Rubén Osorio Juniga for a new translation of the Antonio de Espejo entrada narrative.[3] Their new translation does not mention bison or cattle hides as sources for clothing. The farming tribes encountered by Espejo were irrigating cotton from the Río Conchos and Rio Grande and wearing cotton clothing, a much more sensible choice in the hot Big Bend. However, in the classic Herbert H. Bolton translation of the Espejo narrative, the native inhabitants are using robes from "buffalo" even as far south as northern Mexico.[4] The Spanish word actually used by Espejo (who was a cattleman himself) is "vaca," meaning cattle, rather than "cibola" or "civola," meaning bison, an animal he may refer to much later in their journey when describing leather shoes worn in the New Mexico pueblos.[5]

These details seem like insignificant trivia except when they are considered historical fact and influence modern politics. Bones from an extinct shrub oxen found in a cave in the Guadalupe Mountains[6] present the possibility that hides could have come from this now extinct animal. The hides could also have come from escaped Spanish livestock, since Espejo followed Coronado by some forty years. On the other hand, bison hides could have been available quite far south through trade with migrating Indian tribes called "Ciboleros" or "Cibolos" who spent part of their year hunting in what is now New Mexico or east of the Pecos River, which was often called "Río de las Vacas" by early explorers. According to paleontologists, bison congregated along the Pecos River, probably never grazing farther than one drink away, and never inhabited the dry, almost water-less Big Bend region. The Comanche trails were littered with the bones of stolen livestock, which had been driven too long and far between water sources. Vernon Bailey, chief U.S. naturalist at the turn of the twentieth century, says, "In 1901 I could find no one in the Great Bend country who had ever heard of buffalo in that region, nor could I find any evidence to indicate that they had ever inhabited the extremely rough and arid country along that part of the Rio Grande valley."[7] Not until windmills brought dependable water to the surface was the dry Trans-Pecos probably capable of supporting large herds of herbivores or permanent human populations.

In any event, paradise is usually associated with herds of wild animals, and we often imagine paradise as having been lost once the noble savages acquired domestic animals. In *Goodbye to a River*, John Graves says, "During all human time, it seems, the Comanches, like their cousins the Tartars and the Cossacks and the Huns, had been awaiting that barbaric wholeness the horse was to give them."[8] Historians credit Anglos with bringing domestic livestock into the Southwest in the 1890s, but horses, cattle, and sheep, as already mentioned, actually arrived four to five hundred years earlier from the South—not the East—with the early Spanish explorers.

Further complicating the idea of a once harmonious and peaceful paradise, Charles Baker in his summary of West Texas geology reminds us that this particular paradise was born in violence, not grace. He describes the Big Bend as a geologist's heaven where, within twenty-five miles of Marathon, exists every kind of mountain known to man. Richard Phelan describes the Trans-Pecos as God's country: a place man has changed less and occupied less than any other part of the state. He reminds us that Guadalupe Peak, the highest desert mountain in Texas, was once an ocean reef, making moot any claims of native plants or animals in the area. As a matter of fact, ecocritic Frederick Turner, discussing imaginary representations of nature in *The Ecocriticism Reader: Landmarks in Literary Ecology*, calls the idea that the North American continent was a complete and balanced paradise immediately preceding European invasion a form of "'scientific' creationism."[9]

In another collected essay, Aldo Leopold, while hiking in Mexico's Sierra Madre, finds a pristine mountain paradise and projects a noble savage innocence onto Mexican parrots as they fly "happily" to meet him. He calls the parrots a "discovery" and assumes their life is so carefree that their early morning chatter is simply about "whether this new day which creeps slowly over the canyons is bluer or golder than its predecessors, or less so." Like an early explorer, he cannot understand their language and wishes for a parrot dictionary. Leopold also worries what will become of the friendly parrot once the tourist-with-a-gun arrives in paradise.

Much of the language associated with wilderness as paradise is associated with loss and uses female-gendered metaphors (mother earth, virgin land) and verbs of abusive sexual conquest (penetration, rape, ravish),[10] as literary critic Annette Kolodny has pointed out. Typical of much natural history writing, Roland H. Wauer, like Leopold, finds a semivirginal Sierra del Carmen paradise disappearing fast, its nesting habitat for imperial woodpeckers about to be raped and ruined forever by loggers. His trip represents a "the last white man's" glimpse of paradise before it is lost to the sound of axes.[11]

Although rape of the land is usually associated with extractive industries such as mining, logging, and grazing, industries such as tourism and subdivision are also guilty. Just as women are often valued primarily as a visual spectacle, tourism is being criticized as a highly visual method of objectifying nature, which turns cultures into caricatures of themselves and substitutes seasonal and low-paying service jobs for traditional occupations. Mary Lasswell's adventuring tourist perspective is written in a purple prose style popular with the romantics. With breathlessly rapid New York sentences, she relies on urban metaphors to describe colors on the canyon walls as inspiration for silk, velvet, textile, drapery, upholstery, and carpet. The cliffs remind her of architecture and she uses classical music to describe the feeling of being within those walls. She sings arias to produce self-aggrandizing echoes, says Rio Grande cows drink "afternoon tea," and believes the Spanish dagger is "begging for some sympathetic hand" to bring its "waxen bells" inside the houses. In stark contrast to her tourist's eye view, she also quotes the most eloquent description of the Big Bend ever uttered; for over a century, filmmakers, poets, and essayists have admired this quote from a supposedly illiterate Mexican vaquero. He called the Big Bend the place where rainbows wait for rain, where the river is kept in a stone box, and where the mountains go away at night to play with other mountains.

Quite often, viewing the Trans-Pecos as a paradise depends on when the pilgrim first sees the country: during a relaxing visit with credit card in hand, during a year of good rains, during October's Indian summer, just at dawn or sunset, or under a full Comanche moon. Big Bend homesteader J. O. Langford (excerpted in Chapter Six) says he was forced to leave behind a "paradise" of grass and water during bandit raids in 1915. He returned in 1929 to find a paradise lost: "And now, where once I'd thought there was more grass than could ever be eaten off, I found no grass at all."[12] Discouraged, he left again for good in 1942, just a few months before the desert bloomed again.

Ironically, his often quoted words parallel exactly the cycles of good rain and the terrible drought of the Dust Bowl thirties which Lasswell's droughted-out ranchers lament. She asks them: "When did you last have grass?"

"Nineteen forty-one. It rained good. Not enough to flood, but enough for grass."

"When was another good year?"

"Lessee. Nineteen-fourteen was fine!"

Paradise came again in 1986, but we haven't seen it since. According to river guides, paradise disappeared "forever" in 1990, the last time truly "big water" came down the Rio Grande. But even in 1901, as Robert T. Hill notes, some of his advisors said he would drown, while others said he'd need a buggy, not a boat, to explore the usually dry Rio Grande. Those who first see the Big Bend at high noon in mid-July when the rains haven't come for years see a hot, rocky, barren hell. Those who stay occasionally see it turn into a paradise, knee-deep in grama grass and wildflowers. Those who stay for generations learn to love both extremes.

The last three essays in this chapter expose different perspectives toward owning a piece of paradise. Martin Dreyer recognizes the universal human dream to claim or own a mountain as a way to escape civilization's stress and find a primitive utopia "out there" somewhere. Barton Warnock finds paradise in small, hidden nooks and crannies, protected from overtourism by private land, fences, torturous dirt roads, and a hot three-mile desert hike.[13] David Alloway, on the other hand, finds paradise can be "owned" by the poorest of people because it comes in fleeting moments, often seen only by those who must be at work before dawn. One rainy morning, driving in the dark to his trail guide job with the Chisos Remuda in Big Bend National Park, he sees a delicate rainbow cast by the light of a full moon.[14] The rainbow, as the old vaquero predicted, had waited patiently for rain, but in the clear air and bright desert moonlight, it finds no need to wait for the sun.

NOTES

1. Gary Paul Nabhan, "Cultural Parallax in Viewing the North American Habitats," in *Reinventing Nature? Responses to Postmodern Deconstruction,* ed. Michael E. Soule and Gary Lease (Washington, D.C.: Island Press, 1995), 92.

2. See Edward Said's introduction to *Orientalism* (New York: Vintage, 1978) for a good example.

3. Dr. Osorio Juniga has a medical degree from Universidad de Puebla in central Mexico, practiced for many years in Chihuahua, and today is considered one of the top authorities

on the Mexican Revolution in northern Mexico. He is the author of *La familia secreta de Pancho Villa: Una historia oral (The Secret Family of Pancho Villa: An Oral History)*, (Alpine, Tex.: Center for Big Bend Studies, Occasional Papers no. 6, 2000). Klingemann served as translator for Osorio's book, has dual citizenship, was raised in Terlingua, and is now curator for the Museum of the Big Bend in Alpine.

4. The classic translation of Espejo's journey by Herbert E. Bolton says that bison robes were found in northern Mexico, before the party ever reached the Rio Grande. However, no words either for cows or bison appear in the original archaic Spanish (which often uses *f* for *s* and *v* for *u*):

> ". . . [Patarabues] en todas las quales auifados los vnos Caciques de los otros falian a recebir a los nueftros fin arcos, ni flechas, y les trayan muchos mantenimientos, y otros relalos y dadiuas, en efpecial cue los camuças muy bien adereçados, y que no les excedian en efto las de Flandes."

Bolton evidently chose to embellish Espejo's account, probably from the George Hammond and Agapito Rey 1929 translation of an account of the same journey by a member of Espejo's party, Diego Pérez de Luxán. However, he fails to note that, at this particular spot, Hammond and Rey state that "these people ordinarily go after the meat and skins where they [the buffalo] roam, which is about thirty leagues from this province" (George P. Hammond and Agapito Rey, *Expedition into New Mexico Made by Antonio de Espejo, 1582–1583*, Los Angeles: Quivira Society, 1929, p. 57). I have not seen the original Spanish version of this account of the journey. I think the tendency of translators to embellish—perhaps by stereotypically including buffalo robes whenever explorers encounter Indians—should be investigated further by scholars.

5. According to another new translation of Espejo's entire journey by Wallace Moore (not collected herein), the word cibola (or civola) never appears in the Espejo narrative, although he does talk about "cattle whose skins looked like cotton" after the explorers reached central New Mexico pueblos where bison were known to roam. Moore teaches Spanish in Kermit, Texas. His translation has not yet been published.

6. See Frederick R. Gehlback, *Mountain Islands and Desert Seas: A Natural History of the U. S. Mexican Borderlands* (College Station: Texas A&M University, 1981), 106; and C. B. Schultz and E. F. Howard, "The Fauna of Burnet Cave, Guadalupe Mountains, New Mexico," *Proceedings of Natural Science, Philadelphia* (vol. 87, 1935), 273–289.

7. Vernon Bailey, *Biological Survey of Texas,* North American Fauna no. 25 (Washington, D.C.: Government Printing Office, 1905), 69.

8. John Graves, *Goodbye to a River* (New York: Knopf, 1960), 18.

9. Frederick Turner, "Cultivating the American Garden," in *The Ecocriticism Reader: Landmarks in Literary Ecology,* ed. Cheryll Glotfelty and Harold Fromm (Athens: University of Georgia, 1996), 40.

10. Annette Kolodny, *The Lay of the Land: Metaphor as Experience and History in American Life and Letters* (Chapel Hill: University of North Carolina Press, 1975).

11. Wauer was chief park naturalist for Big Bend National Park from 1966 to 1972.

12. J. O. Langford, *Big Bend: A Homesteader's Story* (Austin: University of Texas Press, 1952), 153.

13. Dr. Warnock authored numerous field guides on wildflowers of the Big Bend. He was a professor emeritus at Sul Ross State University. The Texas Parks and Wildlife Barton H. Warnock Environmental Education Center at Lajitas is named in his honor.

14. Alloway was formerly chief park naturalist for Big Bend Ranch State Park and now operates his own desert survival business.

RUNNING THE CAÑONS OF THE RIO GRANDE
Robert T. Hill

1901

SO FAR AS MAN'S CONCEPTION OF TIME IS CONCERNED, THE AMERIcan desert is, always has been, and always will be. Its vast oval area of sterile plain, relieved here and there by mountain ranges, extends between higher bordering crests—those of the Rocky Mountains on the east and the Pacific Sierras on the west—from British Columbia to the end of the southern plateau of Mexico. Of the feeble streams which originate within the great desert, only three cross the barrier sierras and ultimately reach the sea. These three are the Columbia of the north, the Colorado of the southwest, and the Rio Grande of the southeast.

The wonders of the Colorado of the West were made known to the world through the dangerous trip of Major J. W. Powell in 1869, and are now brought within easy reach of the Pullman-car tourist. The cañons of the Rio Grande are longest and least known; they have been and still are the least accessible to man, and have not hitherto been fully described.

Before describing the passage of the cañons of the Rio Bravo, the middle portion of the Rio Grande, let us glance a moment at the country through which they pass—the matrix, so to speak, out of which the cañons are carved. The widest and lowest part of the great American desert closely follows the international border, and is traversed by the Southern Pacific Railway. The railway on the north and the Rio Grande on the south enclose a vast triangular area known in Texas as the Big Bend Country.

Away from the railway the Big Bend—sometimes called the Bloody Bend—is known as a "hard country," that is, one in which, through lack of water, civilization finds it difficult to gain a foothold. Although abundantly supplied with water works, such as scarped and cañoned streamways, it possesses a minimum of water. These great arroyos are mocking travesties which suggest that nature became tired of making this country before turning on the water.

Every other aspect of the Big Bend Country—landscape, configuration, rocks, and vegetation—is weird and strange and of a type unfamiliar to the inhabitants of civilized lands. The surface is a peculiar combination of desert plain and volcanic hills and mountains, the proportions of which are increased by the vast distance which the vision here reaches through the crystalline atmosphere. There is no natural feature that can be described in familiar words.

There are no true forests except upon the tips of the highest peaks, but shrubby plants abound, which are as strange and unfamiliar as the names they bear. Each of these plants is armed with thorns. You are wounded, caught, held, or anchored by this spiteful vegetation at every step away from the beaten trails first made, long centuries ago, by the Mescalero Apaches and the Lipans. One is also roasted unmercifully by day by 130 degrees of sunshine, and cooled almost to the freezing-point at night. These great extremes of temperature shatter even the very rocks into fragments.

Around the southern side of the Big Bend Country flows the Río Bravo, separating this hard portion of Texas from a similar and still harder portion of Mexico. Between two republics the river serves as a permanent frontier which is virtually impassable. Few Americans realize the impregnability and isolation of this frontier, or that it represents a portion of our national boundaries which heretofore has never been completely traversed or explored.

When the expedition was first announced, many witty remarks were made concerning it. The idea was ridiculed that there were either mountains or cañons in this region, and one facetious correspondent said he had lived upon the Rio Grande for twenty years, and added that owing to the absence of water in its sandy bed, the only way the river could be explored was in a buggy. As I drew nearer the region, more serious obstacles were suggested. As we reached San Antonio, the already familiar story that the trip could not be made for want of water began to be supplemented by other dangers. At the Pecos we first heard from old frontiersmen what proved to be the truth, that too much water was to be dreaded rather than too little, which coming in sudden floods would be likely to dash to pieces any craft that entered the stream. At Alpine and Marfa, the only two villages of consequence in the desert stretch of three hundred miles between Pecos and El Paso, graver warnings were received. One man who had spent considerable time upon the river stated that huge obstacles had fallen into the cañons, which made them utterly impassable; others warned us that smallpox was ravaging Presidio del Norte, our proposed point of embarkation, and that in the semi-open country along a portion of the river below Presidio there were murderers, thieves, and bandits, who would destroy any one invading their domain by shooting volleys at night into sleeping camps. These stories of danger, apparently from authentic sources, grew in magnitude as we neared our destination, so that when we finally reached the river two men who had engaged to go upon the expedition backed out from sheer fright.

Many obstacles had to be overcome in order to undertake the journey. Lumber for the boats, purchased at San Antonio, was shipped one hundred and fifty miles by rail to Del Rio, where it was made into three strong, flat-bottomed rowboats, each thirteen feet long and three feet wide, their bottoms protected with longitudinal cleats to provide against the constant scraping over rocks. The finished boats were sent nearly two hundred miles by rail to Marfa, where they were placed upon hay-wagons and hauled overland seventy-five miles due south across the desert to the river at Presidio del Norte.

For the trip, a crew of men who could shoot as well as row a boat had to be provided. By great good fortune we secured the services of James MacMahon, an old time trapper, and of Henry Ware, both of whom were frontiersmen of great strength, inured to hardships, skilled with oar and gun, and capable of unlimited endurance. These, with my nephew Prentice Hill, a lad of nineteen who was in for any venture, an extra boatman, a Mexican cook, and the writer, made a party of six, two men to a boat.

At Marfa, tents and other camp luxuries were packed and shipped back to Marathon. We carried only photography and surveying apparatus, guns, ammunition, and supplies. No personal baggage was permitted except such as one could roll in his bedding. Tents may seem superfluous in the arid region, but, strange to say, it rained for five nights in succession after we disposed of them. These rains proved a blessing, for they caused a sufficient rise in the river to save us an incalculable amount of drudgery in dragging boats over the shoals.

As far as Shafter our road to Presidio was over grass-covered but waterless plains of not unpleasing aspect. Beyond Shafter the road suddenly descends from the upland grassy plains to one of the horrible ocotillo deserts characteristic of the outer basins of this portion of the Rio Grande valley. These basins are old alluvial plains, covered with gravel and yellow adobe soils, extending far away from the river in successive terraces and reaching five hundred feet above it. They are covered by a spiteful, repulsive vegetation, the chief feature of which is the ocotillo, a plant with small green leaves on long and slender stalks that reach above a substructure of lechuguilla, cactus, sotol, and other thorny plants, like serpents rising from a Hindu juggler's carpet. In this belt lies Presidio del Norte, a village with a few miserable adobe houses opposite the older and larger Mexican town of Ojinaga.

Just above Presidio the Río Conchos enters the Rio Grande from Chihuahua. This is a long stream, and brings the first permanent water to the main river. In fact, the Conchos is the mother stream of the Rio Grande. Above the mouth of the Conchos, the Rio Grande was a dry sand-bed. Below, it was a good stream one hundred feet wide, with a strong current, which was to carry us along at a rate of three miles an hour. At this season of the year, the Conchos is flooded by the summer rains that come from the Pacific. Our plans were based upon the assistance of one of these rises, and we were not disappointed. Two days after our arrival at Presidio the river rose a foot, giving exactly the desired stage of water.

At noon, October 5, 1899, we pushed out into the river at Presidio and started on our long journey into the unknown. I do not claim to be the only man who has traveled the tortuous and dangerous channel of the frontier stream; for one man, and one only, James MacMahon, has made at least three trips down the river. Mine, however, was the first exploring expedition to pass the entire length of the cañons, and, with the exception of MacMahon's, was the only attempt that succeeded. Others, like Gano and Neville, have passed the fearful twelve miles of the Grand Cañon de Santa Helena. The only government expedition, the International Boundary Survey, pronounced the cañons impassable and gave up the attempt to survey them, except the lower hundred miles of the course, which Lieutenant Micheler passed through.

MacMahon was interested neither in science, exploration, nor travel. He ventured the stream without knowledge of its dangers, and merely because, as a lifelong hunter and trapper, he knew that the beaver probably lived along its unmolested banks. These animals alone interested him, and a map made by him, if he could make such a thing, would note only beaver banks and danger-spots, for these were all that he saw. Unguided and alone, he loaded his boat with traps, placed it in the stream, and slowly drifted down to Del Rio, braving a thousand dangers and making the first successful passage. This man, whose name has perhaps never before appeared in print, had spent his long life in such exploits and is one of the few old-time trappers still to be found in the West.

The finding of MacMahon was the first of the dozen fortuitous circumstances which made my trip possible, and there was not a day that his knowledge of the dangers of the stream did not save us from loss and destruction. Always kind and unobtrusive, he was as cautious as a cat, being at times apparently over-careful. He was ever on the lookout for a safe channel in the treacherous current, beaver slides on the banks, and border Mexicans in the bushes.

Hardly had we begun to enjoy the pleasant sensation of drifting down the stream when a roaring noise was heard ahead. This came from seething and dangerous torrents of water foaming over huge rounded boulders of volcanic rock which everywhere formed the bottom of the river. Reaching the rapids, we had to get out of the boats and wade beside them, pushing them off or over the stones, or holding them back by their stern-lines. This process had to be repeated many times a day for the entire distance, and, as a consequence, all hands were constantly wet. The swift current and uncertain footing of the hidden rocks made these rapids very dangerous. A loss of balance or a fall meant almost certain death. It was our very good fortune not to upset a boat or lose a man. Ware was especially cautious at such places, for only a year before, while upon a hunting and fishing expedition on the Lower Rio Grande, his companion had been drowned in a place of this character.

The first twenty miles lay through a low, broken desert country. The river-banks were of muddy silt, with here and there a lone cottonwood or willow. Ahead of us loomed the Bofecillos Mountains of Texas and the San Carlos Sierra of Mexico, closing in upon the river.

This region is infested by thieves and murderers, and MacMahon was watchful. Our loaded rifles lay beside our oars, and every bush and stone was closely scanned for men in ambush. The special objects of terror were a famous Mexican, Alvarado, and his associates. Alvarado possessed a mustache one side of which was white and the other black. From this he was called "Old White Lip." To his hand had been charged the murder of several men who had attempted the river route, and it was he who, MacMahon avowed, the year before had riddled his sleeping camp with rifle-balls. At night we secreted our camps in thickets of carrizo, a kind of cane which grew on the low sand-banks, and each man slept with a loaded Winchester beneath his pillow.

The second morning we reached the appropriately named village of Polvo ("dust"), the last settlement for one hundred and fifty miles. It consists of half a dozen dreary adobe houses on a mud-bank, the remains of the old United States military post of Fort Leaton. Here the hospitable storekeeper, an agreeable white man who for some unknown reason had chosen this dreary place of exile, entertained us by showing us the splotches of blood upon the floor and wall behind his counter, where his predecessor had been robbed and murdered the year before, supposedly by Alvarado and his friends. Before I saw this gruesome sight I had not entertained sufficient respect for MacMahon's precautions. Thereafter I was more careful to keep my firearms handy. While at this store, remarks were made by some of my men which led me to suspect that they were secretly planning to retaliate upon Alvarado. Here was a possible motive for undertaking a journey the dangers of which they depicted in vigorous terms. In vain I protested that this expedition was for scientific purposes, and not for vengeance. They only replied that they would shoot Alvarado on sight, "like any other varmit."

A few miles below Polvo the huge chocolate-colored cliffs and domes of the Bofecillos Mountains began to overhang the river, and before night we entered the first of the series of cañons of the Rio Grande, in which we were to be entombed for the succeeding weeks. This bears the cheerful name of Murderer's Cañon, for here, a year or two before, the body of a supposed victim of Alvarado was found lodged on a sand-bar. This and the Fresno Cañon, a few miles below, are vertical cuts about six hundred feet deep through massive walls of red volcanic rock. All the other cañons are of massive limestone. The rocks are serrated into vertical columns of jointed structure, and when touched by the sunlight become a golden yellow. The sky-line is a ragged crest, with many little side cañons nicking the profile. When evening came we were glad to camp on a narrow bank of sandy silt between the river and its walls. Lying upon our backs and relieved of the concentration of our wits upon the cares of navigation, we were able to study and appreciate the beauties of this wild gorge.

The river itself, here as everywhere, is a muddy yellow stream. In places, patches of fine white silt form bordering sand-bars; about twenty-five feet above these there is a second bench, covered by a growth of dark green mesquite. The whole is enclosed by vertically steep, jointed rock walls. The thread of water and the green ribbon of the mesquite bench are refreshing sights, for immediately above the latter, on both sides, the desert vegetation always sets in.

Toward sunset I scaled a break in the cañon to reach the upland and obtain a lookout. Above the narrow alluvial bench forming the green ribbon of river verdure, I suddenly came upon the stony, soilless hills forming the matrix out of which the valley is cut, glaring in the brilliant sunshine and covered with the mocking desert flora. The sight of this aridity almost within reach of the torrent of life-giving waters below, the blessing of which it was never to receive, was shocking and repulsive. It also recalled a danger which ever after haunted us. Should we lose our boats and escape the cañons, what chance for life should we have in crossing these merciless, waterless wastes of thorn for a hundred miles or more to food and succor?

Below the mouth of Murderer's Cañon the rapids were unusually bad and dangerous and it required all hands but one, who stood guard with cocked rifle, to wade beside the boats and preserve them from destruction. As this cañon suddenly ends, its vertical walls continue north and south, as the front of the mountain which it has crossed. We then entered a valley which presents a beautiful panorama of desert form and color. The hills are of all sizes and shapes. Those of the outer border are dazzlingly white, chalk rocks, surmounted here and there by black caps of volcanic rock. The slopes are vermilion foot-hills of red clay. Still lower are the river terraces of the desert yellow clay and gravel, the whole threaded by the narrow fringe of fresh green along the river.

In this wild country lived the notorious Alvarado. Only a most fortunate mistake prevented my men from carrying out the threat to exterminate this bandit. Alvarado had a surname as well as a Christian name and when they were told that the next ranch down the river was Ordóñez's, they did not understand that this was another name for Alvarado until after we had passed him with an infant in his arms, serenely watching us float down the stream. I breathed easier on finding this out, but the men swore audibly and long at their misfortune in not recognizing the supposed monster.

Still lower down the river this region becomes more weird. Immediately adjacent to the stream there are great bluffs of a dirty yellow volcanic tuff, which weather into many fantastic, curvilinear forms. One of these, two hundred feet high, stands out conspicuously from its surroundings, as an almost perfect reproduction of the Egyptian Sphinx. This, with the sterility of the surroundings and the dirty mud colors, constantly recalled the character of the Nile.

We were relieved to see before us the entrance of another vertical "shut-out," or cañon, into which we passed at about four o'clock in the afternoon, and found a suitable camping-ground, hemmed in on each side by vertical walls and out of rifle-range from above. This cañon was only a mile or two long, and was very similar to Murderer's Cañon in its scenic and geologic features.

The next day the river followed a sinuous course through a most picturesque district, which we named the Black Rock Cañon. This was a widely sloping, terraced cañon cut one thousand feet below the summit of a level plateau. The edges of this plateau were lozenged by erosion into symmetrical buttes with great flat caps and scarp lines above terraced slopes, the graceful curves of which wound back and forth from the river's edge. The tabled tops and lower slopes of these buttes were thick strata of dazzling white chalk, while between them was an immense bed of black lava, which always occupied the same relative position between the white bands, as if kind nature had painted a stripe of black about the hills to break the monotony of the desert glare. All day we wound through these hills, now beneath vast bluffs at the water's edge, and then again in more open places, each revealing a new and more beautiful vista.

Toward evening a graceful sweep of the river brought us into a more open basin opposite the mouth of the San Carlos Creek. This stream, which can barely be said to flow, comes in from the Mexican side and is the only flowing tributary of the Rio Grande that we passed between the Conchos and the Pecos. Near its headwaters in the wild and rugged San Carlos Mountains is a little settlement of Indians, the remnant of a once famous, desperate tribe from which the creek and the mountains take their names. Opposite is a wide, sloping plain of limestone, from the center of which rises a wonderful symmetrical butte a thousand feet high, the summit of which is a head presenting the profile of an old man, which we named the Sentinel, from the watch which it kept over the entrance of the Grand Cañon.

We traveled fully one hundred miles to this point by river, but as the crow files it is only about fifty miles below Presidio. We camped upon the Texas side, beneath a limestone bluff. A mile below us down the river was a fast mountain wall, the vertical escarpment of which ran directly north and south across the path of the river, and through which the latter cuts its way. The river disappears in a narrow vertical slit in the face of the escarpment. This mountain is the Sierra de Santa Helena, and the rift in its face is the entrance to the so-called Grand Cañon of the Rio Grande. Why this particular cañon is called Grand is not known, for many of the cañons below were not only as deep but far longer and in every way equally deserving of the name. But Texas is poor in topographic names; most of the features are without names at all. This was the case even with the great mountain through which this cañon passed. Later the Mexicans told us that the feature was called the Sierra de Santa Helena, and this particular cañon will be spoken of as the Grand Cañon de Santa Helena.

The Sierra de Santa Helena is an elongated, quadrangular mountain block half a mile high, twelve miles wide, and fifty miles long, and lies directly across the path of the river. Its summit is a plane surface slightly tilted to the west. The edges are precipitous scarps. Imagine this block cut through vertically with the finest saw, and the rift of the saw will represent the cañon of the river.

Before entering the cañon, let us look at it as did Dr. G. G. Parry of the Mexican Boundary Survey, who, deeming it impassable, climbed the heights and saw it from above. The general surface of the plateau represents no indication of a river-course, and you are not aware of its presence till you stand suddenly on its abrupt brink. Even here the running water is not always visible, unless advantage be taken of the projecting points that form angles along the general course of the river. From this dizzy height the stream below looks like a mere thread, passing in whirling eddies or foaming over broken rapids; and a stone hurled from above into this chasm passes completely out of sight behind the overhanging ledges. From the point formed by its last projecting ledges the view is grand beyond all conception. You can here trace backward the line of the immense chasm which marks the course of the river till it emerges from its stupendous outlet.

The next morning, after the customary involuntary wetting at the rapids by which we made our nightly camps, we rowed straight for the narrow slit in the mountain. The river makes a sudden bend as it enters the cañon, and almost in the twinkling of an eye we passed out of the desert glare into the dark and silent depths of its gigantic walls, which rise vertically from the water's edge to a narrow ribbon of sky above. Confined in a narrow channel less than twenty-five feet wide, without bench or bank upon which to land, our boats glided along without need of oars as we sat in admiration of the superb precipices which hemmed us in on each side. The solemnity of the scene was increased by the deathlike stillness which prevailed and by the thought of those who had tried the journey and either lost their lives or narrowly escaped destruction. The walls rose straight toward the sky, unbroken by bench or terrace and marked only by an occasional line of stratification in the cream-colored marbles and limestones which composed them. The waters flowed noiselessly and swiftly through this cañon, with hardly a ripple or gurgle except at one place. Their flow is so silent as to be appalling. With the ends of our oars, we could almost touch either wall. The solemnity and beauty of the spectacle were overwhelming.

We had gone only a few miles when a halt was suddenly forced upon us. Directly ahead was a place where one side of the great cliffs had caved away, and the debris spread across the narrow passage of the river. This obstacle was composed of great blocks of stone and talus rising two hundred feet high, which, while obstructing the channel, did not dam the waters but gave them way through the interstices of the rocks. The boulders were mostly quadrangular masses of limestone fifty feet or more in height, dumped in a heterogeneous pile, like a load of bricks from a tip-cart, directly across the stream. At this place, which we appropriately named "Camp Misery," trouble began. Although the obstruction was hardly a quarter of a mile in length, it took us three days to get our boats across it.

A landing was made upon the rocks, and scouts were sent out to explore a route across them. In the course of three or four hours we found that it would be necessary to pack the contents of the three boats over these stones, first uphill to an altitude of one hundred and eighty feet and then down again to the stream below the obstruction. Crevices were found between the boulders where a foothold could be obtained, and the articles were passed hand over hand to a height of one hundred feet. Our faithful Mexican, with ax in hand, then cut away the thorns and daggers and made a path along the base of the cliff for the remainder of the way. It was not until the following night that the last piece of baggage was transferred.

The handling of the equipment was an easy task in comparison with a greater difficulty that lay before us. The three boats, each weighing three hundred pounds, were yet to be lifted over the vast cubes of limestone along the immediate course of the river, around and between which the water dashed with the force of a mill-race, and where a slip of the foot on the smooth rocks meant certain death.

Foothold had to be sought on these great stones, and often precious hours were lost in seeking a means to ascend them. This was sometimes accomplished by throwing lariats, the dangling ends of which were scaled hand over hand. Once upon the summit of the rocks, the boats were pulled and pushed up by the exertion of all the crew. Three days were consumed in this task before we passed our final night at Camp Misery, ready to resume our journey the following morning. At the place where we ate and slept there was not a foot of flat earth to lie upon, and we sought such perches as we could obtain upon the sharp-cut edges of the fallen limestone blocks, above danger of flood. For myself, by a liberal use of the geologic hammer, I widened out a crevice in the stone, in which, by lying crooked, I managed to pass the nights.

During our three days' stay at Camp Misery we had abundant opportunity to observe the majestic features of the great gorge in which we were entombed. The scene within this cañon is of unusual beauty. The austerity of the cliffs is softened by colors which camera or pen cannot reproduce. These rich tints are like the yellow marbles of Portugal and Algiers, warmed by reddening tones which become golden in the sunlight. The cliffs are often rigid and geometrically vertical, but usually the severity is modulated by gently swelling curves which develop at the edges of the horizontal strata or vertical joint-seams. In many instances, the profiles are overhanging or toppling. This was forcibly illustrated on one occasion when, having selected a spot upon which to make my bed, my attention was directed by the men to an immense boulder so delicately poised upon the very edge of the cliff immediately above me that the vibration of a rifle-shot would apparently have dislocated it and sent it thundering down.

Here and there the surging waters at the angle of a bend, beating straight against the limestone, have bored great caves beneath the bluffs at the water's edge. In places gigantic columns five hundred feet high have been undermined and dropped down a few feet without tumbling, so that they now lean in uncertain stability against the main wall.

From above, the sky-line was of never ceasing interest, whether bathed in sunshine while shadows filled the vast crevices below or flooded with the glorious moonlight which is one of the characteristics of the desert.

Frequently there were vast caverns a hundred feet or more below the crest-line, into which we could look from below and see their other ends opening out upon the plain above. Castellated and turreted forms in natural mimicry of the feudal structures of the Rhine were frequent. One of these, opposite our camp, was so natural that upon awakening one moonlight night and seeing it above me, it took several moments for me to dispel the idea that it was a genuine castle, with towers, bastions, portcullis, and port-holes.

A striking feature of this cañon was the absence of animal life. There was little sign of bird, rabbit, wolf, squirrel, or other animal, so common upon the uplands above. The only indigenous creature we saw was a small species of bat, new and unknown to me, which fluttered about at night. A single covey of blue quail, which in some manner had made their way into these depths, were so frightened of our intrusion that is was pitiful to see their vain attempts to fly out to the cliffs above. Time and again the mother bird called her flock together and led an attempted flight to the summit. The quail is not noted as a soarer, the trajectory of its flight being almost as flat as that of a rifle-ball. They rose two hundred or three hundred feet, with a desperate whirring of their wings, and then fell back almost exhausted into the rocky debris of the cañon.

While buried in this cañon at Camp Misery we were constantly impressed by the impossibility of escaping from it in case we should lose our boats or be overwhelmed by sudden floods. Leisure moments were devoted to looking for some possible manner by which the vertical walls could be scaled. For its entire length there is no place where this cliff can be climbed by man. In order to reach its summit, after finishing my river trip, I made a special overland journey from Marathon and succeeded in surmounting its north end some ten miles from the river and in making a photographic view of the cañon from above.

Having finally succeeded in crossing the obstruction early one morning, we transported our baggage to the boats, preparatory to leaving. Before the boats were loaded a tremendous roaring sound like distant thunder was heard up the cañon, and we saw that what we most dreaded was happening—the river was rising. A big flood of the ordinary kind would have veneered the dangerous rocks with water, and our prospects for escape would have been small. We hastily piled our baggage into the boats and sprang aboard. It was either stay and starve or go and chance it. Fortunately, this particular rise proved to be a small one, just sufficient to give the desired impetus to our craft, and our course through the cañon was rapid. The walls increased in altitude as we descended the stream, and just as they reached their greatest height, some seventeen hundred and fifty feet, our boats suddenly emerged into the sunlit desert.

Looking back, the beautiful outlines of the east cliff of the plateau of Santa Helena, from which we had emerged, were seen. We lingered long in contemplation of this most remarkable feature. It is an abrupt escarpment of massive limestone which rises in a vertical wall to a height of seventeen hundred and fifty feet and extends northwest and southeast for sixty miles, fifty miles in Mexico and ten miles in Texas. Its sky-line is as square-cut and horizontal as the top of a table. The face of the cliff appears absolutely vertical, although it is marked by one slight bench. Nicking the summit here and there at wide intervals are deep V-shaped rifts of minor waterless cañons whose mouths are suspended in the air. As bold and extensive as is this mountain, it has hitherto found no place or name on published maps. For a week after passing out of the cañon this great escarpment could be seen behind us.

This majestic wall of rock forming the eastern escarpment of the Santa Helena owes its contour to the geologic process known as faulting. Along a great fracture developed parallel to its face, the rocks have dropped down over five thousand feet. Some forty miles to the east there is another scarp line, parallel to that of the Sierra del Carmen. This faces in the opposite direction, or toward the west, so that these gigantic cliffs oppose each other. Between these two walls of rock the strata once met in an arch, making the great crest of the regional mountain uplift. The intervening region, or lower country, represents a down fallen wedge. Such a country constitutes a rift valley, just as if a longitudinal slide were made in the crust of a watermelon and then pushed in until its area was below that of the remaining surface. In this case it was the arch of the Rocky Mountains which had dropped down, constituting a peculiar belt of country, into which we suddenly emerged as we left the cañon and which may be called the Terlingo Desert.[1] Although this desert is only forty miles wide, the river pursues a circuitous course through it of fully one hundred miles. For days we followed vast beds or ox-bows until we had made the great south bend of the river.

The Terlingo Desert is one of the most bizarre pieces of landscape that can be imagined. Though called a plain, this is only out of courtesy to its more mountainous perimeter. Its surface is covered by nearly every form of relief within the topographic category, including stretches of level plain, vast terraces, deep arroyos, lava-capped hills, necks and dikes of old volcanoes, huge mesas, summits, and small mountain-ranges, collectively forming one of the hottest and most sterile regions conceivable.

The crowning feature of this desert is the lofty and peculiar group of peaks known as Los Chisos ("the ghosts").[2] These weird forms are appropriately named. They are ragged points of a reddish granitic rock, weathering into yellow and orange colors like those from which the Yellowstone derives its name; they rise almost straight into the air to a total altitude of nine thousand feet, or sixty-five hundred feet above the river. The vertical slopes of the peaks, rifted here and there by joints and streams, give to them the aspect of being clad in filmy drapery. Wherever one climbs out of the low stream groove, these peaks stare him in the face like a group of white-clad spirits rising from a base of misty gray shadow and vegetation. Many are the weird forms and outlines which the peaks assume. Two specially conspicuous rocks are known as "Mule Ears," and, seen from a distance of twenty miles or more, are remarkably suggestive of the objects for which they are named. They are separated from the main summits by a valley which, from its inaccessibility, the cow-boys have named "Cow Heaven." Surrounding these peaks on all sides is an area of lower hills and old terraces covered with desert gravel and vegetation, some of which are black-capped volcanic hills; others are of dazzling yellow sandstone; still others show stripes of stratified vermilion and chocolate colors.

Day after day we drifted through this weird desert, hemmed in by low bluffs of dirty yellow soil and seeing few signs of human habitation. One day we ran across three or four Mexicans leisurely driving a herd of stolen cattle across the river into Mexico. This is the chief occupation of the few people who choose this wild region for a habitation.[3] A little later we were greeted at our camp on the Mexican side by a white man accompanied by seven or eight Mexicans, all fully armed. Ware recognized him as a notorious ex-convict known in Texas as "Greasy Bill." Later, upon my return to Marathon, I learned from the Rangers that he was the outlaw most wanted in Texas and that only the year before he had murdered an old man named Reed, who kept a store on the Texas side.

We were now nearing the apex of the Great Bend. The river had never been correctly meandered, and we naturally looked for the point where the stream which we had followed so many miles in a southwesterly direction should turn toward the north. Five times we came to the southern apex of bends in the stream, each time thinking we had made the turn, before we finally reached the most southern point in our journey. Our general course then changed from southwest to a direction, which we were to follow for many days.[4]

Just after making the turn we entered the first of the two cañons known as the Little and the Big San Vincente cañons respectively. These cut through a long, low sierra within the general area of the Terlingo valley.

Directly through and across the front of the sierra, a vertical black line could be seen marking the vast chasm through which the stream makes its way. As we neared the entrance, the river presented the appearance of apparently plunging into a seething hole without visible outlet. This cañon, like the Grand Cañon de Santa Helena, is cut through limestone, but the strata are tilted and bent into many picturesque effects. The bends of the stream in its depths are more numerous, and the walls are broken by the entrance of many lateral cañons presenting pinnacled and terraced cream-colored sides.

In this cañon we saw a Rocky Mountain sheep far above us upon an inaccessible ledge. Serafino took one shot at him, and he tumbled back in a majestic leap.

The passage of the San Vincente cañons took only a few hours, and at noon we found ourselves in the eastern or Tornillo extension of the Terlingo Desert, near the ruins of the old Mexican Presidio de San Vincente. These ruins were seen in 1852 by the Mexican Boundary Survey, and were apparently as ancient and deserted then as to-day. They consist of extensive roofless walls of old adobe buildings standing in an uninhabited region, upon a low mesa a mile or two from the river. The people of the Big Bend region have a tradition that in the days of the Spanish regime, they were the site of a prison where convicts were kept and worked in certain mythical mines in the Chisos Mountains. They are the ruins of an old Spanish frontier military post.

The following morning we passed another short cañon, through a mountain region similar to that of San Vincente, which was picturesque in every detail. Beyond this we arrived at the village of Boquillas, where we encountered the first and only American civilization upon our expedition.

At this point, and for about fifty miles down its course, the river is reinforced by a remarkable series of hot springs bursting out of vertical fissures. The first noted of these was in the middle of the stream, and its presence was made apparent by the beautiful limpid water welling up in the midst of the muddy current. Roughly estimated, the volume of the stream is doubled by springs of this character as it passes through these mountain gorges.

Boquillas is a widely divided settlement that owes its existence to a near-by silver mine in the adjacent mountains of Mexico. Upon the American side there are a store, a custom-house, and a post-office. These are connected with the Mexican side of the river by a great wire-cable carrier a quarter of a mile long, terminating in Mexico at a smelter where enterprising Americans are reducing the ore found in a vast pocket twelve miles away in the Sierra del Carmen.

Two miles below the smelting-works is a densely crowded village of two thousand Mexican inhabitants. This, like other Mexican towns along the Rio Grande, presents none of the neatness or artistic suggestion of the villages of other parts of Mexico. There is no sign of stucco, whitewash, or of ornamentation of other kind. Streets and walls and interiors are all a continuation of the dirty adobe soil of which the houses are built, made no less repulsive by the filthy pigs, burros, chickens, and other inhabitants which seem to possess no separate apartments. It is rumored that the ore is becoming exhausted and that within a few months the industry will cease. Then the inhabitants of the three Boquillas will disperse like the flakes of white cloud that sometimes dot the sky, and the solitude of the desert will again reign the entire length of the Big Bend.

East of the Boquillas group of settlements the wonderful western escarpment of the Sierra del Carmen rises straight above our path. Although the crest, which makes a gentle arch, is less regular than that of the opposing escarpment of the plateau of Santa Helena, it is higher and of grander relief. Surmounting the center of the arch of the plateau is a single steeple-like peak, which may be termed the Boquillas Finger. This landmark, like the Chisos summits, was often in sight from points one hundred miles away.

Across the center of the Sierra del Carmen, which rises seventy-five hundred feet above the sea, the river cuts another vertical chasm, which is even more worthy of the name the Grand Cañon than that of the Sierra de Santa Helena. The Mexican Boundary Surveyors, upon encountering it, were obliged to make a detour of fifty miles around the mountain to approach the river again, where they finally gave up the attempt of further exploration and reached the lower Texas country by a long journey through Mexico. The cañon profile presents a summit nearly five thousand feet above the river. The river itself, in approaching this mountain, first turns from side to side in short stretches, as if trying to avoid the mighty barrier above it, and then, as if realizing that it is constantly becoming involved in the maze of foot-hills, suddenly starts across the sierra.

In crossing this mountain the river pursues a tortuous course made of many small rectangular bends, around each of which a new and more surprising panorama is presented. The walls of the cañon are the same rich cream-colored limestone rocks as those which make the cañons of Santa Helena and San Vincente. Owing to the dislocation of the strata, the rocks are more varied in form and are broken into beautiful pointed salients and vertical columns. Wonderful indeed are the remarkable forms of rock sculpture. Among these was a vast cylindrical tower like the imaginary pictures of Babel, standing outward of the cliff-line and rising, through perspective, far above. Upon the opposite side was another great Rhine castle. Frequently lonely columns of rock five hundred feet or more in height stood out from the front of the cliff in an apparent state of unstable equilibrium. Caverns of gigantic proportions also indented the cliff at many places. Again, the great yellow walls were cut from base to summit by wonderful fissures filled with white calcite or vermilion-colored iron ore. Huge piles of talus here and there encumbered the bases of the cliffs.

The moon was full while we were in this cañon, and the effects of its illuminations were indescribably beautiful. Long before its face could be seen, its light would tip the pinnacles and upper strata of the cliffs, still further gilding the natural yellows of the rocks. Slowly this brilliant light sank into the magma of darkness which filled the cañon, gently settling from stratum to stratum as the black shadows fled before it, until finally it reached the silent but rapid waters of the river, which became a belt of silver. Language cannot describe the beauty of such nights, and I could never sleep until the glorious light had ferreted out of the shadows from every crevice and driven darkness from the cañon.

After several days our boats suddenly drifted out of the shades and beauties of the Carmen Cañon and emerged into the last of the open desert basins. As we did so, we suddenly came upon a thousand goats, accompanied by their shepherds and dogs, which were drinking at the water's edge. Startled by the unusual appearance of boats, they quickly fled.

In this small desert, known as Stillwell's Valley, which is only ten or twelve miles across, we again see the remarkable alluvial deposits of the Rio Grande rising in wonderful terraces back to the bases of the mountains. The human mind is almost incapable of conceiving the vast quantity of boulders which in times past have poured out of these vertical cañons into such open plains.

Evidence of animal life, hitherto so rare, now began to appear. A lizard was noted, and two immense ravens, half-hopping, half-flying, defied us to shoot them. Everywhere along the muddy banks beaver slides were found, and the willows had been cut by them. Three deer were also seen, while now and then a covey of blue quail scrambled up the stony banks and scattered in the cactus-shrub. A mocking-bird sang in the thorny bush. Only one who is accustomed to the animal life of the desert can imagine the joy with which we greeted these lowly friends.

Beyond the little Stillwell Desert we entered Temple Cañon. The severity of its walls was frequently broken by ravines, so that at nearly every bend there stood before one a beautifully sculptured mountain, golden in the sunlight, with pinnacled summits, and cliffs carved into exquisite panels and grottoes.

Our journey was just half accomplished, and we had crossed to the eastern side of the Cordilleras and were upon the Atlantic slope. The general direction of the river now bent due north, and although the true mountains of folded structure had ceased, the stream continued to be indented to a depth of two thousand feet or more in cañons of limestone cut out of the great plateau which flanks the eastern side of the Mexican sierra. This lower course is almost a continuous cañon to Del Rio, and from an esthetic point of view is even more picturesque, and beautiful than the portion of the river already described.

Beyond Temple Cañon the cliffs recede, leaving a valley from one to five miles in width between the distant walls. Through a huge gap in these the mouth of Maravillas Creek has been cut. This is a horrible desert arroyo, leading northward for one hundred miles or more to Marathon. It has a channel sufficient for the Hudson but is utterly devoid of water. Now and then, in the intervals of years, great floods pour down its stony bottom, giving the boulders and other desert debris a further push toward the Rio Grande and the sea. Such floods, however, are so unusual and sporadic that I have never found a man who knew this stream to run from source to mouth. No profounder testimonial to the slowness of nature's great geological processes can be found than these vast waterless waterways. The mouth of Maravillas Creek marks the end of the great northerly stretch of the Rio Grande, and from there on the algebraic sum of the direction of the river's course is almost due east to the mouth of the Pecos.

Below the mouth of the Maravillas the river continues in a narrow valley between the now more widely separated cliffs of the cañon, which are great buttes and mesas, the dissected fringe of a high limestone plateau above us. These cliffs are cut into many lobes and buttes. Occasionally one of these stands out and apart from the main cliff-line in lonely grandeur. Of this nature is Castle Butte, a notable landmark. This rises fully fifteen hundred feet above the river. Its circular, flat top, the square-cut escarpment cornice, and the gracefully sloping pediment are beautiful illustrations of the wonderful symmetrical sculpture seen along the river. These wider vistas are only of brief duration. Soon the rocky walls again approach each other and the stream resumes its crowded channel between vertical walls, presenting only at rare intervals a place where one can land and find a small spot to camp.

We had now been nearly a month on the river, and the necessities of the occasion forced us to push on as fast as possible. In the steep cañons

there had always been a tense feeling of anxiety, accompanied by a long-
ing to escape the dangers as soon as possible. This feeling, as well as our
limited commissary, ever drove us onward.

Shortly after making the turn to the east, and in the depths of a beautifully terraced cañon, we came upon another copious hot spring running
out of the bluff upon a low bench, where it made a large, clear pool of
water. We reached this place one Sunday noon. The sight of this natural
bath of warm water was tempting to tired and dirty men, and here we
made our first and only stop for recreation. After lunch, most of the party
proceeded to the warm pool, and stripping, we literally soaked for hours
in its delightful waters, stopping occasionally to soap and scrub our linen.
While here the party indulged in guessing the height of the enclosing
cliffs. The air was so clear in this country that one always underestimated
the magnitude of the relief. None of our estimates exceeded five hundred
feet. Seeing a good place for the first time in all our course to scale the
cañon walls, I climbed them and measured the exact height, which was
sixteen hundred and fifty feet. The view from the summit was superb, revealing the panorama of the uplands, which is completely shut out while
traversing the chasm below.

In the eastern course of the river the rock forms and sculpture become
more varied, and one is constantly surprised by new types of sculpture
and scenery. For miles we passed through a perpendicular cañon, the cliffs
of which were serrated by rough and cavernous indentations and great
vertical seams, between which the ledges were molded into ragged forms
like the Bad Lands of Dakota. Below this, in another cañon, the sculpture is marked by queer, eccentric pinnacles projecting above the ragged
sky-line—spires, fingers, needles, natural bridges, and every conceivable
form of peaked and curved rocks.

About the center of the eastern stretch of the river, the altitudes of the
cañon walls decrease slowly and almost imperceptibly until the river completely surmounts the great limestone formation which has been the chief
matrix of its prison walls. These walls, to their termination, lock in the
river securely from approach. In this eastern stretch the immediate gorge
of the river is generally a cañon within a cañon. With a double cañon of
this type MacMahon had once been caught by a flood. He endeavored to
escape to the uplands, in order to make his way to the railway. After three
days of attempt, he finally reached the summit of the immediate cañon,
only to find another wall, invisible from the river, which it was utterly impossible to surmount. Fortunately, the river had meanwhile subsided, and
he escaped by resuming his boats.

There was a break in the continuity of the cañon near where the river crosses the 102d meridian. This interruption is only a short one, for the stream soon begins to descend again into a rock-bound trough. In this portion, and as far east as the mouth of Devil's River, some of the most beautiful and picturesque effects are found. The walls are no longer of orange color but are of chalky limestone of purest white, which weathers into great curves rather than vertical ledges. In one cañon, for instance, the walls are carved into the most remarkable perpendicular pillars, resembling columns of the Egyptian type, each of which is over one hundred feet in height. Unfortunately, the Kodak films were exhausted, and the glass plates failed to receive the impression of this artistic scene. In other places the river has gradually undermined a channel far beneath a great ledge of overhanging limestone, the summit of which projected as smooth, slanting gables overhanging the stream, under which we sailed for hours.

Beautiful as were these cañons, and prolific as they were in game and in caves of wild honey, the hardships we had endured were telling upon the temper of the party, and we no longer appreciated the noble surroundings. We longed only to escape from the walls, upon which we now began to look as a prison. Ten hours of hard rowing each day, every one of which was burdened with the additional labor of dragging the boats over dangerous rapids, constant wetting by wading and ducking, the baking due to a merciless sunshine, the restricted diet, made no better by Serafino's ignorance of hygienic cooking and Shorty's constant additions of bacon grease to every article, together with the ever-present apprehension of danger, had put us all in a condition of quarrelsome, nervous tension, which is a dangerous state in camp, no matter how friendly all may be, and it was with pleasure that we finally sighted a longed-for landmark indicating a point where we could abandon the river.

Opposite the village of Langtry, near the top of a vertical cliff some three hundred feet high, is a small bluff cavern. Poised on the edge of this inaccessible cavern is a huge pile of sticks carefully entwined into what is perhaps the largest bird's nest in America. Since the trans-Pecos country was first known, this nest has been a landmark, and until lately was inhabited by a pair of eagles which here annually brought forth their young. A few years since, however, a company of colored soldiers were stationed near this place, and, with the instinct which prompts men to shoot at every living thing, they killed the birds, which even the hardened frontiersmen had long protected.

We landed the contents of our boats upon a little beach opposite this nest. A messenger proceeded a mile and a half to the village of Langtry and secured a packhorse, which conveyed our belongings to the railway-station. It was gratifying to see once more even the crudest habitation of man. We were received by a famous old frontiersman, whose hospitable house is decorated with a peculiar sign reading:

> Law West of the Pecos.
> Roy Bean.
> Justice of the Peace and Notary Public.
> San Antonio Lager Beer.

We had hardly reached the railway-track when we became aware of the fact that civilization's dangers are sometimes greater than those of nature. A locomotive whistle was heard in the distance, the first time that sound had greeted our ears for over a month. From the fact that this whistling continued fully five minutes we understood that it was a signal of distress, and that a train had become derailed somewhere on the wild and desert prairies. Soon a hand-car appeared. An appeal for medical assistance was made, and my party, with its small first-aid-to-the-injured outfit, was conveyed some five miles out into the desert, where a huge freight-train, pulled by two gigantic locomotives and laden with rich goods for the Orient, had jumped the track and tumbled into a chaotic pile. All night long we attended to the injured and the dead, and it was three o'clock the next morning when we dragged our weary steps over the miles of cactus back to the village, threw ourselves upon the railway-platform, and for the first time within a month we slept away from the roar of the river and free from the oppressive fear of danger which had ever haunted us within its confining walls.

We had successfully navigated and mapped three hundred and fifty miles of a portion of one of America's greatest rivers which hitherto had been considered impassable; we had made a geologic section directly across the eastern sierra of the great American Cordilleras from the interior deserts to the coastal plain, procuring light upon some of our least-known country; we had escaped dangers which had overwhelmed those who had attempted the cañons before; and our little party dispersed contented with its success.

NOTES

   1. Today this is spelled "Terlingua," but because the origin of the name is controversial, I have given Hill's spelling here for the possible interest of linguists.

   2. The meaning and origin of this name is also quite controversial.

   3. Obviously, both of these statements are quite biased and debatable.

   4. The author seems to have his east and his west confused here.

EXPLORING THE RIOS

*Antonio de Espejo, translated by John Klingemann
and Dr. Rubén Osorio Juniga*

1583

[This expedition was mounted following an earlier expedition, in 1851, in which one priest was killed and two other priests decided to remain in New Mexico while the rest of the party returned to Mexico. Antonio de Espejo volunteered his wealth and services to accompany the priests assigned to rescue the priests who had been left behind. Espejo was a wealthy young cattleman and merchant. According to George P. Hammond and Agapito Rey, he had gotten in some trouble by murdering one of his cowboys and needed to make amends with the government."[1]]

THE BEFORE MENTIONED ANTONIO DE ESPEJO TOOK UP THE ASSIGN-ment with such earnestness that in very few days I was able to gather the soldiers and supply of provisions to make the journey, spending on the journey a large part of his hacienda. I left with them from Valle de San Bartolomé the 10th of November of 1582, taking for whatever use 115 horses, and mules, and many arms, munitions and supplies of provisions and some servants.[2]

We set our travels towards the north, and in two days' journey we came upon a large quantity of Indians that are called Conchos in large settlements or populations consisting of houses made from straw. These people, already having known about us and had relations with us from long ago, came out to greet us with signs of joy. The food these people eat and those in the rest of the province, which is vast, consists of the meat of hares, rabbits, and deer that they kill, and there is a great quantity of these animals. They have a lot of corn, which is the wheat of the Indias, squash, and good melons, and all in abundance. And there are many rivers that produce a great quantity of good fish, and of different types. They are all almost in the nude, and the weapons they use are the bow and arrow; and they live under a government, and under the lordship of caciques, like the Mexicans. We were not able to find any sign (i.e., symbols, figurines, etc.) of their gods, nor were we able to understand whom they worshiped, with which reason they easily consented to have Christian crosses placed on them. They were pleased with the crosses after having been told by our men through interpreters about their significance. Through these interpreters we were also able to find out about other settlements that were all populated by people from their nation, to which these before mentioned Conchos guided us for more than 24 leagues. There those people came out to receive us because of news sent by caciques from one pueblo to another.

After having traveled the before mentioned 24 leagues, they came upon another nation of Indians called Pasagüates, which lived like their neighbors the Conchos, who did the same and guided us forward another four days' journey, with the notice of caciques as before mentioned. Our men found on this road many silver mines, it seems by those who knew, of very rich metal. After another day's journey we came upon another nation called the Tobosos, who at coming face to face with our men fled to the sierras, leaving their houses and pueblos deserted. Later we came to find out that a few years before certain soldiers had come through there in search of mines and had taken some of them captive, which had left the rest timid and keen-witted. The captain gave orders in his manner to call on them, reassuring them that no harm would come their way, and he did it in such a convincing manner that he made many return, whom he comforted, gave gifts, caressing them, and declaring to them through the interpreter that we would harm no one. They soon returned to being calm, and consented to have crosses placed on them. After being told of their [the crosses'] mystery, they displayed a great deal of contentment in hearing it. As a result, they accompanied our men, as had done their neighbors until they led us into a land populated by a different nation which was at a distance of 12 leagues from their own. They [the new nation] use bows and arrows and run about nude.

We Carry on with the Discovery of New Mexico

The name of the nation that the Tobosos guided us to was Iumanos [Jumanos] who by another name are called by the Spanish Patarabueyes. They have a large province made up of many pueblos with lots of people. The houses had roofs, built solid and firm, and the layout of the towns was done well. All of the men and women have their faces as well as arms and legs painted with stripes. They are a corpulent people, and of those that were seen to that point, were the cleanest. They had a lot of sustenance, and a lot of game animals from both land and air, and a great quantity of fish because they had big rivers that come from the North, and one is as big as the Guadalquivir, which enters the sea of the North [Gulf of Mexico]. They have a lot of small saltwater lakes that during a certain time of the year coagulate and very good salt can be made. They are a bellicose people, and they would later show it because the first night that our men set up camp they shot arrows at us and killed five horses, badly wounding a few others, and would not have left anyone alive had it not been for the armed men who defended us. Having done this bad deed, they deserted the place and climbed a sierra that was near where the next morning I, with five well-armed soldiers and an interpreter named Pedro, an Indian of the same nation, went to find them. With good reasoning I was able to pacify them, and speaking of peace made them come back down to their pueblo, and houses, and persuaded them to send news to their neighbors that we were men who harmed no one, nor were we going to take their haciendas, all of which I easily did with prudence. And I gave the caciques some strings of glass beads that we carried for the purpose, as well as sombreros and other trifles. With this and the good treatment that was given them, many accompanied our men for some days, walking along the shore of the before mentioned river, which contained many pueblos of Indians from this nation, which they traveled for twelve days' journey. At each pueblo the people would come out and greet us, having received news of our coming from the caciques. They met us without bows and arrows and would give us provisions, and others would give gifts and presents, especially pelts and embellished chamois, of which the ones found in Flanders are no better. They are a people who are totally dressed, and our men found that they had a fire in them for our holy faith, because they would signal to their god by staring at the sky, and they called him in their tongue Apalito, and they know him as señor, who through his skill and mercy they confessed gave them life.

Many of them came along with the women and children to the religious one that we said was with the before mentioned captain and soldiers, who made the sign of the cross upon them and gave them a blessing. He asked them from whom they had gained the understanding of God that they had, to which they responded it was from three Christians and a black man who had passed through there and stayed a few days in their land. And according to the signs they gave, it was Alvar Núñez Cabeza de Vaca, and Dorantes, and Castillo Maldonado, and a black man (Esteban). They had escaped from the armada that Pánfilo de Narváez had entered Florida with and after spending many days as slaves had come upon these pueblos through the miracles of God and through the healing of many sick with his [Cabeza de Vaca's] hands. All of which left them a great name in that land.

All of this province stayed in peace and calmness, which was demonstrated by their company and their service to our men for a few days at the edge of the river before mentioned.

After a few days we came upon a great population of Indians who came out to greet us after receiving news from their neighbors, and they showed us many curious things made from feathers of different colors and many blankets made from cotton and striped with blue and white stripes like those that are brought from China to trade and exchanged for something valuable. Everyone came, men as much as women, and children dressed in good and well-adorned chamois, and our men never knew what nation it was for lack of an interpreter who understood their language, even though they talked through signs. They were shown some rock of rich metal and asked if there were any in their land, to which they responded through the same signs that at five days' walk from there toward the West [el Poniente], there was such metal and in large quantities, and that they would guide us to that place and would show us; something which they did later. They accompanied us for the length of 22 leagues, all populated with people from their own nation. We followed the same river upstream and came upon another people, more than we had previously seen. We were well received and given many presents, especially fish, of which there was an infinite supply due to the large lakes that were near there which produced them in abundance.

We were among these people for three days, during which at night and during the day they performed many dances in their native custom with great joy. The name of this nation was not known because of the lack of an interpreter; nonetheless, we understood it to be large and extended. Among them we found an Indian from the Concho nation, who told us by pointing that 15 days' journey from there toward the West [el Poniente] was a wide lake and near it many large pueblos and houses of three or four stories with well-dressed people, and the land provided many provisions. He offered to take us there where our men could rest, but it was never done because we had to continue with the reason for our journey, which was to go north and give help to the before mentioned religious men.

What we particularly noticed about this province was that there was good weather and rich lands and a lot of wild game, both in the air and on land, and many rich metals and other particular things for our benefit.

From this province we followed our course for more than fifteen days without coming across a single person in the large plantations of pines with cones like those in Castile. At the end of what seemed to us to be 80 leagues, we came upon a small ranchería, or small pueblo of people, and in their houses, which were poorly made and of straw, we found large quantities of deerskins, highly embellished like the ones from Flanders, and a lot of white salt. Afterwards, these same people followed us to some large populations about 12 leagues away, always following the river of the North before mentioned until we arrived at the land they call Nuevo México. The shore of the before mentioned river was full of large groves of white cottonwoods, and in some parts they are 4 leagues wide, and likewise with many walnut trees and grapevines like those found in Castile. After walking for two days in these large groves with walnut trees, we came upon ten pueblos, located in different parts along the shores of the before mentioned river, in which many people lived and which, from what we saw, had more than 10,000 souls.

In this province we were given many provisions and taken into the pueblos where we were given lots of food, and chickens, and other things, and all was given voluntarily. Here we found houses with four stories, well built and with elegant rooms, and in most were stoves for the winter. They were dressed in cotton and deerskin, and the men's as well as the women's attire was like the Indians of México; and the strangest thing we saw was that the men and women wore shoes and boots made of fine leather with soles from cowhide, something we had not seen before. The women had their hair combed and made up, with nothing else on their head.

NOTES

1. George P. Hammond and Agapito Rey, introduction, *Expedition into New Mexico Made by Antonio de Espejo 1582–1583: As Revealed in the Journal of Diego Pérez de Luxán, A Member of the Party* (Los Angeles: Quivira Society, 1929), 28–29.

2. The original Spanish uses third person; however, for ease in reading, the translators and I have changed this to first person in order to better differentiate between the Indians and the explorers (using "we" for the explorers and "they" for the Indians).

GEOLOGIST'S HEAVEN
Charles L. Baker
1989

THE HISTORY OF THE MARATHON BASIN IS LIKE A VERY ANCIENT manuscript, tattered and torn, smudged and smeared, with most pages missing. It begins at a time—some five hundred million years ago—when most of the North American interior became covered by sea. Seas appeared and disappeared various times later but were absent longer than present. They left their records as rocks. When there was land nothing else is known.

During two widely separated times—no record intervening—there were deposits of silicon dioxide called chert, more resistant than rocks below and above, and hence making up the low ridges rising now above more extensive flats. The lower chert is blackish and interlayered with dark gray limestone. The upper is white, like frosting on the cake, a whetstone rock called novaculite, elsewhere in the world known only in the ancient mountains of Arkansas. It is very brittle, shattering into fragments, and so the Spaniards called its ridges Sierra del Vidrio, the name, translated, being now shifted to the nearby Glass Mountains. From chert under the frosting to the basal brownish sandstone are some layers of light brown, very fine grained, waxy-textured limestone having narrow flattened, strip-like animal remains, extinct long since, called graptolites, which once floated in sea water and are found to have been as widely distributed as Norway, Western Canada, and Australia.

Novaculite and dark hornstone layers in sandstones and clay shales in the rocks overlying, now between the ridges, are composed largely of single-celled, microscopic marine animals known as Radiolaria, forms being alive still and floating in the seas. The hornstones have been called Sydian stone, basanite or touchstone, the latter name being given because of their use in determining fineness of gold rubbed upon them. A great mystery yet is why only these minute animals and a few land plants seem-ingly existed here when elsewhere—from the Appalachians to California and from El Paso to the Arctic Ocean—was being made a thick limestone having remains of many kinds of sea animals.

The age when coal beds formed from north-central Texas to Pennsyl-vania had a sea widespread over western America. Clays from it found at the north rim of our basin east of the Fort Stockton road contain many seashells. Then began great movements of the rocks, which were shoved from southeast, from direction opposite, or in both directions, thereby being crumpled into folds mostly becoming overturned to northwest and some broken on that side and then moving farther in sheets. This older mountain belt stretched from the Rio Grande to Newfoundland.

Next—after the folds were much worn away—another extensive sea spread eastward over the land, extending from Mexico to the Arctic Ocean and northeast to Kansas and Nebraska. In it were made the rocks of the Glass Mountains, totaling from five to seven thousand feet in thickness. Dr. [J. A.] Udden's studies in 1914 made them famous. For they were found to contain remains of hundreds of sea animals when then known rocks of the same age elsewhere had been made in either dry or cold re-gions where life was scarce. In the latter part of the period, embayment extending to Kansas had a dry climate in which rock salt, potash, and cal-cium sulphate accumulated. Sea water entering from southwest met that already saturated with salts and dropped in the intermediate zone its lime and magnesia carbonates in a lobate belt extending northeast beyond the Pecos and back again into the Guadalupe, Apache, and Glass Mountains in reefs which, where not buried in the northeast, yield the West Texas and southeast New Mexico oil, and, where exposed, form the mountains named. They are the upper thick cliffs and ridges of the Glass Mountains, and Carlsbad Caverns has been dissolved out of the rock; northeast of the latter are mines of potash necessary for fertilizer and much more valu-able than all the oil which will ever be produced—by the way, another discovery of Dr. Udden besides West Texas oil, he being also credited for much of the Terlingua quicksilver.

Then followed millions of years with no record here, though in the Staked Plains and to west Wyoming sands and clays accumulated on land, Nevada, Utah, California, and western Canada being under sea. Largest of the dinosaurs lived at the end, but rocks in which they are found are in Texas only at the northwest corner of the Panhandle.

Then came back for the last time the sea, which stretched from Cen-tral America to the Arctic, from Utah to Iowa, besides covering the west-ern two-thirds of California and the southeast Atlantic and Mexican Gulf coastal plains to as far north as the mouth of the Ohio River. Mountains of eastern Mexico are thick limestone formed in it and the same rock rims of the Marathon Basin on all sides except the north. It forms the great uplifted block ridges of the Carmen Range, the Rio Grande gashing in it the Grand Canyon of Santa Helena, and lower downstream, the one through Mariscal Mountain, the Boquillas canyons and then a shallower canyon nearly all the way to Del Rio—and the lower canyons of the Pecos and Devils rivers. Marathon Basin likely was a plain flanked by the Glass Mountains ridge when the sea got there, but it was covered by deposits of the sea. The sea vanished before making of the first Rocky Mountains from Colorado to Alaska.

Later on, the region next west had numerous volcanoes, producing the rocks from the Davis Mountains to Cape Horn, world's longest volcanic land. Iron Mountain, north of Marathon, and Santiago Peak southwest are now solidified but once hot molten rocks pushed up through the older. Many volcanoes were violently explosive, belching forth fine dusts carried by winds as far east as Georgia. Volcanic rocks were folded into the Davis Mountains, Ord Mountain being an outlier and the Chisos Mountains a remnant.

Present Marathon Basin is a product of the wear and tear of the last million years. A broad dome (or swell) formed there in the last mountain making. Rain ran down the sides, finally making creeks. Water and wind have carried away the former rock cover, leaving the present lowland with its vestigial looped ridges of resistant chert.

Within twenty-five miles of Marathon there exists every known kind of mountain.

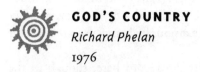

GOD'S COUNTRY
Richard Phelan
1976

"NOW WE'RE IN GOD'S COUNTRY," SAID A FRIEND OF MINE ONCE, AS we crossed the Pecos River westbound. I thought so too, but for a different reason. He was born in Trans-Pecos Texas. To him it was home. For me, it's God's country because man has changed it less, occupied it less, than any other part of the state. It keeps something of Texas's old-time wildness and freedom.

It is big, empty country with few roads, few people, and little water. Its broad stretches of desert—all part of the Chihuahuan Desert—are broken by mountains. There are some thirty named mountain ranges in all, most of them rocky and dry. A few of the biggest ones—the Chisos, Davis, and Guadalupe Mountains—rise into cool altitudes and have pine forests and springs.

Most of the year the Trans-Pecos air is impeccably clear. McDonald Observatory, in the Davis Mountains, has two of the world's major telescopes. Unlike the observatories near Tucson and Los Angeles, it has no problem with the glow of city lights. El Paso, 175 miles away, is the nearest city. . . .

Many Trans-Pecos mountain ranges are fault-block mountains—big chunks of the earth's crust that have come loose and tilted, just as a piece of concrete sidewalk may tilt and settle in the ground, with one end buried and the other sticking up above the surface. Fault-block mountains thus have a steep escarpment on one side and a long, gentle slope on the other.

The mountains have been there a long time, flaking away, dissolving in rain. Once they were much higher, and deep valleys lay between them. As material eroded from them it filled the valleys. Now hot, sandy desert plains and basins stretch from one range of mountains to the next. The peaks themselves are lower, worn down, and the bases of the mountains are buried from one to three thousand feet deep in their own detritus.

This arrangement has created *bolsones,* stretches of desert entirely surrounded by mountains so that no water can flow out. *Bolsón* in Spanish means big purse—something that holds what is put into it. Rainwater streams down the mountain sides, leaching salts and other minerals out of the rocks and washing sand and gravel for miles out onto the desert floor—toward the lowest point of the *bolsón,* of course—and the water and salts collect there, making a shallow lake.

The lake soon evaporates, leaving the salts and minerals behind. Most of the salt is the kind we season food with. With each rain more salt is washed in. The low point is thus a salt flat in dry weather and a salt lake after rain.

The Spanish name for a salt flat is *playa*. The big *playa* just west of the Guadalupe Mountains is crossed by Highway 180, which has ditches on both sides. Sometimes they are filled with clear water. I dipped a mouthful once, experimentally, but decided not to swallow it. It was many times saltier than the sea.

Not much grows in a salt flat, but a few things do. Such plants are called halophytes, which means salt-growers. Wolfberry, sea purslane, and salt grass, for example, grow large in dunes along the Gulf of Mexico, but small in the Trans-Pecos salt flats, where they have plenty of salt but not enough rain.

There were once more *bolsones* in the Trans-Pecos than there are now. Long ago the Rio Grande and the Pecos cut through them and gave them drainage, and their salt flats washed downstream into the sea. One of the best remaining *bolsones* runs north from Van Horn (on Interstate 10) to Guadalupe National Park. It is a long desert valley walled in by the Delaware Mountains on the east and the Sierra Diablo—classic fault-block mountains—on the west. The low point of the basin, white with salt, is some thirty-five miles north of Van Horn on the little Highway 54, which runs along just below the grim Diablo escarpment. . . .

Guadalupe Mountains National Park is so new that for several years it's going to be pleasantly plain, lacking an elaborate visitor center, lacking campgrounds where people can plug into lights and water. Most of the Guadalupe range is in New Mexico. Only the part which extends into Texas has been made into a national park.

The Guadalupes are limestone mountains, laid down as a reef about 200 million years ago when the area lay under a Permian sea. It is the best preserved fossil reef on the planet, a superb museum of Permian marine life. Fossil plants and animals are embedded even in the highest peaks, now nearly 9,000 feet above sea level.

The present crude campground and ranger station (a wooden shack) are high on the mountain's flank, near the old stage stop called Pine Spring. Below lie miles of desert. Above are the mountain heights, with trails leading up, and fifty-five miles of rough hiking trails in the higher country.

The trip that everybody wants to make (and many do) is up Guadalupe Peak, the highest point in Texas. It is not a hard climb. Any good walker can make it, provided he goes at an appropriate pace.

Comfortable shoes, a canteen of water, and a sandwich are all the equipment needed. A camera is nice too, for the view from the peak reaches northward far into New Mexico and southeastward to the Davis Mountains, eighty miles away.

Below Guadalupe Peak are salt flats, large ones, the low point of a huge *bolsón* that lies in both Texas and New Mexico. To the south, traffic slides silently up and down the steep grades of U.S. 180 like beads along a wire. And precisely on the highest point in Texas (8,751 feet) is what many people, including me, consider an offensive piece of litter.

It is a shiny metal pyramid about five feet high, anchored there by American Airlines in praise of its early, low-flying pilots who managed to get past the Guadalupes without crashing into them. (Other pilots have not been so lucky. The Guadalupes are full of old plane wrecks.) The few people who live in the country below have a kind of affection for the commemorative pyramid because it reflects the sun at various times of day and can be seen for miles as a glittering point of light.

Except for this marker, there was not a scrap of litter on Guadalupe Peak when I climbed it. The people who take the trouble to get up there apparently care enough about the place to leave it clean. Wildflowers bloomed among the rocks, and coarse, lush grasses were flourishing after summer thunderstorms. The air had a delicacy and freshness that I thought I might be imagining, but I wasn't. Others noticed it too.

El Capitan is the imposing rock face that travelers see from fifty miles out on highways approaching the park. Many people think it is Guadalupe Peak, but the highest peak lies inconspicuously just behind El Capitan, to the north. A staggering huge chunk of bare biscuit-colored limestone, El Capitan rises for thousands of feet, two thousand of which are vertical, above the desert. It can be climbed, but you don't make a frontal attack. You go most of the way up the Guadalupe Peak trail and then approach El Capitan from behind—from the mountain mass out of which it juts like a headland. It's a good idea to get some information from the park rangers before trying the climb.

The forests in the high Guadalupes are far from dense, for the soil is rocky and dry. Hikers must take water on their backs—a gallon a day per person. The main trees are Ponderosa pines and Douglas firs. Merriam elk once lived in the Guadalupes, but were killed off soon after white settlers came with cattle and rifles. The present animals are American elk, established in 1928 with a small herd brought from Colorado.

They are worth seeing, though not easy to see. A big white-tailed deer weighs two hundred pounds; a big elk seven hundred. You can try waiting for them to come and drink at twilight at a place called the Bowl. You can, that is, if there is water in the Bowl. Often the high country is totally dry, and the wild animals come down at night to drink from various springs which break out of the limestone two or three thousand feet below the summits: Smith Spring, Pine Spring, Guadalupe Spring, etc.

A few black bears and mountain lions remain in the Guadalupes. Bobcats, ringtails, coyotes, and turkeys are common. Porcupines may gnaw the salty straps of your backpack when you are camped. And Texas's only chipmunks live in these mountains and perhaps in the nearby Sierra Diablo. . . .

Smith Spring is a pretty place that even the most sedentary can walk to. In a canyon hung midway between the dry desert and the dry peaks, the little stream supports wildflowers, dragonflies, ferns, and shade trees. The walk back from Smith Spring is best toward sundown, when birds are watering at the pond near the trail and the distant mountains to the south are emerging from the daytime glare and turning eight or ten shades of blue.

The park's pride, and its carefully protected showplace, is big McKittrick Canyon. It is several miles long and several thousand feet deep, and enclosed by fawn-colored cliffs full of caves and pinnacles. The trail keeps to the bottom for two miles or so before it starts to climb.

Here plants from several life zones are sociably mingled: pines and firs from above, yucca and cactus from the desert below, walnut and big-tooth maple which really belong in temperate forests hundreds of miles to the east. The little stream in the canyon helps make all this possible. In isolation from the rest of the world, a number of species have developed which grow nowhere else—a honeysuckle, a mint, and a columbine, for example.

The Texas madrone also grows in McKittrick Canyon, and near the Pine Spring campground. Here and there in the Trans-Pecos, in exactly the right conditions, this strange and beautiful tree hangs on. Its trunk and limbs are red—cherry-red, or orange-red, or sometimes the lavender purple of cream that has been poured over blackberries. With red limbs, shiny green leaves, white blossoms, and edible red berries, the madrone seems to have escaped from some gentle enchanted forest.

A few people are so taken with madrone trees that they dig a small one up, unaware that the trees will not live outside their present range. They are in fact an endangered species, because young madrone seedlings no longer survive in the wild—no one is yet sure why. Some botanists think that the present heavy populations of deer and goats eat every young sprout while it is tender, and never give it a chance to become a tree. Whatever the reason, there is a possibility that when the present mature trees are gone there will be no more.

GUACAMAJA
Aldo Leopold
1949

THE PHYSICS OF BEAUTY IS ONE DEPARTMENT OF NATURAL SCIENCE still in the Dark Ages. Not even the manipulators of bent space have tried to solve its equations. Everybody knows, for example, that the autumn landscape in the north woods is the land, plus a red maple, plus a ruffled grouse. In terms of conventional physics, the grouse represents only a millionth of either the mass or the energy of an acre. Yet subtract the grouse and the whole thing is dead. An enormous amount of some kind of motive power has been lost.

It is easy to say that the loss is all in our mind's eye, but is there any sober ecologist who will agree? He knows full well that there has been an ecological death, the significance of which is inexpressible in terms of contemporary science. A philosopher has called this imponderable essence the numenon of material things. It stands in contradistinction to phenomenon, which is ponderable and predictable, even to the tossings and turnings of the remotest star.

The grouse is the numenon of the north woods, the blue jay of the hickory groves, the whiskey-jack of the muskegs, the piñonero of the juniper foothills. Ornithological texts do not record these facts. I suppose they are new to science, however obvious to the discerning scientist. Be that as it may, I here record the discovery of the numenon of the Sierra Madre: the Thick-billed Parrot.

He is a discovery only because so few have visited his haunts. Once there, only the deaf and blind could fail to perceive his role in the mountain life and landscape. Indeed you have hardly finished breakfast before the chattering flocks leave their roost on the rimrocks and perform a sort of morning drill in the high reaches of the dawn. Like squadrons of cranes they wheel and spiral, loudly debating with each other the question (which also puzzles you) whether this new day which creeps slowly over the canyons is bluer or golder than its predecessors, or less so. The vote being a draw, they repair by separate companies to the high mesas for their breakfast of pine-seed-on-the-half-shell. They have not yet seen you.

But a little later, as you begin the steep ascent out of the canyon, some sharp-eyed parrot, perhaps a mile away, espies this strange creature puffing up the trail where only deer or lion, bear or turkey, is licensed to travel. Breakfast is forgotten. With a whoop and a shout the whole gang is a-wing and coming at you. As they circle overhead you wish fervently for a parrot dictionary. Are they demanding what-the-devil business have you in these parts? Or are they, like an avian chamber-of-commerce, merely making sure you appreciate the glories of their home town, its weather, its citizens, and its glorious future as compared with any and all other times and places whatsoever? It might be either or both. And there flashes through your mind the sad premonition of what will happen when the road is built, and this riotous reception committee first greets the tourist-with-a-gun.

It is soon clear that you are a dull inarticulate fellow, unable to respond by so much as a whistle to the standard amenities of the Sierra morn. After all, there are more pine cones in the woods than have yet been opened, so let's finish breakfast! This time they may settle upon some tree below the rimrock, giving you the chance to sneak out to the edge and look down. There for the first time you see color: velvet green uniforms with scarlet and yellow epaulets and black helmets, sweeping noisily from pine to pine, but always in formation and always in even numbers. Only once did I see a gang of five, or any other number not comprised of pairs.

I do not know whether the nesting pairs are as noisy as these roistering flocks that greeted me in September. I do know that in September, if there are parrots on the mountain, you will soon know it. As a proper ornithologist, I should doubtless try to describe the call. It superficially resembles that of the piñon jay, but the music of the piñoneros is as soft and nostalgic as the haze hanging in their native canyons, while that of the Guacamaja is louder and full of the salty enthusiasm of high comedy.

In spring, I am told, the pair hunts up a woodpecker hole in some tall dead pine and performs its racial duty in temporary isolation. But what woodpecker excavates a hole large enough? The Guacamaja (as the natives euphoniously call the parrot) is as big as a pigeon, and hardly to be squeezed into a flicker-loft. Does he, with his own powerful beak, perform the necessary enlargement? Or is he dependent on the holes of the imperial woodpecker, which is said to occur in these parts? To some future ornithological visitor I bequeath the pleasant task of discovering the answer.

MADERAS DEL CARMEN
Roland H. Wauer
1992

WE HEARD THE PEREGRINE TIERCEL (MALE) CALLING TO HIS MATE long before we saw him. We also heard the responsive cries of the peregrine haggard (female) somewhere on the face of the gigantic cliff directly across from our lofty perch. I turned my binoculars toward the deep canyon below and searched for an invisible dot that would be the eyrie-bound hunter. Another call from the depths below somehow directed my search a little to the left. There he was! The tiercel was flying swiftly in a direct course towards the eyrie and his waiting mate.

I watched that incredible bird with all of the respect he so well deserved. He was returning to his eyrie with food that he had caught in the desert far below. His flight upward was at an angle of at least forty-five degrees. Yet the weight of a bird almost his own size—either a white-winged or mourning dove, I couldn't be certain—did not seem to hamper him. The peregrine's powerful wing strokes drove him upward.

Three of us watched the tiercel every stroke of the way after my first discovery. We knew when he was nearing the eyrie because of the increased calling of both birds. Then suddenly he disappeared from view into a hidden crevice within the rhyolitic fortress. We understood what was taking place as he shared his kill with his mate and, perhaps, three to four downy youngsters.

A few minutes later the tiercel reappeared, flying out and upward toward the top of the cliff, another six hundred feet or so. There in full view and perched on an old weathered snag, he rested. We watched him preen, ruffle his feathers, and finally settle down as if to stand guard on his Maderas del Carmen homeland.

We had hiked from our camp at Los Cohos Spring to the summit of Loomis Peak earlier that morning. Roseann Rowlett, David Ligon, and I had been standing in awe admiring the grand scene before us when our attention was caught by the peregrine's calls. And we continued to admire that incredible bird from afar for some time before we again turned our eyes to the scenery around us.

The view from the top of Loomis Peak (8,960 feet) may be one of the finest in North America. The desert lies to the west, below the 5,500-foot escarpment. On a clear day the Chisos Mountains stand out to the northwest. They seem almost touchable although more than fifty miles away. On dusty days they glimmer like a mirage against the far horizon. To the north are the other peaks of the Maderas del Carmen, and the flatland that lies beyond is the uplifted limestone portion of the range.

More of the Maderas del Carmen stretch out in a wide semicircle northeast to southeast from Loomis Peak. A dozen or more plateaus and canyons form parallel lines, one after another, all the way to the shimmering desert beyond. Because of the distance involved, one cannot pick out details in the desertscape below the cliffs on the west. The eastern side of the Maderas del Carmen forms a series of gradually descending steps that eventually terminate on the desert floor.

The high peaks to the south of Loomis Peak fall sharply off toward the west. And there below the southern rampart are the white scratches of Los Cohos Mine (at 6,300 feet elevation). Until 1976, western access to the highlands was available only by trail from the mine. A rough ore road provided access to that point.

The Sierra del Carmen forms a massive limestone and volcanic mountain range east and south of Big Bend National Park, Texas. That range arose from the same geologic past that created the prominent topographic structures that jut out of Big Bend's desert landscape. In about the center of the 801,000-acre park is a volcanic mountain range known as the Chisos. To the west is a broad limestone mesa that was sliced in half by the Rio Grande to form spectacular Santa Elena Canyon. South is Mariscal Canyon that forms the elbow of the Texas Big Bend Country. And to the east are the Sierra del Carmen and Boquillas Canyon.

The Sierra del Carmen comprises three rather distinct units. The northern end of the range forms the east side of the Big Bend National Park and usually is called the Dead Horse Mountains or, in Spanish, Caballo Muerto. This region is a series of extremely arid limestone ridges and valleys. South of Boquillas Canyon in Mexico the uplifted limestone ridge forms gigantic horizontal layers that provide a magnificent backdrop to the park's Rio Grande Village and the settlement of Boquillas in Mexico. South and slightly to the east of these limestone slopes is a higher series of volcanic peaks that run north-south for about twenty-five miles. This portion of the Sierra del Carmen range is known as the Maderas del Carmen.

The Maderas del Carmen contains seven peaks over 8,000 feet in elevation. Approximately 115 square miles lie above 5,500 feet. By contrast, just ten square miles of the Chisos lie above 5,500 feet; Emory Peak, the highest point in the Chisos Mountains, is only 7,835 feet elevation. An important difference between the Maderas del Carmen and Chisos Mountains is in the amount of annual precipitation the two areas receive. More than twenty inches is rarely recorded in the Chisos, but the Maderas del Carmen usually receives forty inches or more. This mountain mass is closer to the Gulf of Mexico and storms often diminish over the del Carmen before reaching the Chisos.

Mexico's Sierra del Carmen is more than an extension of the Texas Big Bend country. It contains all of the same ingredients that have made Big Bend National Park one of the world's greatest wilderness preserves—and then some. The park was dedicated in 1984 as one of North America's first international biosphere reserves, a status bestowed upon it by the Man and the Biosphere program (MAB) of the United Nations Environmental Program (UNEP). Yet the mountains south of the Rio Grande, which have received only minimal recognition, contain an even greater assortment of wildland flora and fauna, and spectacular scenery.

The desert that surrounds the Sierra del Carmen is typical of the arid lowlands throughout most of the Chihuahuan Desert region of Coahuila and eastern Chihuahua. For those who understand the desert it is a gentle and exciting place to be. But for the uninformed it can be harsh and deadly; daily summer temperatures can easily exceed 100 degrees Fahrenheit. The desert is more than a transition zone between the Rio Grande's line of greenery and the grasslands of the del Carmen foothills. It is the start of the mountains, the bottom of the pyramid.

On the warmer southern slopes, grasslands occur between 3,500 and 6,500 feet elevation, but the same habitat occurs at somewhere lower elevations on the cooler north-facing slopes. This habitat is relatively indistinct on the west side of the Sierra del Carmen, where the escarpment rises rather abruptly from the desert to the sheer cliffs of the mountaintops. The western escarpment ascends 5,500 feet in less than two miles. But on the east side of the del Carmen mountains, the same elevational change is stretched out to approximately twelve miles. The eastern side, therefore, not only provides easier access to the highlands but allows greater use by ranchers, loggers, and hunters.

Chisos agave is one of the unique succulents found within the del Carmen grasslands; until the 1960s it was considered endemic to the Chisos Mountains of Big Bend National Park. A second and even rarer agave occurs above the grasslands on the rocky cliffs and ridges of the Maderas del Carmen. It is known to occur only within the mountains of northern Coahuila—the del Carmen, Encantada, and Santa Rosa ranges. This is *Agave potrerana*, a heavy-stemmed plant with a beautiful rosette leaf base. Yellow flowers appear in late July and, like all agaves, the plant dies at the end of the first flowering season. It takes agaves from fifteen to thirty-five years to bloom.

A woodland of pinyon pine, junipers, and oaks occurs above the grasslands. This pinyon-juniper-oak habitat forms rather extensive woodlands on the eastern slopes of the numerous ridges and mesas and within the midelevation valleys. On drier slopes this habitat may reach up to 7,000 feet. Fingers of oak, hackberry, and other broadleaf trees follow canyon bottoms to about 4,000 feet elevation. But somewhere between 6,500 and 7,500 feet begins a more extensive montane forest that runs to the very tops of the highest pinnacles.

The real treasures of the Maderas del Carmen occur in the highlands. The forest crowns the rhyolitic castles and hides the fragile meadows and clear streams. Southwestern white and ponderosa pines blend with an amazing variety of oaks on open flats and ridges, and Douglas fir and Arizona cypress are more common in narrow canyons and other protected niches. Coahuila fir grows in some of the highest and most out-of-the-way canyons.

The new road, which is unpaved and extremely rough, climbs above Los Cohos Spring and crosses the divide into Madera Canyon (locally called Cañon Cinco). From that point, an old road follows the canyon bottom eastward all the way to the desert.

Near the top of Madera Canyon is a peaceful, straw-colored meadow set in a cathedral-like setting. Except for an assortment of wildflowers at various seasons, needlegrass is by far the most common groundcover. A slight breeze ripples the tawny stems like a field of summer wheat. But this field was not planted by farmers. It is a product of the rains, the soils, and wildfires. The meadow grass feeds deer, pocket gophers, and a variety of rodents. One of these—the yellow-nosed cotton rat—occurs only in meadows of needlegrass, in places left unabused, and where nature is still in control.

I was awakened one very early morning in a nearby meadow to the low whistles (a descending call that sounded as if it might come from a canyon wren—eastern screech-owl hybrid) of Montezuma quail. Nowhere have I found this beautiful Cyrtonyx as abundant as it was in the Maderas del Carmen. The theory that this species does better on ranchlands in the United States is certainly refuted by the del Carmen population. It must reach its greatest abundance on these native mountain grasslands.

Sierra del Carmen Whitetails

I surprised a mountain lion stalking a deer in the Madera Canyon meadow on one trip. My sudden appearance frightened the lion from its venison meal. The deer of the Sierra del Carmen is a small race of whitetail named after these mountains and occurring only in the del Carmen and Chisos mountains and adjacent wooded "islands," usually above 4,500 feet elevation. The various populations once were contiguous, but desert now separates these upland areas.

Philip Wells studied woodrat middens (dens) found within dry overhangs in the foothills of the Chisos and Dead Horse mountains. His 1966 report on his research described pieces of pinyon foliage more than 20,000 years old found in the middens. According to Well's chronology, until about 10,000 years ago the woodrats lived in a woodland environment quite similar to that found in the mountains today. Then the vegetation began to change to a more xeric type and finally to true desert. These studies suggest that the Chihuahuan Desert invaded northern Mexico as recently as 9,000 or so years ago.

The Sierra del Carmen whitetail deer apparently followed the tree line upward when the desert became established. Today, the Chisos and del Carmen mountains are like islands surrounded by an ocean of desert. And sometime in the last few thousand years mule deer have moved into the lowlands.

Cañon del Oso

My favorite place in all the Sierra del Carmen is Cañon del Oso (Bear Canyon). It is the greenest and most peaceful of all the beautiful canyons within the Maderas del Carmen. On the canyon floor is a stream that flows between grassy banks and trickles over rocky ledges. Numerous pools are spaced here and there where mossy boulders have lodged on some previous high water to dam a place or form a new meander. We bathed in some of the deeper pools in Cañon del Oso. The temperature of the water was almost too cold for us to stay submerged for more than a few moments. But the sunshine was warm and relaxing.

We were not the first people to use the delicious waters. At the head of Cañon del Oso is Cañon Tres, which contained remnants of an old logging camp. Weathered board houses still lined a relic roadway in one part of the canyon, and a pile of decaying slash marked the site of a long-forgotten mill. Beyond the pile of waste were narrow gauge tracks that led away from the mill site into a side canyon that still showed scars from logs dragged off the hillside to be torn apart and cut into boards.

It seemed incredible that such a place really existed within Cañon del Oso, incongruous, given the wild character of the canyon and the wilderness setting. The logging camp took on an almost surrealistic character as I wandered about. A rusty tool here and a piece of glass there brought ghosts back to that tiny village for a while. I was amazed at the idea that timber was so valuable during the 1930s that this remote sanctuary was breached. And the route used to transport machinery and equipment to the site, and to haul boards and logs away from the mill, was just as unreal. The roadway followed the canyon bottom for more than ten miles, over boulders and rockfalls, around narrow bends and down steep grades.

In places a log road had been constructed within the canyon bottom but high above the cascading water.

Only remnants of the roadway still existed, where huge planks were high enough above the canyon for a flash flood to pass underneath without disturbing the roadbed. In other places the rushing waters had totally torn away the roadbed and no sign of human endeavor remained.

The logging camp itself—Campo Tres—had been built at the end of the roadway in a little valley that lies between a high rocky cliff to the north and a high plateau to the south. A spring flowed from a grassy bank at the head of the valley and followed a shallow gully past two rows of houses and a tremendous pile of slash and sawdust. In one side of this pile was a deep hole where a black bear had recently dug for either shelter or food. Bear tracks led toward the high plateau via a steep side canyon.

Birdlife

I spent almost an entire day wandering on that forested plateau. The timber was tall once again, but I could not help imagining what it might have been like before the loggers came and changed things. I searched that day for trees that had been used by a woodpecker larger than those I already had seen throughout the forest. Acorn woodpeckers were common within the lower woodlands and ponderosa pine stands, and an occasional hairy woodpecker was found, too. Northern flickers were present in the highlands, as well. But I was looking for evidence that the imperial woodpecker, North America's largest, existed within the Maderas del Carmen.

The initial idea of these mountains containing imperials began on my first visit to the Maderas del Carmen in 1969. The Mexico highlands had enticed me ever since 1966, when I first went to Big Bend National Park as chief naturalist. My hopes of seeing the del Carmen highlands finally transpired when six of us climbed the steep burro trail above Los Cohos Mine into a different world. We camped at Los Cohos Spring and hiked out each day to explore the scenic wonders and learn what we could about the local flora and fauna.

One afternoon, high above camp on the western rim, I found three ponderosa snags with large, oblong holes in the trunks twenty-five feet above the ground. I was surprised at the size of the holes and took several photographs. I assumed at the time that the holes were remains of pileated woodpecker activities. Since that bird had never before been recorded in these mountains, I intended to document its presence. It was not until later that I learned that pileated woodpeckers do not occur in Mexico. The only large woodpecker that frequents habitat like that of the Maderas del Carmen was the endangered imperial, a bird known only from the

Sierra Madre Occidental highlands, far to the west. Like the ivory-billed woodpecker of the southeastern U.S. lowlands, the Mexican imperial is more of an enigma than a reality. And yet, there in the Maderas del Carmen was possible evidence of its existence far out of its previously known range.

Three weeks later I returned to the Maderas del Carmen highlands to try to find the bird or hard evidence of its existence. I found additional nesting trees, although every one was old and not adequate proof. I attempted to climb to one of the nest holes, hoping that an ancient feather had been left behind, but a near fall reduced my enthusiasm for that method of discovery. If I had known then that those trees were the last bit of nesting evidence I was to find, I would have risked my neck again and again until I retrieved any clues that remained in the nesting cavities.

One more piece of circumstantial evidence came my way on that second trip. I met a bear hunter wandering along Madera Canyon early one morning. We struck up a conversation and he soon was telling me about the local wildlife. I learned about the bears and *panteras,* as well as the deer and fox. I opened my Peterson field guide to the plate on hawks and falcons and asked him if any one of those birds lived in these mountains. With only a moment's hesitation he pointed to the Cooper's hawk, goshawk, and peregrine falcon. Although I was a little uncertain of the goshawk then, I later found it nesting in Madera Canyon. I next turned to the plate on western warblers. Again, he was correct. He pointed only at the painted redstart and Colima and olive warblers.

The only picture I had found of the imperial woodpecker at that time was in Ernest Edward's 1968 bird-finding book. I had photocopied that plate and it had reproduced quite well. I took that copy from the back of my book, unfolded it, and asked the bear hunter if any of the birds on that plate lived in the Maderas del Carmen. He looked at all of the illustrations. Then he pointed at only one, the imperial woodpecker.

I asked him how recently he had seen one. He said it had been a long time, maybe four or five years ago; he said he used to shoot them for food because they made a very good dinner.

I have returned to the Maderas del Carmen seven times to search for the imperial woodpecker, but since 1970 have found no new evidence. My last visit to the Maderas del Carmen was in 1976 and with the same amount of anticipation as I had experienced on that second trip. Two friends—Joan Fryzell and Grainger Hunt—had told me of seeing a "large crested woodpecker" in Cañon del Oso the previous year. Joan, Grainger, and I revisited the site in 1976, but I again returned without proof.

However, the highlands of the Maderas del Carmen were once again being invaded by woodcutters. The old logging camp in Madera Canyon had undergone a complete restoration. I counted thirty-four Mexicans busy with their projects of cutting the timber, dragging it off the hillsides and down the canyons to newly constructed roads, and trucking the logs to the mill to be cut into boards for transportation to Musquiz and Sabinas.

It is impossible to know what the Maderas del Carmen were like during the centuries before the first loggers cut the forest. I believe that the imperial woodpecker lived within these forested highlands. And I cannot help but wonder what other forms of life will be destroyed by the new logging activities.

Over the years, the birdlife of the Sierra del Carmen has commanded greater attention from scientists than any of the other wildlife. However, no investigations were done before the area was first logged. Alden Miller was first to describe the del Carmen birdlife, in 1955. Dave Ligon and I compared the area's breeding birds with those of the Chisos, Davis, and Guadalupe mountains in the 1970s. Although the Maderas del Carmen bird population is similar to that of the Chisos Mountains, there are several significant differences.

The greater variety of breeding raptors, undoubtedly the result of the much larger land mass, is most important. Golden eagles, redtails, zone-tails, goshawks, sharp-shinned and Cooper's hawks, peregrines and prairie falcons, and American kestrels are known to nest. One night at Los Cohos Spring I heard four kinds of owls calling: eastern screech, flammulated, northern pygmy, and northern saw-whet. Great horned and elf owls nest lower down the mountain.

I found the Maderas del Carmen montane forest habitat to be very similar to that of the Chiracahuas of southern Arizona. The brown-throated race of the house wren was abundant and seemed to sing from every pile of downed logs and brush. If behavior and vocalizations are any criterion for being a separate species, this bird deserves that status. Yellow-eyed juncos (earlier called Mexican junco) were just as numerous within the forest. Pygmy nuthatches were common in the stands of ponderosa pines. And high in the foliage of the pine and fir communities were olive warblers. In more open places, painted redstarts busied themselves flycatching in typical redstart manner.

Plans for Resource Protection

During the pre–Big Bend National Park days of the 1930s, a grand plan for an international park that would include the mountains and desert on both sides of the Rio Grande was encouraged by U.S. officials and other interested persons. Early park planners made a serious attempt to include the Sierra del Carmen in the planning process. The U.S. National Park Service sent biologists to both sides of the river to make initial surveys. Botanist Ernest G. Marsh, Jr., visited the del Carmen mountains and prepared a 1936 report on his findings, encouraging the establishment of a comprehensive national park comprising the best of both countries.

After Big Bend National Park was designated in 1944, biological surveys continued. As part of an ecological study of the new Texas park, a team of scientists including Walter P. Taylor, Walter B. McDougall, Clifford C. Presnall, and Karl P. Schmidt visited the northern half of the Sierra del Carmen in spring 1945 and reported on this survey the following year.

A Mexican "national park" was finally identified during the 1970s, and several Mexican maps included a park boundary line for the Maderas del Carmen park. However, the area received no administration or management and only minimal protection; and I discovered that local residents were unaware of park status.

Throughout the 1980s there was considerable communication about a "companion park" across the Rio Grande from Big Bend. According to Jim Carrico, Big Bend National Park superintendent at the time, Coahuila governor Eliseo Mendoza Buerreto was very supportive of the establishment of a major park for the Sierra del Carmen. The governor or his staff "discussed designation proposals and their implications" of a companion park with U.S. Park Service officials five times during 1988.

Superintendent Carrico presented a paper on this issue at the November 1988 Triennial Conference of the George Wright Society, in which he reported that much of the initiative for the Sierra del Carmen park is now coming from Mexico. He said that "members of the Coahuila Governor's staff have indicated that an area of approximately 1.6 million acres will make up the study area" in Coahuila. On September 7, 1989, an official program document, called "Programa de Desarrollo de Boquillas y Maderas del Carmen," complete with an exhibit of photographs and small scale models, was presented to Mexico's minister of tourism.

U.S. officials informed me that they believe that "high level SEDUE officials have personal interests in seeing the Sierra del Carmens receive protected status as well as proper management." SEDUE (Secretariat for Urban and Ecological Affairs) is analogous to the Department of Interior or Agriculture in the United States. However, only time will tell whether or not the good intentions expressed will become reality.

I hope that Mexico's policy makers will soon realize that the resources of the Sierra del Carmen are more important to the Mexican people if they are retained in their wild character rather than logged and hunted and mined. Mexico has a gold mine of another kind! A well-planned national reserve can do more for the economy and opening up of the northern frontier than any logging operation or hunting program could possibly accomplish.

It may someday be possible for people from all parts of the world to enjoy the beauty and resources of the Sierra del Carmen. More than one million visitors annually travel thousands of miles to see Big Bend National Park. These same people may someday visit a companion park across the Rio Grande. And, perhaps, a few of them may stand on top of one of the massive cliffs of the Maderas del Carmen's west side and marvel at the kind of view that raises mind and spirit above the routine concerns of our petty world.[1]

NOTE

1. In 1999 Alberto Garza Santos established a private nature reserve called Museo Maderas del Carmen, A.C. (www.maderas.org.mx).

COLORATURAS IN THE CANYON
Mary Lasswell
1958

EVEN THOUGH FACT AND REASON REASSURED ME, WHEN I SAW THE grandeur of the Big Bend, I kept saying to myself: Can this be Texas? Have I not fallen asleep and wakened in the high sierras of Mexico? Here was a Texas beyond anything dreams could produce—and the dream was a reality.

Where is the Big Bend?

That is a controversial question. There are as many answers as there are inhabitants. Each Big Bender feels that his own boundary description of the region is the official one. And why not? You can stand on any peak and look over your shoulder at yesterday and look ahead of you into day after tomorrow. In the desert section, centuries of sand and dust swirl around you. When the gray eddies and whirlpools die down, it would not be surprising to behold the Sphinx. A Mexican vaquero of nearly a century ago described the Big Bend Country something like this:

> You go south from Fort Davis
> Where the rainbow waits for the rain,
> Where the river is kept in a stone box

And the water runs up hill,
And the mountains tower into the sky
Except when they disappear to visit other mountains at night.
There is nothing down there for the cows to eat
So they have learned to live without eating.
There is room for a thousand cows
But not for ten thousand.
And how far is this?
One hundred miles. Possibly two.
¿Quién sabe?

The soul of Spain is here. Santa Elena Canyon is the stone box and the mountains in late evening light do appear to double up for night. The distance is roughly a hundred miles if you go by Alpine and was surely twice that a hundred years ago, by the tortuous path the vaquero must have taken from Fort Davis. The Big Bend region gets its name from the great dip to the south made by the Rio Grande about fifty miles below Presidio. The broad arc of the river cradles a region unparalleled in the United States in that it is an almost unaltered area of mountainous Mexican border wilderness. The solitude and ruggedness deepen as one winds into the heart of the Big Bend National Park in the Chisos Mountains.

Most of Brewster County, Texas' largest with almost 6,000 square miles, is considered Big Bend Country—yet the population is so sparse that rarely are more than fifty votes cast in the lower Big Bend.

Laura Gilpin's book of photographic studies, *The Rio Grande: River of Destiny,* contains superb photography of the Big Bend. To look at the pictures is the next thing to being there, for her camera reproduces not only the face of a mysterious region but its heartbeat as well.

How many times did the unknown vaquero-poet see in the black, volcanic evening a ghostly full moon rise over the jagged rock of the sierra on his right, while a blood-red sun low down in the west dipped into the purple sea of the horizon on his left?

This have I seen, and like Joshua, commanded the sun to stand still, and with as little success.

Along the side of the road, in the rocky chips, wild mint and creeping sage send out puffs of incense. A bell rings silently inside the beholder, and he begs: "Thy blessing, Lord."

The ritual ends. An unseen hand snuffs out the cathedral candles and the traveler pushes on, restored. Warm, enormous stars stand out, almost close enough to touch.

From mysteries such as these the ranchers, men and women, gather strength to face the unequal struggle with the capricious seasons. They call up a more fortunate rancher who has grass, tell him how many head they want to run, and ask, "How much?" Then they nail up the doors and windows, put the brake on the windmill, and start "riding the chuck-line route": visiting more fortunate friends.

"We'll go back when it rains," they say calmly. "We're drouthed-out. Might's well admit it."

"When did you last have grass?"

"Nineteen forty-one. It rained good. Not enough to flood, but enough for grass."

"When was another good year?"

"Lessee. Nineteen-fourteen was fine!" They turn their backs on what has been home through fat years and lean, and go into town, some to do carpentry, or drive buses, or some to write books, a few to work on magazines and newspapers, or to fry steak in roadside cafes. The spiritual strength and beauty of these men and women matches the great region that produced them.

"The atomic fission boys might knock off a few chips and splinters, but by the Almighty God that made them, they won't make much of a dent in them rocks." So runs the sentiment in the region of the Big Bend. What could the atom split that extremes of temperature had not done long ago?

The A-bomb or the H-bomb might reduce the Santa Elena Canyon to rubble, but they could never carve out anything comparable to the grandeur produced by the bold strokes of violent and sudden temperature changes. Rocks and mountain fastnesses were split asunder as though with a giant wedge, by the molten fire of noontide and the deadly freezing drop at night countless aeons ago.

The glory of the Big Bend National Park starts at Persimmon Gap, the northernmost entrance to the park, and to my mind, ends only when the beholder dies. Maybe not even then. I make no comparisons to the other natural wonders of the western United States. What I saw was entirely within the picture frame of Texas, and contrasts only with other parts of this state: that is to say, from sea level at Brownsville to eight thousand feet at Guadalupe Peak. The mood was set for me outside of Marathon on the way to the Park: five antelope of indescribable grace bounded along in gentle parabolas parallel to the car, leaps Nijinsky would have loved. The soaring of the antelopes was contagious to the human spirit, and I had that same feeling of primordial peace that comes from Rousseau's paintings of animals.

In the Park itself, my main impression was much the same: unspoiled, natural beauty. Grandeur, not just bigness. Great craggy copper-rose cliffs rise sheer and majestic on every side. The rosy red of the mountains is brocaded with the deep black-green of the vegetation clinging to a precarious toe-hold. The effect is of a heavy rust-colored silk with an exotic pattern of blackish-green cut velvet superimposed on it. High soar the peaks in shapes to stagger the imagination. Cathedrals, palaces, Valhalla. Those and many more: one the unmistakable image of the Alamo, high in the clouds, immortal as its history.

Colorful immensity and primeval magnificence fill the beholder with a great sense of upheaval, a feeling that gods older than ours clapped their hands to command the canyons into sudden glorious being. The pedestrian mind of man is linked for an instant with the force that created man and mountain.

Up among the craggy cliffs and precipitous ledges there is a sense of gigantic turbulence. One feels that the gods are still engaged in a primordial rough and tumble, an Olympian roughhouse that gouges and rends chasms through the heart of the mountains.

The scene before me, like much of Texas, was simultaneously my inspiration and despair. How should I attempt to picture such vastness of space and spirit? Beethoven, in a super-symphony, might have succeeded in communicating the glory. Fate would need to knock loud and long before this majesty would open the door.

A year after this section was written, an article on Texas by Ludwig Bemelmans appeared in the *McCall's* Magazine, in which he too expressed the thought that only Beethoven could capture the essence of the Big Bend. It was interesting to me that two practicing gourmets whose writing has been largely of a humorous nature should reach into the roster of the Immortals and seize upon the same genius as the only one who might have captured and put into imperishable form the Big Bend of the Rio Grande. Unless a titan endowed with musical power, imbued with melodic nobility, emerges from the amorphous cacophonists of the present, the symphony of the Big Bend will never be written. Beethoven has no more of a successor in sight than has Shakespeare.

The haze-crowned beauty of the Park is awesome and ennobling. Here *genus homo,* the litterbug, has not yet left his spoor. His ugly, mendacious signboards have not marred the pristine spaces of the Park and Chisos Basin.

The wild garden of the Big Bend is exciting. Where have the enterprising textile designers been all these years? Instead of hideous wagon wheels and cattle brands, twisted wooden ropes, and beastly, abnormal blossoms in garish colors, a whole related series of prints, drapery materials, upholstery fabrics, and carpetings could be worked out combining the natural colors and designs of the rocks, plants, and flowers, against various backgrounds. The century plant, seemingly carved of antique green-bronze iron beautifully corroded by age, holds up its branching candelabra to the sky. The waxen bells of the yucca, the giant Spanish dagger, are all begging for some sympathetic hand to set them to work, to bring them inside our houses.

Throughout the Park, the cinnamon-pink bark of the madrona and the Texas persimmon trees, their lovely round dark blue-green leaves, and intriguingly shaped trunks, twisted and gnarled stand out as colorful accents in the landscape. Here and there clumps of ocotillo rise in breathtaking splendor; their great dark green stems reach out like slender fingers clutching bunches of red firecrackers, holding their scarlet bursts of flame against the sky. There is no end to the intricacy and beauty of the plant life in the Big Bend.

The Park, and most of the Big Bend region, is little known because of inaccessibility. I think there is something in the atmosphere that is more than a little frightening to hot-shot extroverts, so the Park is unspoiled. So far.

Those who love and respect the Big Bend suffer a feeling of ambivalence toward publicity: they want everyone who can to come and enjoy the Park, but at the same time they want to preserve the primeval quality that sets it apart. There is nothing there that will attract the undesirable tourist. If the Park Boards, National and State, maintain the same high standards of taste and ethics they have shown up to date, there will be small danger of week-end hell-raisers appearing there in numbers large enough to matter. They want liquor and honky-tonks. The drive is too long for them in the first place. Scenery, nature trails, riding, exploring, and the creative arts of writing, sketching, or photography hold no appeal for them.

"Seems like I've heard of the Big Bend National Park," Texans have been heard to say, "but if I was gonna drive that far, I'd wanta go some place where I'd feel like I'd bin somewhere: Las Vegas or the Carlsbad Caverns!"

Castalon and the Canyon of Santa Elena—these I would see. The Chisos Mountains' wild wonderland would be the background.

Where were the human figures? There were not too many in sight. I felt certain that those we might ferret out would not be disappointing. Man and the way he has stacked up against the combined beauty and malevolence of the country would give perspective and contrast, add to the meaning of the scene. The mountains are higher, the sky farther away, and distances more vast when the forked radish draws himself up to his full height against their background. Man is magnified or dwarfed by the canyons. He is tried in the crucible of unpitying and implacable nature. No man has altered that country, but it has altered many a man.

Over the chalk-white, dusty roads full of ruts we drove to Castalon, pretty much the end of the world. The river flowed serenely by a lush cotton field. Across it rose the great Mexican cliffs. Castalon Peak stood out in bold relief. After seemingly endless jolts we came to La Harmonia, to the store that is one of the three buildings in the town: ranch owner's house, manager's house, and the store. It is post office, drugstore, dry-goods emporium, grocer shop, hardware store, filling station—the works.

They had sold the last huge bear trap in stock. That was a disappointment, as I had heard of the size and businesslike quality of the trap. They still had wooden wheels better than five feet in diameter for oxcarts; rope made of *lechugilla,* strong and beautiful. All the appurtenances of life in the outposts, for two nations. There were patent medicines for every imaginable ill, saddle blankets and sewing thread, shoes, scythes, and hemp *bosales,* hackamores, halters for leading horses and donkeys. Oil lamps and candles. A few artificial flowers. Cosmetics, and the candy that is universal, hard and tasteless, but highly colored.

Two Mexican men stared at me and discussed me as though I were in the next county, just as they did when I was a child. I conversed in Spanish with Mr. Uranga, manager of the store. The onlookers listened and commented on the color of my skin, hair, and eyes with all the freedom in the world. "This *huera* has stolen our idiom," they agreed. "It is a marvel, these women of writing. I have seen one in Mexico. But brunette." The store smelled ancient, and of the Border: coal oil, dusty seed corn, and loud candy.

I felt a great desire to pitch a tent by the river, under the cottonwoods, and stay in such a peaceful region until I was glutted with quiet and repose. "How lovely," says the Mexican, "to do nothing and then rest." Castalon is the place for it.

Down the dusty, choking roads again to catch the sun just right on the Santa Elena Canyon. My hair felt as though it had been in a plaster cast overnight. The cement-like dust has an adhesive quality, a kind of inanimate perversity. As I fought the chalky powder, I could scarcely believe that between the hours of sunrise and sunset I could drive from due West to deep East—to a woodland of lush, velvety pines, growing out of thick sandy loam covered with pine needles and ferns, myrtles and hollies. Later, I did just that and fixed forever in my mind the two major divisions of Texas: climate, scene, and a way of life. Brown West. Green

East. And each with its own charm. The West Texan, inured to hardship, tough as a boot, his hide cured to the color and texture of jerked beef, and his heart as big as Brewster County. The East Texan, an easygoing old Plantation person inhabiting the replica of the Old South he has created, can afford to let nature take its course with fifty inches or more of annual rainfall. He can lie under a tree, move his chaw of terbaccer from one cheek to the other, grin up at you and say: "I'm too lazy to hit a lick at a snake!" As I studied the chasms and gorges, I kept reminding myself that there was another side to the Texas coin.

In the late afternoon, without having seen another living soul, we drove up within walking distance of the river. I picked up a good sized stick and charged off through the underbrush of willows and *tules* to see the famous canyon.

Just as I got my first glorious sight of it, something crashed through the brush behind me and I froze in my tracks, expecting a dinosaur. It was only a bald-faced cow, annoyed at having her afternoon tea interrupted. I waved the stick and shouted "Huy!" and she charged off again.

Pictures of the Santa Elena are many and beautiful; adjectives are louse-words to begin with, but the Big Bend makes them excusable. They were all used up. I was fresh out, and a good thing, too. Nothing in the way of description—and I have read some good ones, is adequate. The impact of the first sight is a thing to be experienced. It defies adequate description. It is a little like looking into the nave of a gigantic cathedral, with the river flowing through the middle of it. An old hymn mentions "the beautiful, the beautiful river, that flows by the throne of God." That's as close as I can come, and it's not original.

Since Bob Pool was far off, busy with cameras and film, I indulged a secret yen that had nibbled at me for a long time to try out a real, live rocky echo. What was to stop me? The cows wouldn't mind. I felt absolutely certain that there were no other human beings within forty miles. The first timid, rusty notes of Thrane's "Norwegian Echo Song" came back not once, but twice. Magnified and incredibly improved. Like certain microphones, the echoing crags improve voices, conceal defects, and intoxicate the performer with his own golden notes. I shifted into high gear. It was many years since I had attacked the Queen of the Night Aria from *The Magic Flute;* I knew I should never again have such an uncritical audience nor such acoustical assistance.

As in Robert Nathan's *One More Spring* when the fiddle player shows his old press clippings, and the hero of the book says, "You should have stayed in Albany. In Albany you were 'adequate,'" coloraturas should stay in the canyon. The echo was flattering enough to lure me on and on. The time lag between the emission of the notes and the return of the phrase by the echo allows the performer to hear himself. A crashing sound behind me almost stopped the music. I brandished the stick behind my back at the cows, who must have responded in classic fashion as they did to Orpheus' lute. I kept swinging the stick wildly behind me till something made me turn. A man of about seventy, his decent gray-haired wife, and their son and daughter (or so they looked to me), neatly dressed tourists who might have come from Des Moines, were gaping at the Laughing Loon of the Big Bend. There was nothing left to do: I waded into the river and sat down on a rock looking like the Misogynist Monkey on the cover of *Life*.

A MOUNTAIN FOR SUZY AND FOR YOU
Martin Dreyer
1965

IN THE WEST TEXAS TOWN WE SAT AT THE RESTAURANT WINDOW and watched the sunlight moving down the craggy face of the mountain. Orange to pink to purple. Sunset's display that ended in the dark glory of mountain etched against the deepening sky.

We sat watching and eating. Our waitress stood at the far end of the window, gazing out raptly at the distant mountain.

"Suzy, some more coffee," I called.

This efficient waitress didn't know we were alive. She gazed out the window and her thin face seemed to glow as if a light had been switched on inside her.

I called to her again and finally she pulled out of it. She brought us more coffee. I asked her what had seized her.

"Oh, I get that way." She hesitated, then took on a teasing tone. "That's my mountain."

"Tell me," I said.

"Suzy's Mountain," she said, still jestingly. "Doesn't that sound wonderful? A mountain all of my own."

She told about it, slowly, simply. It was the reason that she stayed in this small town. The mountain was her temple. There she worshiped, found spiritual comfort, saw the light. She went into this mountain, climbed it, sprouted wings to fly over it. It was rugged and wild and broodingly beautiful. It was the grandeur of nature reaching out to her like a lover.

So we moved on, travelers along the desert and mountain country of

West Texas. Everywhere we went we saw Suzy's Mountain and Tom's Mountain and Bill's Mountain. There were mountains for everyone, some with peaks like far-off forts and castles, and there were majestic canyons that have been carved through the many centuries by the Rio Grande's hungry flow, and there were deserts splashed with the brilliance of the flowering cacti and Spanish dagger.

Something for everyone, for all who wish to pay court to Nature and revel in her untouched splendors. Big Bend National Park, Santa Elena and Boquillas canyons, Chisos, Guadalupe and Davis mountains, the Permian Basin, the trans-Pecos country, ghost towns and the giant sand dunes of Sandhills State Park.

What was our desire? There was hiking and horseback riding up mountain trails. Fishing and hunting and camping and a view from lofty guest cottages of the phenomena of mountains and desert and plains merging.

It was all there, for all us travelers, a mountain, a canyon, a sand dune that we could call our own.

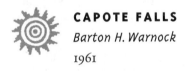

CAPOTE FALLS
Barton H. Warnock
1961

THERE ARE MANY PLACES IN THE BIG BEND THAT ARE OFF THE USUAL trails. They are not too well known, and are not so easy to reach and to explore, but offer interesting rewards to the person who spends the time and effort necessary to reach them. One such place is Capote Falls, located in the Tierra Viega Mountains southwest of Marfa. The falls, which have never been known to dry up, reach a height of over a hundred feet, which makes them the highest permanent falls in Texas. They are made by numerous small seep-springs developing in the cienega, a grassy meadow, of the rimrock country near Capote Mountain. During drought years the stream of water, which tumbles over the side of the mountain into a box canyon, has carried particles of calcium and other minerals and has slowly formed a wide-based stalagmite that narrows upward to the place it fuses into the volcanic walls of the canyon. Grooves have been cut into the stalagmite by the water, making folds that resemble the folds of a robe or cape, thus the Spanish name "Capote," which means robe or cape. The robe is hollow and it is possible to climb between the stalagmite and the walls of the box canyon. Indians camped at the base of the falls, as evidenced by pieces of pottery, grinding stones, and arrow points found nearby. Ash trees line the sometimes clear pool of water that sprays out from above. After a heavy rainfall the pool may be cleaned out and be well over fifty feet long and fifteen feet deep, extending back to large boulders that have tumbled into the canyon, but usually the pool of water at the base of the falls is only about three to six feet deep, making it an ideal swimming hole during the summer. A small, sandy beach usually surrounds the pool. Maidenhair fern grows abundantly on the lime-encrusted crevices of the canyon wall near the falls, and columbine with long yellow spurs are common in early summer or late spring.

Capote Falls can be enjoyed most by observing the falls from below. To reach the canyon from below, one must travel a dirt road from the town of Marfa for about seventy miles. The road will take the traveler over one of the most scenic parts of Texas, with several historical spots en route. As you turn off the paved road from Marfa you pass by the remains of old Fort D. A. Russell, which was a cavalry post for many years. Traveling in a generally southwesterly direction you cross beautiful rolling hills covered with grama grass, and spotted with basketgrass which was used by the Indians to weave baskets and sandals. After traveling about forty miles you will suddenly leave the grasslands and enter the wild canyons leading from the rimrock country to the desert vegetation along the Rio Grande. At the start of the winding road down Pinto Canyon (painted canyon), you will notice loading corrals where the ranchers from the land below drive their animals to load them on heavy trucks that would have difficulty driving out from below with a load of sheep or goats. You will be impressed with the bigness of Chinati Peak, the principal mountain to the left. On the top of the peak is a grassy knoll surrounded by junipers, which is used as a landing field for airplanes.

When you reach the bottom of Pinto Canyon you will cross a small stream of water which flows intermittently through the lazy canyon. Soon you will come to two adobe houses that were used in filming the movie "High Lonesome," so named because of a lone windmill set on a high hill overlooking the rim rock country to the west. A few large cottonwood trees make a pleasant place to stop for a picnic or a cool drink of water.

The first village you will encounter as you continue on the road to the Rio Grande is Ruidosa (Roaring Waters). The Rio Grande is not always a roaring stream, but during the rainy season of July and August it is often swollen and sometimes reaches flood-stage. Ruidosa is a small settlement of some fifteen or more adobe houses, a small school, one store, and an old abandoned church. You will be able to obtain gasoline only if the gas truck has visited the river country on time.

As you leave Ruidosa you will travel in alluvial sandy river bottom country along a dusty and usually rough dirt road. You will see numerous mesquite and salt-cedar trees, and often the California quail will dart across the road in front of your car. About ten miles from Ruidosa you come to the settlement of Candelaria, where you must stop and visit the old mercantile store that handles the various commodities that were needed by the people who live along the river. Above Candelaria you will see the "jail-house," which is a steel cage with a steel top about seven feet on all sides; you will see the beautiful white church as you enter the village; and you can look cross the river and see the Mexican village on the other side.

About two miles from Candelaria you enter one of the most picturesque canyons along the river country, the one made by Capote Creek, which carries water from the falls. As you travel through the eroded painted desert you will cross the creek several times. This trek is interesting to a photographer or an explorer as there are remains of an Indian shelter, a wall about twelve feet high which is the remains of a sedimentary dike, which appears to be man-made, but which actually was made by erosion, and there are numerous interesting desert type plants such as the Mexican screw-bean, which is kin to the mesquite and which furnishes the uniquely shaped screw-bean that is used in making jewelry and lapel decorations.

As the road finally becomes almost impassable, you will make camp at an old mining site where the foundation of an old mining building still may be seen, and you will leave your car and travel the remaining three miles on foot. After a good night's sleep the three mile walk along the beautiful stream of water, usually partly shaded by ash trees, will be a pleasure and you will be rewarded for your time and energy by beholding the marvelous beauty of Capote Falls.

WHERE RAINBOWS WAIT FOR RAIN
David Alloway
1989

THERE IS A SAYING ABOUT THE BIG BEND THAT IS SO POPULAR IT IS on the edge of being overused and clichéd. The reason for the phrase consistently appearing in print is because it is probably the best description of the Big Bend ever spoken. Attributed to an old Mexican vaquero of the nineteenth century, it goes: "You go south from Fort Davis until you come to the place where the rainbows wait for rain, and the big river is kept in a stone box, and the water flows uphill. And the mountains float in the air, except at night, when they run off to play with other mountains."

To those who do not know that portion of Texas, it is a fanciful rendition. Movies and television lead one to believe that Texas is so flat that if you stand on a stepladder you can see the water tower in Omaha, Nebraska. But west of the Pecos, the area called Trans-Pecos Texas is a mountain and basin region where deserts surround wooded peaks. At the extreme southern portion of the Trans-Pecos, nestled in a bow in the Rio Grande, lies the Big Bend.

Some people drive through it one day and lament its barrenness, never stopping to see how cleverly nature provides life to complement the rugged terrain. Those who stop to observe find it almost beyond expression, until they hear of the old vaquero's description.

The river *is* kept in a stone box. The Rio Grande lazily flows muddy, until it hits one of the canyons the Big Bend is famous for. Then it roars between vertical cliffs up to 2,200 feet high, the sky a narrow ribbon of blue overhead. As the water tries to cut its way out of confinement, the river creates its own stone box in the process. At places, from the rims of the canyons the river does give the illusion of flowing uphill. In the Big Bend, things are often not as they seem.

Long desert flats can heat air and cause it to rise in broad waves. Looking across the flats, a mirage can reflect the sky at the base of mountains, giving the illusion that the range is floating on air. Other times the mountains can be reflected skyward, making it appear that the peaks are separated from their bases or that the bases are precariously balancing on their own peaks.

Sometimes a layer of dense clouds shrouds the base of the Chisos Mountains, making them look like castles floating on clouds in a fairy tale. Standing on the South Rim, I have seen clouds so thick below me that I felt as if I could jump off the precipice, land softly, and take a stroll over to Elephant Tusk.

And rainbows do wait for rain. Perhaps the colors are stored in the banded formations near Maverick Road, which become vibrant when wet, or in the blossoms of the pitahaya, ocotillo, and cenizo, which explode in blooms after a rain.

Rainbows often choose a feature that is already dramatic, such as Casa Grande in the Chisos Mountains, and add a halo to provide an ethereal effect. Sometimes they run in pairs, twin arches working extra hard to grace an otherwise monotonous flat. One time a rainbow did not even wait for daylight.

The summer of 1986 I was working in the Basin as a guide for Chisos Remuda, the saddle horse concession in the National Park. Riding horses in the majesty of the Chisos Mountains gave plenty of time for inspiration but little occasion for socializing. Any time spent with a caring female companion was done in the short summer nights between horse feedings.

There was a lady in Lajitas, some fifty miles by road, who understood that my job only allowed for romance with a true sense of urgency. She also understood one or two of the other wranglers who worked at the Remuda as well, but that glorious summer night she was full of understanding only for me.

I left Lajitas at four in the morning to make it in time for chores, soporific from a fourteen-hour workday and a seven-hour courtship. The morning feeding took place at 5:00 A.M., and on the western edge of a time zone in daylight savings, that time of the morning is *dark*.

There was a full Moon setting in the west and a cloudbank in the east occasionally discharging flashes of heat lightning at its top. Heading for the storm, I worried. If it was raining and the creeks were running, I would be late.

The clouds, however, were merciful. They sent down a light drizzle to soak into the thirsty desert instead of dumping their burdens into flash floods racing to the Rio Grande.

The Moon behind me cast a light on the desert, causing it to glow as if it were phosphorescent. The clouds reflected the light and accented the effect with their static discharges. As my eyes adjusted I saw that while rainbows wait for rain, one was becoming impatient.

It was a Moon Rainbow. I will call it that because I have never heard of one before and have no other reference than my own experience. In the mist below the clouds, delicate in the blackness, was an arch. At first it appeared as only a pale curve of moonlight, a shimmering soft white.

I stopped for a second and turned off the headlights. Standing along the road I looked at the phantom arc. I could see a blue tinge and a rosy color. The yellow, already pale in daytime displays, was absent to the naked eye, but a rainbow glowed in the night.

For fifty miles I followed the sight, turning off my headlights in the few straight stretches of road. The setting Moon was at a perfect angle to illuminate my way, and to refract in the mist to keep the rainbow at a constant distance from me, even though I chased it through the night. Under the clouds and far to the east, the sky was the pitch black I was accustomed to this time of morning, but the Moon Rainbow spanned it with a gentle sweep of color and light.

When I turned onto the road to the Basin, the rainbow traveled alongside me, still keeping its distance. Then the moonlight fell on the north-western slopes of the mountains, wet with the summer rain and reflecting the light of the full Moon. At Lost Mine Peak the rainbow took on its grandest form.

Hovering above the mountain, the arc was at the height of its brilliance. The soft hues of blue and red spanned the peak, whose wet cliffs shimmered in the moonlight. The sight was inspiring but also gave me a chill in its supernatural illusion. After all, this is the place some people refer to as "Ghost Mountains"—mountains that run off to play with other mountains.

I had a fellow witness to this phenomenon named Lynn Carter. Besides being my employer, his appreciation of the Big Bend made him one of my closest friends. Lynn was standing on the screened deck above the bunkhouse with his daughter, Lynnene, when I pulled in.

After watching the rainbow for a few minutes over cups of coffee, he asked if I might be able to catch it with my camera. I replied no, because it would take a very long exposure, the Moon was about to set, and the dawn would soon break. Even if I could run back and get a picture of a rainbow in the night over Lost Mine Peak, I would only be accused of creating a darkroom hoax. As far as I know, our three memories are the only record of the Moon Rainbow.

They have yet to make a camera lens that can capture the Big Bend and hold its image true to form. Human memory and the Big Bend are the perfect companions, for I can to this day close my eyes and see the delicate hues defying the dark of a summer storm. For this I am grateful, for I expect never again to see a Moon Rainbow in my life, even in an enchanted place like the Big Bend—where rainbows wait for rain.

AUTHOR'S NOTE

On December 13, 1998, Lynn Carter went to see the other side of the rainbow. This essay is dedicated to his memory.

TWO

Nature as Devil's Advocate

TODAY ANY FORM OF TROUBLE IN THE BIG BEND IS OFTEN blamed on the border, but this region of the Chihuahuan Desert was a nest for trouble long before a border ran through it. One wonders if something about the violence through which the land itself came into being remains in the air. Some mysterious force seems to be at work here, inspiring a stalwart lawman to smuggle drugs, inspiring a well-trained Marine to become jittery enough to shoot an unarmed fifteen-year-old Hispanic goat herder, inspiring someone to shoot a river rafter from the high canyon cliffs. Husbands beat wives, wives shoot husbands, best friends betray one another, as our newspapers regularly report. Bandits and smugglers have always lived on both sides of the Rio Grande; they spring from all races, often mixed, and often speak at least two languages. Does the place attract them or raise them?

West Texans are famous for their contrariness, which is perhaps representative of some defiant spirit of place since, as Walter Prescott Webb describes, even our river has done what no other river has ever been able to do—cross the continental divide. Born in a country where every other stream of water headed dutifully west to the Pacific, the Rio Grande followed the Rocky Mountains southwest for seven hundred miles, looking for a hole in the fence. It found a weak spot at El Paso del Norte and bravely shot through the fallen mountains into the very gates of hell. Why the river would rather slice through several mountains in order to empty into the Gulf of Mexico only the river knows. Webb calls the Big Bend an "earth-wreck" and says the "Bloody Bend" is a geologist's "despair" which "fell from the hands of its Creator."[1] He says, "Perhaps order once prevailed there, but some mighty force wrecked the place, shook it down, turned it over, blew it up, and set it afire." His account describes how the river easily steals three thousand rounds of ammunition from a company of Texas Rangers and forces them to kill thirty horses and mules with an ax.

In humorous excerpts from John C. Duval's *Adventures of Big-Foot*

Wallace, even the animals appear to be on the Devil's side.[2] The wolf plays his stereotypic villain's role by "hatching a plot" against Big-Foot. In the tall tale storyteller's tradition, the old Indian fighter soon begins to suspect "foul play" and "mischief" from the "devils" who are running in a huge gang. The wolves trap him in the trunk of an old oak tree where he fights them off all night with his knife. Like all devils, they melt away into the chaparral with the light of day. In other tales, while poking fun at a tenderfoot author who travels across West Texas with him as he delivers the mail, Big-Foot adds javelinas, the weather, snakes, and bumblebees to the list of Devil's advocates found in the Trans-Pecos. Even the "timid, innocent" deer turns out to be a devil in deer's clothing. The tenderfoot writer finally decides that James Fenimore Cooper was nothing but a humbug who probably never actually met a real deer or spent a night trying to sleep in the rain.

Pecos county judge and pioneer surveyor O. W. Williams[3] often wrote down the oral tales told to him by his Mexican compadres. In one tale collected here, his friend Juan tells about an unforgiven all-thorn plant that continues to pay dearly for its part in Christ's crucifixion. Williams calls the plant honca but it must be either holacantha or junco, or what most of us call Corona de Cristo. In another tale a friend named Natividad tells about the way the wind has eaten the bones and protectively plays the Devil's friend by hiding the old Comanche trails from all but "a few of us."

In an excerpt from *The Land of Journey's Ending,* Mary Austin also discusses the old forgotten trails. She says one stretch of the north-south trader's route became known as the Jornada del Muerto because the heavy pack trains and wagons, loaded with gold and silver, pineapples, and combs for the ladies' hair, drew bandits, Apaches, and wayfarers like flies. She says that although the Rio Grande has been designated an international boundary, it feels no responsibility. Instead, it seems to delight in moving ranches and settlements from one country to another overnight, defying sovereignty, law, and order.

The Rio Grande has appeared in numerous westerns as the outlaw's savior. Cross the Rio, so the legend runs, and the baddest of the bad will fall into the waiting arms of the Devil himself, who lives on the other side—either side, depending on which side the outlaw starts from. Humorously, Eugene Manlove Rhodes, perhaps the most authentic of all writers of westerns, exposes this irony. Bransford, the hero of the book from which this excerpt comes, has been falsely accused of robbery and crosses the river into Mexico, not to escape justice, but to patiently await justice. Instead of pretending not to be a fugitive, he immediately admits that the devils who live on the north side of the river have a price on his head. So the little town on the south side welcomes him as a "guest of the city."

Edward Abbey, a famous Devil's advocate himself, crosses the Rio looking for a virgin paradise with which he and his three friends hope to have consensual intercourse. However, with typical Abbey obnoxiousness, he finds the barrancas of Chihuahua's Copper Canyon confusing, crawling with peaceful but irritating Tarahumara farmers and goat herders. He finds the barrancas impossible to hike—at least with full packs and two dang (we can safely assume unvirgin) women. The food is bad, the beer is good, and the series of willow-shaded, cascading pools carved into rose-colored bedrock that they name "Little Eden Camp" is good too—at least until they foul it for several days with sex, alcohol, and human defecation. The Devil always takes the spoiler's side.[4]

Michael Jenkinson describes the way the Rio Grande defies would-be pleasure boaters with obstacles. Its "informal" border crossings and trails seem more welcoming to ne'er-do-wells, cutthroats, smugglers, and renegades as it carves its canyon walls into goblins and trolls. Legends of lost mines, murders, and missing persons abound. Heat, rattlesnakes, panthers, javelinas, flash floods, and broken legs round out the Devil's bag of tricks that are used to inflict misery and fear on the just while providing a safe haven for the unjust. However, there is a saying in the Big Bend when people start arguing about whether it rains on the just or the unjust. The saying goes that if it would only rain on the unjust, we could easily carry water in a bucket to the just.

NOTES

1. Webb was a consulting historian for the National Park Service when this article was written.

2. Although John Crittenden Duval (1816–1897) characterizes the author who followed Bigfoot Wallace around as an umbrella-toting dude, that author could easily have been Duval himself, and he was no dude. Fighting alongside Wallace every step of the way, he was a veteran of Goliad and the Civil War. He was also a ranger in Jack Hay's famous company. His father, William Pope Duval, was the first territorial governor of Florida. His tales are based on fact and serious action, but he would misrepresent the spirit of the frontier if he told the tales without comic relief. William A. "Big-Foot" Wallace (1816–1899) came to the Southwest to avenge the deaths of a brother and a cousin. He had come from pioneering Scottish ancestors, and his stature as a folk hero grew taller and taller through the years. He could out-shoot, out-smart, out-yarn, and out-eat any man living. Indian fighter, Texas Ranger, and hunter, he also carried the mail from San Antonio to El Paso in the 1850s. Both men lived and died as bachelors.

3. Two books by Williams have been published: *Historic Review of Animal Life in Pecos County* (1908; reprint, Dallas: Martin Stationery, 193–?) and *Pioneer Surveyor-Frontier Lawyer: The Personal Narrative of O. W. Williams, 1877–1902*, ed. S. D. Myres (El Paso: Texas Western College Press, 1966).

4. In addition to this essay ("Sierra Madre") and an essay collected in Chapter Five

("Disorder and Early Sorrow"), Abbey wrote four other major pieces about the Trans-Pecos area: "On the High Edge of Texas" in *Beyond the Wall* (New York: Henry Holt, 1984, 125–136); "Big Bend" and "Round River Rendezvous: The Rio Grande, October 1984" in *One Life at a Time, Please* (New York: Henry Holt, 1988, 127–141; 150–157); and "On the River Again" in *Abbey's Road* (1979; reprint, New York: Plume, 1991, 98–106).

WRECKED EARTH
Walter Prescott Webb
1937

THE PROPOSAL TO CREATE THE BIG BEND NATIONAL PARK AND A COR-responding Mexican National Park just across the Rio Grande in Mexico has at last focused public attention on the most isolated, and one of the most interesting, spots in Texas. It is this remoteness and the causes that contribute to it that qualify the Big Bend for the dignity of a National Park. Though it is today the least known region of Texas, it would, as a National Park, become the best known. The Big Bend would be for Texas what Yellowstone is for Wyoming; what Carlsbad Caverns is for New Mexico.

The present isolation may be explained superficially by saying that the Big Bend, until now, has been cut off geographically from the main currents of travel; from the railroad and paved highway that form the bowstring and northern boundary of the bending river. But there are other reasons why railroads and paved highways have not penetrated the southern arc. These reasons are fundamental, inhering as they do in the quality of the land and not in its position.

The physiographic order of the Big Bend is somewhat like the order of a great city built of stone and brick—wrecked by an earthquake. Perhaps order once prevailed there, but some mighty force wrecked the place, shook it down, turned it over, blew it up, and set it afire. Evidences that all this happened exist on every hand, making the land the finest example of earth-wreckage in Texas. The result is that the Big Bend is not only isolated from the outside world, but from within. Though the land has been "known" for centuries, and by the Texans long enough for men to have grown old there, it is doubtful if any one man—cattleman, ranger, game warden, missionary or bandit—has seen it all, explored its canyons, climbed its mountains, found its caves and all its hidden vegas. If anyone has done this, the experience left him inarticulate, for no man has proclaimed publicly that he has seen the whole country.

The first impression of the country—one that does not wear off—is that of magnificent confusion. It is difficult for the geologist to visualize the plan before the wreck destroyed it, and he is constantly having to suppose and to admit that there are gaps in his knowledge. The biologists can help him a little but not much. The historian has less chance than either of these to assist in the restoration. The best he can do is to attempt a generalized picture of the place, much simplified, and with the full knowledge that there are exceptions to every statement he makes.

Men of literature may create the atmosphere and circumstance in which human beings move like microbes across the brilliant yet awesome landscape which they can not conquer or change much; which they have in several centuries scarcely changed at all; but men of literature can not confine on the printed page the essential quality of the land, or convey the sense of unreality and romance that overwhelms the spectator and leaves him with a recurrent nostalgia for a land in which he can not live.

The artist can catch fragments of the form and color, but his canvas is too small and his arm too short to do justice to even a fragment of the scene. Tall mountains with tumbling foothills are described by those who fly over them as "wrinkles"; and on the artist's canvas these become lines, shades and tones. The combined efforts of the scientist, historian and artist to carry the Big Bend to the outside world are painfully inadequate. The task is impossible.

The visitor can not be critical of those who failed because he feels his own inadequacy in the presence of the spectacle. It is this feeling, perhaps, that lifts him in awe and admiration, that tantalizes him into a desire to stay longer, to travel farther, to seek more earnestly that he may be able to comprehend. Finally, he has to leave for the solemn business of making a living, and when he goes, he carries his sense of inadequacy with him and is likely to be constantly haunted by a desire to return, to prove that he is adequate, competent. In short, he is by spells homesick for a land that was never his home and can never be his home. . . .

I described the Big Bend as an earth-wreck in which a great section of country was shaken down, turned over, blown up, and set on fire. It was this wreck that made the river bend in such an unusual way. The Spaniards called it the Río Bravo del Norte, the Brave River of the North. We Americans call it the Rio Grande, but we might call it the Patient River of the South, for by its patience it did something that no other western stream has done; it made its way eastward *across* or *through* the Rocky Mountains. How many millions of years it took, only the geologist can guess at; and his time approximation is such that only an astronomer can comprehend. To understand the Big Bend one must keep in mind that the river came through the mountains.

The Rio Grande rises in southern Colorado on about the same meridian as the Colorado of the West. Both rivers are on the *west* side of the Rocky Mountains, supposed to form the watershed. The natural thing, apparently, for the Rio Grande to have done, was to flow westward to the Pacific. Instead it turned southward and for seven hundred miles followed the western base of the mountain chain, passing entirely through New Mexico, and at the gap at El Paso—the river started to cross the mountains.

Below El Paso the mountain chain now swings a little east but continues southward into Mexico where it rises to great heights in the Del Carmen range. For this entire distance there seemed little chance that the river could get out to the east, and with the mountains rising still higher in Mexico, the prospect of crossing became more remote.

The geologists tell us that where the Big Bend is now was once an ocean. At the time when it was an open sea there were many forms of life in existence. Oysters three feet in diameter have been found by geologists working in the region.

What seems to have happened was that the mountain cracked open, letting the water through to the eastern side of the watershed. Where the river came through the mountain, turning to the left as if to go through a gap in a fence, or as a highway turns at an underpass, and then to the right to continue southeast to the Gulf, constitutes the Big Bend.

To say that the mountain merely "cracked" open to let the river through makes what happened obviously too simple. It explains that the river got through, but does not explain the interior condition of the Big Bend country. The mountain not only cracked open, it did something far worse, far more interesting. A whole section of it, a link fifteen or twenty miles in width crashed down to a lower level, making not a crack, which would have been a canyon of splendid proportions, but a fallen block. On the Texas side this block seems to have fallen from two to three thousand feet, but across in Mexico where the Del Carmens rise to greater height, the fall was six thousand feet or more.

We do not know what set off the blast that wrecked the mountain. Lava pushed up the earth, turned over the hills, tumbling them into new valleys. The lava bubbles cooled and weathered, and erosion has left the barren colored peaks such as the Mule Ears, Sentinel, Castalon, and others. Elsewhere upended rocks were left which now resemble the fins of a giant fish buried under talus slopes. These formations are called dikes.

The whole country within the fallen block is a jumbled mass of marine and lake deposit, of volcanic products, and of desert weathering which with the air of a clear atmosphere emphasizes the grotesque. In the debris have been found bones of the dinosaur, giant turtles, huge oysters and petrified trees, indicating that forests and extinct forms of animal life must have abounded at one time.

Near the center of the fallen mass, the Chisos Mountains rise to culminate in Emory Peak, 8,000 feet above the sea, and 6,000 feet above the river. Some think it may have once stood much higher above the sea when it bridged the gap that now separates the mountains of Texas from its neighbors in Mexico. The most southern point of the Big Bend is made where the Rio Grande swings southward around the Chisos.

Before considering any of the numerous details of the fallen mass, let us take one more general view of the scene. This may be obtained by standing on the crest of the precipices that were left intact after a section of the mountain fell in. Let us consider the mountain as a long roof with a steep and rugged ditch to the East and to the West. Let us suppose that a block has been sawed through the roof, and that this block has tumbled to the ground to form the debris that is the Big Bend. Now suppose that we take our position on the point of the roof that remains and look across the chasm to the opposite section.

The point chosen on the north side, in Texas, is the Dead Horse Mountain, or as it is commonly called, Sierra del Caballo Muerto, which rises nearly 5,000 feet. Outdoor men have lived in the vicinity of the Big Bend all their lives without having climbed Dead Horse, and it is doubtful if any white woman has ever seen it. It can be reached only by horseback or on foot, and after a perilous climb of some twelve miles from the river. Though the price of getting to it is great, the view is worth all it costs. One reaches the crest to find a mesa that is almost level. The view is as yet restricted and the stranger has no hint of what is before him. Suddenly he comes to the vantage point at the edge of the precipice and without warning a view spreads out before him that defies description. Across the chasm from him lies the stone face of the Del Carmen, rising three thousand feet above his position and 8,000 feet or more above the sea.

If the sun is shining against the face of the cliff, as it does all the afternoon, the face of Del Carmen becomes a delicately colored screen a mile high and twenty miles long on which nature gives an incomparably magnificent picture-show which is without doubt the most gorgeous view to be found in Texas, if not in the entire West.

Though the name Del Carmen suggests colors, it can not even suggest the rich tones, the varying hues, the ineffable palpitating beauty of Del Carmen as seen from Dead Horse under the splashing rays of a desert sun. The effect changes every moment, and as the shadows lengthen they darken the face of Del Carmen. Before sunset comes the grand finale when somberness creeps up the cliff and imperceptibly draws the shade of darkness over all, leaving a black outline against a star-lit sky. I have not seen this country in the moonlight but am told that the effects are overwhelming.

But let us go back to the sunlight. From Dead Horse across the chasm to Del Carmen the distance is fourteen miles. If it were not so great, we would have here a canyon that would rival the Grand Canyon of the Colorado. Far below and between these two outposts of the mountains lies the desert, which spreads out to the right and left threaded by the patient river which bends and turns many times under the eye.

There is another gorgeous view, even greater in extent, from the South Rim of the Chisos, which is more accessible at present than Dead Horse. It differs, however, in that one stands in the middle of the Big Bend, near the fallen peak—Emory Peak, still nearly 8,000 feet—and finds an unlimited view to the North and South. To the north are the Davis Mountains, more than one hundred miles away; or one can look across the river into Mexico and see the Front Range (Fronterizas) and beyond them peaks more than a hundred miles away. In other words, the vision sweeps an area two hundred and fifty or three hundred miles in extent. This trip to the South Rim can be made only on horseback or on foot. It requires at least seven hours to make the round trip, a distance of fifteen miles.

So much for the general views of this country. I now consider some details.

From what has already been said, it is perhaps needless to point out that the Big Bend is a "geologist's paradise" and his "despair": his paradise because he finds on the surface such a variety of formations; his despair because he can hardly classify them, much less explain how they came there.

The biologists are almost as fortunate. Both look upon the Chisos Mountains as an "island." Vegetation forms are found in the mountain that can not possibly exist in the desert that surrounds it. These life forms have been cut off here for millions of years to develop undisturbed by outside influences, and the same is true, though to a less extent, of animal life.

Hardly a year goes by that scientists do not come from institutions all over the United States and from Europe to study the Big Bend, to help unravel or to deepen the mysteries that are a part of the area to be included in the proposed Big Bend National Park. Evidences of human habitation are to be found in the caves. Mr. and Mrs. Elmo Johnson, who own a ranch and inn at the southern point of the Big Bend, have made a collection of baskets taken from the caves. The anthropologists estimate that some of these are from three to four thousand years old, the remains of the Basket Makers who disappeared before the white man set foot on the land.

The casual tourist will be interested in the scenes that I have described, from Dead Horse and the South Rim. He will find in the lowlands much else to attract him. For example, the dikes that stand up here and there in the desert like the fins of a giant fish. Echo Dike is remarkable not only for its size and form, but for the echoes of the human voice. The road passes within two hundred yards of this dike, just the right distance for the best sound effect. When a rifle is fired there, four seconds elapse before the echo returns. One can count five, or say short sentences, such as "What are you doing?" "Where are you going?" and have every syllable returned clearly. The unusual thing about these echos is that the tone and inflection of the voice come back so that one may recognize his own voice as well as his words.

Echo Dike is as yet known to few people. It was discovered by Pete Crawford and others when Pete was a game warden in the Big Bend. At that time there were some wild burros in the Chisos, and the stockmen decided to kill them because they destroyed the grass needed by cattle. These burros were sighted on the mountains by the hunters and the men opened fire on them with Winchesters from the road in front of the dike. They were amazed to hear a second report of their guns come booming back to them from the dike.

The river itself is a vital interest to all who see it. In finding its way through the debris of the sunken block, the Rio Grande does all sorts of queer things. To an easterner, accustomed to full flowing streams, it does not seem to be much of a river. In dry seasons it may dwindle to a thread of winding water, and except in floods a horse can wade across it at frequent intervals. To the people of the West, of the Great Plains, and the arid region, it appears a mighty stream. To those who dwell by it, the Rio Grande is a life giver, a Nile.

In a few places the river has built alluvial benches where irrigated farms have been opened. The Eugene Carteledge farm is one of the best known, comprising perhaps two hundred acres of irrigated land. Of more interest than the farms are the canyons which the river has cut. The three notable ones are Boquillas, Mariscal, and Santa Helena. Locally the last is known as the Grand Canyon of Texas. Before reaching this canyon, the river is flowing along the base of a high fault, or block, which appears to have no break in it. Suddenly, the river disappears in what seems to be a crack in the face of the cliff. It is twelve miles through this canyon and the passage is so treacherous that the people who have made it are indeed very few.

The walls rise sheer on either side for 1,500 or 2,000 feet and are so close together that one sees only a long ribbon of sky above him.

The difficulties in passing through this canyon are due to the shallow water, the rapids, and the danger of a rise with little possibility of escaping up the perpendicular walls. The greatest obstacle, however, is a heap of rocks that have fallen from the Mexican side, a jagged pile through which the water finds its way. The explorer is compelled to carry his boats over this mass, a job that, in 1899, detained Dr. Robert T. Hill so long that he named the place Camp Misery.

We do not at this time know how many people have made the passage through the Grand Canyon. Mr. E. E. Townsend of Alpine has compiled a list of about a dozen parties or individuals who have gone through — including some who *did not,* but further investigation is needed to discover just how many have made the attempt. . . .

In December of 1881, and January of 1882, a surveying party led by John T. Gano navigated the Big Bend in boats. This party was accompanied by Captain Charles Nevill and a number of Texas Rangers. It was on this trip that the Texas Ranger fired the last shot at an Indian. Though they killed no Indians, they captured nine horses and mules which they killed because they could not take them out. Captain James B. Gillett of Marfa remembers this incident, and that one high-strung ranger, Joe B. Irving, refused to kill the horses. The ammunition of the party had been depleted, and Captain Nevill had the horses and mules knocked in the head with an ax. It is said that the killing of the horses gave the name, Dead Horse Mountain, to the near-by rim.

This is one of the few cases on record where the Texas Rangers operated in boats, and it proved more dangerous than riding on horseback. Captain Nevill reported that one boat capsized on December 23 and that on the last day of the year another was wrecked on a snag in "a very swift riffle." Captain Nevill, evidently a better Ranger than navigator, was in the wrecked boat, supposed to be then in Santa Helena. In his report to General King, dated February 4, 1882, he wrote:

"I barely escaped drowning as I had on my pistol and belts, coats and boots. I lost my Field Glass and 3,000 rounds of ammunition."

. . . In conclusion, I wish to say that there is something very precious in this wild country, and that it is a place of temporary escape from the world we know. Here is a place where the spirit is lifted up as it must have been when the white man found America and before he had time to mar it with his improvements.

The very names of the landmarks carry the aroma of romance, the suggestion of bold, though not always estimable, deeds. Across the face of the barren mountain we see a white thread passing from Texas into Mexico, the Contrabanda Trail. Here is Strawhorse Trail, and here, high up like an eagle's eyrie, is Robbers' Roost. There are Boot Canyon and Boot Spring, and of course Terlingua, said locally to be a corruption of *tres lingua* or three languages, Indian, Spanish, and English, which have been the languages of the country.

On Terlingua Creek, which enters the Rio Grande just at the mouth of Santa Helena Canyon, people were farming and practicing irrigation when a small boy named Columbus was swinging his bare feet off the wharves in Italian ports and dreaming of going to sea. And on that day, so unchanging is this wild country, the Big Bend looked almost exactly as it looks today. Man has marked it, but he has not marred it.

The fact that man has not seriously disturbed the Big Bend recommends it as a National Park site. If it were thickly settled, it would be out of the picture. But there it lies in its gorgeous splendor and geological confusion, almost as it fell from the hands of its Creator. Because it seems to be made up of the scraps left over when the world was made, containing samples of rivers, deserts, sunken blocks of mountain and tree-clad peaks, dried up lakes, canyons, cuestas, vegas, playas, arroyos, volcanic refuse, and hot springs, it fascinates every observer. Three life zones exist from the base to the summit of the Chisos Peak to delight the lovers of wild plants and animals.

The human interest value of the Big Bend comes from the fact that two contrasting civilizations face each other across a river that constitutes a boundary but not a barrier, and both rest upon an age-old Indian culture that partially survives. Men have not always lived in peace here, as one can learn today by sitting in camp and listening to the border men— Texas Rangers, border patrol, river guards, game wardens, and cowmen.

When Dr. Robert T. Hill visited the region nearly forty years ago, he referred to the "Bloody Bend," an illuminating footnote on the background and history.

How fitting it would be if the Big Bend of Texas, and the wild region opposite in Mexico, could be converted into an international park devoted to the pleasure and enlightenment of man, and to the promotion of peace and understanding between neighboring nations.

MR. COOPER WAS A HUMBUG
John C. Duval
1936

HAVE I EVER TOLD YOU, ASKED BIG-FOOT, ABOUT THE "TUSSLE" I HAD with the wolves a short time after I came to Texas? It was a sort of initiation fee paid for entrance into the mysteries of border life, and I don't think I have ever been as badly frightened before or since. It happened in this way:

One very cold evening, two or three hours, perhaps, before sundown, I concluded to take a little round in the woods, by way of exercise, and bring home some fresh venison for supper; so I picked up "sweet-lips" (his rifle) and started for a rough broken piece of country, where I previously had always found deer in abundance. But, somehow, the deer didn't seem to be stirring that evening, and I walked two or three miles without finding a single one. After going so far, I hated to return without meat, and I kept on, still hoping to find the deer before it got too dark to shoot; but at last I had to give it up, and turned my course back toward home again.

By this time the sun was setting, and I hurried up as fast as possible, to get out of the chaparral and into the prairie before night came on. All evening I had heard the wolves howling around in an unusual way, but I had no fear of them, as I had been told they seldom, if ever, attacked a man in Texas. When I had gone back perhaps half a mile or so, a large gray wolf trotted out into the path before me, and commenced howling in the most mournful manner; and, in an instant, he was answered by a dozen other wolves in the hills around us. Thinks I, old fellow, if you are hatching a plot for my benefit, I'll make sure of you anyhow; so I brought "sweet-lips" to range on his shoulder-blade, and at the crack of the gun he gave one spring into the air and dropped as dead as a hammer in his tracks.

But, somehow, although I can't say I felt any fear of them, my suspicions were aroused as to foul play on the part of the gentlemen who were answering him from the hills, and I loosened "old butch" in the sheath, and rammed another bullet down "sweet-lips" and as soon as I had done so, I put out for home again in double-quick time. But the faster I went the faster the wolves followed me, and looking back after a little while, I saw twenty-five or thirty "lobos" (a large fierce kind of wolf, found only in Mexico and Texas) trotting along after me at a rate I knew would soon bring them into close quarters; and in the bushes and chaparral, that bordered the trail I was traveling, I could see the gleaming eyes and pointed ears of at least a dozen others coming rapidly toward me.

I saw in a minute that they meant mischief, but I knew it was useless to try a wolf in a foot-race. However, I resolved to keep on as long as they would let me, and when they closed in, that I would give them the best ready-made fight I had "in the shop." So I stepped out as briskly as I could, and the wolves trotted after me, howling in a way that made my hair stand on end and my very blood run cold. A dozen times I wished myself back again safe in "old Virginny," where a man might travel for a hundred miles without meeting up with anything more dangerous than a 'possum; but wishing didn't stop the wolves, so I let out my "best licks," hoping that I could make home before they could muster up courage enough to attack me.

But, I "reckoned without my host," for one big fellow, more daring or hungry than the rest, made a rush at me, and I barely had time to level my gun and fire, for he was touching the muzzle of it when I pulled the trigger. He fell dead at my feet, but, as if this had been a signal for a general attack, in an instant the whole pack were around me, snarling and snapping, and showing their white teeth in a way that was anything but pleasant.

I fought them off with the breech of my gun, for they didn't give me any chance to load it, retreating all the while as rapidly as I could. Once so many of them rushed in upon me at the same time, that in spite of all my efforts, I failed to keep them at bay, and they dragged me to the ground. I thought for an instant that it was all up with me, but despair gave me the strength of half a dozen men, and I used "old butch" to such a good purpose that I killed three outright and wounded several others, which appeared somewhat to daunt the balance, for they drew off a short distance and began to howl for reinforcements.

The reinforcements were on their way, for I could hear them howling in every direction, and I knew that I had no time to lose. So I put off at the top of my speed, and in those days it took a pretty fast Spanish pony to beat me a quarter when I "let out the kinks." I let 'em out this time with a will, I tell you, and fairly beat the wolves for a half mile or so, but my breath then began to fail me, and I could tell by their close angry yelps that the devils were again closing in upon me.

By this time I was so much exhausted that I knew I should make a poor fight of it, more especially as I could perceive, from the number of dark forms behind me and the gleaming eyes and shining teeth that glistened out of every bush on the wayside, that the wolves had had a considerable addition to their number. It may be thought strange that I didn't "take to a tree," but there were no trees there to take to—nothing but stunted chaparral bushes, not much higher than a man's head.

I thought my time had come at last, and I was almost ready to give up in despair, when all at once I remembered seeing, as I came out, a large lone oak-tree, with a hollow in it about large enough for a man to crawl into, that grew on the banks of a small cañon not more than three or four hundred yards from where I then was. I resolved to make one more effort, and, if possible, to reach this tree before the wolves came up with me again; and if ever there was good honest running done, without any throw-off about it, I did it then. The fact is, I believe a man can't tell how fast he can run until he gets a pack of wolves after him in this way. A fellow will naturally do his best when he knows that if he doesn't, that in twenty minutes he will be "parceled out" among as many ravenous wolves, a head to one, a leg to another, an arm to a third, and so on. At least that was the effect it had on me, and I split the air so fast with my nose that it took the skin off of it, and for a week afterward it looked like a peeled onion.

However, I beat the wolves once more fairly and squarely, and not much time to spare either, for just as I crawled into the hollow of the tree, which was about as high as my head from the ground, the ravenous creatures were howling all around me. At the bottom of the hollow I found a "skunk" snugly stowed away, but I soon routed him out, and the wolves gobbled him up in an instant. He left a smell behind him, though, that was anything but agreeable in such close quarters. However, I was safe there, at any rate, from the attacks of the wolves, and all the smells of the city of New Orleans couldn't have driven me from my hole just at that time.

The wolves could only get at me one at a time, and with "old butch" in my hand, I knew I could manage a hundred in that way. But such howling and yelling I never heard before or since but once, and that was when I was with the Keechies, and a runner came in and told them their great chief "Buffalo Hump," had been killed in a fight with the Lipans! They bit, and gnawed, and scratched, but it wasn't any use, and every now and then a fellow would jump up and poke his nose into the hollow of the tree; but just as he did, he caught a swipe across it with "old butch" that generally satisfied his curiosity for a while. All night long they kept up their serenade, and, as you may well suppose, I didn't get much sleep. However, the noise didn't matter, for I had got several severe bites on my arms and legs and the pain I suffered from them would have kept me awake anyhow.

Just at daylight the next morning the wolves began to sneak off, and when the sun rose not one was to be seen, except three dead ones at the root of the tree, that had come in contact with "old butch." I waited a while longer, to be certain they had all left, when I crawled out of my den, gave myself a shake, and found I was all right, except a pound or so of flesh taken out of one of my legs, and a few scratches on my arms. I hobbled back home; and for a long time afterward, whenever I heard the howling of wolves I always felt a little uneasy.

I found out the next day, why the wolves had attacked me in the way they did. I had a bottle of assafoetida in my trunk, which somehow had gotten broken and run out among my clothes, and when the wolves pitched into me I had on a coat that had been wet with the confounded stuff, and smelt worse than a polecat. I had often heard that assafoetida would attract wolves, but I always thought, before this, that it was sort of an old woman's yarn; but it's a fact, and if you don't believe it, go some dark night into a thick chaparral, where wolves are numerous, and pour about a gill over your coat, and then wait a little, and see what will turn up; and if you don't hear howling and snapping, and snarling, I'll agree to be stung to death by bumble-bees.

•   •   •

I was satisfied, the Indians having had so much the start of us, that it was useless to "hurry up" with the expectation of overhauling them before they reached the country they intended to occupy permanently. I determined to travel along leisurely, and keep our horses in as good plight as possible for the long "scout" that I knew was ahead of us; so we traveled only about twenty-five miles that day, and encamped just before sundown in a little valley where there was a bold running creek and plenty of good grass for our horses. When we had got some supper, we staked our animals, placed the usual guard over them, and laid down under the trees upon our blankets, the author and I occupying one bunk together.

In a little while after we had "gone to roost," the author said to me:

"Captain, what is that roaring I hear like a charge of cavalry?"

I rose up and saw a dense black cloud coming rapidly toward us from the north, and I knew we were about to have one of those sudden squalls common at that season of the year in the hilly country, and invariably accompanied by a heavy fall of rain.

"We're in for a ducking, my friend," I said, "unless you can manage to protect us with your umbrella."

"Oh, I can do that," said he, jumping up; "and you will find that an umbrella is not such a bad article to have on a scout, after all."

So he unstrapped it from his saddle and hoisted it over us; but scarcely had he done so when the squall struck us with the force of a tornado, and the first gust of wind turned the umbrella wrong side out, wrenched it from his hand, and carried it out of sight in a moment.

"Captain," said he, "what's to be done now? The umbrella has been whisked off like an old witch upon a broomstick, and we shall be drenched to the skin."

"I know it," I replied, "but there's no help for it, and all we can do is to 'lay low' and take it quietly."

"Why, Captain," he answered, "it will be the death of us! I never caught a wetting but once in my life, and then as soon as I got home, I didn't feel safe until I was tucked into bed with the 'sheets aired,' and had swallowed a couple of hot toddies. Oh, dear! The water is running down my back in a stream now, and I shall certainly perish from such horrible exposure."

"Not a bit of it, Mr. Author," I replied, "you'll wake up as fresh as a lark in the morning. There's a stream running down my back, too, but it isn't quite as big as the Colorado, and I'm not the least afraid of its drowning me. All you've got to do is keep quiet, and you will very soon be comfortable enough."

"Well," said he, after a while, "if this is what you call 'comfortable,' your ideas and mine differ very widely on the subject. The water is half-way up my sides. I begin to think," he continued, shivering and scroung-ing closer to me, to borrow a little of my warmth, of which in fact I hadn't much to spare—"I begin to think there was a good deal of humbug about [James Fenimore] Cooper, after all, for in all his descriptions of the woods and frontier life, he never says a word about a fellow's having to sleep in a puddle on the ground, with a damp blanket smelling of horses over his shoulders, and a stream of cold water trickling down his back. When people 'bivouac' in his novels, the nights are always serene and clear, the stars twinkle overhead, and the turf is green and soft (there's a boulder as big as my fist exactly under my hip), and everything is pleasant and agreeable. I'm losing my confidence in Mr. Cooper rapidly."

In about an hour the rain ceased, the puddle disappeared from around us, and notwithstanding his "uncomfortable" situation, our author slept like a top the balance of the night.

The first thing we saw in the morning, when we woke up, was the "um-brell" on the top of a mesquite bush where the wind had lodged it, about fifty paces from where we had slept. The men discovered it about the same time, and as they wanted to fire off their guns and pistols, which had got damp in the rain, they pretended to think it was a turkey on its roost, and every one took a crack at it. As soon as the firing ceased, our author went out and lifted it from its roost with a long pole, and though sadly damaged by the bullets and wind, he carefully strapped it on his saddle again.

That day we traveled only about twenty miles on the trail, to a small creek where I thought it advisable to camp, as I knew it was doubtful about finding any water for a long distance beyond it. The sun was two or three hours high when we got to the creek, and several of the men went out hunting, and so did our author, though what he expected to kill with his little bird-gun is more than I can say. He had been gone but a short while when we heard both barrels of his gun go off quickly one after another, and soon afterward we heard him halloo a dozen times in rapid succession.

Supposing something extraordinary had happened to him, I seized my rifle and hurried off in the direction of the sound. When I had gone about half a mile, I came to the top of a ridge, and looking over the valley beyond, I saw our author dodging from one side to the other of a small mesquite-tree, while a big buck trotted around it, every now and then making furious lunges at him with his horns. Our author, however, displayed more activity and skill in dodging than I had given him credit for, and thinking he was in no immediate danger, I walked along very leisurely toward him.

When I got within about fifty yards of him, he sang out to me, in the most pleading tones, "to make haste and shoot the buck."

"Hurry, Captain," said he, "and shoot the outrageous thing, I can't keep up this dodging much longer."

But the fact is, I was in no hurry to shoot, for it was rather a funny sight to see how spry the little author would "squirrel" round the tree whenever the buck made a pass at him. At last he lost all patience, and sang out:

"Captain, why in the world don't you shoot? Shoot, and that pretty quick, if you don't want to see me murdered in 'cold blood' by this horrid beast."

"That's hardly possible, Mr. Author," I said, "as you certainly have taken exercise enough to warm it up a little."

But the buck kept him so busy he paid no attention to anything I said, but continued to sing out:

"Shoot, Captain! Shoot the horrid beast!"

The little author was amazingly expert and nimble at dodging, but fearing he might accidentally get hurt if the game was kept up too long, I raised my gun, deliberately took sight at the buck, and fired. At the crack of the rifle, he made one last desperate plunge at the author, grazing him so closely that he carried away a piece of the tail of his hunting-shirt on his horns, and then fell as "dead as a door nail" a few feet from the root of the tree.

Our author threw himself on the ground, completely "beat out," and panting and blowing like a stag-hound after a long chase. I walked up to where he lay, and as soon as he could catch his breath a little, he said:

"Captain, will you please tell me exactly how long it took you to walk from the top of that hill to this place, and how long you took sight at that buck after you got here? I am anxious to know, for I wish to make a note in my book of the 'slowest time on record.'"

I saw in a minute that our author was mad as a hornet (and no wonder, either), so I said:

"Until I got up close to you, I actually thought you were after the buck, and not the buck after you; that it was the buck dodging round the tree, and you were trying to get hold of him to cut his throat." (Big-foot "stretched his blanket" considerably here.)

"Well," he replied, "it may have looked so to 'a man on a hill,' but it was just the contrary, I can tell you. If you had put off shooting one moment later, the world would never have seen the conclusion of the 'Way-worn Wanderer,' and you would have been responsible to posterity for the loss they would have suffered in consequence. But it's all owning to Mr. Cooper," he continued, "for I never would have ventured to attack a beast with such a head of horns if it had not been for him. In all his novels he describes the deer as a 'timid, innocent animal, that is startled at its own shadow in the sun.' I only wish he had been here in my place! Why, sir, I never saw so furious a beast in all my born days, and I am pretty well convinced now that Mr. Cooper was a humbug; and as certain as I live I will expose all his fallacies in the 'Wayworn Wanderer.' He has imposed on the world quite long enough."

"That's all right, Mr. Author," said I; "but how do *you* intend to describe the deer?"

"Just as he is," he said, "a peaceable-looking animal enough before you attack him, but, the moment you fire upon him, a great fierce creature, with a head of horns like a brush-heap, eyes as green as grass, and his hair all turned the wrong way, and so active that nothing but a monkey or a squirrel can dodge fast enough round a tree to keep out of his way."

"That's a description, sir, that for truth and correctness would do to go in 'Goldsmith's Animated Nature.'"

While our author was running on in this style, I proceeded to skin the buck, and to cut off some choice pieces to carry back with us to camp.

When I got through, I pretended just then to discover the tail of our author's hunting-shirt hanging to the buck's horns.

"Hello!" said I, "what's this?"

"Oh, that," he said, "is nothing but the tail of my hunting-shirt, which that 'timid, innocent animal, that is startled at its own shadow in the sun,' carried away on its horns when he made the last furious lunge at me. I'll thank you to hand it over to me, if you please, and I'll splice it on when we get to camp. Mr. Cooper's a humbug, sir!"

•   •   •

We had traveled but a few miles, when our trail led us into a narrow pass in the hills, and after going up this two or three miles farther, we came to one of the most beautiful little valleys I had ever seen, through the midst of which there ran a bold stream of water, bordered by fine large cypress and pecan trees. The grass in the valley was luxuriant, and the Indians we were following had just come through, as was evident from the quantity of bones and other offal around their camps. As our horses had had but little grass for the last two days, I thought it would be good policy to follow their example, and rest them here until the next day. So we picked out a suitable place for a camp-ground, in a grove of pecans, and staked the animals out to graze.

Our author was a great geologist, I think he called it, as well as a book-maker, and would frequently talk to me about the "stratas" and the "primary" and "tertiary" formations, though I told him I did not know anything of such matters; and whenever we stopped to camp, he would frequently "boge" about for hours among the caverns and gulches, hunting what he called "specimens," and come back with his pockets filled with rocks, which he would sort out and label, and then store them away carefully in his saddle-bags. On one occasion I heard one of my men say to another, "Bill, what in the thunder do you suppose the 'author' has got in his saddle-wallets, that makes them so heavy?"

"Don't know," said Bill, "unless they are nuggets."

"Nuggets?" said the other; "they are rocks just like these you see laying all around here. I know it is so, for I looked into them this morning!"

"Why," answered Bill, "what do you reckon the fool is packing them about for?"

"No idea," said the other, "unless he has no faith in that 'bird-gun' and 'pepper-box' he totes, and intends to fight with them when we catch up with these Ingens. The truth is, Bill," he continued, "the fellow is as crazy as a bed-bug, sure, and if he only had any weepins about him that could hurt a body, I should keep my eye skinned on him, certain."

In fact, by this time the belief was prevalent among the men that our author was really "unsettled" in his mind, which supposition proved, in the end, of service to him, for of course they could not hold a crazy man responsible for anything he did.

As soon after our halt as he had unsaddled and staked his horse, he went out, as usual, hunting "specimens" in the ravines and gullies among the hills. I was just settling myself upon my blanket, to take a comfortable snooze, when we heard him "halloo" repeatedly about half a mile from camp.

"There," said one of the men, "there is that crazy chap got into a scrape with another buck, I suppose, and somebody will have to go and help him out of it."

"Yes," said another, "and the first thing he knows he will have his 'hair lifted,' 'boging' about alone, with nothing but that 'pop-gun' of his to fight with. He had better trust to his 'umbrell.'"

I was satisfied, however, it could not be a buck that was after him this time, for I had noticed, when he left camp, that he did not take his "pop-gun" along with him, and as he continued to "sing out" louder and louder, I at length picked up my rifle, and started off to see what sort of scrape he had got into. At the bottom of a deep ravine, I found him sitting on the top of a chaparral bush, with his memorandum book in his hand, and about a dozen Mexican hogs around him. He was barely out of their reach, and ever now and then, one of them would make a pass at his legs, whenever he stretched them down to relieve them a little from the constrained position in which he was compelled to keep them.

As soon as I appreciated the situation of affairs, I scrambled up into a mesquite-tree, about thirty paces from where our author was roosting, for I knew very well these "havilinas," when excited and roused, were the most dangerous of all our wild animals. When in considerable numbers, they frequently attack a man with great ferocity, and are almost certain to cut him to pieces with their terrible tusks, unless he can effect a timely retreat, for they are much more active and swift on foot than the common wild hog.

When I found myself safe from their attacks, I called out to our author to know what he was doing on that bush.

"Hallo! Captain!" he called out. "Is that you?" (For the hogs had kept him so busy he had not noticed me until then.) "I am as glad to see you as I was when the buck was after me. I hope, though, you will not be quite so deliberate as you were on that occasion."

"Yes," I answered, "but what are you doing on top of that bush?"

"Doing!" said he. "Can't you see that I am trying to keep my legs out of the reach of these outrageous wild pigs, and it is as much as I can do at that. There! Did you see that scoundrel make a pass at me?"

"Why don't you drive them away?" I asked.

"Drive them away!" replied our author. "I have thrown all my specimens at them, and everything else I had about me except my memorandum book, and it only makes them worse. They are not afraid of anything."

Said I, "Mr. Author," fixing myself comfortably on a limb, "this reminds me of a scrape I once got into with these 'havilinas,' that would do for a chapter in the 'Wayworn Wanderer'; and as we are comfortably fixed out here, all by ourselves, I could not have a better chance of telling it to you."

"Comfortable!" he exclaimed. "You have strange ideas of it, if you think a man can be comfortable, sitting on the top of your abominable Texas chaparral, with his knees drawn up to his chin, a thorn in each leg as long as my finger, and a dozen wild hogs making lunges at them whenever he stretches them down for a moment's ease. For heaven's sake, shoot them," he implored, "and let me out of this nest of thorns."

"I can't," I replied. "I have only the bullet that is in my gun, and if I shoot one of them, it will make the rest ten times worse."

"You don't tell me so, Captain," he answered; "then what in the world shall we do?"

"Why," said I, "the only thing we can do now, is to be patient, and wait until the moon rises to-night, and I think then the 'havilinas' will leave us."

"Oh, don't talk to me about the moon's rising. It won't be up till 12 o'clock, at least, and I can't stand this fifteen minutes longer, no how. Crackey! That fellow gave me a grazer! He has taken off the heel of my boot on his tusks!"

"You see, Mr. Author," I continued, pretending not to hear what he said, "it was about six years ago, that Bill Hankins and I were out 'bear-hunting' on the head-waters of the Leon, when—"

"Plague take that fellow, he brought blood that time, certain!" said our author. "Their teeth are as sharp as razors."

"As I was saying," I went on, "it was about six years ago that Bill Hankins and I were out bear-hunting on the head-waters of the Leon, when we fell in with a large drove of these 'havilinas.'"

"They are knawing my bush down," said our author, in a pitiable tone; "they will have it down in less than ten minutes."

"As I was saying," I continued, "it was about six years ago that Bill Hankins and I were out bear-hunting on the head-waters of the Leon, when we fell in with a large drove of 'havilinas,' and before we were aware of our danger—"

"Shuh! you devils," said our author, flinging his last missile, his memorandum book, at the hogs, as they made a general rush on his bush.

"Mr. Author," I said, in an offended tone, "you are not paying the slightest attention to what I am telling you. You might learn something even from the Indians in this respect, for, according to Mr. Cooper, they never interrupt a man when he is talking."

"As I was saying," I continued, "it was about six years ago that Bill Hankins and I were out bear-hunting on the head-waters of the Leon—"

"Oh! bother Mr. Cooper and Bill Hankins and the head-waters of the Leon," said our author, losing his temper at my persistence in relating the anecdote. "Cooper's a fool. Oh, my! There's a thorn clean through my back, into the hollow!"

"But, my friend," said I, changing my tactics, "you ought to bear your troubles with patience, for you should remember what a thrilling chapter you will be able to make out of this adventure for the 'Wayworn Wanderer.'"

"Oh, yes," he said; "but who will there be to write it, when I am chawed up by these infuriated pigs like a handful of acorns? Oh, dear! They'll have me directly. I can feel the bush giving way now. Captain," said he, "you will find the manuscript of the 'Wayworn Wanderer' in my saddlebags. Take it, and publish it for the benefit of the world, and tell them of the melancholy fate of the poor author. But tell them, for mercy's sake, that I was devoured by a lion, or a panther, or a catamount, or some other decent sort of beast, and not by a gang of squealing pigs. It won't sound romantic, you know."

"I'll do it, Mr. Author," said I; "but I hope you will live long enough yet to tell them all about it yourself. You have a first-rate chance now to study the habits and appearance of these 'havilinas,' and can write a chapter on them that will be very interesting, and true to nature. How will you describe them?" I asked.

"They look to me," he answered, "like a couple of butcher-knives about as long as my arm, stuck into a handle covered with hair and bristles!"

"And can you tell me," I said, "what particular tribe of animals they belong to?"

"Captain," he answered, "I don't feel inclined to discuss the subject just now, particularly as the subject is so eager to discuss me; and besides, to tell you the truth, I think you have selected a most unsuitable time for propounding your questions in natural history. Oh, my! There goes the leg of my pants and a strip of the hide with it!"

"Mr. Author," I said, pretending not to hear his remarks, "I recollect once reading a chapter in one of Mr. Cooper's novels, in which he gives a very interesting account of the immense droves of wild pigeons that were migrating from one part of the country to another, and—"

"Oh, bother Cooper, I say!" said our author, becoming perfectly frantic, as a thorn touched up in the rear, and a pig made dash at his legs in front. "Cooper is an unmitigated humbug, and I begin to think you are not much better. Oh, I can stand this no longer," said he, "and I'll make a finish of it at once"; and I verily believe he would have jumped down right among the hogs in another moment; but just then I saw several of my men coming toward us from camp and said to him:

"Hold on a minute, Mr. Author; there come some men to help us, and we'll soon rout the beasts."

Seeing that we were both treed by some sort of "varmits," the men hurried up, shot several of the hogs, and the balance, finding we mustered too strong for them, quickly retreated into the chaparral.

Our author came down from his roost, and threw himself at full length upon the ground, for the purpose, as he said, of getting the tucks out of his legs. After he had rested himself for a while, and picked out all the thorns that had been left sticking in his flesh, he rose up considerably refreshed in mind and body, and we walked back toward camp.

"I am afraid, Mr. Author," said I, as we sauntered along, "you will begin to think you are paying pretty dearly for the information you are collecting in the wilderness."

"Not at all, Captain," he answered, "for I know that no great undertaking was ever accomplished without labor and many difficulties to be overcome. A novel such as I intend the 'Wayworn Wanderer' to be cannot be written except by one thoroughly posted on the subjects of which it treats. I will confess, however, that once or twice since I came out (particularly when I was in that disagreeable position on top of the chaparral-bush), I have wished I had never undertaken the job; but that, you see, was only a momentary weakness, and I shall not give way to it hereafter. 'Richard's himself again,'" he said, flapping his arms across his breast like a play-actor.

Now, there was one thing of which our author was exceedingly afraid, and that was a snake. He was in constant fear of them, day and night, and, like all people who have a great dread of snakes, he could find more of them in the course of the day than any six men in the company. He was forever finding snakes, at all times, and in all localities, where nobody else could have found one if he had hunted closely for a week. Now, it so happened that just as he made his last heroic speech, and in the very act of flapping his arms against his breast, he put his foot upon a large rattlesnake that was coiled up in a bunch of grass. The snake rattled, and struck his teeth into his buckskin leggings.

"Oh! oh!" he sang out, dropping his feathers like a strutting gobbler when he hears a gun go off, at the same time making a most extraordinary leap to one side. "I am gone now to a certainty. This reptile has bitten me to the bone."

When the snake struck him, the fangs penetrated partially into the tough, spongy buckskin of his leggings, and as our author sprang off he dragged the snake with him. The moment he discovered that the snake was fastened to him, he kicked out frantically with his legs, and exclaimed, in the most piteous accents:

"Take him off, Captain, for heaven's sake; take him off before he swallows me alive."

The snake was torn loose after the first vigorous kick; in the excitement of the moment, however, our author never noticed it, but continued his kicking until at last he fell to the ground from pure exhaustion, where he lay rolling and squirming apparently in the greatest agony. I ran up to him, and taking hold of him, said:

"Mr. Author, are you bit?"

"Bit!" said he. "You can't put your finger on a place that isn't bit. I'm poisoned from head to foot by the reptile! The jig is up with me now, certain. Oh! what a fool I was to venture out into this howling wilderness, where you can't go forty yards from camp without running a great risk of being devoured by some wild beasts nor put your foot down without treading on a snake."

I really feared at first that the snake had bitten him, and I hastily rolled up his leggings and looked for the wound, but couldn't find the slightest sign of one, except some scratches made by the thorns of the chaparral bush.

"Mr. Author," said I, "you are all safe; the snake hasn't even grazed the skin."

"Are you sure he hasn't bit me?" he asked.

"Yes," I replied, "I'll warrant your life for a gingercake. Why, Mr. Author," I continued, "you are in luck to-day. You have scarcely finished your adventure with the 'havilinas' when here you are collecting material enough for another thrilling chapter of the 'Wayworn Wanderer.'"

"Yes," said he, "that's true enough, and I can work up a very interesting chapter on 'snakes' out of this, there is no doubt; but, let me tell you, I don't want to collect 'material' quite so rapidly. I would rather these incidents would occur a little wider apart, and give me time enough to catch my breath. 'Enough is as good as a feast.' I am willing to make a martyr of myself now and then for the sake of immortality, but I can't afford to do it every fifteen minutes in the day."

THE HONCA ACCURSED
O. W. Williams

1919

AN HOUR'S RIDE HAD CARRIED US FROM THE HILLS TO A WIDE VALLEY that lay between the mountain ranges. That hour had transported us from one vegetable world to another, as if we were in the hands of the genius of some New World Aladdin's lamp. The sparse mountain oaks and junipers, with their stunted and dwarfed bodies, had disappeared, and we were now among the inhabitants of the valley, a floral people even more stunted and dwarfed and of forms infinitely more strange and grotesque than their kin of the mountains. We had left a people of Quakers, wearing garments of peace and harmony; we had come among a people of war, frozen by some magic with sword in hand and armor buckled for the fray. Lance or sword or dagger peeped out from almost every bush, and where we saw a shrub without weapons in sight we scrutinized it with a strong suspicion that somewhere in its drab or russet bosom there lurked some secret deadly missile ready to be thrust into the rash intruder.

For this was the flora of the arid region, and our scientists tell us that this extraordinary and varied development of leaf, stipule, and stem into thorn is the result of an age-long struggle on the part of the plants against their competitors and enemies. Now the dagger, sword, and lance would avail little in the struggle for life against their competitors, who carry on their operations chiefly under the ground, vegetable sappers and miners who in darkness and depth steal the moisture and life away from the beleaguered citadel. But against their enemies, the birds that steal away the seeds and the animals that browse on leaf and stem, these weapons would avail much. So we understand that the panoply of war which these plants wear is not put on for service against their neighbors of the flora, but against the predatory animal life that feeds on them.

Yet, as one gazes over this troop born of the dragon's teeth, that has sprung armed from the ground, the imagination easily falls into the thought that it is a picture of war of neighbor against neighbor, class against class, brother against brother, and we can even picture to ourselves certain resemblances among the plants to characters of the Middle Age, that age when every man was an Ishmael whose hand was raised against every other man. Over yonder stands the courtly *palma,* whom we may liken to the Knight Errant, kindliest of all the spirits of this war-like array, and the earliest doomed to disappear. Within its coronet, dagger guarded, the crow in safety rears her brood. Under its straw colored armor the lizard hides, and in the shade at its feet the hare sets his form. When it is decked in its white plume the desert bee sucks desert nectar from its snow-white bells. And when it finally falls in the battle, the *termite*—the cowled monk—shrouds it in its dusky pall.

And here stands the *gatun,* the robber baron, with curved claws thrust out from his castle; claws that never loosen when once fastened, that grasp meat or raiment regardless of distinction, for everything is prey that comes his way.

Over there is the *tasajillo,* Italian bravo, hiding under cover at the street corner, eager to thrust his stiletto into his unsuspecting victim, ready as he does so to draw back into obscurity.

Here is our leech, the *hoja-sen,* sober of garment and wise of countenance, offering as a remedy for every ill, whether of fever within or wounds without, the one sovereign remedy of the leaf.

And there, hid away in the shade of some strong hand, like the *gatun,* its treasure guarded by gnarled roots, is the *tasajo,* the hermit monk. Meek and mild, its drab stem is pointed to heaven with cross uplifted, while hidden underground and warded above by castle walls lies its store of worldly wealth. In darkness it blooms, and charms with its sweetness the spirits of the night, spirits too meek and lowly to court the light of the sun.

And down on the sandy barrens lie, waiting for unwary feet, the *peritas,* the crabbed essence of bristling barbarity, corded and knotted with fiery barbs, the caltrops of this fiendish infantry. No subtle spirit of distillation can charge a human weapon with more painful humor than carries this humble, crawling porcupine of the sandy dunes.

Here too is our outlaw, the *biznaga,* living apart and alone, a law to himself, and disdaining alike the power of the robber baron and the balmy night sweetness of the hermit monk. But through all its coarse and roughened hide now and then there breaks forth a brilliant bloom of star-like purity of color, an emblem of what may come from the lowliest and loneliest human.

Just so, too, amid all this scene of desolation, flits our Prince of the Red Hat, the cardinal bird, preening his feathers in the shade of the *gatun,* picking insects from the bells of the *palma,* or plucking the red berries from among the thorns of the *tasajillo.*

But nowhere in all this throng shall you find those spirits of peace and good will to man, the yellow-buskined wheat or the more gallant corn with his golden tasseled cap and his green plumes. We miss these burghers. To find them we must go, just where we find them in the Middle Ages, to the water's edge, whether in the hills or on the plains.

Now among them all there towered up here and there a lone figure in Lincoln green, presenting to every front an unchanging face of thorns, and for it I could recall no suitable figure. It was what Americans term the "All-Thorn." It is well named, for stipule, leaf, and stem seem to have alike gone to thorn, so that at its outer perimeter it is difficult to make out the particular thorn, which is the true stem along which runs the center of growth. As I did not know the name given to it by the Mexicans, I asked it of Juan.

"The *Honca* Accursed," was the reply.

I know of no reason, logical or grammatical, why there should be a difference of meaning between "The *Honca* Accursed" and "The Accursed *Honca*," yet in the local parlance there is a difference implied. And if you will substitute for "Accursed" the old stage-drivers' favorite equivalent—beginning and ending with "d"—you will easily catch the distinction. When the participle precedes the noun, the imprecation is a personal one prayed for or pronounced on its object by the party speaking. But when the participle follows the noun it is rather the reiteration of a curse already pronounced by a higher authority.

Having this in mind, I asked of Juan why it was that he designated the shrub as "Accursed."

"Has the Señor never heard?" was the surprised answer.

I told him that I had not.

"Then it must be that the Protestants do not have the same Bible that we Catholics have. Or it may be that the Señor has never had his Padre tell him the story of how the wicked Jews crucified Christ."

"Yes, I have heard the story, but what has it to do with the *Honca* Bush?"

"That will I now tell to the Señor in my own way, as I have heard it from my Padre, with maybe a little more as I have heard it told among us by the campfire.

"You must know that long ago the Jews had Christ among them. They wanted a king among them who would take them out to battle, and who would place his foot on the neck of every nation on earth, and they believed that their old Books had promised them such a king. Christ claimed to be their Promised King, and they saw that he did have great power. But he taught them that they should not go to war; that were a man to be struck on the right cheek, he should offer the left to be struck in the same way. This kind of teaching would never bring the King of the

Jews to place his foot on the necks of every people on earth, and they came to consider Christ as an evil spirit—a deceiver—who plotted evil to them. Then they planned to kill him.

"Now when the Jews had gotten Pilate to deliver Jesus unto their hands that they might crucify him, they set about to mock him as they led him to his death. On the way (Via Crucis) they passed a goodly thorn tree. This they cut down, and of its trunk they made the Cross on which to crucify him, while of its branches they made a crown of thorns and set it on his head to make sport of his Kingship. And so they went on scoffing and reviling at him, while the blood dripped out of the broken and bruised ends of the thorn tree.

"This thorn tree, Señor, was the *Honca* Bush, and for its part in the sin of that day it stands accursed for all time. Like the Wandering Jew, it can never lay down its burden, but must go to the end of time accursed and hated by beast and man. From a tree it withered and shrank, blasted to a shrub; leaf nevermore grew on it to shelter its trunk from the fierce rays of the sun. The sap in it ran out on that evil day, and there was left to feed it only a foul poisonous oil. Because its thorns had pressed as lightly as they could on that sacred brow there was given it to bear a tiny blossom and to ripen a very small berry. But no bee hunts that flower, and only a dark brown moth, by night and in stealth, visits it in shame and penance. No bird or insect tastes that berry, and it is left to wither on that hated stem until the angry winter winds blow it away to be hidden in the merciful dust.

"The *chonte* never sings from its branches, nor does the *mariposa* sip from its flower. The *liebre* never sits in its shade, nor does the *codorniz* take to its cover when pressed by the hawk. The spotted thrush does not build its nest in its limbs, the snake never climbs the naked trunk nor does the hawk dart on its outskirts. The *hormiga* hunts the little green bug in the tops of shrubs and weeds, and your wise Doctor has told us that it milks the bug, as we milk the goat, and lives on it. It may be that the wise man was making sport of us, for he might as well tell me that I could live on the milk of a *conejo,* and the little green bug could not live on the juiceless ends of the *honca* thorns, or if it could even do so, no ant could live on it. So the ant never climbs the *honca,* nor makes its home near its roots.

"Never in social union lives the *honca.* The *tecumblate* grows in great clusters, bush and bush side by side, with branches embracing in brotherly love. The *gatun* plants its roots near to its kin and rejoices in the fragrant bloom of its neighbor. But the *honca* lives an outcast, solitary and alone, shunning its own kin and hated by all plants. The *tasajillo* nestles under the *hoja-sen,* but never will you find its buried treasure guarded under the *honca.*

"No wayfarer will use the *honca* for fire unless in evil plight, for its hateful odor and dire smoke carry its curse. It burns with a fierce and brilliant light, but the curse goes into the torch as well.

"So, living or dead, the *honca* is shunned by all. When life departs from the leafless limbs, it goes so steadily and shamefacedly that no one knows when it has escaped its rider. For years the bare dead limbs will steadily but hopelessly face the winter storms and summer heat, disappearing piece by piece no one knows how or when, until at last there only stands the bare trunk. When finally the withered trunk lies on the ground, it is not given the burial that comes to all plants in the grace of God. For plants, like men, have their friends who see that they have burial after death. The little blind *hormiga blanca* kindly feels its way in darkness to the fallen bodies of the giants of his home, and patiently working day and night, little by little covers the dead with earth. But it never covers the body of the *honca* in decent burial, but lets it wither and char in sun and storm, until finally, how or when no one knows, there is no more any sign of the accursed shrub. Perhaps it has gone to feed the fires of Hell. *¿Quién sabe?*"

At another time, we had camped for the night by the side of a rock cliff, which presented to us a front as regular as that of a wall laid in Flemish Bond. Our nightly campfire had dwindled down to one or two sticks, and the flickering light therefrom threw a shadow of an "aigrita" bush on the wall in a sort of fantastic resemblance to a dancing human being, or human jumping-jack. To our comrades, given to dolorous memories, it suggested recollections of the convulsive movements of a man dying under the hangman's care. This in turn suggested to someone the "Juez de Colorado," of the other side of the river — the Rio Grande — whose name and whose summary power of administering death without trial or hearing, hinted strongly to us of a "cord" or "rope."

After some discussion, I asked, "Natividad, what is the name of the present Juez de Colorado at San Carlos, Mexico?" San Carlos was a town lying some sixty miles away.

"They haven't any, Señor," he replied. "They have not had any since I caught the last one."

There was plainly a story behind this, a story in which Natividad delighted, if one could judge from the wrinkles about the big mouth and the dancing of the little black eyes. "The Señor must know that I keep very closely to the American side of the river, and even when the General

Naranjo was about to sell his land over the river, and was carrying around that lot of Kickapoo Indians to show them the land, and sent for me to come over and show the corners, and sent word to me by his messenger that I would be safe for he would protect me, yet I did not go over. Now, Señor, I was born in that land; the *amigos* of my youth are scattered over it; and I could not find a house over there, save one, where I would not be welcomed to eat and smoke. I know those *terrenos* as a bird knows the *chaparro prieto,* in which its nest is built. And it comes about that I do not go there now, just because I knew it so well in my time.

"The Señores must know that the line between the states of Chihuahua and Coahuila runs into the Rio Grande at the Paso del Chisos, which the Comanches used in the times long ago—when they came into Mexico in the old days to rob and kill. They came in by Lajitas and Santa Helena. I was then a boy at San Carlos and many a time have I seen them. There was old Tave Pete, the old woman captain—so old that when she rode, she had to have a thick woolen cord tied around her throat to keep her jaws from clattering together. Often have I heard her call out her commands to her people from the belfry in the church, in front of the plazita in San Carlos, and have seen the warriors disperse to do her commands. There I saw the two *pelones,* her sons, so called by our people because they cut their hair short, instead of wearing a long scalp-lock like the other Indians. There have I seen Mauwe and Tave Tuk contend to see which could shoot the strongest arrow. Ah! Tave Tuk was a man! We called him Baja el Sol—which means 'Under the Sun,' and he made his boast that there was no man like him for courage under the sun. I have since heard that he died in the Sierra Del Carmen, fighting the Apaches single-handed.

"Now these Comanches came into Mexico by San Carlos, in September of each year. They robbed and plundered until they were ready to go back. By this time they had captives, horses, mules, and even cattle, to carry back in great numbers, so they had to travel slowly. Now to return by their pass at the Lajitas was to bring them within forty miles of the soldiers at Presidio del Norte, and, as they did not wish to have the soldiers to follow them, they took to crossing the river further east, and forty miles further away from the soldiers, and thus returned along the east side of the Chisos Mountains. This pass came to be known as the Paso del Chisos. I saw it after I was a grown man, and at that time the trail leading to and from the ford was a great wide trail, covered with the bones of animals in great number. I would have thought then that the trail could have been followed by the line of bones for a thousand years to come. Well, the Comanches ceased to come, and our horses and cattle rejoiced once more. And in time those who knew the Comanches and their ways died off until now there are few of us living who ever saw a Comanche ride into San Carlos, with his *chimal* on his arm and his spear across his horse. During this time the bones along the old trail to the Paso del Chisos began to disappear. None knew how. Some said the wind covered them with dust and the rain washed them into holes. Others said the wind ate them as we eat bread; that the bones flaked into little thin pieces, and the little whirlwinds that came dancing over the country in the spring picked them up and ground them into the air. I do not know how this is, Señor, but the bones disappeared long ago so that there was nothing to mark the spot where the trail crossed the river at the Paso del Chisos. But there were still a few of us who knew where the old pass had been."

JORNADA DEL MUERTO
Mary Austin
1924

BELOW EL PASO, THE RIO GRANDE CARRIES AN INTERNATIONAL BOUN-dary on its flood, but not with any sense of responsibility—or perhaps with a sense that outreaches our appreciation. Through the soft, deep alluvium of the coastal plain it loops and wriggles. Flood-plain ranches of years' standing are drowned in a night; whole settlements, that were American or Mexican when they began, find themselves shifted to the other bank. Clearly, international boundaries must not be carried so lightly. Elephant Butte Dam was built to curb the willful Rio—three years' flood will scarcely even fill it—but not without due consideration for both its borders. During the years that loose-thinking Americans were talking about intervention in Mexico, Mexico quietly reached out and ac-quired a visible stake in us. Between San Marcial and Elephant Butte, the Rio is constrained by the United States, in the State of New Mexico, to serve equally Texas and Chihuahua. Below San Marcial the river runs in red with the silt of mountain and mesa; over the dam's vast apron it runs out in shining arcs as clear as glass.

Many years ago, when I began to know the Rio Grande, it was some-where about this green thread of river plain, at the bottom of the stopped waters under Fray Cristobal. I recall brown huts and strips of tillage, young leafage and the rosy glow of peach-blossoms against the warm adobe walls. And on the winding river road a teamster walking at the team's head, singing—and that was the first time I heard it—the team-ster's song beginning,

Cliffs of yonder lofty mountain . . .

I think it must have sprung from hereabout, both song and melody, taking the rhythm of slow-plodding oxen.

Ay, Peña Hueca
No me vayas a olvidar!

There is a Hueco range over beyond El Paso; Spindle Mountain is, in fact, apt enough for any of these vertically streaked mesa fronts, like ancient Spanish doorways. But there sticks in my mind a queer feeling for the place of hearing, as lying now at the bottom of the checked river waters, so that I think of it all going on there still—the creaking axle, the tender note of the blossoming peach, and the song rising through the clear water . . . Ay, Peña Hueca, forget me never more! . . . as I think some passionate plaintive note of the Spanish occupation must continue to rise along through our strident modernism.

The Rio goes on below Elephant Butte, threading a series of fertile intervales: Paloma, Rincon, Mesilla, and beyond El Paso, the valley of Juárez. But the highway is forced up over the black lava wall to follow the Jornada del Muerto.

This is how the last lap on the El Paso road was called when the only transportation was the heavily loaded *atajo,* or the ox-drawn, solid-wheeled *carreta.* The mesa here is said to be the oldest land in the world, and looks it; burnt scoria and ghostly sand of the long *medanos* patterned by the wind, stiff bayonet-pointed yuccas and low, lifeless-looking grass. Once there went great country-colored bands of antelope, swift as the shadows of clouds, but now nothing stirs except the sullen rattler, or the coiling and uncoiling *torneos,* that, while the traveler watches, seem mercifully bent upon covering the bones of dead men and pack-animals, exposed by the shifting *medanos,* only to turn in an unsuspected moment to fling their torrents of pulverized grit in his face.

Of all the *pasears* down the Rio and over the Jornada del Muerto, the most memorable was the annual *conducta.*

At the time of the year when, rising early, you catch the footsteps of the morning on the wings of the magpie for good luck, men whose business was the management of trade caravans, trail masters, *arrieros,* armed escorts, gathered at the rendezvous below Socorro; to whom resorted trappers with mule-loads of skins, *cibolleros* with sacks of jerked buffalo meat, *hacienderos* going down to exchange bales of homespun blankets for blooded stallions to improve their stock, miners with ingots of smelted silver and bowl-shaped, government-stamped lumps of soft New Mexico gold, pueblo graders with turquoises and *osha,* that aromatic root which, bruised and sweetened in a hot decoction, gives such delicious comfort to your perturbed insides, beaver-skins and *serapes de Navajo.*

From the first that we heard of them, Navajo blankets were especially esteemed, though they knew no color then but natural black and white wool, dark blue of a forgotten dye, and red which the women picked out of the crimson lining of Spanish officers' cloaks and rewove, the demand for which made such a scarcity of officers that the Government bethought itself and made *bayeta,* as the crimson cloth was called, a regular article of trade. The *conducta* went armed and cautiously along the Jornada del Muerto. At the waterholes in the Organos Mountains, which the *atajo* must visit or die, they were quite certain to find Apaches in ambush, to see that they died horribly. Some weeks later, when the *conducta* returned with silk and cutlery, pineapples and carved leather, high Spanish combs *por las señoras,* and brazil-wood for dyes, it was all to be risked over again. There were also government supply-trains going up with gold coin to pay the official salaries and gold altar furnishings to content the missionaries, drawing bandits out of the mountains that to this day are called Los Ladrones.

At the ford of El Paso del Norte the Jornada and the Rio Grande come together again, but there was nothing on the north bank when the foot-sore refugees of 1680 reached it, nothing much on the other but a mission founded in 1659 to the honor of Our Lady of Guadalupe, and the indefatigable Father Ayeta, who settled them in three groups about where the city of Juárez now stands. Nor was there anything on the north bank but a trail through the mesquite and sand in 1883, when Zebulon Pike came riding down; nothing, in fact, until Texas tore herself free from Mexico, and then only a trading-post until after the Lone Star of Texas became fixed at last on the flag of the United States.

El Paso is now the chief city of our Southern border, but if you go there you will be astonished to discover how few of its citizens can tell you what journeys passed or came to an end there. For El Paso is a city whose journey is but just begun. There is little besides a date or two, and the fragmentary clans of the Piros at Isleta del Sur, to connect it with the Spanish occupation. Cabeza de Vaca is supposed to have forded the Rio here, making his troubled way across the Big Bend Country; and down about the *entrada* of the Río Conchos, the village of Almaden crossed on its unauthorized adventure up the Pecos. For the rest of its four or five hundred miles, the river has no history. But you cannot live beside the Rio Grande and not know it for a history-maker.

CROSSING TO SAFETY
Eugene Manlove Rhodes
1913

"IT LOOKS AWFUL WIDE, JEFF!"

"Oh, I'll be all right—swim it myself if the horse plays out—and if I don't have no cramps, as I might, of course, after this ride. Well—here goes nothin'! Take care of the little horse. I hope he brings you good luck!"

"Well—so long, then!"

Bransford rode into the muddy waters. They came to the horse's breast, his neck; he plunged in, sank, rose, and was borne away down the swift current, breasting the flood stoutly—and so went quartering across to the farther bank. It took a long time. It was quite light when the horse found footing on a sandbar half a mile below, rested, and splashed whitely through the shallows to the bank. Gibson swung his sombrero. Jeff waved his hand, rode to the fringing bushes, and was gone.

Los Baños de Santa Eulalia del Norte, otherwise known as Mud Springs, is a Mexican hamlet, with one street of about the same length. Los Baños—all that—lies in an ox-bow of the Rio Grande, half a day in mere miles from El Paso: otherwise a contemporary of Damascus and Arpad.

Thither, mindful of the hot springs which supply the preliminaries of the name, went Mr. Bransford. A stranger to the border custom might have simulated illness as an excuse for a modest life, and so retired from public view—in which case there would have been whisperings; but Jeff was in their bosoms, bone of their bone; he cunningly gave it out that he was from the American side, a fugitive with a price upon his head. Suspicion thus disarmed, he became the guest of the city.

SIERRA MADRE
Edward Abbey
1979

OUR PILOT IS IKE RUSSELL. AGAIN. WE'RE FLYING IN HIS OLD WRIN-kled Cessna from Tucson and Nogales south-southeast to a little logging town known as Creel in the state of Chihuahua. Named for the Mexican entrepreneur and politician who helped establish the Ferrocarril de Chihuahua al Pacífico—that fabulous railway which runs from Chihuahua City across the western Sierra Madre to Los Mochis and Topolobampo (perfect name) on the west coast of Sonora.

The sky is extremely hazy this afternoon in spring, full of windblown dust and the smoke from forest fires to the east. Northwest Mexico, like the American Southwest, has been suffering a prolonged drought. Below, I see the barren desert hills rising gradually toward the crest of the Sierra Madre Occidental. Brown, burnt, sere, denuded hills, stripped of grass and largely waterless. Somewhere down in there, in the meager shade of cactus and mesquite, the cattle are dying by the thousands from thirst and starvation. The Sonora newspapers call it, appropriately, a disaster area.

The hills become bigger, rougher, with deep vertical escarpments facing the west. We fly over the trenchlike canyons of the Río Moctezuma, the Río Papigochic, the Río Yaqui, mere threads of water winding among the foothills. Somewhere up around the headwaters of the Río Yaqui there may be—maybe—a surviving remnant of the once-numerous Mexican grizzly population. No one seems to know for sure. The great bear survives mostly on rumor.

Although the approaches are rugged, the range ahead of us lacks any prominent peaks. Some points rise 10,000 feet above sea level, but from the air this part of the Sierra Madre ("Mother Mountains") presents only long ridges and high plateaus with a rolling surface, all trending in a northwesterly-southeasterly direction. There are no snowy summits here or any snow in sight at all. Arid, arid country. The scenic grandeur of the region lies not in the mountains but in the canyons or *barrancas* carved by the rivers, where the vertical relief may often exceed 5,000 feet. According to unverified report. Northwest Mexico has never been mapped in a thorough and scientific manner. Stories of canyons deeper than Arizona's Grand Canyon must be regarded with suspended judgment.

We fly over the forests now, thin but extensive growths of jack pine, scrub oak, yellow pine. Everything I can see appears to be well logged; the land is overlaid with an intricate network of dirt roads. According to Russell, who has been flying over, exploring, and prospecting the Sierra Madre for twenty years, there is almost no virgin forest remaining.

Fires are burning in many places, apparently unattended. As an old-time fire lookout, my instinctive reaction is to grab the radio mike and sound the alarm to all points—but down here, who knows? Maybe nobody cares. Let them burn. In any case, we are beyond my jurisdiction. Furthermore, Ike tells me, while some of the fires below were probably lightning-caused, the majority are deliberate, started by the Indians to clear the ground for the planting of their corn and beans, the slash-and-burn economy.

That forested range below is plainly not uninhabited. Everywhere I look, I see not only logging roads and fires but also the *milpas* of the Tarahumara Indians, small clearings of one to two acres scattered about on every bench and swale of land with a slope of less than fifty degrees off the perpendicular. You might call it wild or primitive country, but as in most of Mexico, the land is occupied to the limit of its carrying capacity by human beings—and by their cattle, burros, goats, dogs, chickens, pigs. To the limit and then some.

Ike flies on, holding his course steady. We pass above the tracks of the Chihuahua al Pacífico, and suddenly more great breaks appear—the barrancas. Hard to make much of them through the smoke, the dust, the glare of the midday sun. I see craggy drop-offs, the serrated edge of rimrock, brushy slopes descending at precipitous angles into obscure depths, out of which a few buttes and pinnacles rise into the light. Water glints far below. The cornfields, the corrals and granaries, the little stone huts of the Indians are perched on the edge of the barranca and on the open slopes far down within it. Barranca del Cobre, Ike tells me; "Copper Canyon." That faint hint of water down in the shadows must be the Río Urique.

To call it a canyon is not quite exact. There is a distinction of meaning between "barranca" and "canyon," both of them, of course, Spanish words. The term "canyon" refers to a long and narrow defile, well defined, walled in by cliffs, usually though not necessarily with a stream running through it. "Barranca" means, literally, a "break"; in Spanish landform terminology the word functions as a broader, more inclusive term than "canyon," denoting any area where the land falls off steeply from one level to the next in an irregular, very rough, highly eroded fashion. For example, Santa Elena in Big Bend is clearly a canyon; Bryce Canyon in Utah is not a canyon at all, but something that better exemplifies the word "break" (like Cedar Breaks, also in Utah) or "barranca."

The Barranca del Cobre, as I can see from the air, huge as it is in itself, is only one barranca among several in the vicinity. Easy to see why this portion of the Sierra Madre has been for so long a formidable barrier to east-west traffic. Even today, from the Arizona line down to the Durango-Mazatlán highway, a distance of 700 miles, there is no paved road across the range. The railroad is still the only reliable transportation from one side to the other.

We make a pass over the right-angled bend of the Río Urique, then turn north past the town of Creel for a quick aerial look at the Cascada de Basochiachic on the little river called Chinipas. Basochiachic is a waterfall with a straight pour-off a thousand feet down, making it one of the highest single-jump falls in North America. But it's been a dry winter in the Sierra Madre, and the waterfall, as we approach it, is not in good form. The volume of water that pours from the brink of the falls is not sufficient to reach the plunge pool below; blown sideways by the wind, the veil of falling water dissolves into vapor halfway down.

Banking east and south again, we return to Creel. Ike buzzes the Hotel Nuevo twice, hoping to rouse the management to the advent of gringo tourists without reservations, then drops us off at the airstrip five miles south of town.

There is nothing here but the strip itself, a limp windsock, a few Indian huts, a few gaunt cattle munching weeds. The Indians stare. The dogs bark. Ike takes off and disappears. My wife Renée and I shoulder our packs, climb the hillside to the road, and start marching toward town. We've walked a mile when a flatbed truck comes grinding along, headed our way. I stick out a thumb and we've got a ride. There are four or five adults in back. We join the crowd on the bed.

One of the passengers is an old man, a Tarahumara, with a big gray Zapatista mustache. His handsome, leather-skinned face looks as if it has faced the mountain sun and mountain winds for a century. He wears the conventional Tarahumara dress: straw hat, white shirt, red bandana around the neck and a loose white baggy sort of dhoti around the loins. His lean brown legs are bare; on his feet he wears homemade thong sandals, the soles cut from discarded auto tires. Huaraches.

I am fascinated by his feet. The old man owns the most beaten-up, stone-battered, cactus-cured, fire-hardened pair of feet I have ever seen on a human being—so cracked, splayed, and toughened they almost suggest hooves. No doubt he has gone barefoot most of his life, the sandals being for dress-up occasions, for Saturday night in the big town: Creel, population . . . 2,500?

The Tarahumara are famed for their long-distance running. Their races are said to go on for fifty miles, sometimes 200 miles. This old man whose feet I am gaping at may be, in his world, a once-great racer.

Though it's rude to stare, I cannot help but look again at his weathered face, the map of his soul. The expression there is attractive and appealing—serene, far-seeing eyes; a calm and easeful smile. Where have I seen that kind of face before? And I remember: yes, among old folk in Appalachia, in west Texas, in Norway, in Calabria. The sign of honor, an interior victory of some kind that cannot be won in less than seventy years—the Biblical threescore and ten. The faces of beautiful old men and women around the world.

We enter Creel, a little mountain logging town 7,000 feet above sea level. We pass the mill, its conical sawdust burners belching woodsmoke, with little boys stacking boards, dragging slab lumber out of the sheds as spinning buzz saws bite with a snarl into fat logs of ponderosa.

Into the town. Rutted dirt streets. Stone cabins, slabwood shacks, log huts. Children swarming everywhere—filthy, ragged, snot-nosed *mocositos,* shouting, screaming, laughing, and happy. Despite the food shortages, the alarming rise in the price of such staples as corn and beans, these children seem to be adequately fed, active, irrepressible. What does it take to sober a child? I don't want to know.

Renée and I check in at the Hotel Nuevo, opposite the railroad station. Despite the name, it is the oldest hostelry in town, definitely second class, maybe third. Still it has that south-of-the-border—what shall we call it? Style? Authenticity. Reputation. (Friends in Tucson had insisted upon it.) The rooms are small, dank, dingy; the beds sag like hammocks; the lighting is erratic; and the hotel food (American plan)—ah, that Nuevo cuisine—perturbs the imagination. Peculiar looking vegetables, unidentifiable. Stringy bits of flesh, obscure in origin, wrapped in limp and greasy folds of dough. Everything disguised, the flavor—if any—buried beneath a mucous membrane of melted cheese and last week's tomato sauce. You can always count on the tomato sauce: Every dish comes immersed in it.

I am glad we've brought with us a week's supply of dehydrated All-American ersatz. Once we get out in the woods we'll *eat*. But there was a better reason for that than mere gringo caution and fastidiousness: By bringing our own feed we will not be competing with the natives for something to eat, will not be helping to force up the price of local foods. The *rico* tourist may think, when he pays the extravagant bill at a Mexican restaurant, that he is at least contributing to the welfare of the workers in the local economy. False. A few will benefit, but the majority, deriving no income whatsoever from the tourist racket, find they are paying higher prices for their daily tortillas.

Turismo is always and everywhere a dubious, fraudulent, distasteful, and in the long run, degrading business, enriching a few, doing the rest more harm than good.

Next morning we are joined by old friends. Bill Hoy and his Argentine wife Marina arrive by train from Ciudad Chihuahua. The four of us plan a walk together down into the Big Barranca—el Cobre—by a new and unknown route. We spend the day packing our packs, inspecting Creel, eating the Hotel Nuevo dinner, recovering, going to bed. Next morning, early, we are off in the hotel jeep for a ride to the head of a side canyon—unnamed on our map—that leads to the Río Urique and Barranca del Cobre. Our intention is to hike down this canyon to the river, follow the river upstream to the next tributary canyon, and walk out to the Creel–La Bufa road, completing the loop. We carry food for five days.

The trek begins down a Tarahumara footpath along a pretty stream. On either side of the stream are corn patches and bean fields of the Indians—tiny, cultivated plots that don't look big enough to support a flock of chickens, let alone a human family. Early May: The corn is a foot high, green and fragile. There is no attempt at irrigation; all depends on the summer rains. Each miniature field is fenced in with brush, rocks, or logs, presumably to keep out the animals—the burros, pigs, cattle, and flocks of voracious goats that swarm like hooved locusts across the hillsides. Subsistence agriculture, close to the margin of survival: One must credit the courage and faith of these peasant Indians. Each year they gamble their lives on a few acres of sand and dust, a rocky hillside for their beasts, the rainclouds. An earnest and serious wager, for there is no public welfare system in the Republic of Mexico. The losers simply disappear.

We tramp in single file between their fields, four big gringos with grotesque packs on our backs, while the Indians near their huts review our parade, shyly, furtively, from a safe distance. Quite likely they have never seen such a procession before. We are shy ourselves, fully aware of the incongruity of our presence here (Vietnam!), the pounds of luxury foods in our backpacks, the goosedown sleeping bags, our big solid boots, the Vibram tracks we leave on the trail. The Indians squatting around small fires, cooking their *pinole,* or cornmeal mush, in handmade clay pots, watch without a word as we go by. But their yellow curs bark vigorously enough, vicious yet prudent.

What the hell *are* we doing here? Sightseeing? Not very dignified. Call it exploration. Science, that's the word. We are exploring a canyon that, according to the manager of the Hotel Nuevo, no gringo has ever trod before. Certainly no self-respecting Mexican would come down here. And even the Indians' trail will peter out long before we come in sight of the Río Urique.

Onward, over the goat dung, through the dust, over the shelves of smooth volcanic rock that skirt the stream. I notice that the fields are protected from floods by flimsy barricades of brush. I think of the heavy logging now taking place in the upland forests, of the vast excavations for a new truck and tourist highway, of the hordes of hungry cattle scouring the clearings and hillsides for a blade of grass, a bite of browse. What will happen when the dry spell breaks and the rains finally do come? When all that runoff water and all that grazed-off soil come pouring down these narrow canyons in a flood of muck and mud? The 35,000 Tarahumara have survived in this rough, beautiful "undeveloped" land for centuries, with their hard and beautiful way of life; but things are happening to their country now that they have never had to deal with before.

Indians, Indians, the goddamned Indians. As if we don't have enough to worry about without them on our hands, and hearts and minds as well. The one thing we could do for these people, I am thinking as I trudge along at the rear of the column, the one and only decent thing we could do for them (and by "we" I mean mainly the Mexicans and the Mexican "authorities," but include gringo Americans and Europeans, too), is leave them alone. Throw out the teachers, the missionaries, the government doctors and public health technicians; close off the roads and stop the road building; stop the logging; shut down the mines; burn down the hotels; tear up the airstrips; throw out the totalitarian fanatics from so-called Third World politics; ban all tourists, including us; and let these people alone. *Leave them alone.*

But leaving them alone is the one thing we will not do. So the Indians are doomed. The Tarahumara, unless saved by a quick collapse of the world industrial megamachine now moving in on them, haven't a chance. Like the Tupi of the Amazon, like the Kurds of Iran and Iraq, like the herdsmen of Tibet, like the Hopi of Arizona, like a hundred other small and once-independent tribes around the globe, these Indians are going to be . . . incorporated. Assimilated. Extinguished.

Well, it's not my problem. We march steadily on and soon leave the Indians and their milpas and their tedious troubles far behind, out of sight, out of mind. The goat paths continue on for a few more miles, but the huts become fewer and fewer, and the few we see appear to be unoccupied. We have a final glimpse of a goatherd—a woman—trying to hide from us in the brush; she is the last Indian or other human being of any variety that we shall see for days.

The stream descends, growing bigger, augmented by springs, seeps, and tributary runs, through a canyon walled by ragged, brush-covered formations of volcanic origin—consolidated tuff interbedded with thin strata of conglomerates. Dark, broken, craggy rock reaching far above us, perhaps 1,500 to 2,000 feet high. I am reminded of the canyons in the Gila Wilderness of New Mexico. Every slope short of bare-rock vertical cliff is terraced by animal paths. Domestic animals. Not surprisingly, we find little sign of wildlife, except for lizards and a few minnows in the pools and the birds.

Many birds. A multitude of birds. Some of them, like the coppery-tailed or elegant trogon and the solitary eagle (their proper names), I have never seen before, anywhere. Marina Hoy, a keen observer, the most able birdwatcher among us, will identify sixty-three different species before this walk is done.

The trogon, as its full name implies, is a striking and colorful bird. But shy: We catch only glimpses of it flitting among the trees. A pair of nesting solitary eagles (for even the solitary must sometimes mate—and these, like other eagles, mate for life) give us a much better show. We lie on our backs at the side of the path for half an hour, watching them soar

and circle over the cliffs, alighting on trees and taking off again, screaming from time to time, no doubt disturbed by our presence, even though
we are hundreds of feet below the focus of their domestic operations. We
apologize for the intrusion, but they are beautiful birds in their black-and-
white regalia, hard to give up watching. Furthermore, it takes the four of
us, passing binoculars back and forth and consulting Marina's field guide,
that much time to determine to our satisfaction that we are indeed looking at solitary eagles and not at their similar-looking cousin, the Mexican
black hawk. Birdwatchers are a fussy, eccentric lot, especially perpetual
beginners like myself, who seem condemned never to find a bird, anywhere, that corresponds precisely to its description and illustration in the
bird books. A failing, on the part of the bird, difficult to forgive.

Finally, we go on, leaving the eagles in peace. Our bird list continues
to grow. Even I spot a few I can recognize: a robin, a common flicker
(all flickers are now classified as one species by the avian authorities),
some kind of hummingbird, and a buzzard. Marina helps me find some
of the more special, unusual, or beautiful: a caracara, a Cassin's kingbird,
a crested flycatcher, a Townsend's solitaire, a painted redstart, a black-
headed grosbeak, a red crossbill. But those rarest and most spectacular
of Sierra Madre birds—the thick-billed parrot and the imperial woodpecker—are nowhere to be seen. It is possible that the imperial woodpecker is now extinct and the thick-billed parrot close to extinction.

Despite decades of heavy overgrazing and overbrowsing, a great variety
of plant life still survives in this nameless side canyon of Barranca del
Cobre. There is yellow pine (*Pinus ponderosa*), Arizona cypress, manza-
nita, alligator juniper, tamarisk, willow and bamboo along the creek, sil-
verleaf oak, a fig tree (introduced) growing by an ancient stone hut,
Apache pine, the wine-colored madrona, Emory oak, palmetto, a few
small aspen on the slopes (this surely must be near the southern-most extension of the aspen's range), some type of maple, some species of locust.
And on the lower, south-facing, hotter and drier slopes, a mixture of typical desert flora: prickly pear, hedgehog cactus, aloe, sotol, flowering agave,
and yucca. We see a woody shrub blooming with what look exactly like
sunflowers. Impossible but true. And air plants, orchids, flourishing on
the pines. And many other plants, the identity of which we can hardly
even guess at.

"What is it?" we ask, meaning what is its name? This odd quirk of
the human mind: Unless we can name things, they remain for us only
half-real. Or less than half-real: nonexistent. A man without a name is
nobody. A man's name can become more important than his person. A
plant, an animal, a thing without a name is no thing—nothing. No won-

der we humans like to think that in the beginning was — the Word. What word? Any word. Any word at all, anything rather than the silence and terror of the nameless.

We don't get far this first day. We spend more time ogling birds or bushes or the rocky walls upstairs, or talking and eating and resting, mainly resting, than in serious businesslike hiking. Compatibly indolent, we call a halt in midafternoon and make our first camp, much earlier than strictly necessary, on a nice, pebbly beach with sand pockets, sleeping-bag size, by the side of the stream.

After our supper of reconstituted freeze-dried glop, we lie about the evening fire sipping rum, listen to the poorwills and whippoorwills (both), and watch the little lights that float through the dusk around us. *Molto misterioso.*

The first light I saw, from the corner of my eye, startled me. Unimagined and quite unanticipated, a small globe of furry luminescence drifts unblinking toward my face. For a moment I think I'm seeing one of Carlos Casteneda's Don Juan magic-button spooks: a spirit from some separate reality incarnated for my very own spiritual benefit in the form of low-wattage bug. No, not so; the bug blinks, and I recognize our old friend the firefly.

Alas, occult visions seem to come only to those who believe in them beforehand. First the faith, then the hairy little miracle. First the pill, the tab, the wafer, the space capsule — then come the ruby-eyed, six-legged alligators swimming through your psychedelic dome.

To hell with mysticism.

Next day we push on, at a comfortable pace, downward and deeper into this jungle-brush, jumbled rock-slide canyon. Where is the Río Urique? There is no longer any trail, only a welter of animal paths following the contours of the terrain and winding among the boulders that nearly choke the stream bed. No easy way. We follow the rock shelves, we climb over and around the boulders, we scramble up and down the brushy slopes, our hands on tree trunks for support. At one point, far beyond the last of the Indian fields, we discover a long-legged boar wallowing in the water, enjoying himself. Half-wild or maybe wholly wild, he scuttles off like a javelina when he finally sees us. I dislodge a stone; a red scorpion scurries under the leaves. Four piebald burros high on the slope watch us pass; they have long dark eyelashes, like movie starlets or cocktail waitresses; they do not bray but *cough* at us.

We're not making much progress, I suspect, and God only knows where the Río Urique and the Big Barranca are; but it doesn't seem to matter. There's plenty to look at and feel, plenty of time to think about where we are. The growing consensus among the four of us is, "If we get there we get there and if we don't we don't." To hell with science too. Thus the ambience of Mexico infects our nervous systems: Montezuma's revenge in its subtler form.

In late afternoon we come to the loveliest scene yet: a series of pools big enough for swimming, joined to one another by noisy cascades pouring through sculpted grooves and polished chutes in the rose-colored bedrock. Tall willow trees shade the sand and stone at the water's side. Thickets of oak on the slope higher up promise good fuel for cooking. Against the blue, on either side of us, behind and ahead, rises a metropolitan skyline of towers, blocks, pinnacles, and spires of unknown height, though the pine trees on the rim suggest by their scale that the distance must be at least 3,000 feet.

A good, clean well-furnished campsite, with a view. Here we shall camp tonight, and the next night and yet another. Too fine a place for only an overnight stop. We unload the pig iron from our backs, strip, and plunge into the clear green pools, then sit in the sun on the smooth pink andesite and study our creased, coffee-stained topographic map, trying to determine where we are. The map is a Xerox copy of a copy, printed in Mexico on recycled tortilla paper with iguana piss for ink. Hard to read. We end up guessing we may be halfway to the Urique. No matter. No sweat. We build a fire of oakwood in a cove in the stone, cook supper, uncap the Ron Bacardi, contemplate the coagulation of twilight and the assembly of our organic lanterns afloat on the warm currents of evening—the fireflies, the lightning bugs. I remember from childhood that a firefly stays luminous even when ducked under water—it should lure trout? But there are no trout in the tepid waters of this creek; nothing but chub, carp, dace, mudsuckers. The biggest fish we've seen so far was six inches long.

Morning. We have decided to make this stopping place a base camp. Bill and I, leaving our packs in camp, plan a fast reconnoiter down-canyon to see if the river and main barranca are within reach; Renée chooses to spend the day at home; Marina accompanies us part way, then drops back for photography. Bill and I go on alone.

We find that the canyon gets rougher the farther we go. A few miles beyond base camp it becomes a narrow gorge, walled in by rotten-rock cliffs a couple of hundred feet high. Above the cliffs are benches and talus slopes covered with brush and forest, then the higher cliffs. The complexity of the landscape, with its lavish growth of vegetation, reminds me of scenes depicted on Chinese tapestries. Hoy, the shutterbug, cannot resist pausing for more picture taking. Click, click—we hasten on.

Fallen slabs big as boxcars lie tumbled and heaped across the creek, jamming the gorge from wall to wall. We climb over and through the cracks between and under them. The gradient becomes steeper, which may or may not mean we are getting close to the Urique. Waterfalls tumble ten, fifteen, twenty feet down to emerald basins. We belay one another off the vertical pitches, climb down trees, in one place descend, chimney-style, between a giant slab and the canyon wall.

We realize that we are not going to crawl down through here with full field packs on our backs plus a pair of girls not too keen on bouldering. Our proposed loop expedition is hereby canceled for this year. Bill and I go further, but by two in the afternoon, after rounding several more bends without seeing any hint of the main canyon through the hazy vistas beyond, we admit defeat. We are not going to reach Barranca del Cobre by this particular side canyon. That much is clear.

In cheerful ignominy we stop, rest, eat some gorp and jerky, then turn back without regrets, retracing the route up rocks and trees and chimneys, boulder hopping back to camp. Taking our time. We don't talk about it, but I'm sure Bill is as conscious as I am of the trouble we'd be in if one of us bent a bone or tore a cartilage in here. Why, you couldn't get even a burro down into this shattered maze.

We spend two more days and nights in Little Eden Camp before starting the long walk back to the Indian farms, the dusty road to Creel. On our return, we pause to examine more closely a Tarahumara plow, left leaning against the wall of an unoccupied stone hut. The plow has been carved—whittled, rather—from a single big chunk of oak, with one root still attached serving as the handle, much like the one-handled plow that Hesiod tells us the ancient Greek farmers used. The plowshare is simply the frontal tip of the oak, chipped to a point and hardened in fire. In the center of the beam a square hole has been cut or burnt (somehow); inserted in this hole is a square peg by which, apparently, the implement is drawn when hitched to an ox. Primitive? From the Indians' point of view, quite up to date: The plow was introduced into Mexico by the Spanish only 470 years ago.

A day later we're riding the ferrocarril, the "iron road" from Creel to the west coast of Mexico. But we stop for two days at a point on the rim of Barranca del Cobre called Divisadero, meaning "overlook." Before hiking off into the woods, we check out the local facilities. Divisadero is the Grand Canyon Village of Mexico and that is bad, but not the worst thing I can say about it. Perched on the extreme rim of the barranca, just like Bright Angel Lodge, is a brand-new hotel, built Holiday Inn style for the accommodation of tourists. A fat black sewer hose, leading from the hotel, dangles over the cliff in full view of the principal lookout point, dripping its contents into the next terrace down, about a hundred feet below.

The air is filled with the roar of a diesel generator nearby, busy making electricity for the lodge, bellowing continuously night and day. The building is surrounded by a barbed-wire fence, seven strands high—obviously a people fence, meant to keep out the Indians who have gravitated here in hopes of selling their clay pots and wooden fiddles and other trinkets to the passing trade. Against this fence the wind has piled a solid layer of papers, trash, junk.

We go into the hotel restaurant for cold beer. The Cerveza Bohemia is good—Mexican beer is better than most American commercial beer—but we foolishly make the mistake of ordering sandwiches to go with the beer. Half an hour later, after long whispered consultations back in the kitchen, the *mozo* in his red monkey jacket brings us each what is meant to be a gringo sandwich: two slices of pale Kleenex balloon bread, exact imitations of our own back-home unspeakable Holsum, Wonder, and Rainbo, between which are concealed a transparent sliver of tomato, a film of mayonnaise, and a token wisp of cheese; with each sandwich we get one green olive impaled on a toothpick.

The tab for this affront (including the beer) comes to eighty-four pesos—$6.72. Adding injury to insult. Got to learn Mexican for "rip-off." Walking out, I inquire, from curiosity only, how much the rooms are; the desk clerk says thirty dollars a night for two. Fred Harvey would love this place.

We clear out, evading the temptation to provoke an international incident, hoist backpacks, and walk several miles along the rim until we are well beyond sight, sound, smell, and taste of Divisadero. We set up camp on slab of rock cantilevered over the edge of a 500-foot drop-off. There we relax, perusing from above the impressive depths of the Barranca del Cobre.

How deep is it anyway? As I mentioned before, no exact surveys have been made in this part of Mexico. Boosters of the barranca claim it is 6,500 feet deep in the Divisadero area. Arizona's Grand Canyon is a mile deep, if measured from the South Rim, 6,000 feet deep if measured from the North Rim. The trail from near Divisadero to the Río Urique in the bottom of the barranca is eighteen miles long, according to Michael Jenkinson in his book, *Wild Rivers of North America*—making it comparable to the walk down into the Colorado River from the North Rim. Of course, the length of the trail has no necessary correlation to the depth of the descent.

To me the barranca does not look as deep as the Grand Canyon. But

Bill Hoy thinks it does. Subjective, chauvinistic prejudices play a role here: The Grand Canyon, for me, is part of my backyard, home; Hoy is queer for Mexico and all things Mexican.

Which is bigger? The Grand Canyon is 285 miles long from Lee's Ferry to the Grand Wash Cliffs; the Barranca del Cobre is approximately 150 miles long. If its length is added to that of the neighboring barrancas, however, we get a combined barranca system that may be four times the length of the Grand Canyon.

Which is more impressive? They are different. The Grand Canyon descends steeply and dramatically to its inner gorge, revealing more varied and colorful rock strata than the barranca, which is wider, generally brushy, and formed mostly of dark, broken volcanic rock.

Which is wider? Once again, such comparisons are difficult and maybe useless. The Grand Canyon, except for Phantom Ranch, Supai village, and the nearly continuous stream of tourist boat traffic on the river during half the year, is uninhabited. The Barranca del Cobre and the other barrancas are settled in every tillable nook and cranny by the Tarahumara Indians. But the Grand Canyon is surrounded by the general asphalt-covered, electrified terrain of industrial U.S.A. The barrancas of the Sierra Madre make up a far vaster area, mostly roadless (except for logging and mining roads); most of the interior is far, far from any town, telephone, or Park Service comfort station.

We spend the evening with our feet hanging over the edge of the abyss, spying on the Indians down below. How slowly they seem to move among their huts and fields and stone corrals, along the winding threadlike paths that lead from one tiny settlement to the next. A life in slow motion. Illusions of distance? But what's the rush? The Tarahumara live deliberately, wasting no movements; and when they run, they run all day, all day and half the night. We hear roosters crowing, dogs yapping, the tinkle of goat bells, the sound of somebody playing a tune on a wooden flute. I think of southern Italy, Crete, North Africa.

The Río Urique, studied through field glasses, looks from our perch on the rim like a trickling stream hardly larger than the one we'd followed down the side canyon a few days earlier. It has indeed been a dry winter. The barranca floor is full of rocks, boulders, fallen debris, through and under which the water moves. A river of rocks. Parts of the Urique have been run by boaters with kayaks, in early spring after a winter of normal precipitation in the mountains, but the feat looks impossible now. . . .

RIVER OF GHOSTS
Michael Jenkinson
1981

AT THE SOUTHERNMOST TIP OF THE BIG BEND, MARISCAL MOUNTAIN blocks the course of the river, and again the waters plunge through a spectacular canyon. Boats can be shoved off at either Pantera or the abandoned Talley Ranch, reached by rough backcountry roads. Road conditions should be checked when fire permits are picked up from rangers at Panther Junction, and, as when doing any desert travel, several gallons of extra water, a shovel, and towrope should be tossed onto the load.

Mariscal and Santa Elena canyons have a number of similarities. Both were formed by the river cutting through limestone as it was gradually uplifted; both begin abruptly without preamble—the river simply slipped into narrow cracks wedged by towering rock. Like Santa Elena, Mariscal Canyon has a rockslide not far from the entrance.

The Rockpile in Mariscal is just a hundred yards inside the opening. It is much less formidable than the Santa Elena version; nevertheless, river runners should beach on the gravel bar a little upstream from the rocks on the Texas side and look it over. A number of boaters, ignoring this ritual, have been unceremoniously dumped into the water.

About one-half mile below the Rockpile, a massive block of stone has fallen into the river, forcing the water to churn through a 5-foot gap on the left and a 10-foot gap on the right. Like the Rockpile, this, the Tight Squeeze, has caused a number of unplanned swims. The left-hand gap is not recommended. Current in the right-hand slot piles up on another rock, forcing a tight right turn to the left. It is best to enter the right-hand slot from close to the Mexican side, which gives one the best angle for avoiding debacle or outright disaster. Inexperienced boaters can line or portage boats along the rocky Mexican shore, a practice followed by even the most seasoned boaters in highwater. When the river is running 5 feet high or more, it surges over the midstream rock, creating a dangerous waterfall.

Below the Tight Squeeze, the river is mild, and although dunkings do occur, they are occasioned by boaters rubbernecking the soaring delights of this canyon to such an extent as to forget the equilibrium of their craft. In places the walls are from 1,500 to 1,800 feet high. White boulders rise from the shores, polished by centuries of silt-laden floods.

Midway through the canyon the sheer walls drop away for about one-fourth mile at The Break, a great rift caused by folding and faulting. It is as though a giant finger had been drawn down the length of the mountain while the rock was soft and doughy. There is a shallow rapids here and, on the Mexican shore, some sod dugouts that have been occupied from time to time in the past. This is a lonely place. When the night wind swoops down the dry creekbed on the Mexican side, shaking spiny yucca and whistling against the cliffs, it seems a thousand miles from the nearest streetlight or well-trimmed lawn.

Yet the crossing here is an old one, and the trails that wander up the rift on either side of the river, splitting into numerous smaller paths back on the mountain, have been used often, usually at night. No one knows for how many centuries Indians have walked the trails, but on a boulder of the west wall of the dry creek petroglyphs representing turtles, centipedes, a cross, and other, more obscure, designs have been pecked into the rock. Comanche war parties used the trail when raiding Mexican ranchitos for horses and other livestock; they were followed by former buffalo hunters, renegade sheriffs, and ne'er-do-wells from shanty towns of the southern plains, who also took to running off Mexican ponies. In turn, gangs of Mexican cutthroats stormed up the rift, seeking Texas longhorns and Indian babies which could be sold into slavery.

In more recent times, the trails have been used by a variety of smugglers who, moving their pack trains by night, carried illegal firearms, gold, liquor, and wax from the candelilla plant. Originally, the pale green plant was considered useful only as a rustic cure for venereal disease, but the wax now commands good prices as a component for candles, phonograph records, floor wax, and shoe polish. The trail heads at the north end of Mariscal Mountain are largely concealed with brush; from lookouts the smugglers can scan the surrounding desert for members of the Border Patrol or others who might be inhospitable to their ventures, before proceeding northward or making contact with buyers.

Rangers at Big Bend National Park estimate that three to four pack trains bearing illicit candelilla wax cross the border and pass through portions of the park each month. In remote camps, mostly on the Mexican side, the gathered candelilla plants are dumped into fifty-five-gallon oil drums cut lengthwise. The vats contain boiling water laced with a small amount of sulfuric acid, which causes the wax to separate and float to the top. It is then ladled out, allowed to harden, and packed upon burro trains. The Rangers, of course, have no mandate over customs matters, but they are concerned over the gathering of the plant within the park boundaries, principally on Mariscal Mountain and Mesa de Anguilla, and must apprehend pack trains for not possessing a commercial license to operate within the park. Recently, six horsemen escorting forty-three loaded burros were arrested in the park. Such men are usually armed. They are poor; the animals represent most of their material wealth, and the wax can be the result of weeks or months of hard work. Confiscations are not lightly regarded by either side.

Below The Break the river glides smoothly between high walls, which through one stretch have been eroded into a fantasy of pinnacles and towers, like a setting for goblins and trolls. There is a good campsite about one mile below The Break on the Mexican side, a high sandbank with a view of the pinnacles. The river breaks abruptly out of the depths of Mariscal Mountain to wind sluggishly through rolling desert country. It is about 2 miles to the site of Solis Ranch, usual take-out point for Mariscal Canyon float trips.

Most float parties leave a shuttle vehicle at Solis and then drive around the north end of Mariscal Mountain to either Talley Ranch or Pantera. En route they pass the ruined processing plant, offices, and residences of the Mariscal Mine, a cinnabar (mercury ore) mine that has largely been inactive since the 1920s. Hardier souls can leave their vehicle at Talley Ranch, drift through, cache their boats, and then hike back over Mariscal Mountain. The trails are unmarked, faint, and waterless; but experienced and prepared backpackers will find the trek enjoyable—there are spectacular views of the canyon, at least one former smuggler's house, and a number of large bat caves. The Mariscal Canyon trip is 7 miles long, and can be done in four or five hours (with, of course, additional hours needed for shuttle driving).

Between Solis Ranch and Boquillas the Rio Grande cuts through two other canyons, San Vicente and Hot Springs, with a stretch of fairly open country between them. Although they are not sheer-sided gorges like Santa Elena or Mariscal, their eroded cliffs do display interesting formations. There are only two rapids in the entire run, neither of which should present problems. After passing through San Vicente Canyon, one quickly reaches the rapids of the same name, created by boulders washed down by flash floods in Glenn Draw. The other fastwater is at Hot Springs Rapids, located at the mouth of Tornillo Creek. Here an island splits the river. The Mexican channel is recommended.

In these canyons, one occasionally sees the brush huts of a candelilla camp or flocks of goats scrambling along cliff-sides, and where the banks are gentle there are scattered farms on the Mexican side. The small Mexican hamlet of San Vicente was originally established as a fort in 1774. On the other side of the river, San Vicente, Texas, is today marked by ruined adobe and stone houses as well as a graveyard on a gravel hill to the north. A short way downriver, there are other reminders of the past—the abandoned store and somewhat primitive tourist courts of Hot Springs, which operated from 1909 to 1942. There are a number of warm springs trickling into both sides of the river, and on the Mexican side, some people have created their own spas—small bathing pits dug in the riverbank silt.

San Vicente and Hot Springs canyons are usually run as an extension of a Mariscal Canyon float trip—two or three days would be ample time. A good take-out place is Boquillas Ford. The trip can be shortened by taking out at Glenn Draw, reached by rough road (four-wheel drive recommended), or at Hot Springs, from which an improved road leads back to blacktop.

Boquillas Ford may well be the most informal border crossing in the country. American tourists camping at nearby Rio Grande Village are ferried back and forth across the river on burros provided by barefooted Mexican boys.

At one time this was country where most people carried a gun and expected to use it. Max Ernst, who in 1908 was justice of the peace for the area, stopped a bullet while returning home from business in Boquillas. He managed to reach a neighbor's house before dying. In his pocket, his wife found a note he had managed to scrawl: "Am shot, I expect by one of Solis at gate. First shot hit, two more missed." Although Martin Solis and his four sons were sharply questioned by a grand jury, the case was eventually dropped.

Eight years later the community of Glenn Spring was besieged by sixty or seventy bandits from south of the border. Glenn Spring, a village of about sixty people, was situated a few miles up the wash from the mouth of San Vicente Canyon. There were nine U.S. soldiers camped at Glenn Spring the night of the raid, and during some lively gunfire, four of the soldiers, the son of the storekeeper, and several raiders were killed. After looting the store and putting the torch to three other buildings, the bandits headed back toward the dry mountains of Mexico.

Below Boquillas, the river winds through the middle of the Sierra del Carmen. Schott Tower, highest peak in the range, rears up from the Mexican side of the water; it is visible from a number of places in the canyon. The Boquillas Canyon run is excellent for novice boaters or family outings, as there are no rapids of any consequence. The canyon itself is 17 miles long, and it is 25 miles to the customary, and best, take-out at Stillwell Crossing. This should be an overnight trip at the minimum, and most backcountry aficionados will want to take three days, allowing time for exploration of the side canyons. Some of the canyons contain exquisite glens and wildly eroded rock formations.

At Stillwell Crossing there is an old cable footbridge. . . .

Stillwell Crossing is a gateway to one of the loneliest stretches of river anywhere. From here a man could drift for a week—all the way to Langtry, over 130 miles downriver—without seeing another human being. Canyon after canyon slashes through gaunt, dry ranges; sunsets flame over tortured rocks where no one has ever walked; coyotes yip at dusk and dawn; and the press of immense solitude is either exhilarating or vaguely ominous to the infrequent traveler. Senses sharpen. A distant tumbling pebble, kicked loose by a lizard or a roadrunner, can be heard distinctly. The muggy smell of the river and damp-rooted plants beside it rises strongly through the warm air. In caves and alcoves of the mountains, panthers sprawl during the afternoon heat, waiting for the cool and darkness of night to hunt. Bands of peccaries, far more dangerous to man, root up side draws. Close to the river, the bird the Mexicans call *brasita de fuego* (little coal of fire), darts between willows at water's edge, black wings fanning against red body.

Such a setting would seem almost flawed without a lost mine, and, of course, there is one. Back in the 1880s four brothers by the name of Reagan had a ranch that was roughly defined as running upstream from the canyon now bearing their name to the mouth of Maravillas Canyon, an amorphous spread where cattle simply drifted to wherever they could find any sort of thornless plant to chew on, like as not across the river on the Mexican side. One morning a valuable horse was found to be missing from the remuda. Lee Reagan and Bill Kelly, a cowhand who was half Negro, half Indian, set out to find the horse—Reagan covering the American side of the river, Kelly the Mexican. At dusk they met, as arranged, near the mouth of Maravillas Canyon. When the rancher asked Kelly if he had spotted the pony, he shook his head and then grinned in the failing light.

"I've found something better." He reached into his *moral*—saddlehorn pouch for small objects—and pulled out a lump of ore. "I've found a gold mine. Right over there! In a canyon just wide enough to ride a horse through."

Reagan, for whom at that time all rocks were just a diabolic device to keep feed from coming up, could not have distinguished between gold ore and petrified wood, and was damn sure his employee knew even less. A good sight less. And so, far from sharing Kelly's excitement over the rock, he was merely irritated that they had not found the horse.

Kelly hung on to the ore, and after a time hoboed a freight train to take it to his friend Lock Campbell of San Antonio, a conductor for the Southern Pacific. Campbell, as it turned out, was out on a run, but Kelly left the ore sample with a mutual friend and returned to the Reagan ranch.

Campbell had the ore assayed. Results were $80,000 to the ton, enough to induce gold fever in the most stolid man. As soon as he could get leave from the railroad, he hurried down into the remote Rio Grande canyon country, seeking Kelly. He never found him. About the time word of the assay results reached the Reagans, Bill Kelly disappeared. Foul play was strongly suspected.

As might be expected of men with a bonanza somewhere in their sprawling back yard, the Reagans began to take a lively interest in minerals, but for all their ceaseless prowling were never able to locate the strike made by their departed cowpuncher. Lock Campbell probed for the mine, as did a number of other hopefuls, finding nothing but spectacular country and intriguing clues.

Will Stillwell, who with his brother Roy ranched upriver from the old Reagan spread, may have actually found the Lost Kelly Mine. Around 1914 or 1915, he encountered an old, sick Indian woman while on a cattle-buying trip into Mexico. The woman seemed close to death, but Stillwell and his companion, a Mrs. Murphy, managed to nurse her back to health. In gratitude, she gave them directions to a gold mine. Up a certain canyon, she related, they would find a large boulder with a tomahawk buried on one side. The mine was farther up the canyon, covered with poles and dirt.

The finale to the episode was later related to Virginia Madison. She describes in it her book, *The Big Bend Country:*

> . . . they found the boulder and they found the tomahawk. They knew they were almost to the mine then, but they were without water. The nearby tinaja was dry and a water seep a little farther up the canyon was not enough for their horses. They had no tools to dig with and bandits were hot on their trail, so they were forced to abandon their hunt and retreat across the Rio Grande to Texas. They decided to stay out of Mexico until the revolution had died down. Will Stillwell was certain that he had, at last, located the rich gold mine.

Stillwell apparently gave the author no particulars as to where the mine was located, although he did tell his brother Roy. Soon after, Will joined the Texas Rangers and was killed in a fight, and Roy died as the result of an accident while hauling feed to his ranch.

In more recent times an American gold-seeker, Xanthus "Kit" Carson, and a Mexican, Guerra Menchaca, plodded over a faint trail that once connected the Stillwell Ranch with the Mexican village of Musquiz. Menchaca had spun an interesting yarn. He had been a soldier with the Mexican army, which in 1910 was skirmishing with revolutionaries in the Big Bend country. He became friendly with a prospector named Virgil Ellis, who lived in Musquiz, where, some three decades before, Bill Kelly had also made his home. Ellis made a tidy living packing gold out of a remote mine he had discovered, the location of which he described to Menchaca.

Fearing pillage by revolutionaries, the prospector suspended operations for a time, concealing the entrance with rubble from dynamite blasts. He was killed in an accident not long after. Menchaca, for rather obscure reasons, had sat upon the secret for forty years.

For Carson the treasure hunt was apparently as perilous as Stillwell's had been years before: there was some doubt whether Menchaca, suffering from heart trouble, would endure the strenuous hike; the heat was withering; and they had to "fight the hordes of rattlesnakes in the cactus patches every step of the way." In a narrow, sheer-sided canyon, they found boulders inscribed as Menchaca had said they would be. The mine itself was covered with rubble from flash floods and Ellis' dynamite blasts, rendering development prohibitively expensive. There seems little doubt they had found the Ellis diggings, and there are strong arguments that the site was the one approached by Will Stillwell and is the Lost Kelly Mine to boot. Kelly would have used this route in passing from the Reagan Ranch to Musquiz.

Yet lost-mine stories are rarely wrapped up that neatly, especially when the gold remains hidden. A member of a float part may yet, while hiking up a side canyon, stub his toe upon a fortune, and it just may be the one that Billy Kelly never collected.

Bob Burleson of the Texas Explorers Club once said of the lower Big Bend canyon: "[There are] many tough rapids, some of which require a portage, and almost a continuous canyon for three-fourths of the trip. This trip is for properly prepared and experienced river runners, and could be a very arduous and miserable trip for the careless or ignorant adventurer."

Bill Kugle, another member of the Texas Explorers Club, elaborates: "I have often thought of the bad situation which could result if someone broke a leg. There would be no other way to get an injured person out other than to float out over a period of several days. It would be extremely difficult to float an injured person out in a canoe without capsizing several times. The discomfort attendant upon being thrown into the rapids with a crudely splinted broken leg can hardly be described. For this reason I have strict instructions to the members of our expedition before leaving: 'Don't break no legs.'"

A run through these canyons, in terms of both rugged scenery and whitewater challenge, offers one of the great adventures in American wilderness boating. . . . Although most float trips start at the Adams Ranch at Stillwell Crossing, there are a number of possible take-out points, including one at Bone Watering and another at the Bootleggers Highway. Prior permission must be obtained from ranchowners to use any of them.

Not far below the Adams Ranch one can see the Dow fluorspar plant at La Linda, Coahuila, and pass under the bridge over which fluorspar is trucked to the Marathon railroad depot. As soon as the bridge fades from sight you are in wild country, immediately running Horse Canyon, short but deep, and then drifting into a more open stretch with mountains looming back from the river. This is lost-mine country. The narrow canyon which Xanthus Kit Carson and Guerra Menchaca explored slices through the rimrock on the Mexican side. A few miles beyond is Maravillas Canyon, where Bill Kelly is said to have displayed his ore sample to Lee Reagan. Maravillas Canyon is usually dry and wide, filled with white boulders. There is a burned ranch house at the mouth of Maravillas, and a rough road leads up the creek to Black Gap Headquarters—a 20-mile hike and the last thread back to civilization for at least four days.

One shoves off. Across the expanse of Outlaw Flats, famous for mirages, the flat-topped bulk of El Capitan lifts a sheer 1,000 feet above the desert floor, shimmering like a mirage itself. Downstream the water quickens, funneling into Big Canyon, where the river breaks loose into several fine rapids. And then comes Reagan Canyon, which twists through the rock for some 40 miles and thunders through the most dangerous rapids on the lower river: Hot Springs, Burro Bluff, Horseshoe Falls, and Panther Canyon. Here and there warm springs rise at riverbank, and occasionally one spots a ruined cabin or a cave. . . .

Below Reagan Canyon there are other deep gorges, strange rock formations, hot springs, and whitewater. Then, gradually, the country becomes more open and cattle can be seen grazing; now and again a ranch road will come right down to the river. . . .

THREE

The Wild and Domestic Border

I LIVE IN WEST TEXAS, SO I WOULD NOT CALL THE WIDE open spaces here wilderness, but if I traveled to East Texas and tried to find my way through the trees, then I might call all those trees a wilderness because I am not familiar with that place. In contrast, an East Texan might look at all the vast grasslands around Marfa as wilderness. Antelope to me are tame because some of them hang around my house all day and seem to greet me when I come home from work. On the other hand, alligators seem exotic and very wild to me because I have never been around them. We imagine those places, plants, and animals close to our homes and cultures as domestic, and those places, animals, and plants we are not familiar with as wild. Certainly the aboriginal Indian people of North America who raised their families in the deserts and forests never considered those places wilderness, nor did they invent such a word in their language. Dividing places and inhabitants into categories like wild and domestic seems to be a very European habit that began on this continent as a way to imagine the landscapes as unclaimed and uninhabited, therefore ready to settle. In addition, the so-called domestic animals and plants are descended from wild ancestors, and most can quickly revert to a feral state (depending on how they are treated).[1]

Boundaries and borders between wild and domestic places and animals blur the more one looks into the subject and the further back into prehistory one delves. Because all of the Trans-Pecos was once under sea water, once had a wet and tropical climate, and once was home to "wild" camels, elephants, shrub oxen and horses—the question of wild and domestic or indigenous/native/exotic becomes quite interesting and controversial. Whether one is talking about animals, plants, rocks, or people, the Trans-Pecos seems to be a somewhat violent melting pot whether one wants to melt or not.

This chapter collects various perceptions about the wild/domestic categories. Bob Burleson and David H. Riskind describe "domestic" houses made of "wild" desert materials. Is a house made of lechuguilla wild or domestic? How about a tarantula's house complete with "satin sheets" and an open- and close-able door that hangs from "hinges," as described by Kathryn Williams Walker?[2] J. P. S. Brown's wild corriente cattle are probably descended, at least on this continent and in this period of history, from stock imported in the sixteenth century by the Spanish—but maybe not. According to paleontologists, wild cattle and horses roamed the West Texas grasslands millions of years before the arrival of Indians, bison, and wolves. Both supposedly became extinct toward the end of the Pleistocene and thousands of years before European settlement. Domestic varieties of horses and cattle were reintroduced by the Spanish in the early 1500s. Some of these animals escaped, became feral, and were considered wild animals once again.[3]

Herds of wild horses roamed much of the Big Bend during the late 1800s, and many ranchers of that period gathered their ranch horses from those herds. According to Frederick Olmsted, the Texas mustang attracted a class of ne'er-do-wells who made their living trying to catch them.[4] He also claims that although these wild horses could be tamed, they could never be trusted and would revert to a murderous wildness even after twenty years as a broken animal. His deep-seated prejudices against the land, the mustang, and the mustangers seem almost humorous today.

Camels too were prehistorically wild and native to the desert Southwest, but the camels described herein by William H. Echols were domestics that had been imported from the Middle East as part of an experiment to see if they would prove valuable as prospective military animals.[5] Their ability to withstand long marches without water was exceeded only by their ability to withstand the pain of sore feet and backs. Although the experiment was successful, the camels were abandoned and gradually disappeared. However, Big Bend Ranch State Park has recently reintroduced domestic camels and is currently offering camel caravans as a tourist attraction. Ironically, reintroduction of the camel (which is a genuine native) does not create the same headlines as reintroduction of the wolf (which may or may not be truly native to this continent).

The wild and domestic labels are often associated with native (wild) and invader (domestic). Strangely, even our state flower, the Texas bluebonnet, which blankets much of the Big Bend National Park and enjoys full protection of the law, is not a native plant. Ralph A. Selle describes its immigration from the Mediterranean, its quick adoption as a favorite food by migrating bison, and its quick inclusion into Indian legends. The bluebonnet is often planted along highways so tourists can enjoy Texas' "wild" flowers, it enriches poor soil—like its cousin alfalfa—by fixing nitrogen, and it can be fed as hay to livestock. So, is the bluebonnet then wild or domestic?

Thoreau wondered about the call of the domestic rooster, saying, "The note of this once wild Indian pheasant is certainly the most remarkable of any bird's, and if they could be naturalized without being domesticated, it would soon become the most famous sound in our woods. . . . No wonder that man added this bird to his tame stock."[6] We consider chickens domestic, but what about quail who come for food to a human's call? Rancher's wife Evelyn Mellard writes about blue quail as though they were friends and neighbors. Her depth of personal observation and relationship with many coveys of these wild birds far surpasses that of the more typical nature writers who get their information from field guides and occasional single sightings. Her writing is somewhat anthropomorphic, but both scholars and scientists have recently begun to reinvestigate the worth of such projection.

Although personification, anthropomorphism, and pathetic fallacy— all the many ways of imposing human emotion and characteristics onto nature—have been frowned upon in the recent past, writers, critics, and even scientists are reevaluating that perspective. Peter Fritzell, in his 1990 book *Nature Writing and America,* argues that our insistence on dehumanizing animals is actually a defense mechanism which keeps us feeling special and separates humans from nature.[7] In a 1994 *Mosaic* article about romanticism, Onno Dag Oerlemans suggests that rules against anthropomorphizing cause humans to view nature as an "otherness subservient to human needs."[8] A recent article in *The Chronicle of Higher Education* states that many of today's scientists feel that a little healthy anthropomorphism could actually help research in animal behavior.[9]

So, is it anthropomorphic to imagine that birds actually enjoy human company or just true? Phoebes prefer to nest in garages, towhees like oatmeal boxes, and many bird species from wood ducks to purple martins prefer human-constructed birdhouses to those that nature provides. In one essay collected herein, Roy Bedicheck recounts the cliff swallow's preference for domestic architecture rather than wild canyon walls.[10] The swallows, he says, especially favor tall public buildings. Although this excerpt ends sadly with the eviction of the swallows from the Sul Ross State University administration building, they still return regularly to the Alpine campus. Efforts to discourage them aside, several still build tenaciously under the high eaves of the university's red brick buildings.

Although most of us today expect all animals, birds, and plants to be classified as either wild or domestic, even the inanimate can be divided into these imaginary categories. The Marfa ghost lights have long been the center of a controversy over whether their origin is domestic or wild. Kirby Warnock tries to find out whether the lights are simply car lights on the Big Bend highway, ranch security lights, or something wild and natural.[11] He concludes that since they were seen before either cars or electricity were invented, their wildness, and therefore their value to tourism, seems assured. Interestingly, the same phenomenon appears in Boulia, Queensland, Australia, where the mystery lights are called the Min Min Light.[12]

Finally, wild, natural, and native metals are considered domestic, at least in the U.S. imagination, because the domestic is usually associated with the economic. Kenneth Ragsdale describes the mythic discovery and early mining of the rich red cinnabar ore, which may often have been the red pigment used by Indian artists to draw much of the rock art found in the Big Bend.

These imaginary divisions between wild and domestic have caused much political, religious, and economic grief. Like all borders, this division was designed to support an agenda that nature seldom recognizes or supports.

NOTES

1. For readers interested in the wild/domestic argument, I recommend my book *The Wild and the Domestic: Animal Representation, Ecocriticism, and Western American Literature* (University of Nevada Press, 2000).

2. Katherine Williams Walker is a daughter of O. W. Williams, also excerpted in this collection.

3. The corriente makes cameo appearances as an indigenous animal in the work of numerous nature writers, including Leslie Marmon Silko's *Ceremony* (New York: Penguin, 1977), 74–75, and Edward Abbey's *Beyond the Wall* (New York: Henry Holt, 1984), 138–139.

4. Olmstead was born in Hartford, Connecticut, in 1822. As an eastern journalist, he was one of the earliest tourists to journey into Texas and write of his experiences. Although his travels never actually took him much farther west than Eagle Pass, the mustangs and mustangers he describes did range into parts of the Big Bend.

5. Lieutenant Echols led the experimental Hartz camel expedition through West Texas in 1860.

6. Henry David Thoreau, *The Portable Thoreau*, ed. Carl Bode (New York: Penguin, 1975), 378.

7. Peter Fritzell, *Nature Writing and America* (Ames: Iowa State University Press, 1990), 98–99.

8. Onno Dag Oerlemans, "The Meanest Thing That Feels," *Mosaic* 27, no. 1 (1994): 1–32.

9. Kim A. McDonald, "Scientists Rethink Anthropomorphism," *Chronicle of Higher Education*, February 24, 1995, A8.

10. A 1903 University of Texas graduate, Bedicheck wrote his first book at 70 years old while living in a cabin on Walter Prescott Webb's Friday Mountain Ranch.

11. Kirby Warnock is the editor of the *Big Bend Quarterly*. This essay was first published in that magazine.

12. Alf Wilson, "Seeing the Light," *Outback,* April/May 1999, 114.

RURAL HOUSING
Bob Burleson and David H. Riskind
1986

WE ARE NOT ARCHITECTS AND DO NOT PRETEND TO KNOW THE proper names of all the various styles of Mexican houses. This brief section is only intended to make you aware of some of the construction materials, techniques, and styles of the owner-built homes of rural Mexicans. Most of these houses are made with locally available materials, whether animal, vegetable, or mineral. They usually cost nothing except time and labor. Generally speaking, they are best suited for hot to moderate temperatures, since really cold weather is not that common in Mexico except at high altitudes. Therefore, when a blue norther blows across Texas and it freezes in the Rio Grande Valley, you can bet your boots that there are some cold *gente* huddled under whatever cover they have available to them.

Although these houses may appear at first to be nothing more than hovels, and totally unsuitable for human habitation, they are often happy homes and a source of genuine pride to the inhabitants. Look carefully and you often find that the woman of the house has managed to maintain a small garden, or pots of flowers or herbs used for seasoning. Generally, except under the worst conditions, the dooryard is swept clean daily with a homemade broom, and bedding is aired in the sun. Most semipermanent homes have a small kitchen garden (if water is available) in which are grown beans, chile peppers, cilantro, and other food and seasoning plants. Herbs are gathered in *el monte* and can be seen drying under the roof edge or in the rafters. Where conditions permit you will find caged birds and lard cans used as pots for flowering plants. All are carefully tended by the *ranchera.*

Most of the houses are rather dark inside, since electricity is uncommon and windows of the sort we have are generally not available. Instead, there are either no windows or the unscreened openings are shuttered. In foul weather, the house is closed tight and any of a number of forms of heating, all dangerous, are used. A 55-gallon drum (*tanque*) may be cut in half, the bottom filled with sand, and used as an open hearth. Or a 55-gallon drum may have a door cut in the side, a pipe attached, and serve as a stove. Some homes have commercially made kerosene heaters, or woodburning stoves. A few of the older ones made of rock have a fireplace and chimney, but this is a real rarity except on old ranches. Now and then a propane hotplate or space heater is seen. Propane bottles must be carried many miles to be refilled.

General styles of houses range from the desert adobe to the house near the river made of polished, flood-worn boulders from the mountains. On formerly large ranches, many houses of ledgestone remain, the stones usually having been laid with only mud for mortar. Some of these have fireplaces. We have not seen much new construction of rock houses, indicating that less permanent types of housing have come to the fore. In the mountains, particularly near sawmills, houses are made of slabs of fresh-sawed lumber, often roofed with the exterior slabs of bark. In other areas where tall evergreen timber is found, traditional log cabins are raised. If caves are handy, they are often walled up and used for homes. Dugouts are made if a cutbank is handy.

A friend decided to climb up to one of the caves in Indian country to see if it had been recently occupied. He called out loudly and got no reply; then, thinking the cave unoccupied, he started up the steps hewn into the rock wall of the canyon. About halfway up, a fist-sized rock came arching out the door of the cave, barely missing him. He decided that someone was surely claiming that cave and did not insist on his visit!

In several areas we have visited, where large piles of weathered granite boulders are found, homes have been constructed under huge boulders, the builder simply walling up sides and front and having a solid rock rear wall and roof. A more snug dwelling can hardly be imagined. They last a long time as well; one of the best examples, at Rancho San José de las Piedras, Coahuila, has been known to be in existence and occupied since at least 1856, when it was sketched by a U.S. military engineer. It was still the home of a *pastor* when we were last there only a short time ago. Pictographs on the boulders prove that the Indians used the shelters even before the Mexicans adopted them.

Timber is scarce in the northern deserts of Mexico. Most of the streamside trees (particularly species of cottonwood [*álamo*] and ash [*fresno*]) have long ago been cut to provide posts and beams for houses. In some areas where permanent streams support the growth of cottonwoods, the people preserve the main trunks of the cottonwooods and simply cut off the larger limbs from time to time, as if harvesting a crop. This is called in English "pollarding," obviously not a Mexican term. The term comes from the word "poll" for "head," and literally means to "dehorn" the tree, as you might dehorn a cow. Check the cottonwoods and other fast-growing trees near a Mexican village and you will see evidence of this harvest. The limbs go to make structural parts of houses, or for furniture, cottonwood being easily worked. Along the more populated stretches of the Rio Grande, the cottonwood has nearly been eliminated because of overharvest.

Roofing materials also vary widely. Grass and *palma* (yucca) leaf thatching is still used. In mining and lumber camps the primary roofing material is a corrugated black asphalt-felt seen all over Mexico. In some areas, locally made reddish roof tiles are used, either half-round or flat. Again, sheet iron roofs are found where money is more plentiful, and occasionally one sees roll roofing of the sort available in the United States for cheap roof covering. In government housing, corrugated asbestos cement roofing is common, but this is not seen except in the newest *ejido* communities of concrete-block houses with casement windows. Among the most common rural roofs is the old standby, wet earth mixed with ashes. In the tropics split palm fronds prevail.

To make an earthen roof, the Mexicans first frame it out with poles then overlay a solid deck of whatever material is available: small branches, river cane or reeds, bloomstalks of *sotol, lechuguilla,* or other desert plants. Over this is put tar paper if they have it, cardboard if they don't. Sometimes a layer of grass or woven matting—or anything handy, to keep earth from sifting down through the cracks—is used. Over all are piled several inches of puddled (wet) adobe soil mixed with ashes.

Walls of houses not made of brick, rock, or adobe usually start with four poles at the corners, and sometimes a central pole to help support the ridgepole and roof. In between will be placed staves, and more slender branches will be woven between the staves. River cane, if available, will be used for walls, supported by and tied to the staves. We have seen walls made of anything and everything. Sometimes adobe is plastered over the basic wall to seal it against the weather, sometimes not.

The cheapest houses are obviously those of the poorest people. We have seen *jacales* with walls of stacked upright yucca plants and roofs of split dagger trunks (making a half cylinder), with one turned up and the two on either side turned down for a "corrugated" roof.

Nails, bolts, metal hinges, and the like are very rare, and to the Mexican not necessary. . . . We watched the construction of such a home from the ground up, and not a single nail or piece of wire went into a serviceable house for a family of four, complete with sleeping loft, walls, open windows, and the usual dirt floor. It took two men, equipped with one old axe and a machete, about twenty-four hours to build it. It sure as heck beats slaving all your life to pay for a $90,000 all-electric marvel that you cannot survive in when the power goes of! A close inspection of the Mexican village cannot help but leave one wondering a bit about the validity of many of our ideas of the "necessities of life." Such a house will last several years with no repairs, and for a lifetime with reasonable maintenance. Hinges can be made of wood and often are. Just as often a few strips of old truck tires will be nailed by one end to the doorpost and the other end to the door, making neat, nonsqueaking hinges that last forever. We ran over one of these hinges one time, with the nails sticking up, and it gave us a quick flat tire.

The luxury of glass windows has hardly reached rural Mexico. These are usually found only in the cities and in the country homes of *ricos* (people of wealth). More likely, windows are closed by a wooden shutter or by a blanket, piece of an old tarp, or a goatskin. However, even the most humble *jacal* may have an iron wire strung up as an antenna; battery-powered radios are a source of pride and pleasure.

Floors are almost always unadulterated dirt, the native earth. In some adobe dwellings, a floor of puddled adobe or even of adobe bricks is used, but the order of the day in rural housing is the earthen floor. In areas where timber and sawmills are found, the floors are rough planks, as are the ceilings and interior walls. Flagstones are rarely used.

The idea of double walls or insulated walls is unheard of. The conventional stud wall, slab-on-grade house that we slave all our lives to pay for is never seen in rural areas, except in the more recent *ejidos* or mining areas.

Take the time to look at the housing, at the materials, techniques, and lack of manufactured items that go into them. Consider that each house was built by a family for itself, generally with only the help of neighbors and whatever grew or could be found nearby. There are many valid alternatives to the wasteful and materialistic lives we lead in the United States, and this is one of them.

TARANTULA
Kathryn Williams Walker
1967

THE TARANTULA IS A LARGE BLACK SPIDER WITH EIGHT HAIRY LEGS. It takes its name from a town in Italy where tarantulas are numerous. It usually sleeps all day and comes out at night to hunt for ants and other insects. After a rain it walks high on its legs and presents an appearance as if walking on stilts. I have tried to throw rocks at them from a distance, but with my poor ability and the tarantula's agility in leaping sidewise in different directions I have never been able to kill one.

The tarantula's nest is reported to be an ingenious creation, built underground and lined with fine white material that looks like satin. At the entrance there is a door of sand and gravel held together by a gluelike substance and even having hinges of a kind of thread produced by the tarantula. This door can be opened or shut and is concealed because it looks just like the surrounding ground. The tarantula hibernates in the winter.

In 1933 the men at Iraan planned a public fighting match between a vinegarroon and a tarantula. The combatants were set in a tub, where a battle was raged for about a quarter of an hour. It was reported that the tarantula won. The tarantula secretes a poison which will paralyze insects but is not strong enough to do much damage to a healthy human being.

THE BROWN-AND-WHITE SPOTTED ARISTOCRATIC CORRIENTE

J. P. S. Brown

1970

IN MEXICO THE WORD CORRIENTE *MEANS COMMON OR PLAIN. THE WORD is used to describe the usual run of the cheap and mediocre.*

When applied to cattle, corriente *means native cattle. The* corriente *is a descendent of the cattle the Spaniard brought to Mexico, the same cattle the Texas Longhorn descended from. But* corrientes *are not defunct like the Texas Longhorn. The Mexican* corriente *still abounds in spite of hunter, drought, deprivation, and degeneration.*

Since he is common and cheap to buy, people think he is inferior, a butt for jokes. A joke circulates among cattlemen in Mexico about a cattle buyer who went to see a bunch of cattle and after he looked them over he told the owner he didn't want them after all.

"Why?" asked the owner. "I told you they were corriente *before you came to see them and you said you didn't mind if they were* corriente.*"*

"Yes. I said that," said the buyer. "But your cattle are mucho muy *corriente, very much, too much, corriente."*

"What the devil! Common is common. I said they were common. How can any common thing be too common any more than any aristocratic thing be too aristocratic?" said the owner.

"Now you have it!" said the buyer. "I want aristocratic corrientes.*"*

The cow was poor. Someone had tipped her big horns back with a saw. The swelling rings on her old dead horns showed she had a lot of age on her. Along her backbone, which was very prominent, with each vertebra clearly distinguishable, her dark brown hide was faded and bleached and stretched to a golden brown. She stood in a wash that fell off a mountain of the Sierra Madre of Chihuahua, her belly tight and swollen. It was time for her—the sixth time, for she was seven years old—to have her calf.

The brown cow moved slowly out of the still heat of the open wash into a tunnel of vainoro, the thick spiny brush that grew solidly along the sides of the wash. She probed her way through the unyieldy thorned branches to the dark uncluttered shade next to the trunks. There in the private depths of the vainoro she dropped her calf, a brown-and-white spotted bull calf.

She licked her calf clean. He staggered on weak legs with each swipe of her rough tongue. She nudged him onto her sparse teats and he took the vital first milk, the milk that gave him his mother's resistance to disease. When he had nursed she left him full and sleeping, the tiny head flattened to the ground, the large clean ears down flat against the head, and left the tunnel of vainoro to feed and water.

Later, when the calf awoke alone, he raised his head. Instinct kept him quiet. He moved only his head, ears twitching at the insects that came to investigate his new live warmth. Then his tail began to wring spasmodically on the ground as he examined each new wonder in the vainoro and longed for his mother. Once, the heavy steps of a large animal passed in the wash below and the calf lowered his head to the ground, stretched his neck out along the ground, and stilled his ears and tail.

A few days later it became necessary for the cow to range away from the vainoro and she took the calf out of his tunnel. He trotted out on long knobby legs close at her side, shying at the marvel of a butterfly, a lizard, or the smell and sign of an old bull.

During the ranging the *vaquero* Manuel Rodriguez saw the cow had calved and, with the help of his dog, drove her to the corral of his camp at El Naranjo. He took the calf from his mother. He tied him down. He took out his sharp knife and seized the stiff healthy ear and earmarked the calf. He carved a round hole, called a *balazo,* or bullet hole, in the center of one ear, and he sliced off the whole curve of the underslope of the other ear. The calf now bore the official mark of all livestock of El Naranjo ranch. Manuel shut the calf in a small corral with several other calves. He then turned the brown cow out into a pasture where she joined other cows that were being milked.

Each morning the cows would call at the gate of the corral, bawling for their offspring. Manuel and his son let them in, roped them, hobbled their hind legs, and released the calves to let them suck. When the cows were letting down their milk freely, the men caught the calves and tied them to the fence and milked the cows of all but a small portion of their milk. Then the calves were untied and allowed to strip the cows of the last of their milk. The brown-and-white spotted calf slobbered ravenously over his mother's little udder, butting it in consternation when it went dry, his long black tongue curved around a teat, the pure eyes half-closed in delight.

During this time the calf learned to respect the men. He learned the rope around his neck had an end to it and would jerk him back sharply when he ran against it. He learned to undergo patiently the hunger that was to dominate him for most of his life. He found his corral had bounds but he never respected them. He was always hunting a way out of the corral.

The brown cow was milked for a month and then was replaced by another cow and released to take her calf back to her *querencia,* her favorite range. The calf was now dead of hair and weak from having been robbed of the greater part of his early nourishment. He was stunted and potbellied. With the milk that had been robbed from the calf Manuel Rodriguez's wife had made cheeses and fresh curd *panelas* which they sold. These cheeses paid the biggest part of Manuel's wage and were the reason he worked for the owner of the ranch of which the brown cow and her calf were units of livestock.

Hunger was the rule in the Sierra Madre. El Naranjo was small and overstocked. This part of the Sierra Madre was not cow country, not grass country. Grass grew only from July until the middle of October and had dried up and been eaten by November. Then hunger took over again and got worse each month until the July rains began again.

The owner of El Naranjo was Juan Vogel. He could not live on his ranch because he could not make a living there. He paid Manuel Rodriguez a small wage and gave him the right to milk the cows for the cheeses. Juan took what his ranch and livestock produced as a supplement to his living in town and rarely returned anything to the ranch for improvement.

Summer had begun when the brown cow was released from the milking. The land and foliage of the Sierra Madre were brown. Cattle moved little in the heat of the day and browsed at night on brush, *pechita* beans of the mesquite tree, leaves of the *tuna,* prickly pear cactus, and the *cholla* cactus. Mother cows eating the fierce needle-like spines of the *cholla* would get their cheeks, muzzles, and foreheads covered with pieces of stalks of *cholla.* The spines festered on the cattle and prevented them from browsing and grazing normally. Gradually these cactus eaters became addicted to cactus, as they could eat nothing else. The tips of their tongues split, their mouths filled with thorn until they constantly frothed, expelling valuable fluid. These cattle were able to eat less each day until they became so thin they resembled racks with dusty skins stretched tightly over them. They became bellyless, wild, and covered with parasites. A cowman wondered what sort of soul or spirit kept them alive, certainly nothing requiring food or drink.

Then, when it looked as if there was not another bite of feed anywhere in the Sierra and cattle ranged like goats up on the cliffs in country apparently impossible for a bovine, and every inch of the Sierra had been picked over, the summer rains began and grass sprouted.

The brown cow ranged far from Manuel Rodriguez' camp. She and her calf summered in a tiny meadow on a stream of clear water surrounded by straight pines high on the border of Chihuahua and Sonora.

When winter came the feed was gone in the meadow and the two moved down into the brush country where the spotted calf had been born. Here they ranged until the spring, when the brown cow had her seventh calf, a black heifer calf. The spotted calf was a yearling now. He had been weaned by his mother but still ran by her side.

One day Manuel Rodriguez came for the brown cow again, and she and her heifer calf and the spotted yearling were driven to the corral where the cow was taken for milking again. The spotted yearling stayed close to his mother whenever she was turned out of the corral, but he was becoming accustomed to ranging farther away each day looking for better feed, as there was not enough for him near the camp of Manuel Rodriguez. One evening he stayed away from his mother for the first time in his life. Gradually his visits to his mother became fewer as the rustling for feed became more difficult. He began to hunt new ranges, and when his mother was turned out again the brown-and-white spotted yearling was on his own.

His pointed little horns were growing fast, nearly an inch a month now. The short hair under each eye was black and formed black crescents, a natural protection against the glare of the sun. He was light brown and white over his head, neck, and foreparts, but along his flanks and rear the spots changed to a reddish brown and were small and numerous, like reddish brown grains. He was almost a roan on his hindparts, but he wasn't a roan. He was a *granizo,* with a multitude of distinct freckles on his hindquarters.

The yearling was learning to be alone. He found it natural to hide when a man passed near him. Alone, it was easy for him to climb high in the Sierra and feed in places his mother had not been spry enough to take him. He traveled silently on small rock-trimmed hooves. He picked his way patiently and surely over vertical slopes of smooth rock. He never wasted energy in being curious or calfish, for he had none to waste—his process of making a living in that country took every bit of his nerve and guile. He never passed up a chance to eat; his every waking moment was dedicated to feed. He became as crafty and wild as the pumas, jaguars, and ocelots he encountered in their pursuit of a living.

THE MUSTANGS
Frederick Olmsted
1857

THE MUSTANGS ARE THE DEGENERATED PROGENY OF SPANISH estrays, now as wild and fully naturalized as the deer themselves. They associate in incredible numbers, like the buffaloes, a single herd sometimes covering a large tract, and, if frightened, rushing to and fro in sweeping lines, with the irresistible force of an army. From their numbers are recruited additions to the stocks of Texan and Mexican herdsmen, and the business of entrapping them has given rise to a class of men called "mustangers," composed of runaway vagabonds, and outlaws of all nations, the legitimate border-ruffians of Texas. While their ostensible employment is this of catching wild horses, they often add the practice of highway robbery, and are, in fact, simply prairie pirates, seizing any property that comes in their way, murdering travelers, and making descents upon trains and border villages. Their operations of this sort are carried on under the guise of savages, and at the scene of a murder, some "Indian sign," as an arrow-head or a moccasin, is left to mislead justice.

The wild horses are easily collected, by means of long fences, called "wings," diverging on either side from the mouth of a "pen." Having been driven within this, the mares of a herd are caught with the lasso, and the stallions, which do not repay breaking, turned loose or wantonly shot. Here and there a "ranch" is established, forming a temporary home and retreat for the "mustangers." The herds probably suffer extremely in the dry season, and have been much injured during generations of exposure and hardship. They are narrow-chested, weak in haunches, and of bad disposition, and are worth about one tenth of the price of improved stock, a herd tamed to be driven, selling, delivered at the settlements, at $8 to $15 per head. Many stories are told of the incurable viciousness of tamed mustangs. An old animal which you have ridden daily for twenty years, will, when his opportunity comes at last, suddenly jump upon you, and stamp you in pieces, his vengeance all the hotter for delay.

No part of the immense remaining territory towards the North, seems to possess the slightest value. It is a dry gravelly desert, supporting only worthless shrubs. Such was distinctly its character at the point where we crossed it, and from all the definite description we could obtain from officers who had led trains, or scouting parties, here and there over it, or Texans who had traversed the various routes into Mexico, it nowhere offers more attractive features. Should it become desirable to plant settlements within it, for reasons other than economical, probably a few spots might be selected, where a sufficiently good soil, with wood and water, exists for such a purpose, and it is also true that our acquaintance with it is but limited and somewhat vague; for what one calls a desert, another calls prairie, and what to one is pure sand or clay, to another is a light or heavy soil — the impression depending much upon the soil the traveler has been accustomed to cultivate, as well as especially upon the season in which his observation is made.

The climate, which, throughout West Texas, begins to approach that of Mexico, has here become absolutely Mexican, and is marked by an extreme dryness — rain so seldom falling during the summer, that ordinary vegetation perishes for lack of moisture, leaving the soil to the occupation of such Bedouin tribes of vegetation as have the necessary powers of endurance. There are here a class of worthless shrubs, whose minute limbs are studded with the sharpest spines as if to repel all animal life from seeking to share with their own roots this weak shade. They stand in clumps and patches, leaving intervals which may be traversed with more or less difficulty.

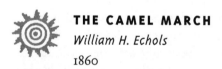

THE CAMEL MARCH
William H. Echols
1860

STATING BRIEFLY MY LINE OF MARCH IN CONNECTION WITH ITS PRAC-
tical state, which began at the point where I left the El Paso road, and twenty-five miles from the head of Devil's River, proceeding toward the Pecos, between which points the course alone will not recommend it to a consideration, but on it I found no permanent water till within two miles of the Pecos, where there is a fine running stream; nothing else of interest. Country very rugged. Then I proceeded directly to Fort Davis; from the Pecos to San Francisco Creek on the Comanche trail, across a jornada of 120 miles, exceedingly rugged and desolate, totally impracticable, and with much difficulty we even escaped perishing; from this point up the trail ten miles to Willow Spring; then to Fort Davis, where the route is

very good indeed, but no permanent water for fifty-five miles; from here I went to the Rio Grande Presidio del Norte, and across the country to the San Carlos trail, the latter utterly impassable for any trail, but water plenty. . . .

The camels are in fine condition; and with some improvements, which my experience with them last year taught me to suggest to be made, respecting the packing of them, such as iron loops on the water barrels to prevent them from shifting, and larger water barrels, which are the most important changes, I hope to be freed of a great deal of delay and vexation which I encountered the previous year. The male camels were all left, with the exception of one. Although much stouter and more serviceable than the females, they occasion a deal more trouble and attention from their belligerent propensities to one another. The command now consists of thirty-one men, exclusive of the herders and camel attendants, with the twenty camels and fifteen mules for packing. . . .

June 30.—Left the Pecos at camp this morning with the intention of making our way across the country to Fort Davis. Proceeded up a cañon which in two miles proved to be an unfavorable one for our purpose. Came to a head in a very few miles. Very rugged high cliffs on the sides, and may be classed among the innumerable inaccessible ones which abound in this region. We retraced our steps. . . . Grass very dry: brushwood. Whilst ascending the mesa two camels fell and bursted two of the kegs and injured several others, wasting about forty gallons of our most appreciated loading. The animals I believe are not injured. One of them lost its foothold, fell, and pulled the others from the trail by the rope attaching the train. Others might have suffered the same fate but for the timely assistance of Lieutenant Holman, who cut the lead line. During the ascent they had to resort to their feat of walking on their knees, which they do when the inclination of the trail is very great and heavily laden, to throw the center of gravity equally over the four legs, or on a slipping trail when their feet slip from under them. Marched 15.4 miles.

July 1.—Did not get as early a start this morning as desired, and again delayed by vain endeavors to proceed on our march across cañons too huge to attempt, retraced our steps. . . . Country very rough, rocky, barren, dry, apparently no rain on the region over which we passed today for a year. Every blade of grass dry and dead, and not of this year's growth. Our mules will not fare well—no forage and a very limited supply of water. The camels have performed most admirably today. No such march as this could be made with any security without them. It is with difficulty that the mules can be kept from the water barrels, particularly when the water is being issued. I might say the same of men. Grass bad; brushwood about the size of a finger. Made 27.2 miles. Gave the mules two and a half gallons of water.

July 2.—Marched westwardly most of the day, and after a long march of 29.4 miles over a rough country, camped dry without any prospects of finding water, in about the poorest prospect of making progress I have ever been situated. We are all very uneasy, not to say a little frightened, for our welfare. The mules must go without water to-night, are broken down now, and some are expected to be abandoned on the march to-morrow. We have only water sufficient for the men thirty hours. The Pecos, Rio Grande, and Fort Stockton, are all too distant to reach, and the water on the Comanche trail, San Francisco creek, or Willow Spring, which we expected to attain, we may be unable to reach for the impassibility of the region. Our march to-day has been rough, and too rough tomorrow, I fear, for the many lives that are now with us to stem. The animals go to the barrels and draw the bungs with their teeth and knaw at the bung holes. The second time in my life I have seen a quart of water priceless, almost. We have sent a man to search for water, to be paid liberally if he succeeds; if not, all the mules we expect to lose.

A canteen of water was issued to the men with enough to make a cup of coffee. This is the fourth day since the camels drank, which was at the Pecos, brackish water, the same that we have, not only brackish, but when the bung is taken from a barrel a stench proceeds; it contains so much filth and impurity, and, being barreled so long. The camels display quite a thirst.

July 3.—Continued our march over very rugged country, retaining our course a little south of west, marched all day with much hope at heart, but very little sign or prospect of success of our only object in life to-day, that of reaching water. The whole command is very uncomfortable with regard to its future prospects. The animals of burden are almost ceased to be talked of, and the topic has become one of self interest alone. Drought depresses the most buoyant spirit, and keeps the mind in full operation and anxiety. Some of the men are very weak, and have several times reported about to give up and no water to drink. All we can tell them is, if they stop, they must risk the consequences, that not a moment can be lost for any one. We have some apprehensions for the safety of the command, and to-morrow a dispersion must take place in small parties to look for water according to individual judgement, to seek one another if successful; if not, never to meet again but by chance. The men have a quart of water issued to-night, and have enough for two drinks to-morrow, but they are so feeble and thirsty that it all would not last them an hour if they could get to it. The mules have stood it admirably, much to the wonder of every one. All are in camp to-night, but cannot graze for their thirst. The camels are continually bellowing, which I suppose, as it is unusual, a sign of a want of water. . . .

July 4.—Although the command was very weary last night, it did not rest as well as I have seen it; the whole conversation was of "something to drink." We had to use our canteens for pillows to secure our water, as none of the most thirsty show much reluctance in emptying any one they may come across at a draught. This morning brought forth many serious and despondent countenances in the command as they prepared to march with their two drinks of water, and not knowing when or where the next was to be had, if at all. After marching four miles one of these was given out, with serious thoughts of dispersion, every one to do the best he could for himself and comrade. When ascending a little rise, to my delight, I recognized looming up in the distance, about fifteen miles, Camel's Hump mountain, at whose base the head of San Francisco creek lies, and all pushed eagerly on to taste the sparkling treasure. No one can imagine the feelings of a thirsty man till he sees one. I would not describe it by a vain attempt, as vain almost as that would be which I might use in describing the region of country just passed over which made them so; a region in its original chaotic state, as if the progress of civilization was too rapid for the arrangement of chaos; a picture of barrenness and desolation, when the scathing fire of destruction has swept with its rapid flame mountains, cañons, ravines, precipices, cactus, soap weed, intense reflection from the limestone cliffs, and almost every barrier that one can conceive of to make an impossibility of progress. . . .

July 30.—This morning I rode down the precipice, at whose base we were encamped to look for a place to cross the precipitous mountain of yesterday. I went down four or five miles, from where I could see about six further, where it was smaller and more broken, but yet presented a formidable obstacle; but not so bad as at the trail. In going up the precipice, as far as I could examine, several miles, it appeared to increase in height. Proceeding up the trail six and a half miles we entered a rough cañon, but short and passable. One and one fifth miles further, we arrived opposite the Sierra Santiago, on whose side is reported a sulphur spring, upon which we had placed much dependence, but, to our sad disappointment, it was dry, which prevented making a halt to examine for another route around the mountain. We had only to push ahead and seek water, and found a nice spring or creek at 7.4 miles from Sierra Santiago. I have named it "Forked Branch." The camels were without water three days; the mules also, except a very limited supply last night; both are beginning to show exhaustion; the mules are lame and halt; the camels have several sore feet; their soles have actually been abraded off to the quick by the sharp cragged rocks, and others have very sore backs, indeed; holes in the humps large enough to thrust in both fists; these sores do not injure them much, being in the fleshy part of the hump, so long as they can be kept from the bones. Camped at Forked Branch. Marched 15.8 miles.

I would recommend to any one using the camels over rough country, in case of tender feet, to shoe them with a piece of (circular) raw hide, gathered around the leg by a slipping cord; this will be found an absolute necessity in some instances. One of the men left the command a short distance yesterday, and has not been seen or heard of since.

OPAL FIELDS OF SHIMMERING BLUE

Ralph A. Selle

1932

THE USE OF A FLOWER AS AN EMBLEM OR SYMBOL OF A NATION HAS been well fixed in history during the last five centuries. Celebrated in song and story—and sometimes on the shield or the banner—the flower becomes a loving token, an emblem about which will rally many people who have common interests, like opinions or an ancestry that can be traced to the same place.

The emblem of England is the rose; of France, the lily; Scotland honors the thistle; and "Green Ireland wears the shamrock." Uncle Sam wears a corn tassel, and Dixie sings of cotton. All of the states and territories now have an adopted flower, or at least a flower that is generally recognized. . . . Long before any official action was taken, the bluebonnet was the popular favorite of Texas. . . .

While the bluebonnet is a descendant of a very old garden flower, it has attained a remarkable development in a restricted area where the soil and climate just suit its peculiar demands. It flourishes best in the "bluebonnet bias," a belt of limestone outcroppings extending from Texarkana to El Paso. This "bias" is by no means regular, but the curves and brakes are not very abrupt; it is from 50 to 200 miles wide and there are isolated areas of bluebonnets, "lakes of bluebonnets," that are entirely out of the belt. Singularly, the great belt of bluebonnets does not extend into Mexico or even into Arkansas.

Brought here from the Mediterranean countries, possibly Europe or Africa, in shipments of grain and clover, it quickly escaped from the fields and took possession of the prairie lands of Texas. The old mission priests called it buffalo clover because the buffaloes fed upon it. For some reason, the Tejas Indians associated the great patches of bluebonnets with the spring migration of buffaloes; they were satisfied with the explanation that the immense herds simply came to eat the blue clover.

The bluebonnet might be classified as a clover; it is a legume and it belongs in the division of plants with the clovers. But it is usually mentioned as a lupine since its botanical name is lupine. It is quite probable that the bluebonnet can be traced to the "bonnet flower" of the Old World, the scabiosa of the old-fashioned gardens.

The bluebonnet improves the soil. Like the other forms of clover, it thrives on the poorest soil. It thrives where the prairie grass is sparse, where the only foothold is red, hard clay; it covers the bare spaces on the hillside with its mantle of blue beauty, and it enriches the soil so that other crops can grow. After a few years of bluebonnet pasture, the ground can be ploughed with the full assurance that it will be rich enough to produce cotton or corn or whatever crop the climate of the locality might justify. It sends its roots deep down and fixes nitrogen in the soil.

Like all other leguminous plants, these bluebonnets (lupines) carry little nodules or tubercles on their roots which fix or hold nitrogen taken from the air. These nodules are due to a kind of bacteria which begins to grow like a parasite; and, it seems that the roots in growing around them, or healing a scar, build up the material of the nodule; since this nitrogen is built in while this process is going on, "nitrogen-fixing bacteria" is an appropriate term.

Since this process of building up the soil was not understood by the early settlers, and bluebonnet land was usually poor soil, they jumped to the conclusion that these lupines impoverished the soil. It required an extensive campaign of education and demonstration by scientific farmers to convince the skeptical natives that bluebonnets actually improved the soil instead of rendering it barren.

A peculiar whim of the bluebonnets is their preference for the barren places, the red hillsides and the hard-pan prairie lands. For a few years, they multiply rapidly, wax abundant and irresistible, then they fade out and give other flowers a chance. This is especially noticeable with Indian paint; blankets of Indian paint crowd into old fields of bluebonnets. Bluebonnet fields are sometimes taken by purple verbenas or creeping charleys. After a term of years, these whimsical blue fields may come again, taller and bluer than ever.

There is a marked difference in the shade of the blue, in the amount and intensity of the red and the relative amount of the white and gray of the bluebonnets of a new field that is coming to its best and an old field that is waning. The deepest, darkest blue does not arrive for three or four years after the field has started, and it will reappear in its fullest richness only three or four years, then it will not be so blue; in a few more years, it will be a pale sky blue. Examined closely, each flower will have less deep blue, the red on the tips of the bonnets will seem more intense and the white and gray will be much more prominent.

There are yet a few people who insist that bluebonnet fields appear the same year after year; they do not recognize the rhythmic cycle which requires 10 to 12 years to complete. To such we can only say, study your bluebonnet fields carefully, make notes on the intensity of the blue, and compare these notes from year to year. . . .

Like peas or beans, the seeds of bluebonnets ripen within the pods. These peas are very rich in protein and they might find a place in the human diet but for the fact that they have a bitter taste. They have been fed to animals, especially cows and hogs, with marked success; and "bluebonnet clover hay," which is cut about the time that the pods are beginning to form, is a good type of provender.

After a dry winter, they will not do so well; only a few of them will appear and they will be short, stunted and very pale blue—in some instances, there will be no traces of red. They appear in about the same condition when the soil is too rich. Like the good everywhere, they grow and expand best where they are needed most. They are doing a great service for the poor soils of Texas by storing nitrogen and making it available for other plants to use. For the benefit of the soil, they should not be harvested, and for the refreshing uplift, the aesthetic appeal and the unbounded invitation of the great outdoors, they should be preserved and protected in their native environment. . . .

The bluebonnet comes down through the ages with an aura of tradition and glory. This wealth of story and romance only proves that the roving Indians and the first white settlers were greatly stirred by the wonderful pageant of blue. Since they could not understand it, they wove it into their superstitions and religious beliefs. They did not, they could not, treat the bluebonnets lightly.

According to tradition, some Spanish priests made a pious pilgrimage to the Holy Land and, from a hillside near the city of Jerusalem, they plucked with their own hands some seed-pods of the "blue blanket," and these were finally planted with much ceremony inside the walls of a Mexican mission. But the flowers flourished and spread and became wild, and like the gospel, they spread to the four winds; and blankets of blue were spread all over the land. . . .

Several of the early accounts refer to these blue flowers as "blue blankets." Probably this is due to the romantic accounts of "Old Chief Blue

Blanket" and his two sons, "Big Chief Blue Blanket" and "Bad Medicine Blue Blanket." Before Old Chief became leader of his tribe, he led a party of warriors in a raid among distant tribes. They brought back much plunder, tents, blankets and weapons, some ponies and dogs, and several squaws that were heavy and slow and dark and sullen; but one of these squaws was slim and quick and light and lively.

Old Chief was already supplied with squaws—probably several of them—but the "blue song bird" took his fancy. She was light as the wind and she could laugh to music. She would sing soft bird songs that would make Old Chief sleepy; and even when she beat the cymbals or the deerskin drum, her stroke was so light that it sounded like a bird calling.

Since she sang so well and beat the drum so lightly, it was not necessary for her to work like the other squaws. Old Chief ordered them to wait on her, and he made dire threats casting down his ax and spear to portend death to all if anything happened to his favorite. When Old Chief was in camp, she was at his side, crooning or singing or chattering; she did not even wait on him, but she would order his pipe to be brought or his blanket to be placed—and the squaws who were heavy and slow and dark and sullen always obeyed her orders.

When Old Chief was away from camp, Blue Song Bird would busy herself making head-dresses, and the ones that she made were more brilliant than any that the tribe had ever known. But she did not make red ones. Red was a favorite color of the tribe, but, no difference; she made blue head-dresses, and Old Chief wore blue. Red was the color of blood, of war, but blue was the sky, the blue bird, a song. Blue became the emblem of the tribe, and under the blue, the tribe prospered.

Old Chief and Blue Song Bird lived to be very old; they did not make war, and other tribes did not make war upon them. Since they thought much of the blue sky, the songbird and crooning songs, their hearts became light; they did not think of war; they wanted everybody to live and be happy. The Great Spirit was pleased with his people. He sent blessings of rain and sunshine, fruits and nuts, fat birds and fur-covered buffaloes; and when his people responded so kindly, even the Great Spirit showed his pleasure by spreading the emblem of his favorite tribe over the hills and prairies—the bluebonnets.

The son was even greater than the father. Big Chief Blue Blanket was wise and peaceful; the people worked and played together; they did not order one another around; and they would all join in singing the "blue bird songs" and the praises of Big Chief Blue Blanket. He lived long, and his departure was grieved; but the Great Spirit made the blue blankets bluer than ever.

It was a sad day for the tribe when "Little Blue Blanket" became chief. He was selfish and cruel, irresponsible and despotic. One of his whims was a hatred for good-looking young women; his squaws had to be wrinkled and ugly and strong to do much work; and he did like to smash the heads of young squaws. It was necessary to keep the young women out of his sight. His people were very tolerant, and they did not kill him until he had committed so many outrageous crimes that he was known as "Bad Medicine Blue Blanket" to the neighboring tribes. Then they took him out and laid his head on a flat stone. Even after "Bad Medicine" had disgraced the tribe, the Great Spirit permitted the blue blankets to spread over the prairies. . . .

According to [another legend], a prairie fire had swept all over the land. The people rushed to the walls of the mission for protection. They were saved from the fire, but there was no food. The people prayed, and the Great Spirit sent a blue bird to be offered as a sacrifice. But the feathers of this bird were not to be burned; they were to be planted on the blackened hillsides, and under no consideration was one feather to be placed within 20 paces of another feather.

The feathers of that little bird were scattered over so much territory that it took all the men and women of the tribe from sun till sun to plant them. When the last feather was planted, the skies were darkened and much rain fell. The black ashes were washed away, and blue feathers grew everywhere—and buffaloes came in great numbers.

[In still another legend] the land of the Aztecs was visited with a plague. The pestilence was so terrible that the people were terror-stricken. They prayed, but the gods would not listen. After a period of anguish, the gods agreed to accept an Aztec maiden as an atonement for the wickedness that had brought about the calamity. The chief's daughter, the favorite of the tribe, offered to make the sacrifice. When the beautiful maiden approached the altar which was built on a high mound, a strong breeze blew her bonnet from her head. Since she belonged to the gods, no one tried to restore the bonnet. Even before the second sun, blue flowers sprang up around the bonnet, but each flower showed a splotch of blood. The gods were appeased and the pestilence disappeared, but the bluebonnets come every year to make people think of the sacrifice of the tribal favorite, and to remind indifferent mortals that beauties and treasures of this world are only whims of the gods.

THEY LIVE HERE TOO — OUR QUAIL

Evelyn Mellard

1977

WHEN WE LOCATED ON LAND NEVER BEFORE THE PERMANENT home of man, we were nevertheless, trespassers on homesteads of the Blue Quail, scientifically labeled *Callipepla squamata,* or Scaled Quail. I had never seen nor heard of Blue Quail and was totally unaware of their existence until well after things had settled down following our building program and I noticed them moving through the tall grasses of my yard, circling wide the house, conversing among themselves. Quite unintentionally I had been feeding them, I subsequently discovered.

In my early experiences of cooking for two, I seemed always to have an excess of bread, toast if I'd made toast, or biscuits or whatever. And what I did was to toss the leftovers outside a short distance from the house. The quail, of course, found the food, experimented, took their first bite of processed bread, liked their discovery, and checked by from time to time for more. They had a reason to be cautious of me, they carried inherited knowledge of the destructiveness of man with gun or other weapons. If I opened a door or made the slightest noise, off they'd be with a whir of wings to safety. I wanted a closer relationship and began leaving bread out on purpose.

We didn't have chickens, and I had never myself raised chickens, but I knew how quickly chickens learned to come when called at feeding time. I wondered if ever I could teach the wild quail to come to my call. I knew what "CHICKIE, CHICKIE, CHICKIE" would produce, chickens running over each other to be first to arrive for the feeding. Would "QUAILIE, QUAILIE, QUAILIE" ever produce the same effect? I called without any sign of success. Still I continued to call, to leave the bread, and to remain hopeful. Maybe, just maybe, someday my "QUAILIE, QUAILIE, QUAILIE, COME ON, QUAILIE" would bring them running to me. What joyful excitement that would be!

Meanwhile, I had done a bit of "research" and had learned from my husband and others something about our *Callipepla squamata,* Scaled Quail, Blue Quail — sometimes designated Mexican Quail. Also, I had been able to have closer sight of them. They are Scaled Quail because of the scaly markings on their breast and back. Their color is gray, somewhat bluish-gray, and they wear white plumed "shakos." Their stance is military erectness, especially when challenging or being challenged. They carry themselves almost perpendicular when running, except when attempting to escape from an adversary, and then their posture is nearly horizontal.

They are ground birds and usually do not fly unless frightened or crowded. Later I discovered they would fly into hackberry trees if there was some bud or seed they wanted for feeding. And years later, at the present time, they fly to the rooftops of all our buildings, mostly to keep an eye on us if feeding time approaches, we think—but that's getting ahead of my story.

My story of my early callings continued without noticeable success for months on end. And then one day, one day well past midafternoon, it happened. I was calling "COME ON, QUAILIES, COME ON, COME ON, QUAILIES," when I noticed motion in the grass bordering the canyon. The quail were there, circling, hearing. I called, I softened my voice, I entreated, I talked just to them. No one else was present, just the quail and I. I so wanted them to come to me, to answer my call. They circled the canyon and on around in front of the house and me, but they were still mostly hidden in the grass. Then to my surprise and excitement, they raced to a tree cactus some fifty feet beyond where I stood and huddled around it.

I let them rest a few minutes and presently continued to talk to them. We were the only ones in our universe. I could see them clearly under the tree cactus and they could see me, standing in the open. I watched their movements. They seemed to be in conference. Clearly a decision was being made. I continued to encourage them and talk to them. They took their time, listening, evaluating, deciding. And then a supreme joy of my life happened.

The leader took front position of the covey. Others fell in behind him, not in single file, but by three or four close-ranked. A moment of quiet hesitation—and here they came, a phalanx of quail running toward me. They never hesitated more, not once, all closely packed together behind the single-file leader, but ran straight toward me on the ground. I scarcely breathed or moved. They stopped but didn't begin eating instantly. It was our moment of mutual trust and confidence. I edged back almost imperceptibly, still saying, "It's all right, quailies, it's all right. No one will bother you! No one will ever harm you so long as I'm here! There's your bread. Eat your supper. It's all right, quailies! It's all right!"

When I had inched back about seven or eight feet, they broke ranks and began feeding with gusto while "talking" among themselves—perhaps congratulating their courageous leader and each other on their daring but successful venture. I was "teary 'round the lashes" as I sat down on a step and watched and listened.

When they had finished, they rose as one, their wings whirring, and settled to earth near the canyon rim. In the future they didn't always come when I called, but they didn't always fail to come either. I even on occasions demonstrated their responsiveness to me by calling them in for guests to see, the guests never allowed outside the house on such occasions, however. I would take no chance of someone inadvertently frightening my quailies.

Guests frequently asked me, "how can you tell a hen from a rooster?" The answer was that many times I couldn't. The hens and roosters are similar, sometimes in a covey impossible to distinguish. Paired off, and quail do pair off in the spring, slight differences can be noticed. The rooster is usually heavier, taller, and fancier in dress and markings than the hen. His plume is more showy. The chief difference, however, is seen in character and attitude. Quail understand the difference between male and female and fulfill the difference accordingly. Positions of males in a covey are fiercely defended or challenged. In acquiring and maintaining status in the covey, all privileges seem to rest on male prowess, temperament, or courage.

The privilege of covey movement no doubt rests with the leader or leaders. Authorities state that the radius of movement of a covey is approximately one mile, not always covered, with some overlapping, each range usually one to one and a half miles apart. Also, it is said that quail do not have to have water, that some coveys in the Big Bend National Park have been seen seven miles from water. Quail drink from vegetation if there is moisture, but I know for certain that they drink daily if water is provided as here it is always. I know they prefer to have water.

Quail belong to Biblical history, as we know, and also to folklore. During my childhood I often heard it said that quail refused to reproduce unless assured that there would be plenty of food for their families, which was to say unless it rained. If only people had as much sense as quail, it was thought, there would be less hunger in the world. What scientists say is that quail *cannot* reproduce unless their diet furnishes vitamin A, hence the waiting for rain, for green vegetation which supplies the vitamin A, making reproduction possible.

A vitamin-protein-mineral supplement feed for all species of wild quail has been developed. Scientifically produced, results in the field scientifically checked and notarized, the following benefits are announced: Reduces loss due to malnutrition, induces earlier mating, increases hatchability of eggs, encourages second laying when first nests are destroyed, and aids in holding coveys to a given area. This supplemental diet is especially important to wild quail during critical periods when natural food is limited in quantity or lacking in proper nutrition.

Quail hunting enthusiasts have defended their sport by saying that quail might just as well be hunted because no more than 20 percent would survive to mate in any case. Not so when a balanced supplemental ration is fed. Quail will live and in the spring will reproduce. Not only that, they will have a richer color, be heavier, and will obtain these results on no more than a gram of the feed per bird a day. Previous research statistics and hunters' opinions to the contrary, quail can be "stockpiled," their numbers increased. We fed our quail this balanced ration, developed and manufactured by a local citizen, until some shortage of ingredients forced closing out the production.

Hunters further defend their sport by stating that coveys should be broken up and forced to intermingle. I am not against the sport or the hunters who enjoy it. I am against the argument. Nature takes care of covey intermingling. A quail's nest is a grass-lined hollow on the ground under a bush. It is estimated that 75 percent of first nests are destroyed—and there is no guarantee that there'll be second nests for such pairs or that a second nest would fare any better than the first. First nests depend on diet, second nests more so. Pairs failing to produce a covey will be forced to join with others during winter and nonproducing months.

Even when all goes well and reproduction occurs, there is no surety that survival will accrue. Quail are the most defenseless creatures on earth, easy prey to predators, hawks, snakes, coyotes, almost any meat-eating bird or animal. Quail lay from nine to sixteen or more eggs per nesting, but as noted, survival or even birth of the young is hazardous. The coveys will intermix. We estimate that we have ten or twelve coveys eating together with us now. It doesn't seem likely that they will sort themselves out, now that mating time is here, and keep to their original segregation. Of course, in large areas where they are protected, as in the Big Bend National Park where one covey may be separated from its neighbor covey by a mile or more distance, no doubt there is little permanent intermingling—but even in the park predators other than man would scatter them. None of their enemies, unless man, is destroyed there.

As the natural habitat of quail—grasslands, brush, arid country—is destroyed or usurped, the quail population diminishes. Even so, in Texas Blue Quail are still found in the Panhandle, parts of the Edwards Plateau, portions of the lower Rio Grande Valley, and in the Trans-Pecos, Big Bend Country. Formerly they also ranged from central Mexico to central Texas.

There is a hunting season for quail with a limit of take per person; but hunting losses, drought, erosion of land, overgrazing of grasslands, natural enemies, all combine to lessen their numbers. Our protection is insignificant in the overall picture, but we do demonstrate what can be accomplished in a relatively short time by mutual human-quail confidence and partnership owning of land. Our quail have protection here where they and we live and they know it, but their enemies are many, their protective friends few.

Sometimes our efforts to protect are futile. In my early days here on the ranch when I was first concerned with the quail, I heard the frightened peep-peeping of a little fellow only a few days old. It was late in the afternoon following a shower and the frightened, lost little one was running and calling frantically. Not a single adult was in sight and no answering response came.

I gathered the tiny infant into my hand, cupped him closely to my breast and talked to him. I walked around a while but no family was seen or heard. As long as I held him close and warm he was quiet. Thinking he might nestle down for awhile, I tried putting him in a cotton-lined box. No success. His call was incessant and frantic. The poor, tiny lost creature! I wanted to feed him and give him a drink. He wouldn't take water or food, nothing that I offered. I recalled a friend's having told me that she had saved a little bird, not a quail, by giving it cornmeal. No help for my little one. He refused all offers and coaxings.

In the evening, I sat holding him cuddled to me for hours as I read. Not a peep. At bedtime, I put him in his box, which I placed on a nightstand beside my bed. I covered him with a thin layer of cotton. The lights out and all quiet, he didn't chirp a peep once. Morning brought the same problem as the day before. He wouldn't eat or drink and continued his forlorn calling unless I held him, which I did as much of the day as possible. I walked about with him outside trying to locate his family—nowhere in sight or sound. If only I knew how to feed him, but I didn't.

At bedtime the second night I put him in his cottony covers and we both went to sleep; he not to wake. When I waked the following morning, my first thought was to check on the frail little one. He had died sometime in the night.

I lined a Sucret box with cotton, placed him on his side, covered him with more cotton and closed the lid. He was that tiny—plenty of depth in the Sucret box. After breakfast we buried him in a border of the yard, my husband framing the little grave with four equal-length pieces of tile left from our building program. Years have passed and the tile framework is still in place, marking the spot where we put the little one away, a capsule of energetic life, lost, loving, afraid. He calls no more.

He calls no more, but day in, day out, successive generations of quail call all around us. I wish I could spell the sounds they make, but I can no more do so than I could spell a musical note or tone. Sometimes the quail conversing together remind me of guineas, and again of the liquid sound I've heard turkeys make. I know the quail calls and their meanings. I know when they are sounding their gathering call, or come to me, come here call, their group-alarm cry, their individual-fright cry, and their conversational notes. Now, when we call them in for feed, they begin "talking" at the sound of our voices—either my husband or I can call them—and these conversational notes are the most joyous, the most musical, the most liquid of all their sounds. A hundred or more quail in a happy, conversing mood create music not otherwise heard. They "talk" as long as we are talking to them. When we return indoors, they become quiet and the business of feeding takes over.

Our friends have said that we should make recordings of quail sounds, especially at feeding time, and we agree, but our interest has never been scientific but merely friendship for fellow travelers in this arid region where we all live. There are so many things I'd like to know about the quail now that spring approaches.

It is March and time for pairing off in preparation for rearing families, those fortunate enough to escape predators and loss of eggs and young ones. During the winter months the quail have been in coveys, several coveys coming together here for feeding. Last year's young ones are among them and many of last year's older ones. Do quail mate for life? Will last year's pairs find each other? I don't know. Ours have not been banded, making identification possible.

What I do know is that this is a critical season. I hear a quail calling now, the come to me call, the here I am call. Roosters will fight for mates and fight to keep mates. Once the pairing has been accomplished, the male permits no visitation privileges with his chosen one, not even if it appears a friendly good morning. It's his responsibility to keep the "marriage" inviolate, and he goes about his duty with dedication. The lady has no recourse to society except his own. Once the busy business of feeding is over, he and she stand together preening themselves and woe unto a careless intruder into their privacy, their ritual as almost it seems. I have never seen a rooster fight his hen to keep her in tow, but I've seen roosters mortally tear into any "gentleman" nosing around her.

For some time I have been trying to discover who or what seals the bargain, the agreement to mate, but I have been trying unsuccessfully. Quail are very private people. There's no chasing of hens as seen among chickens, no necessity of course for mated pairs. Neither is their breeding done in public. In all the years that our quail have been around us—and they literally own the place—not more than four or five times have I seen a pair breed. Those few times have occurred on the feed ground when other quail were present. A pair of quail are much more deliberate about their sexual activity than chickens, take more time, show little if any excitement. It's done, it's over, no other quail show the least interest, and the wedded pair are matter-of-fact in attitude. How often mating per pair occurs I have no knowledge. Once or many times, I don't know.

I have witnessed two aberrations that pose interesting speculation—copulations out of season, in the dead of winter, in January, when the covey was a melded unit. Here is what happened. In both instances a little hen, apropos of nothing, suddenly darted over to a rooster and squatted, back toward him, almost under his beak. He, in no hurry, surveyed the situation, her position and invitation, and obligingly complied. When 'twas over, they parted without so much as a farewell gesture or a thank you, dear. Did the lady see old hubby standing by and decided to remind him of past and future responsibilities? Was she a young thing determined to learn about life? A widow fraught with longings? A married gal that recognized a playboy when she saw him? A hopeful looking forward to spring mating? Or is that the way all unions are decided, the Eve in the garden technique? If I ever find out, I'll tell you!

Whatever the protocol of matchmaking, once nesting time arrives, both partners are busy, and busier still when the little ones are hatched, especially if the brood is a large one. Only in the last few years have parents brought their tiny babes to the feeding ground. Only recently have they felt that much at home. There are good reasons for keeping the young away. Adults fight the newborn. I've seen grown quail peck an infant, lifting it off the ground in their sharp beaks. The parents try to protect their brood but usually are so overcome in their efforts they retreat with family as swiftly as possible.

Another hazard is that babes will follow any grown quail, not because of encouragement, quite the contrary, but simply by instinct to follow. The little ones of course become confused in a crowd and follow any movement, hoping to escape the sudden brutality they have encountered, hoping that parents will take them to safety.

I saw an interesting but pathetic development one morning when a pair with a large brood of infants arrived at the feeding ground, occupied by numerous adults. Mamma went about grabbing a few bites to eat along with having a drink at the waterpan. Papa was on tiptoe with excitement and resentment in his efforts to protect his young from the harsh treatment of ill-tempered adults. He also was trying to keep his chicks from scattering.

Mamma, perhaps aware of the situation, possibly decided to help by leaving the inhospitable grown-ups. She started away from the area, about half of the babes following her. At the same time, a pair of quail without a brood left in the opposite direction, the remainder of the little ones hurrying after them.

Papa was dumbfounded, Mamma with half his family going in one direction, the other half following strangers. He stood straight, head thrown back, seemingly paralyzed for a minute or so. Then he rushed after the young ones following the strangers, but stopped suddenly in his tracks. That half of the family was already vanishing under the fence with the unconcerned adults.

Wheeling about, Papa tore out at full speed and overtook Mamma and her group. Informing her of the dilemma in no uncertain terms and no doubt ordering her to about face, which she did, he turned and ran at a fast clip.

I was not able to see how the reunion was accomplished, but the next day at a later hour the united family returned to the feeding area and found it vacant. The busy parents had peace and time to eat and drink, hover their little ones, and in every way refresh themselves. And they had not lost a babe, it appeared. There were no other broods the size of theirs. I kept thinking that a distraught human father in the same predicament could scarcely have improved on the solution demonstrated by Papa Quail.

If you have ever seen little quail run, you are in a better position to appreciate Papa's situation. The little ones seem to move as UFOs are described, without motive power, just rolling speed. Little quail go so fast—they have to keep up—that you can't see the movement of their tiny legs. Little downy quail are miniature objects gliding like a rolling dollar. It's almost more than two parents can do to "ride herd" on them, but except for predators, storms, or other unavoidable disasters, quail parents will guide their family to adulthood, able to make their own way in a covey, where they are still pecked, until able to establish their own standings.

When a predator strikes, parent quail act as decoys, directing attention to themselves and ofttimes giving their lives for the young. It is not unusual to discover a brood with only one parent, meaning that one was the sacrifice. And again, we've had little ones that lost both parents. Last summer such a situation occurred. The young ones huddled as a brood and traveled together, eventually joining a family with smaller and fewer babes. The elected foster parents pecked at the orphans but were not able to dissuade them from following. It was unusual to see this family arrive with larger and smaller young ones, but we watched them throughout the season until all were lost in the mature covey.

Little quail, like little chickens, are on their feet and ready to go soon after breaking into this world. Quail chicks have to run faster than chicken chicks to keep up with their parents. We wonder how any quail babes survive, what food they could possibly find to give them the speed and stamina needed to follow their hurrying parents, who will from time to time stop and hover them. Infant quail babes want to be hovered often, and it is positively amazing the number that can get under one adult.

A rain shower came on suddenly one day last summer when a one-parent brood was on the feeding ground. Without hesitation the mother brought the tiny ones onto our covered terrace and huddled them against the wall behind a porch chair as long as the rain fell. They were perfectly protected, the several little ones out of sight, somewhere among the parent's feathers. She knew she lived here too! She and her family!

I have mentioned that our many quail living here are all over the place. We see them on top of buildings, sometimes in trees, on the terrace, sometimes sitting in the glider. They're in the corrals, under flowering bushes, on and under the woodpile, on and under the loading chute, on gates, on fences. Some are acting as lookout personnel surveying the landscape. Should danger of any sort, a hawk for instance, be sighted, a warning signal would be instantly given and cover taken by all, sometimes with frightening, hurtling speed. Following such warning signals, dozens of birds have hit the walls of our house under the porch cover, hit the walls and plate glass windows in a fearful effort to escape. Mr. Hawk has never come in after them, but I am sure they have bruised themselves escaping him.

At other times, during bad weather especially—snow and sleet, for instance—numbers of quail come onto the terrace and spend hours huddled under the glider and chairs. It's a hosing-sweeping cleanup afterward—but they're welcome.

Why do we bother with quail when we do not want them for food or for hunters' sport? We're friends now is as good an answer as any, I suppose. We've grown accustomed to their presence, to their waiting at feeding time for us, to their recognition of our cars and the excited chatter they begin, never running or flying away when we arrive as they do when strangers arrive, as one time they did for us. We are accustomed to their calls, happy, sorrowful, frightened.

We think of them when the weather is bad. We recall seeing them wading in snow too soft to hold them up, falling through up to their necks but coming on, certain that we would feed them. We look forward to seeing them arrive with their tiny tots now that they are unafraid of bringing them to us. Once they were. We like having them drop by any time of day to check on the feeding grounds. There might, just might, be something special for them, and often there is. They will eat any and all table scraps, vegetable leaves and peels, cooked or raw meat—all, if I cut my leftovers or discarded bits in small pieces for them. I do, regularly.

Perhaps they just come for water, which is always run fresh for them each morning. Perhaps they just check by to see that all is stable, that we are here and going about our routine. They will know. They look through the patio doors and listen for familiar noises, ours, as we listen for theirs.

When we've been away overnight or for a few days, they seem forlorn at our return, until we begin calling. My husband has been feeding and calling lately, and the minute he calls, a chattering answer begins from those nearby, while those in hearing distance come running or flying in. He calls cattle too. He really has a good calling voice. Cattle and quail know his voice. When the quail hear him, they take special delight. Everybody's home and all's well.

The quail know why we bother with them, and so do we. They live here too! Everybody's home!

THE WING OF THE SWALLOW
Roy Bedichek
1947

MARTINS HAUNT THE HOMES OF MEN; THE LITTLE CLIFF SWALLOW prefers man's public buildings, a preference which makes him more of a city bird than his close northern relative, the eaves swallow, which keeps company with rural folk, nesting in the great barns and other outbuildings of prosperous farmsteads, especially in the North and East.

The books say that the original nesting range of the lesser Mexican cliff swallow extended no farther north than the rough country along the Rio Grande. However, as the country settled up, colonies found their way into the limestone area of south-central Texas and were in all probability nesting in bluffs west of Austin when that city was founded in the valley of the Colorado in 1839.

Here, as soon as buildings of any considerable size became available, their eaves and arches were occupied by colonies which forsook all but the most favorable nesting sites in the wilds, as swallows all over the world have always done, liking artificial structures better than those with which nature provides them.

Frank Brown, in his unpublished "Annals of Travis County and of the City of Austin," noted the appearance of the lesser Mexican cliff swallow in 1865. He says:

The swallows appeared in Austin for the first time in June of this year. They commenced building their nests upon the walls of the capitol. Old settlers asserted, at the time, that these birds had not previously appeared in this part of the country. The bats had theretofore been in possession of the old limestone building, but the swallows put them to flight.

The capitol referred to by Mr. Brown is the First Capitol. This is the first definite reference I can find to the bird's nesting in Austin or even in the Austin area. However, bird observations were few, and the country west of Austin was thinly populated at that time and still subject to Indian raids. The bird may have been in the vicinity at that time without being recorded. Chapman gives the range of this subspecies, after it was separated from the Mexican cliff swallow by Oberholser, as "Texas and Mexico. Breeds in western Texas, the Rio Grande Valley, and through eastern Mexico to Vera Cruz."

The First Capitol burned in 1881. The great granite statehouse was completed in 1888. Even before the state departments were well settled in their new quarters, a colony of lesser Mexican cliff swallows occupied the high arch over the south entrance. At this time Congress Avenue, leading from the river to the capitol, was an unpaved expanse of soft limestone, yielding, under pounding and grinding of horse-drawn traffic, an immense amount of floury dust which the south winds swept in stifling clouds up the main thoroughfare of the city. Thereupon a sprinkler system was established, which soon converted the powdered limestone into a pasty mulch which the swallows found very much to their liking. They swarmed down into the street, traffic or no traffic, oblivious of crowds which stared curiously at them.

While thus gathering mud for pellets, this dainty bird barely touches feet to the ground, supporting most of the weight of his body by fluttering his wings high above his back. Craning his short neck forward, he excavates the raw material with his bill and takes off, working the mouthful into pellet form as he flies. Arrived at the nesting site, he presses the little brick into its place in a jiffy and is off again on another hod-carrier flight. Hundreds of the birds covered Congress Avenue, each intent on getting a supply of the gummy mixture of dust and water which the traffic had providently churned into just the right consistency. Many observers thought the birds were eating mud.

They soon proved to be careless masons, dropping this whitish adhesive material upon people entering the building; and the acceleration of a four-story descent gave the pellet, as it reached the shoulders of its victims, considerable spattering and daubing power. The fire department came to the rescue with high-pressure hose, and the birds were driven from the city streets back into the hills.

Similarly, in 1920, when the main building of the Sul Ross State Teachers' College [now Sul Ross State University], at Alpine, was erected on a slope some miles from the rugged canyons of the Davis Mountains, a colony began building nests in the high arch over the front entrance. The President of the College, Dr. R. L. Marquis, a zoologist and bird lover, proposed to protect the colony; but here, too, it soon became obvious that the enthusiastic little creatures had chosen an impossible site.

No matter how charming the bird may be, coming in from the wilds and putting his trust in welcome from man; no matter how expert he is in destroying mosquitoes and other noxious insects; no matter if he fills the evening sky with "poems of motion"—no matter: he has habits which make him impossible as a guest lodged above the entrance to a public building. President Marquis regretfully summoned the fire department, and it washed down the nests each season until the birds finally gave up and returned to their granitic cliffs, cave entrances, and rock shelters in the mountains.

GHOST LIGHTS
Kirby F. Warnock
1982

I HAVE NEVER BELIEVED IN PYRAMID POWER. IF PYRAMIDS CAN sharpen razor blades and keep your milk from spoiling, then why can't I buy one at K-Mart or order one from a toll-free number on television, like a Veg-o-matic? The Bermuda triangle was interesting until close examination proved it to be more the work of paperback writers than of the devil or sinister forces. *Close Encounters of the Third Kind* convinced me that UFOs were a publicity stunt for Universal Pictures, 10 years in the making. No, there are no more "natural phenomena" left that can baffle the scientists and elude capture.

Unless, that is, you count a certain phenomenon in a remote area of West Texas, near the town of Marfa. Now, here is a genuine wonder of nature; one that not only confounds the scientific community but that can be seen and photographed by almost anyone. These "ghost lights" are known to the citizens of the Trans-Pecos as the Marfa lights. Things don't happen until the sun goes down; then, several lights begin to appear in the desert. The lights pulsate, move around, grow extremely bright, and disappear. The lights are of a white color, not orange (like fire), and can be seen without fail every night of the year. That's about it. No bodies, no missing airplanes, no sinister acts. The lights are just there to be seen and to baffle you. The mystery is what kind of light appears in the desert and why.

Several explanations exist, but thus far no one has been able to come up with a conclusive one. I first saw the lights as an 11-year-old at the Paisano Baptist Encampment near Alpine, Texas. Everyone there knew about them. "Why, you just drive out Highway 67 and park by the old airfield, shut off your lights, and you'll see them," everyone would say.

Usually these instructions were accompanied by a tale of what everyone saw happen when they went out there. Two of the most often repeated stories were that a National Geographic expedition had failed to explain the lights and that people who had tried to chase them had died, usually from a plane or jeep crash and not from the "lights" themselves.

I promptly persuaded my parents to drive us out the next night; I wanted to see for myself what the Marfa lights were all about. We parked our car at the old airfield while my father told us that the site had been used by the Army to train pilots during World War II and that it had been closed just after the war had ended. A friend of his had been stationed at the airfield.

My father shut off the engine, stopped the car, and told my brother and me to watch the desert to our right. After about a two-minute wait, we saw three tiny white lights appear. The endless plains made depth perception almost impossible, so it was hard to tell if we were watching a large light 20 miles away or just a flashlight beam some 50 yards in front of us. Certain of the lights moved, while others remained stationary. Occasionally they would pulsate, grow extremely bright, and then disappear. After a few minutes they would reappear and begin the cycle anew.

I was fascinated and excited at the same time. Here was something that, if properly analyzed and explained, could make an investigator famous for the rest of his life. I could already see the headlines in *Time, Newsweek,* and *National Geographic*—with my picture accompanying them. The first thing that I did was to read everything I could find on the subject. That was no problem, since there were hundreds of newspaper articles and Sunday supplements about the lights, as well as substantial portions of a good number of books. Elton Miles's *Tales of the Big Bend* is the best of those books. He devotes a whole chapter to the subject and includes some of the best legends and explanations, ranging from the far-out (the lights are the spirits of a rancher whose family was tortured to death by Mexican bandits and whose ghost has been searching for them for eternity) to the ridiculous (during World War II several German prisoners who'd been incarcerated at the air base had escaped to Mexico, and the lights are the spirit of Hitler, signaling them the way to escape) to the semiscientific, in the mold of "ancient astronaut" stories (a team of scientists had attempted to drive a jeep up to the lights one night, and the next day the jeep was found burned to a crisp, with no sign of their bodies anywhere in sight). Miles does not allege that the stories are true. Early in the chapter, he warns that most of them are fourth-hand information, and that they should be taken with a grain of salt. But there is one story in particular that had also been cited in several of the news stories I'd read. It reports that during the war, some pilots from the air base flew out over the lights and dropped flour sacks to mark their location. The next morning, when the pilots walked out to the spot, they found no flour sacks or anything else.

As the years went by, I kept up my research and attempted several more sightings. But it wasn't until the summer of 1977 that I was able to begin a sustained study. My first stop was at the home of my uncle, Dr. Barton H. Warnock, in Alpine, Texas. Barton had spent more time in the Big Bend country and was more familiar with it than anyone else I knew. He gave me the names of several people to see; the one that caught my fancy was Fritz Kahl, a Marfa resident. Fritz, he said, had been the flight instructor at the old air base and had been residing in Marfa ever since. "He runs the Marfa airport," Barton continued, "and he's there most every day. If you want to talk to someone about those lights, look him up."

This was the break I had been looking for. Until now, no one had given me a conclusive, or even plausible, explanation for the lights; surely Fritz could.

There were rainstorms moving through the mountains as I drove towards Marfa. The town is located in one of the most remote areas of the state. It hardly looks like a place for an unexplained natural phenomenon. There are broad plains in every direction, rising up abruptly into the Chinati Mountains in the distance. Man is still an insignificant speck in this region—the environment and the natural elements still rule. Water and gasoline are partial equalizers; without either, man is as helpless as a turtle on its back in this remote, forlorn county.

I pulled into a field marked by a large tin-roofed hangar. I got out and entered the structure. Fritz wasn't in. I was told by his helper that he was out counting ducks along the Rio Grande with the game warden and would return within the next hour. I sat and waited.

Finally I heard the sound of a light plane landing, and I watched a burly man with a cap on his head emerge. Fritz Kahl had been a resident of Marfa since 1943, when he came to the air base to train pilots. Since then, he had become the owner and operator of the Marfa Airport, a business that enjoys its biggest activity when the border patrol planes land and take off.

"When I came here as an instructor, we heard people talk about the lights," he told me. "Thirty years ago, it was a lot easier to see the Marfa lights, because there weren't as many lights out there competing with them. There were no electric lights back then and no four-wheeled vehicles, so the lights were easier to see. There are Marfa lights, but they've been overrated and overpublicized. So many asinine stories have come out."

For instance?

"Oh, tales about people disappearing or dying. There have been no tragedies because of the lights. We lost eight cadets during the war, but not from chasing lights or trying to dive under them." Fritz delivered this remark with a thoroughly disgusted air.

What, I asked, about published reports of pilots dropping flour sacks to mark the location for investigators to find the next day? Fritz acted insulted when I asked this.

"No flour sacks were dropped," he scoffed. "I've been either instructing at or running this airport for the past thirty years. If someone would have flown out and dropped flour sacks, I would have known about it."

Fritz seemed adamant in his denials of any supernatural cause for the lights, yet he admitted that they exist. What, I asked, did he believe they really were, and why hadn't he ever found out for sure?

Fritz let out a long chuckle. With a grin, he told me, "The reason people come to see me about the lights is because I chased them in an AT-6 airplane. Me and another pilot got a fix on them and tried to fly to that spot, but when we got up in the air, we couldn't see them. I kept getting lower and lower, until finally the fellow in the back seat started shouting at me to get out of there because we were so low he could see the yucca plants."

So one can't see the lights from the air?

"I have never seen them from the air. A few years back, Sul Ross University did a study on the lights and tried to find out what they were. I had three people in a plane with me, and one of them was the editor of the Alpine newspaper. We didn't see a thing. They had people on the ground who could see them, and those people tried to radio us and tell us where the lights were, but none of us saw a thing."

We were interrupted by a call on the airport radio from a border patrol plane that needed to land. Fritz gave him clearance and sat back down. I then asked him just what he thought the lights were.

"Well, the logical explanation would seem to be either static electricity or geophysical activity. I think the Marfa lights are a local natural phenomenon. Whatever they are may not be that unusual, but they only appear here, not in other countries. Or it may be that they are something common to other parts of the world but very unusual to see in this country.

"We have the right conditions for Saint Elmo's fire in the spring of the year. It even appears on the horns of cattle. The only problem with that answer is, you can see the lights year-round."

In walked John Williams, the border patrol pilot, and Murphy Bennet, a local resident. A rainstorm came up suddenly, then turned into hail. As hailstones banged and echoed off of the tin roof of the hangar, the four of us sat and listened to John relate a story of a friend who had lost some fingers in a planer ("He stuck 'em in a planer, and it planed them") until we got back on the subject of the lights.

Fritz offered a last comment: "I still say the best way to see the lights is with a six-pack of beer and a good-looking woman. But if you still want to talk to someone else about the lights, you need to see this geologist who lives in town. He drives right up to them."

"I've seen those lights ever since I was a little kid," commented Murphy. "They got to be phosphorous. Can't be nothing else."

"You go see Pat Keeney," said Fritz, ignoring Murphy. "He'll tell you about the lights."

I took Fritz's advice.

"I've been around phosphate deposits before, and those are not phosphate," said Pat Keeney, a geologist for the Fort Worth–based Meeker Corporation. When he'd first come to Marfa to check on some oil leases, he had been told of the Marfa lights, and had been fascinated by them. He had then begun a one-man crusade to solve the mystery of their origin. The first thing he'd done was to test out all the popular explanations. Since a daytime check revealed no ranches in the area, the next possibility was car lights on the Presidio highway. Keeney was able to determine with topographic maps and surveying tools that there was one stretch of highway that was visible from the old air base. He located this strip of road with a surveyor's transit and marked the location, from beginning to end, with surveyor's stakes that had highway reflectors attached to them. He lined up three stakes, one behind the other, so as to sight down the tops of them and determine the start of the stretch of road. Then he marked the end the same way. With this arrangement, he was able to sit in a lawn chair at night and, with a flick of his flashlight, to sight the reflectors and determine whether a light in the desert was a car or a ghost light.

"I tried to get a fix on the ghost lights and triangulate on them to get their position so I could check it out," he said. "But I never got a good triangulation, because they are always moving."

Nevertheless, Keeney had a good idea of where the lights were located, and, with another geologist, Elwood Wright, he headed out a small ranch road for a closer look. About two miles down the road, they saw a pair of lights moving out on a flat at a high rate of speed.

"They looked like they were moving at about a hundred-fifty to two hundred miles per hour, but of course I had no way of measuring that. The lights spooked some horses, almost ran into them. Those horses started kicking and running through a cactus patch, trying to get away. The lights came to the edge of this road and stopped. "Several times I had seen lights around this old hangar they had on the air base. Well, one of these lights took off for that hangar, but the other one stayed there by the side of the road. It kept moving around a bush, kind of like it knew we were trying to get near it. It seemed to possess intelligence—it was like that thing was smarter than we were. It was making us feel pretty stupid. It was perfectly round, about the size of a cantaloupe, and it moved through that bush like it was looking for something. When the light stopped moving, it would get dimmer, but as it moved, it got brighter. Finally, it pulled out in the middle of the road about twenty yards from us and just hovered there.

"I had left the engine running, and Elwood said, 'Put it in gear and floorboard it. We'll run over it.' All of a sudden it got real bright and took off like a rocket. It was the damnedest thing I have ever seen. I still don't know what it was that we saw."

Since that close encounter, Pat Keeney has been out to the site of the spotting almost 74 times and has yet to see "them" up close again. Keeney was a spotter for the Navy during World War II, and he is familiar with almost every type of aircraft. He is not a man given to heavy drinking, and as a geologist, he has a very analytical mind. His story cannot be discounted.

On my first meeting with Keeney, it became readily apparent that we both shared the same zeal in trying to find an answer to a puzzle that had turned us into fanatics. Worst of all, none of the local residents seemed to care much about the lights. A typical answer was, "The lights are there, and people have tried to find out what they were before. No one has, and I don't care to waste any more of my time."

We were like inmates in an asylum built for two.

With the help of Pat's secretary, Charlie Rhodes, and her husband, Skip, we undertook a concentrated effort to solve the mystery and come up with some plausible answers. A quick comparison of our collection of newspaper articles and magazine features revealed that several writers had covered the subject but not a one had actually tried to solve the mystery himself. The writers had simply relied on interviews with people who had experienced a "close encounter."

The lights have been seen since the 1890s, when several early ranchers feared that they were the fires of renegade Indians. Several cowboys had attempted to ride up on the lights, all without success. Sul Ross State University, in Alpine, had tried to unravel the puzzle, and on one occasion had engineered a huge "dragnet," with cars linking the road, a party in a jeep, and an airplane, all coordinated with radio communication among the different search parties. The results were fruitless. The lights simply evaded them or disappeared when they tried to get close.

It became apparent to us that other expeditions had failed because of the size of the party involved, or because jeeps or vehicles with engines were used. We felt that two people on foot might "sneak up" on the lights without attracting attention.

It was determined that my brother, Miles, and myself would walk out in pursuit while the rest of the party waited on the ranch road. We would take a camera for a close-up shot (we had photographed the lights several times at a distance), and we would avoid using a flashlight so as not to scare our quarry.

With the aid of Pat's surveying gear, we got a rough fix on the lights, but it wasn't a good one, because, once again, they kept moving. In looking at a topographical map of the area, we determined them to be about two miles from the old airport.

"I just don't believe they're past the Presidio highway," Pat said. "They're probably two to four miles out on that flat, just before it drops off on the south rim, and not up in the Chinatis, like most people think."

Walking around the West Texas desert at night in the middle of summer is some people's idea of suicide; the rattlesnakes of the region like to come out in the cool of the evening after holing up during the day. Pat warned us to obtain some snake leggings. This seemed like good advice, but the only trouble was, none of the stores in the area carried any. Their reason?

"Nobody goes out at night around here. Too many snakes, young fellow."

We were forced to model our own leggings out of some large-diameter

PVC pipe. (We should have a patent on them in the near future, and we plan to sell them on late-night TV.) Looking and feeling more like R2-D2 and C-3PO than like ghost chasers, we suited up and headed out as darkness fell.

Skip and Charlie stayed behind. If they saw an SOS from our flashlights, they were to pick us up in the four-wheel-drive truck. We set out at about 10:00 that night. It wasn't the best of all possible nights to be hiking on the Marfa plains. There were flash flood warnings out, and a thick cloud cover shut out any light from the stars or moon, making it as dark as a sack of black cats. Worse, we had agreed that the flashlight would not be used except in case of emergency or to take a quick compass reading should we become lost. Upon walking just a few feet from the car, we were enveloped in darkness, causing me to imagine that we were actually Captain Kirk and Mr. Spock, set upon some deserted planet trying to make our way back to the Starship Enterprise.

The lights were out, though, and they almost seemed to know what we were trying to do. As if to taunt us, they began to put on a show. First, one would appear and increase in intensity, lighting up the landscape around us, then suddenly split into two lights of equal lumination. The split was not like an amoeba separating, but rather as if one light had been "hiding" behind the other, then suddenly rose up from behind it.

We pressed onward, but after four miles of hiking the lights did not appear to grow any closer than when we saw them from the old airport. But they did seem to be brighter. We had been gone for almost two hours and were beginning to get discouraged in our attempt to gain ground on them when suddenly Miles jumped back and I heard a flutter and whistle. It was a mourning dove that had been roosting on the ground. We chuckled over it and stopped to consider our next move.

Should we walk on to the south rim or go back? We decided to sit and watch for a few moments, then decide what to do. We noticed from our new vantage point that whereas we had seen the lights "go out" while watching them from the old airport, here they dipped down into draws instead, or dropped behind a bush, their glow giving away their location. A moment later, they would rise into view again. They were definitely moving. As we got up and prepared to hike on, they disappeared. They did not reappear during the next hour. Without light to follow, we had nothing to walk towards, so we deemed further hiking useless and turned back. Why go to the barn if somebody's already let the horses out?

Before leaving, I marked our progress with my cap, which I ceremoniously hung from the branch of a mesquite tree. We returned to the car about 2:00 A.M., bone-tired and disappointed. We looked out over the plains one last time. A light mist was falling, and no lights were visible. We were headed for town.

The following night, we returned, but this time Skip recommended that we bring along a spotting scope that he had at the house. He also brought a surveyor's tripod to mount it on, so that we could "lock in" the scope whenever a light appeared. Surely this would answer some of our questions.

We set up in our spot along the ranch road and waited for darkness.

Right on schedule, the lights began to appear. Miles looked through the scope but had trouble finding the light because of the scope's extreme magnification. After much jiggling and cursing, he finally found the light and immediately blurted out another expletive.

"It's got all kinds of colors!" he exclaimed.

I looked through the lens and sure enough, the light was glowing in varying colors of blue, red, green and gold! Skip took his turn.

"What does it look like to you?" I asked breathlessly.

"Car lights," he replied. "They look like car lights."

Surely he was mistaken. I grabbed the scope and looked again. My heart sank. He was right. A pair of headlights could clearly be seen winding down the road. We checked our surveyor's stakes and sure enough, the lights were in the area designated as the Presidio highway. But there was another light that appeared off of the highway, farther up, on a hill. We focused on it. It was so far away that it appeared as a white globe of light, pulsating and changing intensity constantly.

"Let's drive down the highway and look back in this direction," suggested Miles. We piled into the Blazer and took off, marking the spot by a ranch light that was just 500 feet from where we stood.

Upon our arrival on the Presidio highway, a glance back at our old position revealed the ranch light, but no "Marfa lights." However, we could see some other lights to the south of us, on the opposite side of the road. I was beginning to see why Fritz Kahl had given up the idea of pursuing the lights long ago. I was also beginning to see why the residents of Marfa were satisfied with the fact that the lights were there and that was all they needed to know about them.

So that leaves me here at my typewriter. I had intended to get good photos of the lights from close up so as to explain the mystery. I was able to accomplish only half of what I set out to do, but I still have a good story to tell.

My final conclusion is that the lights are there. You can see them on most any night, even through rain or cloudy skies. When you start asking me why the lights exist, you can have your pick of several explanations. I don't cotton to the explanations of static electricity or phosphorescent minerals, or that the lights are mirages. Some residents have tried to say that the lights are swamp gas, but Marfa, Texas, has not had a swamp in several million years. Some of the lights are car lights—but not all of them. Some have suggested that the lights are spirits of the dead, or "ghosts," and there is even a reference to this possibility in the Bible. In Matthew 12:42–43 it says that when a demon is cast out of a man it dwells in the "waterless places" or desert, depending on which translation you are reading. I have a hard time figuring out why spirits or demons would want to hang out in Marfa, Texas. I mean, they don't even have a Dairy Queen in Marfa.[1]

So this is where I'm left. I recounted earlier the attempts of other people to classify or capture the lights, all of them ending in frustration and empty answers. Whenever I read one of those stories, I'd always feel that the people were going about it the wrong way and that I could do a better job. I'm sure you're thinking to yourself as you read this that you could succeed where I and others have failed. Right?

That's just fine with me. Go ahead.

But don't say I didn't warn you to just forget it and stay home. The lights are there for you to see, but after 100 years of sightings and the attempts of even the best of expeditions, I suggest that when you visit Marfa you investigate its fine Mexican food instead. At least you can get your hands on it, and it contains no ingredient of the creepy, frightening or frustrating.

NOTE

1. There is a Dairy Queen in Marfa now.

CINNABAR
Kenneth Baxter Ragsdale
1976

DEEP IN THE BIG BEND OF TEXAS LIES A PLOT OF DRY, RUGGEDLY barren land known to geologists as the Terlingua Quicksilver District. Located some ninety miles south of Alpine, Texas, in close proximity to Mexico, the region possesses a greater geographic affinity to that country than it does to the remainder of the United States. Geologically a part of the trans-Pecos Texas, this is an area of arid, mountainous terrain, characterized by its rugged sierras, high plateaus, and gently sloping plains. The austere beauty of this strange land is delusive and holds many surprises for the newcomer. . . .

From an elevation of 4,500 feet in the Alpine area, the terrain gradually slopes south toward the Rio Grande. Beyond Adobe Walls Mountain the landscape changes abruptly and the smoothly contoured panorama is replaced by rugged, treeless, close-spaced mountains that give an impression of forbidding harshness. Here the thin-soiled, arroyo-scarred land is hardened by searing summer heat, scant rainfall, and high evaporation. This is Terlingua country, the geographic heart of the Big Bend of Texas.

Boundaries in the Big Bend are vague and fluid; it is variously a place, a state of mind, and at times an illusion. Paradoxical views reflect different tastes and different experiences. It is a heaven or a hell, a land of serene beauty or barren ugliness, a place of soothing solitude or haunting loneliness. . . .

Since this is an overpowering land, everyone who enters—if he plans to stay—involuntarily accepts the challenge of the environment. It is a tough land to settle, never changing. It is an unyielding land, giving up reluctantly whatever man, plant, or animal seeks from its crusty bosom. It is a defensive land, buttressed with steep mountain ranges, deep canyons, trackless deserts, and dry arroyos. It is a land of exaggerated dimensions. Searing summer heat occasionally pushes the mercury above the 120 degree Fahrenheit mark, distances seem interminable, and the inhabitants are few and solitary. Sometimes nature in the Big Bend reacts as if it had fallen behind schedule and is rushing to catch up. Thunderstorms appear with startling suddenness, emptying their entire contents within a few minutes. Such cloudbursts convert dry watercourses into raging torrents, and almost anything movable—trees, rocks, earth, and even man and beast—is crushed in its path. Departure is almost as sudden as arrival, and within a few hours the precious water is gone and the arroyos look as dry as usual. . . .

The Big Bend allows no winners; there are only survivors.

Such then is Terlingua country, the land the quicksilver prospectors found. Knowing little of its past they were unequipped to cope with the present. Those who compromised remained; those who did not were defeated and left. But the defeated are not part of this story. Those who accepted the challenge succumbed to a lifestyle circumscribed by a condition of scarcity in a land of isolation. Those two factors—scarcity and isolation—touched every facet of life in Terlingua and gave the quicksilver district its uniqueness and individuality.

Settlement came late to the Big Bend. By the time population had penetrated most other regions in the state, the area around Terlingua

Creek was still unknown, uninhabited wasteland. This was the legacy of the red man. The Apaches and Comanches maintained an effective barrier to settlement in the Mexican borderlands, and for over three centuries the Spaniards, and later the Americans, could gain no more than a tenuous hold on the lands along the Rio Grande.

The Spaniards failed because they challenged the region in a manner least likely to succeed. Motivated by an incongruous blend of religion, greed, and an illusionary belief in mythical kingdoms, they fanned out across the Southwest, but instead of colonists, the viceroy dispatched missionaries and soldiers to convert or subdue the savage tribes. They discovered too late, however, that the pacifist Indians along the Rio Grande could not comprehend a sophisticated religion nor adjust to a sedentary mission life. Instead, the hostile Indians, always a majority, held the balance of power and determined the course of Big Bend history almost until the twentieth century. . . .

Spanish settlement in the Big Bend never exceeded a token effort; it remained largely a region to be explored and crossed, rather than a place for permanent occupancy. During the nearly three centuries of Spanish awareness of the area, this policy changed little. Nor did Spain's exit in 1821 begin a new chapter in Big Bend history. It was still the land of the Apache, whose force went unchallenged. However, change was in the offing and two wars plus new ownership of the land north of the Rio Grande led to a new era of exploration and settlement. . . .

As the nineteenth century drew to a close, reports of a rare mineral discovery in the Terlingua area began to circulate in the Marfa-Alpine region of Texas. It was neither gold nor silver—popular subjects in the American West—as these reports mentioned a strange red formation called cinnabar from which quicksilver, or mercury, is extracted. The mood was one of interest rather than excitement. . . .

Quicksilver is many things to many people, and its multiple terminology used synonymously by the lay public is confusing. Properly stated, "mercury" is the technological term used by the chemist and pharmacist to identify one of the basic chemical elements; "quicksilver," on the other hand, designates the silver fluid metal as an item of commerce. Although both words apply to the same material, their application varies with different fields of endeavor. . . .

Facts concerning the discovery of cinnabar in the Terlingua area are so shrouded in legend and fabrication that it is impossible to cite the date and location of the first quicksilver recovery. Early inhabitants reported seeing aborigine pictographs executed with brilliant red pigment on the limestone cliffs and cave walls in the Terlingua Creek area. Although there is no record of these pictographic treatments ever having been chemically analyzed, students of the Plains Indians state that the aborigines used cinnabar for this purpose, as well as for personal adornment.

Although the region was remote, the native occupants along the Rio Grande were aware of the mineral deposit and had become curious about its worth. . . . This growing interest in minerals stimulated others to seek gold. Lock Campbell, a Big Bend settler, engaged a group of prospectors to search for the precious metal on the Mexican side of the Rio Grande, but, fearing Mexican bandits, they prospected the Texas side of the river instead and found cinnabar in the Terlingua area. Campbell reportedly scoffed at their "worthless" find and instructed them to continue their search for gold. . . .

In 1884 Juan Acosta, another Big Bend resident, brought a specimen of cinnabar to an Alpine merchant named Klein, who identified the ore and knew its potential worth. Klein negotiated an agreement with Acosta to develop the prospect, but before beginning operations they sold their claim to a group of Californians who began the first real mining operations in the Big Bend. They named the site of their claim "California Hill.". . .

Although the Acosta episode is well documented and represents the first discovery that resulted in quicksilver recovery, there was no "rush" to the Big Bend. More than a decade elapsed before the mining journals reported the event. . . .

From the beginning the name "Terlingua" identified the quicksilver producing area, and by 1904 developments in the Terlingua Quicksilver District were reported in the professional engineering and mining journals. "Terlingua" is a corruption of two words, *tres lenguas,* which in Spanish means "three tongues." Folklorists differ on the connotation of the word "tongues." Some believe it refers to the three languages spoken in that area: Indian, Spanish, English. Others maintain it is the three tongues, or forks, of Terlingua Creek. . . .

Surface outcroppings of the cinnabar deposit yielded the first recovery . . . "Nuggets" and "boulders" . . . were discovered, and the Excelsior Mine reported masses of almost pure cinnabar weighing several hundred pounds. . . .

In 1902 the mining methods employed were still primitive, and picks, shovels, hand drills, and sledges made up the usual complement of equipment. By August eighty feet marked the deepest penetration, and the operators employed a crude windlass to remove the ore. However, in shallower workings Mexican laborers surfaced the ore-bearing material in rawhide buckets attached to their backs. These vertical shafts were equipped with notched poles, which the natives negotiated with great agility.

Burro-drawn wagons or carts hauled the ore to the rectors where hand-sorting usually preceded the smelting process. Since widely fluctuating assays required different periods of smelting, sorting became increasingly important. During this early phase of development, Mexicans performed most of this work under Anglo supervision. Labor was fairly abundant at $0.90 to $1.25 per day.

As the operations grew more extensive and results yielded greater financial reward, the miners discovered the magnitude of their undertaking greatly increasing; however, their biggest obstacle still lay ahead. With the penetration of the deeper formations, especially the Del Rio clay, all work was conducted below water level. . . . When pumping and grouting techniques failed, the mine operators were faced with one of the most frustrating ironies of the Terlingua district: the constant lack of surface water necessary for human consumption, and the very present subsurface water that constantly threatened to inundate the rich cinnabar ore.

FOUR

Nature as Antagonist or Protagonist

SOMETIMES THE PLACE WHERE THE ACTION HAPPENS IS simply a background or stage for human drama. Sometimes it is used for "local color" or to impart an exotic flavor. But sometimes the place is also a character and influences the plot as much as any human: as healer, destroyer, political pawn, leveler, mystery, or spirit. The Big Bend country is often cast in the role of antagonist. A description of this natural "den of thieves" from a "D" Western novel by Ben Haas, writing under the pseudonym of Richard Meade, is typical of the way the landscape actually plays a villainous part in the action by thwarting the law bringers. Meade's hero doubts that the posse can "flush the thieves out of the deep Big Bend," a big unexplored place with "probably not fifty honest inhabitants in the whole huge region." The first hint to the reader that the hero has decided to join the posse and head into the "great loop of the Rio Grande" is when he, of course, buckles on his gun. The Big Bend is still a favorite setting for modern detective novel writers because it seems to be such a good place to hide both clues and murderers.

An anonymous article found in an old magazine, *Voice of the Mexican Border,* once published in the Big Bend, casts the Rio Grande as the romantic male lead, tracing him from his birth in the Colorado mountains, to his death in the Gulf of Mexico. Along the way, the river weds the female romantic lead, played by the Río Conchos, and both become less and less pure and carefree, and more and more corrupt, violent, and dangerous, as they travel on. The article was probably authored by the magazine's founder-editor, Alice "Jack" Shipman.[1] In another positive role, William Langewiesche characterizes the U.S. Boundary Commission as antagonist and the Rio Grande as strong, patient protagonist, gradually winning the war that was being waged against it by the commission. A local Big Bend resident tells the author that the river is not a ditch and it will not behave like one.

Writing in 1850, John R. Bartlett casts the "treacherous" Pecos River, the "dreary" Trans-Pecos country, the "tortuous" roads, and the "dreaded" weather as nonfiction antagonists.[2] They provide obstacles and frustration, sapping strength from human and animal alike, placing them all in constant danger of starvation or thirst—and apparently causing extreme stupidity in his horses and mules, who constantly seem to be falling down river banks. Although one may read statements like "As hard as it may be for people to believe, the area around the Pecos river was once covered in grass,"[3] Bartlett found the soil in 1850 already heavily impregnated with salt, making production of the "miserable grass" almost impossible.

Probably the most common antagonists appearing in nature writing are predators and their hunters. The Big Bend has an abundance of both. The most demonized of all was the wolf, or lobo, as it was known in Far West Texas. The last wolf killed in Texas served as mascot for Sul Ross State University's Lobos. The female wolf was poisoned in her pen on the campus in Alpine. Some students were up in arms wondering who could have performed such a cruel deed; others thought it an act of mercy, as they had watched "Miss Sully" grow more and more vicious as her time behind bars increased. Pacing, pacing, pacing the cement floor of a small wire cage was no life for a lady lobo.

Writing in 1908, O. W. Wiliams, in this second excerpt from his work, compares the lobo to a heavy tax and says it would take a "very high powered magnifying glass" to find any redeemable qualities in the "beast." Since bison seldom ever crossed the Pecos River headed west, Williams favors the theory that the wolf came into the Big Bend after dependable water wells were drilled, which in turn made large herds of livestock possible, thereby finally providing a prey base big enough to support wolves. Although rain did not always follow the plow, as promised by early boosters, the wolf always seemed to follow the windmill. Interestingly, Williams says West Texas cattlemen usually did not kill the lobo, but rather drove it away to prey upon their neighbors. Animals have always played a mysterious role in the human psyche, and animal stories, as in the story of Little Red Riding Hood, operate at a subconscious level. Some animals, especially the wolf, represent more than just an animal both to their so-called friends and their so-called enemies.

Roy T. McBride, one of the nation's most highly respected predator hunters and a long-time resident of the Big Bend, describes his pursuit of one of the last of the legendary wolves. His story about catching a lobo named "Las Margaritas" in about 1970 first appeared in a technical bulletin written by McBride for the U.S. Fish and Wildlife Service in 1980. This story generated such instant interest that it has since reappeared under the bylines of numerous well-known writers such as David E. Brown, Cormac McCarthy, and Edward Hoagland.[4] Brown hardly changes a word from

McBride's original version; McCarthy dumbs down McBride's trapping method of using fire to disguise the set trap; and working from his own notes rather than from a published version, Hoagland, misunderstanding Spanish, writes that hunters thought "Las Margaritas" was a female. Actually, the male wolf was named after the Mexican ranch known as Las Margaritas (plural, and translated as "the daisies") where the wolf was first trapped and lost two toes. With regard to McBride's story, I make no judgments about which character is the protagonist and which is the antagonist; I simply admire the arts of capture and evasion displayed in the dance between these two characters, who are masters at reading each other's signs and symbols. Even modern academic thinkers are reevaluating the ancient art of reading sign, saying that the ability to do so may reintroduce humans to the natural world from which they think they have been expelled.

Recently, scholar David Abram has shed some light on this subject with his sophisticated academic argument supporting the importance of being able to read sign in his book *The Spell of the Sensuous* (1996). He treats with great respect the kind of knowledge that people who live or work close to nature accumulate through their senses, saying, "In indigenous, oral cultures, nature itself is articulate; it *speaks*." He compares the marks that trackers who can read sign *see* on the land to what we readers now *see* on the page: "As nonhuman animals, plants, and even 'inanimate' rivers once spoke to our tribal ancestors, so the 'inert' letters on the page now speak to us! This is a form of animism that we take for granted, but it is animism nonetheless—as mysterious as a talking stone."[5]

A. Ray Williams justifies his work as an eagle killer by describing the golden eagle's toll on antelope fawns and bighorn lambs as well as domestic livestock. He explains that hunting them gives him a "great life if you don't weaken."[6]

Two more common villains in American nature writing are agriculture and chemicals. In "Poison, Poison" Frederick R. Gehlback describes the apocalyptic spread of pesticides from Presidio farms into the desert via remolinos (dust devils), lizards, and rabbits. Interestingly, he finds also that national park campers armed with bug bombs can wreak the same havoc on an ecosystem.

Even plants can be cast in the role of antagonist or protagonist and the marvelous maligned mesquite can play both roles. Called "the devil with roots" by cattlemen who claim it drinks more water than any other tree, the mesquite is described by Keith Elliott as a favorite wood for barbecuing, a nitrogen fixer for soil, a cure-all for curanderos, an inspiration for Texas artists, and a favorite wood of wood-carvers.

Finally, Lisa Beaumont identifies with fall tree leaves, as both she and the leaves respond with perceived defiance to their mutual nemesis, old man winter, who usually represents the ultimate antagonist.

NOTES

1. Shipman edited the magazine from 1933 to 1938. She was the daughter of Captain Pat Dolan, a former Texas Ranger.

2. Bartlett wrote of his explorations in West Texas while he was connected with the U.S. and Mexico Boundary Commission.

3. Quoted in a book review in *Big Bend Quarterly* (Spring 1997), 5.

4. Edward Hoagland, *Red Wolves and Black Bears* (Penguin, 1976); David E. Brown, *The Wolf in the Southwest* (U. of Arizona, 1983); Cormac McCarthy, *The Crossing* (Vintage, 1995).

5. David Abram, *The Spell of the Sensuous: Perception and Language in a More-Than-Human World* (New York: Vintage, 1996), 25, 116, 131.

6. A. Ray Williams was a game warden for the Game, Fish, and Wildlife Commission of Texas. In the 1930s he had been instructed to reduce the number of golden eagles and other predatory animals in the Trans-Pecos in order to increase deer and antelope populations. In 1941 golden eagles were removed from the protected list of game birds, making it legal to hunt them by plane. Most of the air hunting was done by Williams and John O. "Cas" Casparis of Alpine.

DEN OF THIEVES
Richard Meade (Ben Haas)
1968

RAMSEY LED THE ANIMAL TO A CORRAL THAT CONTAINED THREE other horses, unsaddled it, wiped it down with a gunny sack, and turned it loose to drink and roll. Leaning on a fence post, he watched the animal flop down, try twice, then go over on the third roll, grunting with the ecstasy of it. But Ramsey was not thinking of the horse.

Maybe not joining the posse had been a mistake. That might have been the one gesture that would have healed all the old wounds, finally bridged the gap between himself and the town. But Denning had thrown it at him too fast; there'd been no time to think, and his first reaction had been to draw back, as he always did. Yes, there was no doubt that it was a mistake, even though going would have jeopardized the work of three months. . . .

The sun slanted low, gilding the sides of hills, buttes, and mesas, painting purple shadows in draws and hollows, touching the sea of good grass with gold.

He could understand the way Denning felt. Revolution flamed and guttered on the other side of the Rio Grande. First, Madero against Díaz, then Huerta against Madero, and now Carranza and the famed Pancho

Villa against Huerta. Almost four years of constant warfare, with Villa dominating, always up to his ears in revolution and counterrevolution alike. And now the northern border of Mexico had been picked clean, and the armies and bandit gangs and combination of both that roved Chihuahua and Coahuila would pay dearly for gringo beef—and, Ramsey thought grimly, gringo horses.

So rustling had become worth the risk again. In Texas the land had filled up and the cattlemen were strongly organized, and selling stolen beef north of the Rio had become so dangerous that cow-thieves were almost something out of the past. But they could not resist the safe and lucrative markets the armies below the Rio provided, and Southwest Texas was beginning to feel the effects of the waves of violence that lapped northward. There was no doubt that Denning and the others were hurting. A fat whiteface on the hoof was about the equivalent of a poke of gold.

Still, he doubted that they could flush the thieves out of the deep Big Bend. Down there, at the southernmost point of the great loop of the Rio Grande that gave the country its name, there were thousands of square miles of uninhabited desert, stark mountain ranges, some never totally explored, and probably not fifty honest inhabitants in the whole huge region. Denning was undoubtedly right—that was where the stolen cattle were going. But finding a gang of twenty or thirty throwbacks to the old wild days down there was a difficult matter—especially since they could jump the border at the first sign of pursuit. . . . Still, Denning was a veteran of the old days himself; if anybody could do it, he could.

The light had faded now, and Ramsey went back into the house. In the tiny kitchen, he cooked bacon and heated refried beans and opened another can of beer and sat down to his solitary meal. He was still nagged by his decision not to go.

And yet, he'd had no alternative. He raised Morgans here, the best, and trained them himself into the finest cow and cutting horses. It was a small operation, but a profitable one, and he didn't dare leave it for more than a day at a time. Not even Denning's offer to send men to run it while he was gone changed that. Nobody handled horses the way he did, and in two weeks ignorant men could ruin them all.

Finishing his meal, he washed up and stowed everything as carefully as any old maid. Then he stripped and took a quick shower under a homemade rig outdoors beside the windmill. Putting on clean underwear, he set the alarm clock, got into bed, read by the light of a kerosene lamp for a half hour, blew out the lamp, and went quickly to sleep. Not long before midnight, the clock awakened him. He arose, splashed water on his face, drank two cups of strong coffee, and dressed.

After he'd buckled his chaps, he took a gun belt from the wall and strapped it on. In the holster was a .45 Colt single-action inherited from his father.

SAVAGE AND SUCCESSFUL
Alice "Jack" Shipman
1933

LET US IMAGINE THE RIO GRANDE AS A SENTIENT BEING—IMAGINE him as a strong man of the hills and desert country and travel with him from the place of his birth to his successful termination.[1] The birth of this lusty youth takes place in that great amphitheatre of the San Juan Mountains in southern Colorado. What splendid parents this child river has. They thrust their mighty heads twelve to fourteen thousand feet into the blue skies and catch the rain and snow, which gives life to their son, who is to become a national and international figure.

Approaching the birth place of this famous child river, one's imagination is fired with noble thoughts and the soul is filled with ecstasy that comes from intimate association with living waters at their sources. Majestically, the aristocratic parents carry on the tradition of the mighty Rockies, proud of their lineage, the Continental Divide. And, too, they feel their son of perfect birth will be a famous character in the western United States.

Lustily the youth capers and cascades from his parent's laps, running with snow white purity past fantastically weird rock formations, which are called the Rio Grande Pyramids. Entering a lake, he pauses a while in order to be a bigger and stronger boy. Like all restless youth, he soon leaps over all bounds and is on his way.

He espies an opening over there in the family chain, Wagon Wheel Gap. Away he races from the arms of his parents to seek adventure out in the big world. Perils await him, as is true of all youth.

The parents look after him longingly and weep, but they, like all wise parents, know they cannot live his life for him. They cannot follow along with him, and know that he must experience good and bad. Their prayer is that he will some way make his way through the problems that are part of every river's life.

As he passes through Wagon Wheel Gap, Rio Grande sees, stretching before him, a very large valley entirely surrounded by mountains, two million acres of rich alluvial land known as the San Louis Valley. Playing happily along this beautiful valley the youth is happy and carefree and without serious thoughts. Then the night wind tells him of high adventure to be found farther south. Again he is on the flow. Leaving his native state Colorado, he crosses the line into the state of New Mexico.

Having arrived at full maturity with all the sweetness and charm of clean youth, evil-minded men and women set to work to destroy that cleanliness that they have irretrievably lost. Where he had seen only good, they pointed out evil. They invited him to join them in seeing the world, and he joined them in riotous living. His path twisted and turned, and his youthful clearness vanished. His life stream became a muddy river, filled with rubble and rocks. He gained strength and started sweeping aside foes, cutting canyons through every mountain of difficulty. He was no longer happy and cheerful. He was equipped for all battles, but gone was his peace of mind.

Up to this time Rio Grande had dealt with his own kind. Then came primitive man. As time passed primitive man learned the art of irrigation, and attempted to divert water from the life stream of Rio Grande to irrigate his little fields. Growing impatient every so often at these minor interferences, the Old Man River would go on a rampage, sweeping men and farms into oblivion.

Passing the Elephant Butte with a rush and a roar, Rio Grande told the Elephant of stone he would cut through the mountains south of him. Accomplishing this task, he dashed on to form the boundary line between the United States and Mexico, and having done this he assumed grave responsibility, becoming an international figure.

Rio Grande, the bold buccaneer, slides through the Paso del Norte, cutting an erratic course on first one side of the El Paso valley and then the other. On his south bank, the Sierra Ventana mountain range holds him in line. Then, when he would turn north, the Quitman Mountains on his north bank send the Pirate of the Desert on his way to Ojo Caliente. Just south of this point he slashes his way through a mountain, making a boxlike canyon suitable for a dam site. Hemmed in on the south by the Sierra del Pinos and on the north by the Eagle Mountains, he heads on to Presidio del Norte, where he meets and weds that beautiful senorita Rio Conchos. The love of the Conchos is consistent and faithful. Enriched and strengthened by this union, the Rio Grande forces his way through the Big Bend proper.

This was the greatest campaign of his long list of battles and he left behind a scarred battlefield.

Unrelenting, he attacked Santa Helena Mountain and sawed it asunder for a distance of eight miles, in places cutting to a depth of two thousand feet.

The Mariscal Range had the temerity to stand in the way and received a deadly blow from the Dusky Giant River, and another inspiring canyon was made. Finishing the task, the Rio Grande was blocked by the Boquillas, a portion of the Mexican del Carmen Range. Hitting this mighty mass of earth and stone with his dauntless courage, Rio Bravo carved the Boquillas to the very base. Emerging from this encounter victorious, he discovered more than a hundred miles of mountains behind mountains standing in his way.

He mustered all his forces and charged these enemies, first cutting a canyon forty-eight miles long, which is Patricia. Pausing for a short time, he then set siege to another mountain enemy and won an outstanding victory. He advanced his battle front eighty-nine miles.

While the Rio Grande had been winning all these battles, another important river, the Pecos, had come into being in the mountains of New Mexico. The Pecos had cut a course south until he joined forces with the Rio Grande at the end of the eighty-nine-mile canyon, and they went through the coastal plain with little effort.

For more than two thousand miles the Savage Rio Grande had won his way and at last led his water army in triumph to the Gulf of Mexico, Master Spoilsman of them all.

NOTE

1. Shipman was the editor-publisher of *The Voice of the Mexican Border,* from which this article is excerpted. I assume she was the author, since no author is listed for this article.

THE RIVER IS NOT A DITCH
William Langewiesche
1993

"I TOLD HER, I'M GOING TO SERVE INDIA BY STAYING OUT OF INDIA."

I interrupted him. "Doesn't it seem odd, if you think back, to find yourself managing this boundary?" I gestured toward the crowd.

He looked annoyed. "In the United States I have always tried to participate in the workings of government. I served on the Las Cruces City Council. Now I serve as commissioner. I am happy such an honor has been bestowed upon my family. A nation needs its boundaries, no?"

I nodded yes. You need a *them* to have an *us.*

We drove downriver to the Free Bridge, so called because no tolls are charged. The Free Bridge belongs to the boundary commission. It spans the Rio Grande at a patch of riverland named the Chamizal, after the desert grass *chamizo* that once grew there. The Chamizal is Mexican territory that was lopped off and delivered to the United States in 1864 by a southward shift of the river. This event kicked off a century of squabbling. The remedy, finally agreed upon in 1963, was radical surgery: 4.3 miles of new concrete riverbed were laid and the Free Bridge was built. On December 13, 1968, Lyndon Johnson came to town, met Mexican President Díaz Ordaz at the border, and diverted the Rio Grande into its new course. Mexico walked away with a net gain of 437.18 acres. On the U.S. side, Johnson has still not been forgiven. The problem is, one nation's gain is another's loss. And the boundary commission is guilty by association.

I learned this within minutes of landing at the El Paso airport, having mentioned to a pilot that I had come to visit the commission. "Those sons-a-bitches," he said. "They're the ones who gave away Texas."

He assumed I shared his sentiment, since I, too, had lived in Texas and had flown the border as an air-taxi pilot. He was less open-minded about Gunaji, whom he had seen on television. He said, "Who the hell is that guy? I can't even understand when he speaks English."

It was not a good week for Gunaji. We stood in the shade of the Free Bridge and watched workmen drilling into the concrete. The bridge was rotting. It was built by the Mexicans, of substandard materials, long before Gunaji's time, but it was his problem now. He had ordered emergency shoring. Yesterday he had banned the truckers who haul cargo to and from the *maquiladoras,* the big American assembly plants in Juárez. Hundreds of these drivers make short runs across the border with Mexican rigs loaded to 100,000 pounds. The Free Bridge is their cheapest and most convenient route. Gunaji had forced them twenty miles downriver to the toll bridge at Zaragosa. People were outraged because, after all, the Free Bridge had not yet collapsed. The American managers of the *maquiladoras* threatened to go to Washington over Gunaji's head. There was talk of a conspiracy and corruption. There was talk of violence. Now Gunaji stood under the bridge with his arms folded, looking alone and defiant. Watching him, I thought I understood the severity of his mood. He was an engineer trying to do his job. Other boundary engineers have certainly been allowed to do theirs.

The remaking of the Rio Grande at the Chamizal was not the first operation of its kind. In the 1930s the boundary commission rectified the river downstream from El Paso. Rectified means this: the meanders were cut off, the river was straightened and run between levees, and the length of the boundary from El Paso to Fort Quitman was shortened from 155 to 86 miles. The two countries exchanged 6,920 acres of land in equal amounts, and none of Texas was lost. Here and there the commission has rectified the Rio Grande all the way to the Gulf of Mexico.

But rivers make old-fashioned, troublesome boundaries. One problem lies beyond Fort Quitman, where the rectification ends and the Rio Grande resumes its natural course between faulted mountains. For 193 miles downriver, past Candelaria to the confluence of the Conchos, the Rio Grande braids through jungles of salt cedar. Salt cedar is not a native plant. It is a bush or small tree, a tamarisk brought to North America from the Mediterranean in 1852, sold in California as an ornamental, and planted in New Mexico to control erosion. By the end of the century it had infested riverbanks through the desert and beyond. It is estimated now that 1.5 million acres of salt cedar grow in the American West. The seeds drift in the wind, and when they land on moist sand, they plunge taproots thirty feet deep into the permanent water that lies below riverbeds. The taproots make salt cedar resistant to drought and flood, the on-again, off-again condition of desert rivers, and allow the plant to dominate the less robust native species. The domination is not all bad: salt cedar provides an ideal habitat for birds and other creatures. However, by clogging established channels, it also forces floodwaters to spread farther and encourages rivers to braid. Braiding is the untidy process by which a current laden with sand and silt relentlessly builds bars, then divides around them. It is a particular problem on the Rio Grande because it makes the location of the channel, and therefore the boundary, impossible to establish. The imprecision bothers surveyors, if not the residents.

In the 1970s the commission decided on an engineering solution: for these 198 miles the river would be made to follow the boundary. The two countries agreed. The commission filed environmental impact statements, compromised with conservationists, promised to "enhance wildlife," and in 1980 unleashed the bulldozers. The work continues today, shared by the two countries. The channel is being "restored" to an angled cross-section six feet deep, sixteen feet wide at the bottom, and thirty-eight feet wide at the top. A V-shape is the most efficient design because it minimizes evaporation and encourages the scouring action of a fast, smooth flow. Floodways fifty-six feet wide are being scraped through the salt cedar along both banks.

Nellie Howard, the old sister in the Candelaria store, was not impressed. She said, "When they channelized the Rio Grande, they forgot it was a river and tried to give us a ditch. Come the first rain, the water went everywhere." Soon after work was completed in Candelaria, thunderstorms burst on the mountains and filled the creek beds with torrents for two days. The Rio Grande went wild and returned nearly to its natural state. Nellie Howard smiled and said, "Those engineers came down here pretending to know everything. We tried to tell them, but they wouldn't listen. The river reminded them who's really in charge."

Gunaji himself must wonder. One warm spring day I accompanied him on a working tour of the banks downriver from Candelaria. Our guide was the boundary commission's local engineer, a burly man named John. He drove us in a Ford Bronco along a recently repaired dike, past fields of blue wildflowers. Gunaji was in another of his expansive moods and sat with his arm over the seat back. He said, "What are those flowers, John?"

"Weeds, Commissioner."

"They may be weeds, John, but they bring color to the country, John."

"Yessir, Commissioner."

Later Gunaji seemed to remember his mission. He turned to me with a frown and said, "You see all this vegetation? We need to mitigate this vegetation."

I asked why.

He said, "It impedes the water."

And the water impedes the boundary commission. The project is years behind schedule. There have been difficulties with earth-moving equipment and international coordination. Floods have washed away the floodways. And salt cedar, which can grow nine feet in a year, spreads as fast as it can be cleared. From the air the river looks like it has always looked. The conservationists must be pleased. They agreed to a compromise, but this is better because the river itself is fighting back.

The engineers, however, show no signs of fatigue. They are armed with a 1970 treaty that resolved all pending boundary disputes, reaffirmed the channel as the dividing line, and forbade any further misbehavior by the water.

HORSE-HEAD CROSSING TO DELAWARE CREEK
John R. Bartlett
1850

OCTOBER 30TH, 1850. AFTER OUR FATIGUING MARCH OF TWO DAYS and one night without rest, we slept pretty late this morning; even the expectation of a fine beefsteak for breakfast could hardly induce either officers or men to turn out. After breakfast, I examined the river with a view of crossing, intending to devote the day to it, and recruit our tired animals. Found the water at the Horse-head Crossing, which was a quarter of a mile from our encampment, to afford the greatest facilities. Here there was a bank about a half the height of the main bank, to which there was an easy descent, and one equally so to the water. It is the place where other parties seem to have crossed, and hence rendered easy access. I noticed a long line of horse or mule skulls placed along the bank, which probably gave it the name it bears.

On sounding the river to ascertain its depth, we found that our ambulances (i.e., wagons mounted on springs) would pass over without wetting their contents. We therefore unloaded all the wagons but those on springs, and placing their contents in the latter, we succeeded in passing all our provisions, baggage, etc., over with but little trouble. The west bank was leveled with our spades, to make the ascent from the water easy. I remained with Dr. Webb and Mr. Thurber until all were over, except one empty wagon. This being quite low, its box would be partly immersed in the water; an ambulance was accordingly sent back for us, and for the contents of my carriage. We entered the stream, which just touched the bottom of the ambulance, but not without some fears, as experience had shown that the best and most gentle mules cannot always be depended upon. When we had reached about two thirds the distance across or some thirty feet from the opposite bank, the mules either lost their footing, or were swept by the current into deeper water, a little out of the course taken by those which passed over before. Unable to contend against the force of the water, which was almost level with their backs, the leaders turned their heads down stream. The teamster, who was mounted as usual on one of the mules next to the wagon, endeavored in vain to bring them to their places with their heads toward the shore. The frightened creatures could not maintain their footing; and in struggling to extricate themselves, they extended their alarm to the other mules, who began to rear and prance in the water. Just at this moment the last wagon, which had been behind, attempted to pass us, the driver thinking the other mules would follow his team; but in the attempt, the current swept his wagon, which was half buried in the water, against ours. This brought his mules nearly abreast of mine, and led to greater confusion and alarm. Every moment we expected to be swept away; in which case our lives would have been in great danger, as it would have been no easy matter to extricate ourselves from the closed wagon. I could do nothing but call for assistance from the party on the opposite bank, who stood watching our progress and critical situation with breathless suspense. Mr. Clement Young, seizing the end of a picket rope which lay on the bank, sprang into the river without stopping to divest himself of his clothing, and came to our relief. With great difficulty he succeeded in attaching the rope to the leading mules. Several other gentlemen mounted their horses and sprang into the water at the same time, some to urge the mules towards the shore, and others to extricate the two wagons. The picket rope was now seized by those on the bank, who, pulling with all their strength, brought the heads of the leading mules towards it. The teamsters then putting on the lash, and the horsemen in the water urging our animals forward, they relieved us from our perilous situation, and we gained the bank in safety.

My carriage was now brought over by lashing beneath it a few empty kegs, with two men in the water to keep it steady. A rope was taken ahead, by means of which the men on the opposite bank drew it safely across. We now pitched our tents, corralled the wagons, and, after a hearty supper, turned in for the night.

October 31st. Struck tents and left camp at 7 o'clock following a north-westerly direction, keeping near the Pecos, the course of which we could occasionally trace by the rushes which grew on its banks. The country continues exceedingly barren and destitute of trees or shrubs, except the thorny chaparral which generally grows on desert spots. A short grass appears here and there, but is now completely dried up, affording but little nourishment to the animals. Beautiful yuccas were seen in many places, seeming to thrive in the barren soil. Our constant companion, the prickly pear, with other varieties of the cactus family, were content, too, to flourish in these dreary abodes.

The only living creatures seen today were a few blackbirds sitting on the mezquit bushes, so near the road that one might have struck them with a cane, and a herd of antelopes. The latter bounded before us, and were lost to view before our hunters could surround them. The ground beneath us seemed to afford habitations for various burrowing animals, judging from the numerous holes seen by the road side; but we had no time or means to discover what they were. I presume, however, that they were the habitations of ground rats and mice, coyotes, polecats, moles, rabbits, rattlesnakes, tarantulas, and other reptiles. As there are no rocky ledges, no thick bushes, or decayed logs or stumps in which these animals can burrow, they must resort to the earth; hence the vast number of holes which are seen in all such barren and desolate regions. Every animal here named I have myself seen, at various times, enter or make its exit from subterranean abodes.

After some difficulty we found a spot near the river which afforded tolerable grazing for the animals, where we stopped, pitched our tents, and formed our corral. The banks of the river being high and precipitous, it was with difficulty that we watered our animals. One of the horses, in his eagerness to reach the stream, fell over the bank, and was extricated only by the great exertions of the party. A mule, which had exhibited symptoms of illness for several days, gave out today and was abandoned. It was a serious loss to us, for we had already lost four; although the weight of our provisions was daily growing less, the weakness of the animals increased still faster, from their long journeys and insufficiency of food. The mercury stood at noon today at 82 degrees Fahrenheit.

November 1st. Determined to make an early start this morning, for which purpose the camp was called at four o'clock. Got breakfast and were off at daylight. A little rain fell during the night. The wind was north; but the weather was warm, and our fears of a "norther," so much dreaded by all prairie travelers, subsided with the appearance of a bright sun.

Our march today has been through a region as barren and desolate as that of yesterday. Continued near the river, avoiding its windings. Noticed large spots covered with a saline efflorescence; in fact, on examination, the whole earth seemed impregnated with it. The water of the Pecos, which here is quite brackish, doubtless derives this flavor from the soil through which it passes. Patches of dry grass and stunted mezquit constitute the chief vegetation. Yuccas and cacti are thinly scattered over the plain; the former, sometimes appearing in groups, seemed like bodies of men; and many were ready to see an Indian in every resemblance to them which our journey afforded. Passed the carcasses of five oxen lying about the road; from which we concluded that they had belonged to some emigrant train, and had dropped down from exhaustion, and perished where they fell. Their lank bodies were dried up with the skins still adhering to them, showing that even wolves do not attempt to find subsistence on this desolate plain. The remains of wagons were also seen along the road, and furnished our cook with firewood, an article which he had had much difficulty in procuring since leaving the Concho River, and particularly since we struck the region near the Pecos. Small brushwood and the roots of mezquit bushes had been our resort for firewood for several days. Perhaps it was well for us that we had no fine joints of meat or steaks to cook, with such fuel; but to fry a bit of pork, to boil some beans, and make coffee, which constituted our chief cooking, a little dry brush answered very well.

We had another windfall today in meeting with two oxen, which were pursued and taken. They proved rather lean; nevertheless they were an important addition to our stock of provisions. Took only their hind quarters, which would last as long as they could be preserved. Meat may be kept in this region by cutting it into strips and drying it in the sun; but we had not time to do this.

Stopped to water, and to our surprise found a beautiful fall in the river, eight or ten feet in height. It flowed between high banks of clay, resting on a base of conglomerate, over which it dashed with a life and beauty which contrasted pleasantly with its usual dark and treacherous flow. The banks near the fall are high and perpendicular, and exposed many thin strata of various brightly colored deposits of sand and marl, presenting a singularly beautiful ribbon-like appearance. A small island or rock, overgrown with rushes, divided the fall. On tasting the water, it was found to be less brackish than at the Crossing. This fall is not noticed on the maps of the country. Passed a stray mule, which, looking plump and strong, I felt desirous to transfer to our wagons. Two or three men went in pursuit of him with lariats; but he out stripped them all, and disappeared in the chaparral. At four o'clock, stopped on the bank of the river, near a rapid, where we found the water accessible, and excellent grass for our animals.

Finding our stock of provisions was fast diminishing, I ordered an account taken of them. There proved to be but three hundred and sixty pounds of hard bread, or about ten pounds for each man, which was accordingly divided in this proportion among all. With the usual allowance of a pound a day for each, there was bread enough for ten days. As we could hardly expect to reach El Paso within that time, each man could govern himself accordingly, and save as much as possible for an emergency. But scanty as was our stock, it was unfit to be eaten, being completely riddled with weevils. Hundreds of these insects were found in a single biscuit. To remove them was out of the question; and there was no alternative but to shut the eyes and munch away. Of salt pork there was about a half allowance for ten days. The coffee and sugar was all gone.

November 2nd. Our route kept on in a westerly course, near the river, which we occasionally distinguished on our right by the rushes and other plants peculiar to salt marshes, which grew upon its banks. The same barrenness continues, with scarcely a living object. A few blackbirds and sparrows are all that have been seen. Passed five more dried carcasses of oxen lying by the road. Fell in with a cow. She could not, however, consent to be driven with the train, when she was tied behind the wagon; but so furious did she become at being deprived of her liberty, that it was found necessary to shoot her. The calf was then followed a mile or more, and shared the same fate. Both proved very fat, and a most welcome addition to our supply of food in its diminished state. Passed several depressions near the river, which appeared to have been filled with water. A white efflorescence on their surface showed the extent of the saline matter with which the soil was impregnated. Crossed an arroyo or dry bed of a stream, covered with the salty incrustations before alluded to, which we took to be "Toyah Creek" of the maps. At four o'clock, encamped on the margin of the Pecos, about two miles from the creek. The shrubbery today exhibits a larger growth than any we have seen since we crossed the river.

November 3rd, Sunday. I was desirous to rest today; and had we been any where except on the banks of the Pecos, I certainly would have done so. But a due regard for our safety rendered it necessary that we should not stop until beyond its waters and the miserable barren region near it. Should a rain set in, it would make the roads almost impassable for loaded wagons, so tenacious is the soil. The grass, too, but barely sustained life in our worn-out animals. We saw around us evidence of what the road would be in wet weather. Some teams seemed to have passed over it at such a time, leaving ruts six inches deep in the soft muddy soil. Every day we noticed the clouds with fear and trembling, and watched each change in the weather. The roads are now hard and smooth, and have been so since we struck the river.

Our route has been over the same flat and desert plain before described. Not a living thing has crossed our path, beast, bird, or reptile, except two large white swans, which were doubtless winging their way to more attractive regions. They lit on a marshy place, which I endeavored to approach; but even in this out of the way spot, which the human foot seldom treads, they flew at my approach. Scattering patches of dried grass, with low chaparral, and an occasional yucca, constituted the vegetation of the twenty-two miles passed over today. In order to find a good spot for our encampment, two or three of the party diverged from the road, and succeeded in discovering a little nook on the river's bank, where there was good grass. Several hours before stopping, we got a glimpse of the Guadalupe Mountains, and a range of hills through which we must pass, although more than 100 miles off in a direct line, in a northwesterly direction. Mounts Diablo and Carrizo, which had been visible to the westward, seventy or eighty miles distant, since crossing the Pecos, today were lost to our view.

Passed the carcasses of four cattle by the roadside; and in another place, where there was a slight depression in the plain, and where water had at some time accumulated after rains, there lay the carcass of five more, which had doubtless mired in endeavoring to satiate their thirst. Portions of wagons, boxes, and barrels were also noticed along the road.

November 4th. Still journeying along the river. Barren plains continue, with fewer mezquit than before. Dried grass and weeds prevail. Many carcasses and skeletons of oxen, and several skeletons of mules, marked our route today, as well as the remains of broken wagons. As the prairie did not furnish us fuel to make our fires, we gathered up the fragments of the wagons and carried them with us for the purpose. Noticed along the road recent tracks of Indians, horses, and mules; or, in the language of the country, "Indian sign." The tracks of the animals showed that they were unshod, which would not have been the case if it had been an American party. Next we observed prints of moccasins, which are easily distinguished from the American shoe, or from the sandal or moccasin of the Mexicans. Then the freshness of the foot-prints and of the dung, showed that the party could not have preceded us more than a few hours. In this belief we were strengthened by seeing large fires some fifteen or twenty miles off on the prairie, early in the evening.

Much sagacity is shown by experienced hunters and frontier men in detecting "signs" on the prairie, when and by whom made, the strength of the parties, their direction, etc., whether Indians, Mexicans, or Americans. So with the places where there have been encampments. These the wary traveler on the prairie inspects with care, to see whether friend or enemy has preceded him. If Indians, he will find poles from their wigwams, fragments of skins, scraps of leather ties, beads, etc.; and a little experience will enable him to distinguish the tribe, whether Comanches, Lipans, or Apaches. The principal characteristic, I believe, is the form of their wigwams. One sets up erect poles, another bends them over in a circular form, and the third gives them a low oval shape. There is also a difference in their moccasins, and the foot-prints they make. I know not the precise form of the Comanche and Lipan moccasins; the Apaches assured me they could tell the foot-prints of the Comanches, the Mescaleros, the Yutas, the Coyoteros, or the Navehoes, and pointed out the distinctive marks of several. Different tribes of Indians have their peculiar fashions as well as civilized races, which are chiefly shown in their modes of dressing their hair and their coverings for the feet. American emigrants or travelers leave many marks to indicate their nationality and character, such as scraps of newspapers, bits of segars, fragments of hard bread, pieces of hempen rope, and other things. Mexicans would not be likely to have either of the articles named, but would be detected by the remains of cigarritos (small paper segars), pieces of raw hide, which they use instead of rope, etc. Or if they left any portion of their camp equipage, or cooking utensils, they would differ from those of Americans. The remains of their food, too, would differ. Tortillas, tamales, frijoles, chili colorado, and dried beef would appear; instead of hard bread, fried pork, beef steak, etc. If a Mexican wears a shoe, it will be very different in form from an American one.

The extent of a party is shown by the number of foot-prints. This cannot be told while it is in motion, as there may be a large number of animals driven in a herd with but few riders; but when the camp fires are examined, the number of persons can be detected with a considerable degree of certainty. The freshness of the foot-prints, the dung of the animals, and other signs show how recently a party may have passed; and there are other marks by which its rate of traveling can be ascertained.

Many are complaining today of illness, from indulging in fresh meat. It is hard to restrain travelers who have been living on salt pork, and but a scanty allowance of that, when a superabundance of fine fresh beef and veal is placed before them.

I have omitted mention of an incident that occurred, one of those which help to make up the chapter of events, and show the difficulties of our mode of traveling. Soon after we retired, there was a cry from the guard of "Turn out all hands, a mule in the river." The men all rushed from their tents, lanterns were lit, and ropes taken to rescue the animal; for we could not afford to lose another. It appeared that in grazing too near the bank, which was here some ten or fifteen feet above the river, and very precipitous, he had fallen over. Several men descended by the aid of ropes, and searched along the bank; but the poor creature could not be found, and it was supposed that he had been swept away by the current. When about to move this morning, a neighing was heard on the opposite side of the river, which proved to proceed from our lost mule. One of the men swam across with a rope, pursued and captured him and forced him over the steep bank, when he was drawn across the river. The bank was then leveled, and, by hard lifting and pulling, the animal was raised up and brought back in safety.

Encamped at half-past three P.M. after traveling hours; our mules coming in greatly fatigued.

November 5th. Intended making an early start this morning; but when we came to hitch up the poor mules, they looked so lank and miserable that we thought it best to turn them out again for a few hours to graze. Again we pursued our course along the river for a few miles, when we left it in the hope that we should not see it again; but we were doomed to disappointment in coming plumb upon it in an hour after. We had now followed its dreary and monotonous banks for six days, and longed for a change of scene. Even the jornada of 65 miles presented novelties which the Pecos had not. The constant fear of being overtaken by a storm, the brackish water, and that always difficult to obtain, the miserable grass, and the deficiency of wood helped to render this portion of our journey most disagreeable; and but for the broken wagons that were providentially left in our way, we could not have procured wood enough to cook our food. The river and adjacent country here present the same aspect as below. In width it now varied from fifty to ninety feet, with steep banks of clay or sand from twelve to twenty feet in height. Its rapidity may be somewhat less than at the Horse-Head Crossing.

On stopping to water our animals at the last halt made on the ever-lasting Pecos, one of our Mexican horses was suffered to nibble at the scanty grass on the river bank, while the party were taking lunch. His dangerous situation was observed by one of the teamsters, who stepped forward to lead him away. Resisting the benevolent intention thus manifested towards him, the animal, as a matter of course, determined to progress backwards; and over the bank he went, nearly dragging the man after him. The bank here was full twenty feet high, one half being perpendicular, and the other, formed of the debris, nearly so. We all rushed to its edge expecting to witness the last struggle of the poor beast, when, to our surprise, we saw him on his feet nearly covered with water. The comical look of the animal, as he rolled up his eyes at us, and the predicament he had placed himself in by his stubbornness, brought forth a hearty laugh from all. A man was let down by a rope, who succeeded in bringing him back to the camp none the worse for his fall and somerset.

Leaving the Pecos we took a direction a little north of west over a range of hills composed of gravel and marl. The road pursued a winding course among the hills and across deep ravines. At one place we stopped to look at some limestone sinks near the road. The earth and stone had caved in, or sunk, in spots varying from ten to thirty feet in diameter. The ground for some distance around appeared hollow and cavernous. The country since leaving the river was well covered with grass, but entirely destitute of trees or shrubs. At four o'clock reached Delaware or Sabine Creek, sixteen miles from the Pecos, and pitched our tents on a spot where there appeared to have been a very large encampment a few months before. Besides the fragments there was one large Pennsylvania wagon nearly complete, numerous ox-yokes, boxes, barrels, etc. These were collected and carried to our camp for fire-wood; and very acceptable they proved, for the banks of the creek did not furnish a bit of wood as large as one's finger. As the grass was abundant here and of the best description, with excellent water, I determined to halt to recruit the animals, and gave orders accordingly. The poor creatures were much in need of rest, for several had already given out and had to be removed from the wagons. Two colonies of prairie dogs were seen today after leaving the Pecos, the first we had noticed since leaving the great jornada beyond Castle Mountain.

November 6th. Was aroused in the night by the whistling of the wind. Feeling a great change in the temperature, I looked out of my carriage window, and to my surprise found the ground covered with snow. There was no sleep after this; as soon as morning dawned, I got up to inspect the condition of the party and the animals, and to see what could be done for their comfort. The dreaded Norther I had so much feared when near the Pecos, had now come upon us with all its fury and in its very worst shape, accompanied with snow. But bad as our condition was, it might have been worse. We had escaped the inhospitable region of the Pecos, where the water was unfit to drink, scarcely any grazing was to be had for our animals, and no wood wherewith to cook our food. Here the grass was excellent and abundant, the water was pure, and the calamities of others furnished us with broken wagons and other articles for fire-wood. But our poor animals had no shelter from the pitiless storm, there being not a tree to break the force of the keen blast which seemed to pierce them to the quick. A few isolated bushes grew near the camp, but nothing that afforded covering. During the day, many wandered off, probably to seek shelter; and at one time, ten men were gone in pursuit of them. Some of the horses had strayed seven miles before they were taken.

The only means to add to our comfort were to bank the earth around the tents to keep out the snow and the cold blasts; to bring our overcoats and India-rubber garments into requisition; and to keep up as large fires as the broken wagons and boxes would admit of.

Finding it very hard to keep warm even by the fire, with the cold wind and snow beating on my back, I laid aside my heavy blanket, put on my India-rubber cloak and long boots, and took my double-barreled gun to see what virtue there was in a little sport by way of exercise. The result proved to be better than remaining still, roasting and freezing alternately by the fire. The excitement and exercise restored the circulation and the satisfaction of procuring several brace of ducks amply repaid the hardship of facing the storm. Removing my India-rubbers I again wrapped my blanket around me, seated myself in my carriage with Dr. Webb, and there spent the remainder of the long day in reading Erman's *Travels in Siberia*, a proper book for the occasion. The young men took it very calmly, spending the time at the camp fires or in their tents. So passed the day.

November 7th. In camp on the Delaware Creek. Passed a cold and sleepless night. The sharp wind found its way through the openings in the carriage, which all the blankets I could pile on would not keep out. The young gentlemen crowded themselves in their tents and lay as close as possible; while the teamsters, laborers, etc., stowed themselves in the wagons. The morning was sharp and cold; the snow continued to fall, and the wind remained at the north, though blowing less than the previous day.

I was desirous to resume our march; but the teamsters and others, whose experience among mules was greater than mine, thought it impractical. To do so, they said, would result in our discomfort and perhaps ruin; for the animals would assuredly give out and leave us much worse off than we were at present. I yielded to their representations and determined to remain a while longer; for we were in a good encampment with grass and water at hand, and the flooring of our tents was dry—a consideration of great importance. No one had taken cold or shown symptoms of illness. Before leaving San Antonio my friends told me that at this season of the year we could hardly expect to escape the Northers, and advised me if overtaken by one not to move, but encamp at once, and keep quiet until it had passed. But in determining to remain I thought it most prudent to send a small party in advance to El Paso, now about one hundred and sixty-five miles off, for assistance.

I ordered another inventory to be made of our provisions, and found nothing remaining but a limited supply of hard bread and pork; everything else was gone. If we kept on, we might reach El Paso by parching the few remaining bushels of corn and taking an occasional mule steak; but if compelled to remain here two or three days we should be reduced to very short allowance. Messrs. Thurber, Moss, and Weems at once volunteered their services to go to El Paso. No time was lost, therefore, in fitting them out. They selected three of the hardiest riding animals; put up four day's provisions, which they put in bags and hung to their saddles; fastened their blankets behind them; and set off in the midst of the storm, two hours after it was determined to send them. One of the teamsters named Pratt, a very useful and energetic man, accompanied them. I gave them the following letter to Major Van Horne, commanding at El Paso:

Mexican Boundary Commission in Camp
Delaware Creek, Nov. 7, 1850
Sir: I reached this place on the afternoon of the 5th instant with a portion of the United States Boundary Commission, having left the main body at San Antonio to follow immediately. My desire being to reach El Paso as early as possible after the first of November, we took provisions but for thirty days.

I now find myself overtaken by a Norther and severe snow-storm; my animals are much reduced by fatigue, and there is a probability that I shall fall short of provisions, in case the storm should continue. Under these circumstances I have deemed it prudent for the safety of my party to send four of them to El Paso, to procure aid to enable me to reach there as soon as possible. In the meantime I shall advance as soon as the weather will permit, and hope to reach the Guadalupe Pass in season to meet the return messenger.

I shall be glad if you can send to my aid the following, viz.: ten mules, to be returned in good condition; and bread, pork, sugar, and coffee sufficient for my party for five days: for which I will pay you on my arrival.

I am, very respectively,
Your obedient servant,
JOHN R. BARTLETT,
Commissioner.
To Major J. Van Horne,
Commanding,
El Paso del Norte, Texas.

November 8th. Camp on Delaware Creek. With great delight I rose from my carriage bed this morning at the first peep of day, to find the weather had moderated. Soon after the sun beamed forth in all his splendor, and with it the hope that we should be able to resume our journey. After a few hours delay in packing tents, arranging our camp equipage, and drying the collars of the mules, the pleasing sound was heard from the teamsters of "All ready!" when we left camp, and, immediately crossing the creek, emerged on the more elevated bank beyond. The dry earth and the warm sun soon absorbed or evaporated the snow, so that our progress was but little impeded. But we had not proceeded many miles before the mules showed symptoms of fatigue and suffering from the effects of the cold. Several gave out entirely, hung their heads, and sank to the ground, or refused to move further. These were necessarily removed from the teams, so that several of the wagons were reduced to two feeble mules. As my carriage mules were in better condition, I had got some distance in advance when word was brought me that the animals were giving out so fast that it would be necessary for us to encamp at the first place where good grass and water could be found. A few miles further brought us again to Delaware Creek, where, finding good grass as well as fuel, we stopped and encamped. Dr. Webb and myself walked the entire distance today. An examination of the mules soon showed that in their present condition our progress must be very slow, not exceeding twelve or fifteen miles a day; and that it would be absolutely necessary to give them a couple of days' rest where there was good grazing. This delay would destroy all my plans of reaching my place of destination within the period required, and exhaust our provisions before the supply sent for could arrive. I determined, therefore, as my carriage mules were in good order, to push on myself. With this in view I made up a party consisting of Dr. Webb, Messrs. Murphy, Cremony, Matthews, Young, and Thompson; these, with my carriage driver and another, made eight persons, a party I believed sufficiently strong to go through in safety. We selected good animals, and made such preparations as were necessary during the afternoon and evening, to insure an early start in the morning. A sack of our remaining corn was lashed to the axle-tree of my carriage for the mules. Some salt pork was cooked, which, with hard bread, was stowed inside, while the unoccupied space inside and out was filled with bedding. A tent could not be taken, as the carriage was already too heavily burdened.

November 9th. Up at four o'clock; took a hearty breakfast, and was ready to move as soon as there was sufficient light to see the road. Started at a lively pace, intending to make a good march. The road was quite tortuous, winding among and over hills, in a direction nearly west, towards the bold head of the great Guadalupe Mountain, which had been before us some eight or ten days. This is a most remarkable landmark, rising as it does far above all other objects, and terminating abruptly about three thousand feet above the surrounding plain. The sierra or mountain range which ends with it, comes from the northeast. It is a dark, gloomy-looking range, with bold and forbidding sides, consisting of huge piles of rocks, their debris heaped far above the surrounding hills. As it approaches its termination, the color changes to a pure white, tinted with buff or light orange, presenting a beautiful contrast with other portions of the range, or with the azure blue of the sky beyond; for in this elevated region the heavens have remarkable brilliancy and depth of color.

The low hills we passed are woodless, and sparsely covered with grass. Limestone occasionally protrudes from the hills, while the soil is hard and gravelly, with an occasional patch of sand. Stopped to water the animals at the head waters of Delaware Creek, probably Walnut Creek, about fifteen miles from camp, when we continued our course toward the head of the Guadalupe Mountain, reaching a boiling spring about five o'clock. There are here three fine springs, one of which tasted strongly of sulphur; the second seemed impregnated with salts of soda, while the third was very pure. Found good grazing in the valley where we stopped, with a little grove of trees, a pretty place to have spent a day in, had circumstances rendered it proper; but while our animals were in condition to move, I determined to press them to their utmost. Estimated distance traveled today, thirty-five miles.

The Guadalupe had been before us the whole day, and we all expected to reach it within a couple of hours after leaving camp. But hour after hour we drove directly toward it, without seeming to approach nearer; and finally, after journeying ten hours, the mountain seemed to be as distant as it was in the morning. Such is the great clearness of the atmosphere here, that one unused to measuring distances in elevated regions is greatly deceived in his calculations. When this mountain was first discovered we were more than one hundred miles off. Even then its features stood out boldly against the blue sky; and when the rays of the morning sun were shed upon it, it exhibited every outline of its rugged sides with as much distinctness as a similar object would in the old States at one fifth the distance. Often have I gazed at the Katskill Mountains in sailing down the Hudson; and though at a distance of but twelve miles, I never saw them as distinctly as the Guadalupe Mountain appeared sixty miles off.

For several miles before reaching the springs we had in vain tried to pick up wood enough to make a fire; but none could be found, not even roots or brush wood. Still, the good fortune which had attended us in our journey did not desert us here. A disabled wagon, with its large box, lay near the springs. This not only furnished us with fuel for the fire, but the box, which was whole, served as a sleeping-place for four of the party. This was placed on one side of the fire, and the carriage drawn up on the other. As we were near one of the notorious lurking places of the Apaches, a strict guard was kept up, and relieved every hour during the night.

November 10th. Two hours before day my carriage driver was out with the mules to give them an early feed, while we managed to make a pot of tea from a canister, which I always carried with me for such occasions. This, with cold pork and hard bread, made our breakfast; but meager as it was, it was taken with relish. We then filled our leather water tank, and were on our journey before the sun peeped over the adjacent hills to our left. No sunrise at sea or from the mountain's summit could equal in grandeur that which we now beheld, when the first rays struck the snow-clad mountain, which reared its lofty head before us. The projecting cliffs of white and orange stood out in bold relief against the azure sky, while the crevices and gorges, filled with snow, showed their inequalities with a wonderful distinctness. At the same time, the beams of the sun playing on the snow produced the most brilliant and ever-changing iris hues. No painter's art could reproduce, or colors imitate, these gorgeous prismatic tints.

Five or six miles, over a hilly though very hard road, brought us to the base of the mountain, where we noticed a grove of liveoak and pines, with water near them; but as it was too early to water our animals, we did not stop. At this spring a train was attacked a few months before we passed, and four men killed. As we now began to descend, I got out of the carriage, preferring to go on foot. I could thus the more readily lock and unlock the wheels when necessary. The road here, after passing through long defiles, winds for some distance along the side of the mountain. Now it plunges down some deep abyss, and then it suddenly rises again upon some little castellated spur, so that one almost imagines himself to be in a veritable fortress. Again we pass along the brink of a deep gorge, whose bottom, filled with trees, is concealed from our view, while the evergreen cedar juts forth here and there from the chasms in its sides. Winding and turning in every direction, we followed the intricacies of the Guadalupe Pass for at least six hours; and whenever the prospect opened before us, there stood the majestic bluff in all its grandeur, solitary and alone. In one place the road runs along the mountain in a bare rocky shelf not wide enough for two wagons to pass, and the next moment passes down through an immense gorge, walled by mountains of limestone, regularly terraced. As we were descending from this narrow ledge, the iron bolt which held the tongue of the carriage broke and let it drop. Nothing but iron would do to repair the injury; and after trying various expedients, a substitute for the broken bolt was found in the bail or handle of the tin kettle which held our provisions. This, being doubled and driven through the hole previously filled by the bolt, kept it in its place, while the tongue was supported by cords. By careful driving, and relieving the weight of the carriage by alighting when going over bad places, we got along tolerably well.

I regretted that we were not able to spend more time in this interesting Pass, the grandeur of which would, under any other circumstances, have induced us to linger; but we had too much at stake to waste a single hour. Many new forms of cacti were seen here; and upon emerging from it, we observed in quantities the *fouquiera* (I know no other name for it) covering the gravel knolls. This singular shrub throws up from just above the surface of the ground numerous simple stems, eight or ten feet high, armed with sharp hooped thorns.

On reaching the summit of the line of hills, which completely surround the Guadalupe range on the western side, we looked down upon a broad plain, stretching out as far as the eye could reach. The Sacramento

Mountains, which are but the continuation of the Guadalupe range, extended from east to west for a distance of more than a hundred miles, terminating, like the latter, in a bold bluff, where another range seems to intersect them from the north. Far to the north-west we could see the *Cornudos del Alamo* like two great mounds rising from a vast plain, while to the south-west the horizon was bounded by a faint blue outline of mountains, with jagged tops. The plain appeared level from the height at which we viewed it, and was interspersed with what looked like silvery and tranquil lakes, glittering in the sun, seeming as it were, to tempt the weary traveler to their brink. Our young men cried out, "Water!" delighted with the idea of again enjoying this luxury after a long day's ride. But the whole turned out a delusion, what appeared to be a glassy surface of a lake or pond being nothing but the saline incrustations of a dried-up lake. The vast plain, or desert, as it may with more propriety be called, as far as the eye could reach, was dotted with these saline depressions.

Before we had got through this pass we came upon another broken wagon, and among its iron work were so fortunate as to find a bolt precisely the size of the one we had broken. The wire was quickly knocked out, and the bolt inserted in its place; after which the driver put on his whip, and we rolled over the hard and excellent road at a rapid pace.

The summit of the mountain appears to be covered with a heavy pine timber; but its rocky sides exhibit no foliage, except in the deep chasms which run from it in every direction. At its base, too, we noticed large trees of pine, oak, cedar, etc.

We had now ridden the entire day without water for our animals, not discovering a spring which is noted on the map as *Ojo del Cuerpo,* and at which I had proposed stopping. Our leather tank was empty, and I began to feel anxious on our account, as the next water laid down on the map is at the *Cornudos del Alamo,* thirty miles distant. The road was now pretty good, and we went over it on a fast trot. On the left we passed a range of hills of pure white sand, the same we saw when the plain first opened to us, and which we supposed to be water, and a few miles further the dry bed of a lake, with a white surface, appearing also like water. It was quite rough and hilly here. Clumps of bushes grew in the intervening valley, which I sent parties to examine, in the hope of finding water, but without success.

While pondering whether to push on or encamp where we were, without water, we discovered far off in the plain, directly before us, what appeared to be a large encampment. Smoke was curling up from many fires; and we decried a long line of white objects. Took my spy-glass, and discovered the white dots to be so many wagons stretching over the plain; all which assured us we had nothing to fear. The pleasant prospect of again meeting with our countrymen quite raised our drooping spirits. The weary animals, who doubtless smelt the water, as mules always do, from a great distance, seemed to rouse themselves to new exertions. A rapid drive of four miles brought us to the encampment, which proved to be a train of about sixty large wagons, with government stores, bound for El Paso. It belonged to Mr. Coons, and left Indianola, on the coast, in April, and San Antonio in June last. After sustaining extensive losses of wagons and animals, they arrived here fifty-six days before us, and were forced to remain, as there was not water between this place and El Paso for so large a number of animals as they had with them. The distance was said to be about one hundred miles. Their wagons were mostly drawn by oxen, which could not travel more than fifteen miles a day, and would therefore require six days to reach their place of destination. The train here was in charge of Mr. Percy, who after waiting several weeks in the hope that there would be rain, had sent a messenger to the commanding officer at El Paso, informing him of his situation, and requesting assistance. Parties were now on their way from the Rio Grande, bringing water in barrels, which were to be deposited at several points for the use of the animals, to enable them to complete their journey.

On approaching the encampment we were surrounded by sixty or seventy teamsters, who ragged, dirty, and unshaven, crowded around us; for, with the exception of Mr. Thurber and his party, who had stopped here the day before, they had seen no one from the "States" since their departure from San Antonio in June. They had had a long and painful journey to this place, and suffered much for the want of water. Their animals had given out in many places, which had caused hundreds to be left behind; and many of their wagons had been disabled or rendered useless for want of means to draw them. Besides draught animals, a large herd, embracing several hundred beef cattle, had been driven with the train; and among these there had been great mortality. The stray cattle we had seen, and a few of which we had secured, were doubtless some which had luckily been left near a spot where there was grass and water, which enabled them to recover their strength.

Mr. Percy, the gentleman in charge of the wagons, gave us a warm reception, and kindly offered to let me have the provisions I was so desirous to procure for the relief of the party I had left behind, on my giving a receipt for them to the U. S. Quarter-master on my arrival at El Paso. Having eaten nothing since daylight, we feasted with a great relish on our cold pork and biskit. Our generous host ordered supper for us, but we were too hungry to wait; though I believe most of the party accepted his invitation, and did full justice to a second meal before retiring to their blankets. Mr. Percy, who had the only tent in his party, gave places to as many as could stow themselves within it. Estimated the distance traveled today to be thirty-eight miles.

November 11th. In camp at Salt Lake, near Guadalupe Mountains. The lake, or rather pond near which we were encamped, is a small body of water covering three or four acres, surrounded on all sides by an open prairie or plain, in which there are scattered bushes, with patches of pretty good grass: no trees are to be seen, nearer than the base of the mountain. The pond is resorted to by wild ducks, plover, and other water-fowl in great numbers; but the continued proximity of so large a body of men as Mr. Percy's party has made them less plentiful and quite shy. Still, I managed to shoot a few before breakfast. . . .

After partaking of a hearty breakfast, provided for us by Mr. Percy, we made preparations to start, determined to press through, believing that we should find water enough for our small party at the three springs, or water-ing places, between us and the Rio Grande, which was yet about one hun-dred and eight miles off. But we had expectations from another source, as Mr. Daguerre, who had just arrived from El Paso, informed me that his wagons were on the way to the camp bringing water for Mr. Coon's train, which they were depositing at certain points on the road; and he most generously gave me permission to use it, if we found none of the watering places and should require it for ourselves or for our animals.

While making our preparations to start, Mr. Percy filled our kettle with some excellent boiled beef, bread, coffee, and sugar—an acceptable addi-tion to our stock of pork and hard bread, which, though very good, was not sufficient to carry us to our journey's end. In fact, but for his assis-tance, we must have come on short allowance at once.

After putting up a barrel of pork, with a quantity of bread, sugar, coffee, etc., which our host undertook to send back immediately to the spring at the foot of the mountain, for the party we had left behind, we took leave of our good friends, and dashed off in fine spirits for Thorne's Wells, in the mountain called the "Cornudos del Alamo," or Horns of the Alamo, thirty-three miles distant, which I hoped to reach before dark. The road was most monotonous for the first twenty miles; the great abundance of yuccas and cacti giving a strange and striking air to the vegetation. We saw splendid specimens of a large tree-like cactus (*Opuntia arborescens*). This is a much branched species, with clusters of yellow fruit at the ends of long, horrible, spiny arms. Specimens were seen from six to ten feet high, and twenty to thirty feet in circumference. The country is slightly undulating, and not a level plain, as it appeared to be from the hills. The soil seemed barren, and in many places was covered with saline incrustations. Several dog-towns were passed. At noon, saw a great cloud of dust arising from the plain immediately ahead of us; which, as we drew near, was found to proceed from ten large wagons of ten mules each, belonging to Mr. Daguerre, on their way from El Paso to relieve the train we had just left. At six o'clock, reached the *Cornudos del Alamo,* towards which we had been journeying since our start this morning; and being unable at this late hour, it being now dark, to find the wells in the clefts of the rocks, we encamped without water. This wonderful mountain, of which it is impossible to convey any adequate idea by description, is a pile of red granite boulders of gigantic size, thrown up abruptly into the plain. The boulders are mostly of an oblong shape, with their largest diameter vertical; they are rounded and often highly polished. The interstices between the rocks form in many places extensive caverns. On the summit I noticed two projecting piles, or masses, which rose many feet above the level of the other portions in a conical form, resembling horns, whence I suppose originated the name "Horns of the Alamo" — the mountain itself being known as the Alamo. After building a fire near a rock (for wood was abundant around us), four of the party took a lantern and scrambled about among the rocks in search of water. It seemed a bold and hopeless undertaking for tiny man, guided by the dim light of a candle, to be probing the deep recesses of the mountain and clambering over these gigantic boulders, which were piled up to the height of four or five hundred feet. But, when urged by his necessities, it is hard to say what he cannot accomplish. Within an hour, one of the party was so fortunate as to find in a cavity of a rock enough water to fill our tea-kettle, which had collected from the melting of the snow a few days before. After a cup of warm tea and a hearty supper, the carriage was drawn near the fire, when all bivouacked around it, and were soon lost in sleep.

November 12th. Being spared the trouble of boiling coffee, for want of water to make it withal, we did not wait for breakfast, but set off before daylight. Before quitting the mountain, we journeyed along it for some distance, close to its base. We thus found a singular gorge, or glen, which led some fifty feet into the mountains, where it opened to the sky. Within this inner cavern-like place was a deep hole, which appeared to have contained water, and which we supposed to be the "Thorn's Well" of which we had been in search; but at this time it was perfectly dry. Some large trees had sprung up in this singular place, and the rocky walls were highly polished as if by hand of man. There were other deep holes near the entrance, which we supposed had been dug by California emigrants in search for water. All around were indications that it had been a camping place for many parties. Near the entrance alluded to were several carcasses of oxen, which had perished here before the well was dug.

Resuming our journey we rode ten miles to the Ojos del Alamo, or Cotton-wood Springs, on a hard and excellent road. Our landmark for this spring was a single cotton-wood tree, about five hundred feet up the side of a mountain, on our left. As the mountain was otherwise bare of foliage, save a few shrubs, the tree was easily seen, though from below it looked more like a bush; still, its light yellowish green distinguished it perfectly from every thing around. Left the carriage at the base of the mountain and clambered up to the springs, of which there are seven. The water was very good, though but little remained. Upon the faces of the rocks were rude sculptures and paintings, made by the Indians. We led some of the animals up to the springs; and others, that would not make the ascent, were watered from the kegs which our friends had deposited at the base. Found a note from Mr. Thurber here, stating that his party had preceded us two days.

Turned our animals out to graze, as the grass was very good, and took breakfast. The Hueco, or Waco, Mountains, our next landmark, lay before us here at twenty-five miles distance, and for them we now set out; but so clear was the atmosphere that they did not appear more than eight or nine miles off. The road, which led over a rolling prairie, was excellent. Not a tree was seen, and scarcely a bush the entire distance. The grass was poor and thin. At two o'clock reached the mountain, and at once entered the pass. Just before reaching it, the road divides, one branch leading to the right, the other to the left of the mountain. I was advised to take the latter, which was five miles shorter than the other, as my carriage could be easily lifted over a very steep place in the defile, which was impractical for loaded wagons. The latter invariably take the longer route. The descent was gradual and easy, and led through a narrow defile along the base of the mountain, which lay close on our right. The road was very tortuous, with small hills and deep ravines to cross, though unattended with difficulties, until, after a long descent, we were obliged to follow an arroyo, or stony bed of a water-course. Here the way was exceedingly rough, so that I feared every moment to see the carriage upset or broken in pieces. We were finally brought to a stand, where the road or path, if entitled to either appellation, led precipitately over a ledge of rocks some ten or twelve feet. How any wheeled vehicle ever got through here it was difficult to imagine. After an examination of the place, it was thought most prudent to take out the mules, which were led around the side of the defile, or through a chasm in the rock. We then took two ropes and attached them to the hind axle-tree of the carriage. Wells, the driver, a stout and athletic man, took the tongue and guided the carriage over the precipice, while we let it carefully down by the ropes. In this way it was got over in safety, and deposited on the gravelly bed of the defile. The mules were now hitched up again, and we continued our journey along the same sort of road for a mile. This was an exceedingly grand and picturesque spot, differing from anything we had seen on our route. On both sides the gray limestone rocks rose perpendicular like walls. From the top and in the crevices of these grew a variety of shrubs. A low range of rounded gravelly hills, covered with grass, but destitute of trees, bordered the defile; while about half a mile or less beyond loomed up the great mountain, and its almost perpendicular sides showing a dark brown granite from the base to its very summit. So steep is the mountain that it cannot be ascended except from the plain above. As we emerged from the narrow gorge, the same terraced and castellated rocks which we noticed at Castle Mountain appeared again, but in more strange and picturesque forms—now a fortification, and again some ruined town. These terraced hills opened into a plain or amphitheatre about three miles across, surrounded by hills and mountains, except on the north. Passing them, we reached the Hueco Tanks, and stopped beneath a huge overhanging rock.

The mountains in which these so-called "Tanks" are found, are two rocky piles of similar character to the Cornudos del Alamo before described. The rocks, however, are thrown together in still wilder confusion, and are of more irregular forms. One mass extends about a mile along the amphitheatre above mentioned, and is about half a mile in breadth. The other, situated to the south, is separated by a narrow pass from that described. It, too, extends about a mile from north to south; but in other respects is very irregular, consisting of several vast heaps, quite disconnected. Much of this is granite in place, while gigantic boulders are piled up like pebble stones at its sides and on its summit. These piles are from one hundred to one hundred and fifty feet in height.

After a little search we found water in a great cavity or natural tank in the rock about twenty feet above our heads, containing about fifty barrels, pure and sweet. This tank was covered by a huge boulder, weighing some hundred tons, the lower surface of which was but four or five feet above the water. Searching along the base of the mountain we found another cavity, where we watered our animals. There remained yet another hour before dark; and as there was no grass near, I thought best to push on a few miles and stop wherever grass should be found.

The road leads between the great rocky masses described above, when it enters a plain beyond. We had scarcely passed the mountain when we met Messrs. Thurber and Weems, who were returning from El Paso with ten mules and two men for the assistance of our train, which had been promptly furnished by Major Van Horne. We bivouacked together, after learning that we should find no grass further on. It was poor here, and only grew in tufts about the roots of the mezquit chaparral; but with the hope of terminating our journey on the morrow, we could rest easy. A supper was cooked with the brushwood of the mezquit; and the evening was spent in asking a thousand questions of our friends about what they had seen, and how civilized people again appeared to them.

November 13th. Breakfasted and resumed our journey before daylight, having twenty-five miles to make before its close. About three miles from the Hueco Tanks we passed a range of hills, when a broad plain opened upon us in every direction. Here we first got a glimpse of Mexico, in a range of mountains which rises ten miles in the rear of El Paso. Northeast of them were the El Paso Mountains, on the eastern bank of the river, which unite with the Organ Mountains or "Sierra de los Organos," whose pinnacles and jagged summits could be distinctly seen about sixty miles to the north-west. To the north, at a great distance, Mount Soledad was dimly seen; while at the south the long line of horizon was only broken by low hills, on the Mexican side of the river. A road branched off just beyond the low hills we had passed, leading to the town of Isleta, in a southerly direction. Our course now lay south-west over a sandy desert plain, covered with low mezquit chaparral. Grama grass grew in tufts or little patches here and there; which, though dry and apparently without sustenance, is eagerly eaten by mules. The country was exceedingly monotonous; and our tired animals could scarcely drag their loads through the deep sand, which continued the whole way without interruption. We kept rising gradually over the undulating tableland which borders the Rio Grande until at length we reached its highest level. Here the valley of that long looked-for river opened upon us. A line of foliage of the richest green with occasional patches of bright yellow and brown marked its course. The first autumnal tinge, which in our northern forests so beautifully indicates the earliest frost and reminds us of the coming winter, is here likewise apparent. But there is not that diversity of hue as with us—no rich crimson, scarlet and purple; which is easily accounted for by the want of variety in the Mexican forest. Here the cotton-wood alone is found. Soon the houses were seen peeping from among the trees; but when the "stars and stripes" were discovered curling in the breeze, a thrill ran through our veins which must be felt by those situated as we were to be understood.

I had often read of the delight with which mariners, after long absence, greet the sight of their national flag in some distant port; and this delight I now experience. It seemed like a glimpse of home, and reminded us that we were approaching not only civilization, but countrymen and friends.

THE LOBO

O. W. Williams

1908

WE HAVE IN THIS COUNTRY A WOLF LARGER THAN THE COYOTE, swifter, fiercer and much more destructive to domestic flocks. It is not more bloodthirsty than the panther, and a single animal of the latter species may inflict in one night much more damage than any solitary wolf would inflict. But the panther may be easily trailed and destroyed after his night of carnage, while this wolf is enabled by his extraordinary cunning to live out his life of rapine to a good old age. Its cunning and its persistent diabolical pursuit of its prey lead one to understand the existence of the French Canadian belief in the werewolf.

This animal was known to the early settlers of our country, and is still so known in the greater part of it, as the gray or timber wolf. But in the Southwest and all along the Mexican border it is known by the name of lobo, and this name has almost entirely supplanted the old Anglo-Saxon name for the Spanish wolf of the Pyrenees and the mountains of Spain, and the reader who has followed Robinson Crusoe through his return by way of Spain, and his adventures with the Pyrenean wolves, must recognize the similarity of that animal in its characteristics to ours, allowing of course for some exaggeration in Defoe's account of the Spanish wolf. Extreme hunger has often caused our timber wolf to pursue human beings, . . . and I am inclined to believe that if our plains were covered every winter for a long time with a deep mantle of snow, and our domestic animals were housed and safe from attack, that any belated traveler by night who should hear that mournful and hungry howl of the lobo would surely make his unfortunate horse suffer, until he found a place of cover, for he might well fear attack. Of all the names belonging originally to European animals which were applied to American animals by the first comers, it is probable that the Spanish term of lobo was the most appropriate. The European wolf was more like its American namesake than any other Old World animal to its American kin. We had two kinds of wolves here, and the Spanish wisely gave the name of lobo to one and accepted the indigenous name of coyote for the other.

Of all the animals which prey upon our herds and flocks, the lobo inflicts the most damage, and gives the most trouble to the stock owners. It is not that it causes any sudden and great loss, but that it is a constant and never-ending source of loss. It is not a calamity such as the invasion of locusts and grasshoppers have proved to be in the West at times, causing great loss and damage for a season, and then disappearing for years. It is more like a grievous tax that is laid on year by year which is to be borne with patience and to be counted on every year as an entry in the columns of "profit and loss." The cattlemen may paraphrase that saying about the poor and lay it down that "the lobo we have always."

Yet these animals are not now and never have been numerous in our country. Twenty-five years ago there was said to be but one pack of lobos in Pecos County, and they ranged then on the Pecos River about 30 miles above Sheffield. Then as now they found sustenance principally upon herds of cattle, and this pack made the cattle of the "S" and Mule Shoe brands its principal prey. It had only been a short time then since cattle had been introduced into Pecos county, and I am unable to say whether or not the lobo had made its appearance here before the cattle. But it was the belief of the early settlers that it only came here after the cattle came. And I am disposed for some reason to think that this may have been the case.

The wolf was peculiarly an inhabitant of wooded country and forests, as its English name indicates. Now our county was and is a country of plains. We have no forests, trees are exceedingly rare, and coverts of small brush are seldom found, and were much more rarely found twenty-five years ago. These were conditions not found in the usual habitat of this wolf, and there must have been some good and sufficient cause to have brought it into such country. Such a cause might be found in the presence of an abundance of the food eaten by it. But the buffalo seems never to have been abundant in this section, at least within historic times, while the deer and the antelope were not very greatly in evidence, and were besides animals pretty well able to escape its pursuit. There was apparently, then, in early times no good place for it in this country in the economy of nature. But when cattle were moved here and ranged in large herds over an immense area of unfenced country, they were necessarily turned loose to take care of themselves with the least possible protection by the hand of man. This was a condition favorable to the entrance and increase of the lobo. It is true the forest and the glade were lacking, but the mesas and the rocky caverns around the mesa borders to some extent supplied this want to the lobo, while the abundance of its prey and the scant protection given to it by the owners gave the wolf every opportunity to thrive.

Such conditions gave rise to a wide extension of the range of the lobo. First we began to hear of its ravages at the "Tunas" spring. Then we heard of it about the old Neighbors ranch. Later it began to make trouble about the foothills of the Glass Mountains on both the north side and the south side. Owing to the nature of the country best adapted to its protection, it early marked out to itself a well-defined area of territory in which it is always found, and out of which its ravages are never or but rarely and transitorily made. The northern and western ends of the country being fairly level, destitute of caves and good hiding places, and without mesas or rocky hills, have remained free from them. But the southern and south-eastern parts of the county are countries of high but small tablelands separated by valleys of various widths, and here the lobo has found a congenial home and safe retreat. If a straight line be drawn on the Pecos County map from the Horse-Head Crossing on the Pecos River to the Glass Mountains, this line will approximately mark the northern and northwestern limits of the damage effected by these animals, and will at the same time mark the area in which this damage has been the greatest. To the north and west of this line the animal seldom appears. To the south and east it is always present.

It was not long after the lobo had made this increase in numbers, and had extended its range over the mesa country which had just then been opened up for cattle by wells and tanks and fenced pastures, that the cattlemen awoke to the necessity of making war on this scourge of the great dry divide. Since then the war has continued, feebly at times, and at others energetically. At times efforts have been made in the hope of completely extirpating the animal, but lack of a common united and unanimous attack has prevented success in such a wholesale undertaking, and the result at present seems to be that every individual cattle owner is trying to protect himself alone, regardless of the manner of his defense.

So it comes about that the plan usually and generally adopted by each individual is to drive the lobo away from his immediate locality and no further. This is done by chasing with dogs, and when the animal has been thus driven away the individual sits down in content until the lobo returns or another comes in, when the chase and exodus is repeated. This is manifestly a case of "scotching" the snake and no more. The lobos are not destroyed, but are simply kept moving from ranch to ranch, and it may easily happen thus that one wolf is driven backward and forward between two ranches like a tennis ball through his lifetime, doing as much damage during his comings and goings as if he had remained undisturbed.

This course of action is explained by two facts: First, the comparative ease with which a lobo is temporarily driven off any particular range by persistent chasing with dogs; and second, the great difficulty and lack of success in any more radical measures attempting the destruction of the animal. For the lobo is not only a very swift animal; it is also exceedingly wary, more so probably than any other wild animal found in these parts. The foxhound is too slow and suffers too much from heat and tender feet to have success in chasing it in this country, while the greyhound suffers in the same way, and is besides not able to cope with the wolf if he is overtaken. The horseman mounted on the swiftest horse fares worse even than the greyhound among the mesas and hills of the lobo's favorite grounds.

I have heard, however, of one occasion on which the lobo was overtaken and killed by cowboys, and as the incident serves to point out the way to an occasional success in chasing the animal, I shall relate it as I have it: Several years ago some cowboys on the Gibson & Baldridge ranch caught sight of some lobos near the Horse-Head Crossing of the Pecos River and immediately gave chase. Though not mounted on swift horses, they were fortunate enough to catch up with and rope three of the animals. This was a very unexpected success which was accounted for by three concurring circumstances. First may be mentioned the fact that the chase occurred in a very level country, and the lobos did not have the advantage of going over hills which the horses could not climb, as constantly happens in a mesa country. Then too, it was found that the animals were young and not fully grown. But the circumstances most potent to the success of the cowboys was shown when it was ascertained that the lobos had recently fed heavily, had then gone to the river and filled up with water, and were returning thus heavily laden when chased and captured.

This last condition probably can rarely be brought about by man for the purpose of the chase, as the animal drinks as well as feeds mostly by night. If it could be planned and carried out, it would be a most effective way of destroying it. As it has been deliberately and often planned here in early days to catch other animals in this way, and the success of a chase under such conditions is well-known, it is reasonable to suppose that the plan has not been adopted in the chase of the lobo because it is not found to be suited to the ordinary habits of the animal. It is a well known way of catching "outlaw" horses in the early days of unfenced range. These horses were kept from watering by night and by day as long as practicable and were then allowed to come to drink. After drinking as much as they desired they were then chased and easily captured. Men familiar with such experiences would not fail to apply the same plan to the chase of the lobo if it were practicable to successfully apply it in that case.

Now if we turn from the chase to other methods of capturing the lobo, we find that there is little better success to record. The coyote is very susceptible to the attractions of a poisoned "bait," but the wary old lobo is exceedingly rarely caught in that way. I have heard of one case where a live sheep was poisoned by placing strychnine in the flesh of the shoulder and placed by night where it was known that a lobo was in the habit of passing. This proved successful, and the lobo was killed. But it is the only successful case of poisoning by bait that I can now call to mind. And the plan of poisoning a dead animal for bait which is so successful with the coyote is a failure with the lobo.

At times lobos become so troublesome that considerable rewards are offered for their scalps by individuals on whose property they are raiding. Only a few years ago the sum of $50 was paid for the killing of a particular lobo which carried on its operations on a large scale about ten miles from this place. And $20 a head is a common price paid by ranchmen for killing lobos on their ranches. This may seem to be a large price. But I have no doubt it is worth much more than that to the ranchmen. I have heard of a lobo about 5 years ago killing 9 calves on 9 successive days on a ranch not far from this town. If these calves were worth only $5 each, that lobo destroyed $45 worth of property in a little over a week and may have done damage during its lifetime that would run up to hundreds of dollars.

In consequence of these rewards, there are men constantly engaged in hunting them. Some follow it for years and get to be pretty expert lobo hunters, and I may say as to some of them that they become of little account at anything else. Others follow it for a short time to fill up temporary lack of employment. I know little about their methods, but I have noticed that some of them pretend to have trade secrets which they affect to guard with the most profound care. They will give out mysterious hints about some recipe of drugs which is supposed to be an infallible "bait" for the lobo, and which is only known to this particular adept. Whether there is any such drug or drugs I know not, but I am skeptical in the matter.

I think, however, that the trap, in various shapes, is the reliance of these hunters. The skill with which they are placed and hidden probably measures in most cases the professional ability of the hunter. One rule seems to be that every effective device to conceal or take away the scent of man from the trap or bait must be adopted. This is effected in some instances by means which seem ludicrous and fanciful and in all cases by some procedure rather surprising to the ordinary man. I sometimes think that a man who follows this business will inevitably fall into that superstitious frame of mind which brought about in other countries and olden times the myth of the "man" wolf.

If this animal has any useful qualities or habits, I have not yet learned of them. If it destroys in any appreciable quantity any noxious animal, reptile or insect, I have no account of it. It seems to be a "specialist" in the profession of carnage and to have brought to the highest perfection the killing of cattle. Possibly it has its uses. But it will require a skillful man to ascertain them, and a very high powered magnifying glass.

LAS MARGARITAS
Roy T. McBride
1980

IN DURANGO AND ZACATECAS, WOLF CONTROL COMMENCED LATER than in Chihuahua and Sonora. Most of the high mountains of Durango were first logged for pine and ranching came later. With the arrival of cattle came the inevitable conflict with wolves. Ranchers purchased traps in the United States and offered bounties for wolves. The most effective wolf trapping method was the blind trap set in known wolf runways. What the cowboy didn't know about the fine art of wolf trapping, he made up for with an excellent knowledge of wolf habits. A crudely set trap, poorly concealed and dirty with rust and blood, would often set for months in a narrow mountain trail. Wind would cover the traps with leaves, rains would wash away the foreign odors, and eventually a wolf would step over a log or rock in the trail and be caught fast in a trap. The few wolves that survived these early efforts displayed remarkable intelligence and some even won the respect, if not the admiration, of their adversaries. The following is an account of one such wolf that defied concentrated efforts to capture it. It certainly ranks with any of the notorious wolves of the United States.

"Las Margaritas" was the name given this particular wolf. He operated over a large territory along the Zacatecas-Durango border, and during the late 1960s began killing yearling steers and heifers at a ranch named Las Margaritas. The wolf had two toes missing from its left front foot and his experience with traps left a memory that served him well. All efforts to poison or trap this wolf were futile, and in the spring of 1970 he moved northward to the Mazatlan-Durango Highway area where he began killing steers.

I was trapping in Durango and had heard about this wolf, but instead of having to go to Las Margaritas, he came to me. I was trying to catch a pair of wolves that were killing at El Carmen and an adjoining ejido, Augustine Melgar. I caught the female and the male left. Depredation started a few weeks later, and I was sure the male had returned, but I saw tracks in a trail and noticed the missing toes of Las Margaritas. During May the wolf left, killed some cattle towards Llano Grande, and then disappeared. In June he returned to Santa Barbara and killed 18 more steers. The wolf seldom used the same trail twice and if he came into a pasture by a log road, he left by a cow trail.

I was sure I could catch Las Margaritas, but I couldn't get him near a trap. In July, he came down a log road and passed by a trap, winded it, turned back, and trotted up to the trap, scarcely missing the trigger with the gap caused by the missing toes. The wolf then left the road. This narrow escape seemed to have frightened him because he did not return until September, whereupon he killed 96 steers and yearling heifers in eight months on one ranch alone.

In October, I found signs of the wolf beside a logging road. I placed a trap at this spot. Two weeks later the wolf passed by the trap, advanced a few steps towards it, and then bolted out of the road. He moved to a new area and resumed killing. In November, a pair of wolves showed up in the area and began killing in the same pasture that Las Margaritas was operating in. Several days after their arrival, I picked up tracks that the two wolves made before the dew. Margaritas' tracks were made after the pair. Finally the pair of wolves came to a trap and I caught the female. When Margaritas came to where the trap was pulled out of the ground, he left the road and disappeared until December.

In late December, Margaritas began killing in a new pasture. Traps were set daily on travel routes of the wolf, but the wolf seldom returned to a trail he had once used. Now convinced the wolf would not go to a baited site of any kind, I set three blind traps in a narrow cowtrail in the gap of a mountain. Two weeks passed and Margaritas came down a mountain divide and hit the cowtrail about 100 yards above the traps. Again, I felt confident I would have him caught. When he got about 15 feet from the first trap, he left the trail and went around the trap. Large live oaks were on either side of the trail and wind-blown leaves had hidden the traps beyond recognition. I had stepped from my horse to a steer hide while setting the traps and the dirt was removed by a sifter. The traps had even been boiled in oak leaves. Much care was taken to avoid disturbance of any sundry objects; the trap could have been born there and not been any better concealed. The wolf then returned to the trail and approached the second trap set on the other side of a pine tree that lay across the trail. Again he left the trail and went around the trap. As I neared the third trap, I saw that the trap was gone but again the wolf had left the trail before getting to the trap site. I located the trap with a coyote in it.

The wolf left and began killing about 15 miles to the west. Almost a year had passed and I was now convinced that I would never catch this wolf. At times, however, I had noticed where Margaritas had investigated a campfire along the road where log-truck drivers had stopped along the way to cook. I set a trap near a road that the wolf was sure to come down if it continued to kill in the area, built a fire over the trap and let it burn itself out. I placed a piece of dried skunk hide from an animal that had been run over months before in the logging road in the ashes.

On March 15 the wolf came down the road, winded the ashes and skunk hide and walked over to investigate. Margaritas was caught by the same crippled foot and the trap held. There was much celebration among the ranchers the following day. In eleven months of intensive effort and several thousand miles on horseback, I had managed to get the wolf near a trap only four times. Just how the wolf could tell the traps were there is something I cannot comprehend to this date.

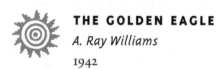

THE GOLDEN EAGLE
A. Ray Williams
1942

THE GOLDEN EAGLE IS ONE OF THE SMARTEST BIRDS OF THE SKIES. IT has the keenest eyesight of any bird that I know of. They are always on the lookout for food and they recognize man as their worst enemy. I have watched these birds sailing and gliding in the sky sometimes 3,000 feet above the earth. When they are hungry and locate a fawn deer or a fawn antelope, they just fold their wings close to their sides and dive down on their prey. When the eagles dive in this fashion, they are coming through the air so fast that they make a sound like air being forced through a pipe. Other times they will perch on a post or hill, waiting until they see something that they want. Then they will fly in and strike with their long sharp talons, and sometimes with their wings close to their bodies. They hardly ever miss catching their prey. I have seen them catch fawns of deer and antelope both.

In June 1930, I killed two old eagles and two young eagles just ready to leave their nest. The old ones had brought 25 antelope fawns to the young eagles to eat from the time they hatched until they were ready to leave the nest.

The eagle takes a heavy toll of Bighorn Sheep lambs and also the lambs of domestic sheep.

In April 1930, Mr. William J. Tucker called me into his office and told me to go to Hudspeth County and find out what it would take to bring back the antelope in the Trans-Pecos. When I reported to him what the eagles were doing to the antelope fawns, he gave me instructions to kill off the eagles. Since April 1930 to the present time, I have killed 2,338 eagles. I have killed eagles in Hudspeth, Culberson, Jeff Davis, Presidio, and Brewster Counties. The ranchers became interested in the eagle control work for the protection of their lambs and wildlife. Cooperation of the ranchers, close law enforcement, and eagle control work have helped the antelope increase to the point where the Game Department has been able to trap antelope in the Trans-Pecos district to send to other parts of the state for stocking purposes.

I am still fighting the eagles to keep the antelope increasing, hoping that some day the season might be opened on the buck antelope. I have killed eagles with poison, trapped them with steel traps, shot them with rifles and shotgun, 12-gauge loaded with BB shot. I have shot eagles while riding full speed on horseback, and from cars. I have spent 1,400 hours in an airplane killing eagles, with an average of one eagle per hour from the plane. Every time an eagle is killed at this time of year, spring, it saves the rancher from 10 to 30 lambs. That means more meat for Uncle Sam, also more wool to make blankets and clothes for our fighting men. It gets the eagle out of action before the antelope fawns begin to come along also.

Killing eagles from a plane in these high mountains gets the pilot and gunner into all kinds of sudden experiences. Sometimes the plane is stalled standing on its tail, and other times while diving at the earth, side-slipping first on one side and then on the other. Sometimes we hit an air current that puts us on our backs and in all kinds of positions while traveling at a speed of from 70 to 150 miles per hour. The ground can come at you fast when an eagle dives for earth and you are right on his tail in an airplane. When an eagle is hit with a load of BB shot under these circumstances, it just explodes, and the pieces are hard to find.

It is a great life if you don't weaken.

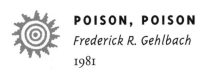

POISON, POISON
Frederick R. Gehlbach
1981

PRESIDIO, TEXAS — THE NAME EVOKES THE IMMEDIATE VISION OF A cold drink! This town is famed for its 100-degree summer temperatures. More than 100 consecutive days of over 100 degrees is not unusual, but Presidio can't match the Gran Desierto on the western end of the Borderlands for heat, as I am later to discover. However, Presidio excels in melons, cotton, and DDT or methyl parathion, so omnipresent that even the jackrabbits may act a little crazy because of it. I know this because pesticide research at Presidio is a classic in teamwork by naturalists, an exemplary study of unnatural history.

Nearly 5,000 acres are under cultivation in the Rio Grande Valley at Presidio and Ojinaga, Chihuahua, across the river. Irrigation agriculture is the mode, and the Rio Grande is potentially nutritive since Ojinaga dumps raw sewage into it. Pesticides are another way of life here—mostly DDT and methyl parathion—about 44,000 pounds in 1965, triple that amount by 1968. The U.S. and Mexican governments have jointly sprayed some ninety miles of the Rio Grande Valley.

When sprayed on cotton to control pestiferous insects, DDT is expected to accumulate in these plants, since it is washed into irrigation water, enters the soil, and is absorbed by plant roots. Even native plants that grow outside the cotton fields take up poisons. Leatherstem is a good example, accumulating methyl parathion in particular. Both kinds of pesticides rapidly decrease in amount from the centers of cotton fields to the peripheries, yet persist up to fifteen miles away.

Physical factors contribute to dispersing the poisons. Cultivated fields at Presidio are at the lowest elevations in the region, hence act as gigantic air-exchange devices. Cool night air moves in through arroyos, heats up during the day, and rises out over the surrounding shrub desert. As it moves, the air picks up dust particles from freshly turned agricultural earth. Dust devils, *remolinos,* the miniature tornadoes that swirl and dance across summer landscapes, are major vehicles of transportation. Moving dust is easily seen, but what cannot be seen are the millions of pesticide particles absorbed on the surface of each tiny dust particle.

Western, checkered, and little-striped whiptail lizards served the pesticide research team in demonstrating some results of pesticide drift and relocation. Specimens taken in shrub desert up to nine miles away from cotton fields contained DDT and methyl parathion in their tissues. Concentrations of the poisons increased during the growing season with continued aerial spraying until August, when a decrease occurred in females. By then up to five times the body tissue amounts were discovered in the lizards' eggs. The pesticides had simply shifted position from mother to egg, as fat energy was utilized for egg production. From eggs to the next lizard generation—the transfer of persistent pesticides may continue. If lizard eggs fail to hatch or hatch into deformed young, as we know happens in some birds, perhaps there will be no next lizard generation.

Whiptail lizards are familiar to anyone who walks awhile in the desert. Would they be missed? Suppose we add small mammals, say jackrabbits, to the list of the missing. Would the decrease in natural diversity then be-come apparent? What about kangaroo rats and pocket mice? The fate of pesticide-poisoned whiptail lizards is conjectural, but I can add a different hypothesis concerning small mammals in the shrub desert community.

Silky and desert pocket mice, Merriam kangaroo rats, and black-tailed jackrabbits were captured by the study teams. Some individuals were marked for reidentification and released. Curiously, individuals were re-captured most often in study plots with high pesticide concentrations. One would expect no difference in recapturability unless something was different about the mammals or their community. The team could find no differences in population sizes, food availability, soils, or climate. But they did find that the small mammals had higher body loads of pesticides in the plots with higher pesticide concentrations.

Methyl parathion in the brain tissue of black-tailed jackrabbits was sig-nificantly higher in such plots. Also, age-class structure of the jackrabbit population showed that addition of yearlings to replace old adults did not occur in the second year of study. Perhaps methyl parathion in the brain interferes with the normal behavior of jackrabbits, so these animals blunder into traps. This would explain the higher incidence of recaptures. And, if a live trap is replaced with a live coyote, the lack of recruitment of yearlings is explained. What will then become of the coyotes?

Proponents of the use of persistent pesticides often argue that the op-ponents' evidence comes only from plants and small animals, not humans. Thus the study team investigated man, the jackrabbit's distant cousin. Two area residents were examined, one with normal exposure to the local poisons, the other without. At the start the exposed fellow had stored a tenth of a part of DDT per million parts of urine. His unexposed counterpart—his control in the experiment—had no DDT in his urine. Two weeks later the first man's share of DDT had increased elevenfold, the second had acquired three-tenths of a part per million parts of urine. A month after that, the first man had twenty-three times the original amount of DDT, the second, six times his original amount. Can this go on until man himself blunders into a trap?

A third human subject, a pesticide spray-plane pilot, stored a third to three times his original amount of DDT just during the course of a day's work. He once complained of nausea following a mission. His doc-tor diagnosed the condition as methyl parathion poisoning and gave him atropine; he recovered. How many other Presidio and Ojinaga residents were affected? We don't know, but jackrabbits should make us cautious, since they are enough like the beagle dogs and white rats used in medical research to furnish an outdoor laboratory example.

Presidio is just one of many well-studied examples of large-scale agricultural use and the resulting widespread ramifications of pesticides. But what about small-scale use—the guy with the bug bomb in his hand? Can the average urbanite poison the Borderlands? Most likely he can, as Howard Applegate concluded in Big Bend National Park, where samples of soil, plants, and animals were collected eighty miles downwind of Presidio. Of nine sampling sites in the park, the four most used by people had the highest pesticide concentrations. Surprisingly, the Chisos Basin campground, 3,000 feet above the desert lowlands and shielded by a 2,000-foot mountain rim, was among the four. It should be isolated from pesticide drift.

It is possible that the DDT and methyl parathion found in the Basin campground were applied by people with bug bombs. Amounts needed to reach existing soil concentrations of DDT were calculated using the following assumptions: that pesticide concentrations were characteristic of the total camping area, not just the particular samples taken, that an acre of soil three inches deep weighs a million pounds, and that a pressurized spray can contains nine-tenths of one percent DDT. Then the size and typical visitor use of the Basin campground and two other camping areas, three of the four most highly poisoned sites, were figured. The Basin site was estimated to contain thirty-eight pounds of DDT, which would require 4,367 spray cans or 1.4 cans per camper during June-to-August season. Boquillas campground indicated 0.3 cans used per person, and Castolon, 1.9 cans in the same prime camping period.

If I hadn't had considerable experience in the Chisos Basin, I would hesitate to accept the figure of 1.4 cans per camper. But I remember this area, Boquillas, and Castolon too, from a time before the modern flood of campers and spray cans. Even in the 1950s, flies were unnaturally bothersome in the Basin campground because of the horse concession nearby. And gnats are a natural pestiferous feature of the summer monsoon. Now campers spray themselves, their equipment, and campside vegetation from March to September; so I believe 1.4 cans per person is a reasonable estimate, particularly when park rangers and concessionaires are included in the Basin's suburban population. . . .

Among the known recipients of pesticides are bats, the most numerous mammals in the world besides rodents. But bats are some ten times more susceptible to lethal DDT poisoning than rodents and perhaps ten times less able to compensate for their loss of individuals. A mouse can produce ten to twenty offspring per year, whereas a bat produces only one or two. Moreover, mice move only a few hundred feet at most in their nightly foraging, while bats fly several miles, can feed on insects over sprayed cropland, and hence can be poisoned outside refuges like Big Bend National Park. So I am not surprised that certain bat populations are declining in the Borderlands, and I believe it legitimate to suspect pesticide poisoning along with natural factors.

The once spectacular evening flight of eight million Brazilian free-tailed bats from Carlsbad Caverns, New Mexico, has all but ceased. Between 1934 and 1973, this population lost 98 percent of its members. Another colony of 25 million free-tails near Clifton, Arizona, declined 99.9 percent between 1963 and 1969. Although pesticides are not proven culprits in either case, proximity of both colonies to sprayed fields and winter migrations into Mexico, where DDT is still widely used, suggest such a hypothesis. Western pipistrelle bats in the same Arizona cave suffered no concurrent decline, but this smaller species does not migrate or travel far to feed and may not encounter pesticides as readily as the Brazilian free-tail. In any case insect consumption by the fewer free-tails in Arizona dropped from an estimated forty tons a night to a mere ninety-six pounds, and I wonder if spraying crops for destructive insects increased accordingly.

Brazilian free-tails remain among the most numerous of bats—*murciélagos*—in Big Bend National Park, and their population dynamics may predict the future of all bats in that refuge. Happily, these particular free-tails show no significant decline in numbers. Of course their summer home is farther from sprayed croplands than the summer haunts of free-tails at Carlsbad Caverns and Clifton, Arizona, but the Big Bend free-tails also migrate into Mexico each winter. Perhaps if pesticides have decimated the Carlsbad Caverns and Clifton colonies, only U.S. agribusiness is to blame, since the Big Bend population seems unaffected by its international experience.

THE MARVELOUS MALIGNED MESQUITE
Keith Elliott
1990

IN FARAWAY PLACES THERE SUDDENLY FLOURISHES A MESQUITE mania. What Texans have known for generations—that the sweet smoke of smoldering mesquite wood lends uncommon savor to grilled meats—has been discovered out yonder, beyond Texas.

Restaurants in New York and Philadelphia, Cleveland and Minneapolis, even London and Paris, are searing steaks—and fowl and seafood—over glowing coals of mystic mesquite. Clearly, yum's the word for mesquite cookery nowadays, and high time. The humble mesquite may be the most maligned, and most misunderstood, tree in the memory of man, notwithstanding the one of Good and Evil. Depending on point of view, the mesquite in Texas is perceived as bane or boon. Its stubborn presence among us is at the least a thorny issue.

On the one hand, there is W. T. Waggoner, pioneer rancher of northwest Texas. He scorned the mesquite as being "the devil with roots. It scabs my cows, spooks my horses, and gives little shade." Still, he admitted forlornly, "it gives the only shade there is, just about."

On the other hand there is J. Frank Dobie, bard of South Texas. He exulted: "No day can be counted entirely lost which begins with the smell of mesquite fire at dawn and the taste of coffee boiled over it."

Old-timers speak of an era in earlier Texas when there were far fewer mesquite trees than today. They, along with some historians and naturalists, believe that the mesquite originated in Mexico. It made its way to the American Southwest, the theory goes, when its seeds were distributed in the excrement of burros, horses, and migratory birds. The hitchhiking, thorn-borne seedpods also broadcast themselves as they rode such creatures and the wind, it is believed.

Well, yes and no, according to Del Weniger, biology professor at Our Lady of the Lake University in San Antonio. He reports that early explorers and surveyors made more than ten thousand references to mesquite trees in widespread parts of Texas between about 1660 and 1860. Thus, Weniger believes, "the mesquite is quite as native to Texas as it is to Mexico. It was abundant throughout western Texas long before the appearance of domestic livestock on the scene."

Weniger's research suggests that mesquite trees flourished in reaches comprising 140 present-day Texas counties in the two centuries before 1860. Captain John Popek, he says, surveyed parts of Texas for a projected western railroad in 1854 and reported forests of mesquite trees that were thirty feet high and four to ten inches in diameter. Railway management need never worry about fuel for its woodburning locomotives, Popek declared, or fret about material for railroad ties.

But such abundance was sadly short-lived, according to Weniger. After the Civil War, during the stirring days of the Longhorn drives and the infancy of the Texas cattle industry, millions of prairie acres were denuded of their *mezquitales*—places where mesquite abounds. "Vast acreages of mesquite were practically eliminated in the Nueces River valley in the 1870s, for example. I read of a single ranch with a fence made of mesquite trunks six feet high, touching each other, that stretched for fifteen miles."

So old-timers who recall Texas as being largely void of mesquite at the turn of the century are entirely correct, he believes. "Trees were burned, grubbed out, and chopped down for use as fuel, lumber, and fence posts. Mesquite makes good fence posts, because it is slow to rot. It's durable, too—some of the pioneers called it 'Texas ironwood.' Did you know that downtown Houston Street here in San Antonio was once paved with mesquite blocks? Bumpy, I suppose, but tougher than concrete."

Mesquite paving blocks lined the streets of turn-of-the-century Brownsville, too. Pioneers used mesquite for the hubs and spokes of wagon wheels and for the ribs and knees of boats. Furniture for the headquarters of the famed King Ranch is made of mesquite. Mesquite was used as timbering in the original Alamo built in 1718. And a cannon fired in Mexico's war against Spain for independence was fashioned by the patriot José María Morelos from a hollowed mesquite log. It may be viewed today in Mexico City's National Museum.

Hardly more than a bush on the far western plains of Texas, the mesquite is often a regal tree in the state's wetter reaches, especially along tributary bottoms. The national champion mesquite, in Real County, has a trunk twelve feet, eight inches in circumference, and its branches form an umbrella fifty-two feet high and seventy-one feet wide.

Many Texans believe the mesquite to be a more reliable harbinger of spring than the robin or the ground-hog. "Plant cotton when the mesquite tree leafs" is an ancient folk saying, and a wise one. When the mesquite buds, there is no longer threat of frost—that is the rural gospel. Warning, though: Trust only the older mesquites. The youngsters may rush the season and try on their finery before the party begins.

In some ways, the mesquite is not an easy tree to love. It is a defiant growth with cruel thorns and impenetrable brush, a come-and-take-it kind of tree. Little wonder that Sunday ranchers bulldoze, root-plow, burn, and grub it from their pastures.

Dr. Peter Felker of Texas A&M University, at Kingsville, disdains the popular view that mesquite depletes precious water. It drinks no more than other trees, he says. "I don't see mesquite as most people see mesquite," he admits. "I see mesquite as a nitrogen-fixing tree, capable of dealing with a lot of drought and capable of enriching the soil. Capable, too, of providing beans that have been a major food source of the Indians of the desert regions before the white men came, and a viable resource for animals."

Pioneers of the Texas Republic had a saying: "With prickly pear cactus apples alone, one can live, but with pear apples and mesquite beans, one will get fat." The mesquite has been a wondrous apothecary over the years. Nearly five hundred years ago, the Aztecs, who named the tree the *miz-*

quitl, ground its leaves to a powder, added water, and used the mixture to heal sore eyes. In rural Mexico, *curanderos* still use the ancient remedy.

Comanches chewed mesquite leaves to cure toothache. Yumas treated venereal disease with the leaves. Yaquis pulped them with water and urine to make a poultice for headaches. Mexican women boiled them with clothes as a bleach. Papagos used the mesquite's inner bark to ease indigestion. Various tribes have used the mesquite's gum, a sweetish amber substance, as a balm for wounds and sores, to mend pottery, to make a black dye, to aid digestion, to brew into a tea for diarrhea, or simply to chew for pleasure. (Old-timers still chew mesquite gum on the belief it strengthens their hearts.)

Authorities say Texas contains about fifty million of the seventy million U.S. acres where mesquites are dominant vegetation. The tree's haphazard and convoluted postures in the wild may seem grotesque to the formalist, but they are gaining favor among artists and artisans. Philip John Evett, native Englishman who is a sculptor and teacher of sculpture in San Antonio, is one of these. He believes mesquite is the most workable of woods for one of his calling. "It is more durable than mahogany," he says, "and its grains are lovely and unpredictable."

Jim Lee, a world-class woodturner from Regan Wells in the Texas Hill Country, says simply, "Mesquite is the king of woods." Not a bad commentary on the most slandered tree of the Texas Plains.

AUTUMN

Lisa Beaumont

1993

AUTUMN. THAT IS THE TIME OF THE YEAR THAT I FEEL THE HIGH energy surges that make me hear the call of the wild. I lust to wander. I want to see new places and meet new people and do new things. I feel so very alive in the Autumn.

There is a tangible taste and feel to the air. It is robust, almost sexual in its headiness. The sun hits the grass from an angle that calls up a golden nostalgia from deep within my being. There is an anxiety about me that sometimes squeezes a moan from my throat. I want something but I don't know what it is.

The symphony of colors is like a dynamic catapult that throws me into an emotional frenzy. I want to laugh or cry. I want to gather the colors to my breast and hold them for hours. I want each leaf and blade of grass that is metamorphosing to rustle around the windows of my dreams.

I love the gaudy and haphazard way the leaves fall and mingle together, then run up and down the streets like children who know they should go home but want to stay just a few minutes more in the soothing balm of an Autumn evening. Autumn is a crusade of movement and gestures.

Then winter's pale and anemic color chart marches up and stiffly replaces the vivaciousness of Autumn. Perhaps it is a stark reminder to me of the way life is. Birth, maturity, overripe maturity, and death. I am in the Autumn of my life. My leaves are beginning to turn. Maybe that's why I want the riot of glorious colors to last a long time.

FIVE

Devil's Playground

TOURISM IS WITHOUT A DOUBT THE MOST LUCRATIVE big business the West has ever produced. Although it has traditionally been touted as a benign form of resource use, that idea is being seriously questioned as tourists have turned beautiful places into trashed, overtrodden, colonialized playgrounds for the leisure class. Extreme sports have produced adrenaline junkies who sometimes treat nature like a scenic gym, used mostly for physical and mental workouts or cooldowns. Called "ecoporn" when used in advertising, an air-brushed nature free of bugs, heat, and death has taken the place of scantily clad women for purposes of arousal and identification.

Tourism causes genuine cultures to become corny caricatures of themselves in order to play to the camera. Local occupations become demonized and forbidden. If locals stay, they are forced into seasonal, low-paying, service jobs while land taxes rise to the point that they can no longer afford to live in the area. West Texas' two national parks, thus far, have had fairly low visitation and have not yet suffered the damaging overuse most U.S. national parks endure, possibly because we have a bit of the "devil's playground" reputation: too hot, too far, not enough conveniences, and not much to do. Our creeks are too hot and dry for trout and our mountains don't smoke or bubble. Even backpacking in the Big Bend becomes a physical test of packing water and hunting shade.

One of the many side effects of tourism seems to be some degree of contempt for the local people. A behavioral science theorist whose ideas are pertinent to travel writing, Edward Said, calls the outsider's condemning view of another culture "Orientalism." Based on European stereotypes of the "mysterious," "strange," and "corrupt" Orient, his theories have also been applied to the Europeans' attitude toward their colonies, the wealthy toward the poor, the environmentalist toward the rural West, and the traveler toward the local.[1] The tourist relationship is a power relationship in which both local people and local places are imagined to exist for the pleasure and entertainment of the visitor. Ludwig Bemelmans' piece is a perfect example of a tongue-in-cheek, humorously contemptuous view of local people by the typical tourist, which many readers find very entertaining. A New Yorker on holiday, Bemelmans compares the Big Bend landscape to a Beethoven symphony, but finds the locals "exactly as they are pictured in the movies." He describes their weather-tolerant cemetery art as "primitive" and, on observing a cowboy crush empty beer cans and "tinkle" his spurs in order to impress some ladies, he compares him to a monkey.

Probably in direct response to, or possibly a cause of, the tourist's contempt for local people is the locals' contempt for tourists. Two prime reasons for this contempt are destruction of rural roads and accumulation of trash. In this chapter, a former Sul Ross State University president, Horace W. Morelock, laments, then solves, the problem of student loss of free access to surrounding ranchland for picnics because of littering.[2] Edward Abbey, in his own ironic way, subtly tries to discourage people from driving fragile desert back roads. His humorous description of totally destroying his former fiancée's new convertible on a washed-out river road is a classic Abbey ramble.

Still another excuse for local contempt toward the tourist is ignorance. Virginia Madison tells a "city hunter" story about a fellow who shot an antelope, thinking it was a deer, during the days when antelope were heavily protected. Antelope were common in West Texas in the 1890s, but their numbers dropped to dangerous lows in 1901. Due to intense management by Texas Parks and Wildlife in cooperation with many local ranchers who voluntarily designated their property as wildlife preserves, imported antelope bucks to improve genetics, and reduced eagle numbers, antelope are again thriving—although the numbers fluctuate due to droughts. Throughout most of the Trans-Pecos, antelope populations are high enough today to support a nine-day hunting season. Ironically, one of the few places where they have not returned is Big Bend National Park.

One of the all-time great avian artists, Louis Agassiz Fuertes, is presented herein as a writer. His 1901 description of birding with a gun in the Chisos Mountains seems quite shocking in these modern days. But we forget that Audubon's bird paintings (which in my opinion take second place to Fuertes' work) were also created through close observation of collected dead birds. Fuertes was traveling with naturalist Vernon Bailey on this trip to the Big Bend. All of the books in which Fuertes' paintings appear were written by someone else, but after this brief taste of his clever and refreshing letter writing, the reader will wish that Fuertes had written the books as well as illustrated them.

Forty years later birders with guns were still at it in the Big Bend.

Herbert Brandt describes "collecting" what he hoped would be a rare Mexican sparrow and even the famed Colima warbler. This not-so-old habit of killing birds in order to prove a sighting or produce a detailed description must have taken a tremendous toll on bird populations. Although Brandt doesn't actually say he shot a Colima, he notes the "bright reddish crown-patch which can only be detected by parting the head feathers." He may have lifted that information from a field guide, or he may have parted the head feathers himself on a dead bird in order to prove his sighting. Although guns are banned today, some birders carry tape recordings of bird calls in order to bring mating birds into view. Many believe this practice confuses fragile species during courtship, and would like to see it outlawed. Tourists, fishermen, mountain climbers, photographers, and even birders can suffer from the trophy-collecting syndrome.

Birds were not the only species collected in the Big Bend. Vernon Bailey, a former chief U. S. naturalist, traveled around the country at the turn of the century collecting everything for the sake of knowledge. In the excerpt collected here, he describes shooting bighorns in the Guadalupe Mountains, even though he says one hunter can wipe them out and he wants to see them protected. Texas Parks and Wildlife is currently trying to reintroduce these animals, now extinct in Texas, into the Black Gap Wildlife Management Area. Their problem today, however, is a hunter who carries no gun: mountain lions seem to consider the bighorns a favorite meal.

Also, so that the reader does not get the false idea that only male naturalists were collectors, Mary Young, a University of Texas botanist, collecting plants on Mount Livermore, packs two guns,[3] shoots rabbits and squirrels for her supper, tries to shoot a bear cub, and quenches her thirst by eating wildflowers. Plant collecting in the Big Bend, both for science and for landscaping, has taken and still takes a toll on the rare and beautiful. Cactus, ocotillo, and Spanish daggers are transported out of the Big Bend by the truckloads to yards and gardens from a half-mile away to Japan.

This chapter also includes several views of river running for pleasure. Mary Humphrey gives explicit directions for running the notorious Rock Slide in Santa Elena Canyon, but warns that one mistake can be fatal and admits that few canoes have run it perfectly. The portage, she says, is a "mankiller," and she mentions as well the danger from carrizo, thorned brush that overhangs the water and causes canoers and kayakers to capsize. In addition, she explains why the Rio Grande should possibly more properly be called the Río Bravo del Norte.[4]

In "Firearms, Exploding Rocks, and a Centipede in Bed," Dudley

Dobie experiences a more friendly section of the river. He and his friends are attracted by a few of the "toys" typical of the Devil's playground: mixing liquor with guns, "lonely" donkeys, smelly buzzards, and hidden rocks. His view of local people, whom he calls "shy children of the desert," at first glance seems somewhat positive. However, outright contempt for another culture and a noble savage admiration for their "simpler" and more "peaceful" existence are both sides of the same condescending coin. As Montana writer Bill Kittredge once said, "Try sitting around while someone tells you how he envies the simplicity of your life."[5]

Finally, Fred McCarty describes a close call when obviously neophyte rafters ignore ranger warnings and listen to locals. The rafters soon find themselves lodged between boulders in the Rock Slide, with the river washing belongings and men out of the raft and ripping off life preservers. Two near-drownings, a two-day rescue, and a many-year recovery make this trip to the Big Bend McCarty's last.

NOTES

1. Edward W. Said, *Orientalism* (New York: Vintage Books, 1979).

2. Morelock was president of Sul Ross State University from 1923 to 1945. His philosophy was that "education is for everyone, not just for a chosen few."

3. According to Marcia Myers Bonta (*American Women Afield: Writings by Pioneering Women Naturalists* [College Station: Texas A&M University Press, 1995], 154), Young carried a .25 Colt automatic that "she concealed in her skirt pocket" and a .22 six-shooter revolver. Although her male assistant is sometimes described as shooting animals also, the guns belonged to Miss Young.

4. The Rio Grande was given numerous names by the early explorers. Coronado called it Tiguex, Alvarado called it Nuestra Señora, Rodríguez called it Guadalquivir or Nuestra Señora de la Concepción, Obregón called it Tibuex, Castaño de Soza called it Río Bravo, and Juan de Oñate called it Río Bravo or Río del Norte. Luxán says they named it El Río Turbio "because it is exceedingly muddy" (George P. Hammond and Agapito Rey, *Expedition into New Mexico Made by Antonio de Espejo, 1582–1583* [Los Angeles: Quivira Society, 1929], 58, 64).

5. William Kittredge, *Owning It All* (Saint Paul, Minn.: Graywolf, 1987), 90.

TINKLING SPURS
Ludwig Bemelmans
1956

LEAVING HIGHWAY 90 AT MARATHON WE CAME TO THE BIG BEND country toward sunset, that part of Texas where the Rio Grande makes a U-shaped bend in its course. In a lifetime spent in traveling, here I came upon the greatest wonder. The mantle of God touches you; it is what Beethoven reached for in music; it is panorama without beginning or end.

No fire can burn so bright, no projection can duplicate the colors that dance over the desert or the bare rock formations that form the backdrop. No words can tell you, and no painter hold it. It is only to be visited and looked at with awe. It will make you breathe deeply whenever you think of it, for you have inhaled eternity.

There is no tree, no house to measure things by. You are in scale with the cactus plant, the stone in the distance—the all-important and the nothing.

As yet there is no interference with this wonderful scene. It is unviolated by signs or other gimmicks. You are left alone to contemplate it, and the only thing to worry about is to take enough gas along, for the service stations here are very far apart.

We drove into Big Bend National Park, and the trip in February when the weather is cold is what the British like to call "a bit rugged." The park is not quite finished yet, and you had better drive carefully. The road rises until your carburetor balks, and you have to drive in first gear—up, up, into craggy wilderness.

The welcome is genuine, but the cabins are built for summer in the High Sierras, not for February. In the center of our little shack there was an oil stove that burned so furiously all night that it shook the place. I left my socks on and put my overcoat over the bed, but still I shivered like a wet terrier all night, and in the morning did not shave or wash. This provided considerable amusement for my wife because when we are at home in New York, I am always complaining that our apartment is overheated.

It is a tribute to American cars that they start in such weather. Still hunched over and breathing on my fingers, I inserted the ignition key into the lock, then drove up to the "Chuck Wagon" for breakfast.

As all breakfasts on any trip through America, we put this one down in the category of first-rate food.

There is a bit of the romantic West up in these mountains. For instance, the young men who take you on pack trains and sometimes help out in the bar are the type, frequently encountered in these parts, who always make me wonder what they sit on. These men measure widest at the shoulders. Lanky and deliberate of motion, slow to smile but wide and handsome in their ways, they are exactly as they are pictured in the movies.

The one who waited on us in the Chuck Wagon had sideburns and a black Western hat with the brim sharply turned up at the sides. The Bull Durham ticket hung out of his chest pocket. He allowed his spurs to tinkle occasionally, and with arms long as a gibbon's and his very extended legs, he changed from one manly pose of relaxation to another. Although casual, these attitudes seemed to be planned patterns. He did not say much, but when a few girls came in and sat down, he tinkled with the spurs and slowly reached over for some empty beer cans, and in a feat that I have not seen equaled, he squashed them in one hand as easily as if they had been overripe persimmons.

With that very elegant weariness that youth and hours in the saddle produce, he ambled over to us and asked us what we would have. I asked for two beers.

"I s'pose you drink it in glasses," he said without condescension, as he placed two cans before us and turned to get glasses.

Compared with what one might pay at a dude ranch, prices in these parts are amazingly reasonable. For instance, a pack trip with mounted guide, both saddle and pack animals furnished, all necessary gear and horse feed, first-aid kit, a cook, food, canteen for drinking water and rain-coats comes to $20 a day for one person. Rates are proportionately less according to the number of people on the trip. Levis may be rented for 50 cents and hats for 25 cents.

As you leave the Big Bend in the direction of Alpine, a road off the main highway leads six miles west to a ghost mining town called Terlingua.

In a landscape which wind and weather have ravaged and the sun of thousands of years has bleached to the color of pepper, this is a place of roofless adobe houses, abandoned machinery and a cemetery.

In the cemetery, romanticism, love and friendship have found their ex-pression in curious wreaths made from old cans. The cans were flattened out and leaves and petals cut from them. Wires were soldered on four stems, and then the metal flowers were brightly painted. The designs are of that rare simplicity which is primitive art. The wreaths lie about gaily in the dusty desolation.

From Terlingua the vast solitude goes on for some hundreds of miles.

KOKERNOT SPRINGS
Horace W. Morelock
1956

THE GROUNDS SURROUNDING KOKERNOT SPRINGS WERE ONE OF THE many strategic points that dotted the Big Bend country during pioneer days.

Immediately to the south of Kokernot Lodge, under towering Chi-nese elms with wide spreading branches and on the bank of a stream that struggles through deep underbrush fifteen feet below, a granite monument was erected by the Texas Centennial Commission, which bears this inscription:

> Burgess Water Hole. Called Lorenzo by Juan Dominguez de Mendoza, 1684, later Charco de Alzate in honor of the Apache Chieftain. After the Civil War given the name of Burgess Water Hole honoring John W. Burgess, pioneer freighter, who here outwitted the Apaches. The immigrant road to California by way of Chihuahua passed this place.

It was on these grounds, during the first quarter of the twentieth century, that "town and gown" met and mingled on "the last frontier" to pool their assets of past experiences and to synchronize their efforts for a greater tomorrow.

During the early days of Sul Ross, the "Scenic Drive through the Davis Mountains" had its origin. The itinerary of something like 100 miles was relieved by a stop-over at Fort Davis to inspect the forts built in 1854; by baseball and horseshoe pitching, and side trips high up in the Davis Mountains; by an inspection of Rock Pile Ranch; by a visit to Bloys Camp Meeting; and then home via Marfa. The pleasure trip was climaxed by a free-for-all barbecue at Kokernot Springs. Transportation was provided by Alpine citizens, and on many trips it required more than 100 automobiles to accommodate the students of Sul Ross. J. D. Jackson always took a fatherly interest in Sul Ross, and he made every one of these trips in his own car. On the way he told many interesting stories of "early days." Jackson Athletic Field was later named for him in recognition of his contributions.

This annual excursion developed in students an urge for week-end picnics to neighboring canyons up to a distance of 25 miles from Alpine. The ranchmen contributed to this relief scene by offering sites along the highways. But by degrees students and others became careless about leaving gates open, by failing to put out campfires, and by forgetting to clear the grounds of sharp-edged tin cans. The ranchmen complained to me. Most of my pleadings [as president of the college at the time] with the beneficiaries for cooperation with the ranchmen fell, as it were, like seed cast by the wayside. I sensed that the day was soon coming when college picnics would be confined to the campus, and the advisory committee of the faculty decided to plant a grove of trees at the east of the campus as a guarantee against a "rainy day." A well was drilled and provided with a gasoline pump, a two-inch pipe was installed and several poplar trees were planted with appropriate ceremonies. But the project proved a failure.

It was then that a vision one night prompted me the next morning to drive down to Kokernot Springs to inspect its possibilities. The thought came to me as I stood under cottonwood trees more than three feet in diameter and lombardy poplars towering more than 90 feet toward the sky, larded with the spreading branches of willow trees, and a clear stream of water meandering through a maze of water cresses, wild flowers, and a network of roots sustaining a variety of trees peculiar to this area—that this idyllic spot might be developed into a community center as a kind of rendezvous for the college and the citizens of Alpine.

Mr. H. L. Kokernot, Sr., was guardian of the John W. and Glen Kokernot estate on which Kokernot Springs was located, and I approached him one day to get his reaction to my idea. He was noncommittal for the moment. But sometime later I met him downtown, and immediately he made me a convert to the portent of dreams: "Go down to Kokernot Springs, select the area that will serve your purpose, set up corners, have the land surveyed, and I will make out a deed to it."

DISORDER AND EARLY SORROW
Edward Abbey
1977

THE FIRST TIME I INVESTIGATED BIG BEND NATIONAL PARK WAS A long time ago, way back in '52 during my student days at the University of New Mexico. My fiancée and I drove there from Albuquerque in her brand-new Ford convertible, a gift from her father. We were planning a sort of premature, premarital honeymoon, a week in the wilderness to cement, as it were, our permanent relationship. Things began well. With all the other tourists (few enough in those days), we followed the paved road down from Marathon and into the park at Persimmon Gap, paused at the entrance station for instruction and guidance, as per regulations, and drove up into the Chisos Mountains that form the heart of this rough, rude, arid national park. We camped for a few days in the Chisos Basin, hiking the trails to Lost Mine, to the Window, to Emory Peak and Casa Grande. Some of the things I saw from those high points, looking south, attracted me. Down in those blue, magenta, and purplish desert wastes are odd configurations of rock with names like Mule Ear Peaks and Cow Heaven Anticline. I was interested; my fiancée was satisfied with long-distance photographs.

When I inquired of a ranger how to get down there, he told me we'd have to backpack it; there was, he said, "no road." I showed him my 1948 Texaco map; according to the map there was a road—unpaved, ungraded, primitive to be sure, but a road all the same—leading from the hamlet of Castolon near the southwest corner of the park to Rio Grande Village at the east-central edge of the park. Fifty miles of desert road.

"That road is closed," the ranger told me.

"Closed?"

"Not fit for travel," he explained. "Permanently washed out. Not patrolled. Not safe. Absolutely not recommended."

My sweetheart listened carefully.

I thanked him and departed, knowing at once where I wanted to go. Had to go. Since we were not equipped for backpacking, it would have to be on wheels. My fiancée expressed doubts; I reassured her. We drove down the old road along Alamo Creek—the only road at that time—to the mouth of Santa Elena Canyon. We contemplated the mouth of Santa Elena Canyon for a day, then headed east to Castolon, where we stocked up on water and food. I made no further inquiries about the desert road; I did not wish to expose myself to any arguments.

A short distance beyond Castolon we came to a fork in the road. The left-hand fork was marked by a crude, hand-painted wooden sign that said:

"Hartung's Road Take the Other."

Staked in the middle of the right-hand fork was a somewhat more official-looking board that said:

"No road."

The left-hand fork led northeasterly, up a rocky ravine into a jumble of desert hills. The other fork led southeasterly, following the course of the Rio Grande into the wastelands of southern Big Bend. One would have liked to meet Mr. Hartung, but his road was not our road.

I pulled up the No Road sign, drove through, stopped, replaced the sign. Our tire tracks in the dust showed clearly on each side of the warning sign, as if some bodiless, incorporeal ghost of a car had passed through. That should confuse the park rangers, I thought, if they ever came this way. My fiancée meanwhile was objecting to the whole procedure; she felt it was time to turn back. Gently but firmly I overruled her. We advanced, cautiously but steadily, over the rocks and through the sand, bound for Rio Grande Village—an easy fifty-mile drive somewhere beyond those mountains and buttes, mesas and ridges and anticlines on the east.

All went well for half a mile. Then we came to the first of a hundred gulches that lie transverse to the road, formed by the rare flash floods that drain from the hills to the river. The gulch was deep, narrow and dry but filled with sand and cobbles. The drop-off from bank to streambed was two feet high. Time to build road. I got out the shovel, beveled off the edge of the cut bank on either side, removed a few of the larger rocks, logs, and other obstacles. Revving the Ford's hearty V-8 engine, I put her in low and charged down, across the rocks, and up the other side. A good little car, and it made a game effort, hanging to the lip of the far embankment while the rear wheels spun furiously in the sand and gravel. Not quite sufficient traction; we failed to make it. I backed down into the bottom of the gulch, opened the trunk, took out the luggage and filled the trunk with rocks. That helped. Gunning the engine, we made a second lunge for the top and this time succeeded, though not without cost. I could smell already the odor of burning clutch plate.

Onward, though my fiancée continued to demur. We plunged into and up out of another dozen ravines, some of them deeper and rougher than the first, sometimes requiring repeated charges before we could climb out. Although the car had less than 5,000 miles to its career, some parts began to give under the strain. The right-hand door, for example had been forced a trifle askew, springing the door. I wired it shut with a coat hanger. My sweetheart, in a grim mood by this time, suggested again that we turn around. I pointed out that the road ahead could hardly be as bad as what we had come through already and that the only sensible course lay in a resolute advance. She was doubtful; I was wrong, but forceful. I added water to the boiling radiator, diluting the manufacturer's coolant, and drove on.

There seemed no choice. After all, I reasoned, we had already disregarded a park ranger's instructions and a clear warning sign. Our path was littered not only with bolts, nuts, cotter pins, and shreds of rubber, but broken law as well. Furthermore, I had to see what lay beyond the next ridge.

In the afternoon we bogged down halfway through a stretch of sand. I spent two hours shoveling sand, cutting brush and laying it on the roadway, and repeatedly jacking up the rear of the car as it advanced, sank, stopped. I could have partially deflated the tires and got through more easily but we had no tire pump, and ahead lay many miles of stony trail.

By sundown of the first day we had accomplished twenty miles. The car still ran but lacked some of its youthful élan. The bright enamel finish was scarred and scoriated, dulled by a film of dust. We made camp and ate our meal in silence. Coyotes howled like banshees from the foothills of Backbone Ridge, gaunt Mexican cattle bellowed down in the river bottom, and across the western sky hung the lurid, smoldering fires of sunset, a spectacle grim and ghastly as the announcement of the end of the world. A scorpion scuttled out of the shadows past our mesquite fire, hunting its evening meal. I made our bed in a dusty clearing in the cactus, but my beloved refused to sleep with me, preferring, she said, to curl up in the back seat of her car. The omens multiplied and all were dark. I slept alone under the shooting stars of Texas, dreaming of rocks and shovels.

Dawn, and a dusty desert wind, and one hoot owl hooting back in the bush. I crawled out of my sack and shook my boots out (in case of arachnids), made breakfast and prepared for another struggle through the heat, the cactus, the rock, and, hardest of all, the unspeaking enmity of my betrothed.

The second day was different from the first. Worse. The washouts rougher than before, the ravines deeper, the sandy washes broader, the stones sharper, the brush thornier. In the morning we had our first flat. No repair kit, of course; no pump, no tire irons. I bolted on the spare tire, which meant that for the next thirty miles we would have no spare. Onward. We thrashed in and out of more gullies and gulches, burning up the pressure plate, overheating the engine, bending things. Now the other door, the one on the driver's side, had to be secured with coat-hanger wire. Sprung doors were always a problem with those old Ford convertibles.

We clattered on. Detouring an unnecessarily bad place on the road, I veered through the cactus and slammed into a concealed rock. Bent the tie-rod. Taking out the lug wrench, I hammered the tie-rod as straight as I could. We drove on with the front wheels toed in at a cockeyed angle. Hard to steer and not good for the tires, which were compelled, now one, now the other, or both at once, to slide as well as roll, forward. They might or might not endure for the twenty miles or so that, according to my Texaco road map and the record of the odometer, we still had to cover.

As in any medical disorder, one malady aggravates another. Because of the friction in the front end I found it harder to negotiate the car across the washes and up out of the ravines. It was no longer sufficient merely to gear down into low, pop the clutch, and *charge!* up the far side. I had to charge *down* as well as *up*. The clutch still functioned, but it was going. I prayed for the clutch, but it was the oil pan I worried about. My fiancée, clutching at the dashboard with both hands, jaw set and eyes shut, said nothing. I thought of iron seizures, bleeding crankcases, a cracked block.

Nevertheless: forward. Determination is what counts.

Cactus, sand pits, shock-busting chuckholes, axle-breaking washouts, rocks. And more rocks. Embedded like teeth in the roadway, points upward, they presented a constant nagging threat to my peace of mind. No matter how slowly I drove forward, lurching over the ruts at one mile an hour, there was no way I could avoid them all. I missed a few, but one of them got us, five miles short of the goal, late in the afternoon of the second day. A sharp report rang out, like a gunshot, followed by the squeal of hot air, the sigh of an expiring tire, and I knew we were in difficulty.

I stopped to inspect the damage, for form's sake, but there was really nothing I could do. Nothing practical, that is, except maybe pull the wheel and roll it on to Rio Grande Village by hand where, possibly, I could have it fitted with a new tire, and roll it back here to the stricken Ford. I suggested this procedure to my one and only. She objected to being left alone in the scorching wilderness full of animals and Mexicans while I disappeared to the east. Did she wish to walk with me? No, she didn't want to do that either.

That helped make up my mind. I got back in the car, started the engine and drove on, flat tire thumping on the roadway, radiator steaming, clutch smoking, oil burning, front wheels squealing, the frame and all moving parts a shuddering mass of mechanical indignation. The car clanked forward on an oblique axis, crabwise, humping up and down on the eccentric camber of the flat. Scraps of hot, smoking rubber from the shredded tire marked our progress. Late in the evening, on scalloped wheel rim and broken heart, we rumbled painfully into Rio Grande Village, pop. 22, counting dogs.

My fiancée took the first bus out of town. She had most of our money. I was left behind to hitchhike through West Texas with two dollars and forty-seven cents in my pocket. The car, as I later heard, was salvaged by my sweetheart and her friends, but never recovered its original *esprit de Ford*. Nor did I ever see my fiancée again. Our permanent relationship had been wrecked, permanently. Not that I could blame her one bit. She was fully justified. Who could question that statement? All the same it hurt; the pain lingered for weeks. Small consolation to me was the homely wisdom of the philosopher, to wit:

> A woman is only a woman
> But a good Ford is a car.

PRONGHORN
Virginia Madison
1968

MANY TOURISTS ARE MOST CURIOUS ABOUT THE PRONGHORN, AND there is no doubt that, of all the animals in the Big Bend, the pronghorn is the most curious about the tourists, and it is his overweening curiosity which has been his undoing.

In the fall of 1934, I was standing in front of the Holland Hotel, in Alpine, when an eastern hunter came out of the hotel to find his car completely fenced in by cowboys and street-corner personnel. It was deer-hunting season in the Big Bend country, and hunters were there from everywhere. The sight of cars with one or more deer tied on front fenders was as common as frijoles on local menus; so, obviously, the group around the car was not agog over a deer.

"Didn't any of you Texans ever see a deer?" asked the hunter. "You can drive out to the edge of town any day in the week and kill one. It took only thirty minutes to get mine," he bragged. He was totally unprepared for the howls of laughter, the bootstamping and leg-slapping which followed his announcement.

One lanky bronc rider turned informer: "Mister, that animal you got draped over your fender there ain't no deer. It's an antelope. There has been a closed season on them around here for about thirty years."

Then a cowboy offered some practical advice: "If I was you, I think I'd *vamos*. If our game warden was to come around that corner right now, I'll bet he'd throw you so far back in jail they'd have to shoot beans to you with a .30-.30 rifle and when you did get out you'd lay a fine of $500 on the line as a going-away present."

"The hell you say!" Then, realizing the monetary worth of the cowboy's advice, the abashed hunter added, "Thanks, fellow," and headed east on Highway 67. The group of spectators, fully enjoying the humor of the situation, began laying bets on how far out of town the hunter would go before he dumped his prize cargo.

It is hard to believe that a hunter could mistake a pronghorn for a deer, but a lot of people are of the opinion that, in this country, they went the way of the buffalo years ago. And so they would have gone had it not been for the cooperative efforts of game departments and ranchers. By prohibiting the hunting of pronghorns for a number of years, and by restocking areas where they had been killed off, they enabled these animals to stage a comeback in the Big Bend country. Since 1941, a limited number of hunting permits have been issued each season, but, of course, none are hunted in the Big Bend National Park.

Whether one goes to the Big Bend country as a tourist, a hunter, or a naturalist bent on the study of wildlife, he will enjoy watching herds of these beautiful animals skimming like the wind over wide, unfenced valleys and along highways and railroads. If he takes time to watch them, he will find, more than likely, that they are racing with his car or with the train on which he is riding. It is only natural to like to participate in the sport at which one excels, and so it is with pronghorns. They can run and they know it, and they make a fair showing, too, even when competing with trains and cars.

So graceful are they in motion that a herd of running pronghorns looks like the undulation of a breeze-swept wheatfield. The speed of the prong-horn is easy to check by automobile. Ray Williams has clocked over two hundred at different times and has found their average speed to be about forty-five miles an hour for the first mile and a half, and after that thirty to thirty-five miles per hour, a pace which they can hold for ten to fifteen miles.

Invariably, they will try to cross in front of anything they are racing with and once they start for a certain point it is almost impossible to make them change their course. Jim P. Wilson, Alpine rancher, said that when he arrived in the Big Bend, in the early 1880s, pronghorns ran in herds of two to three hundred. One day, when trains were new to that country, he saw one of these big herds startled by a Southern Pacific freight, travel-ing east from Marathon. They ran along a drift fence which crossed the railroad and, as they do not stop when once started in a given direction, the herd of animals ran headlong into the freight train and were knocked a hundred feet in all directions. Some were hurled high in the air and lit on top of the train. Wilson and a friend finished off the ones seriously in-jured, but those animals still able to run continued in the direction they had started before the train turned their fright into a carnage.

The pronghorn is strictly a North American animal. He possesses some of the characteristics of the giraffe, the deer, and goat, and the African antelope, yet he is not enough like any of them to be classed in the same family, so scientists created a separate family for him. The pronghorn is the only animal in the world with bifurcated hollow horns, which are shed and renewed every year like the antlers of the deer, yet they grow around a permanent bony core like the hollow horns of a goat or cow. Cutaneous musk glands on the head, feet, and legs, and on the back near the rump patches, working in conjunction with the crupper disks, serve as commu-nication signals. Some observers say that a pronghorn can detect the musk odor a mile away.

Long white hairs on the rump lie perfectly flat when the animals are grazing or resting, but, at the first inkling of danger or when they are angry, these hairs stand erect, giving the impression of a flash of light. Pronghorns are easily identified by those two snow-white chrysanthe-mum-like pompons which blossom on their rumps, giving off a most unflower-like odor when they are angry or excited.

Both sexes are a rich tan color on the back and sides, with pure-white patches on the sides of the face and at the base of the ears. They have black muzzles and the males have a black spot on each jaw, just under the ears. There are two crescentic bands of white across the throat and breast. The entire underparts are white, and they have russet, black-tipped manes, which bristle when they are excited. Their ears are about five inches long, trimmed and tipped with black, prick-pointed, and curving inward at the tip. They have large black eyes, their black horns rooted just above them. Fawns are greyish brown at first, darkening on the face and paling on the back as they grow older. The bucks stand about three feet at the shoulder and are four to five feet long, weighing between 100 and 120 pounds. Does are smaller.

Pronghorns eat almost any kind of plant which grows on their home range. They seem to thrive on grama grass, sagebrush, mesquite beans, weeds, and cacti. In the north, they travel great distances each fall and spring, drifting to warmer climates and better grazing grounds in the winter and back to the north in the spring. However, where the climate is mild the year-round, as it is in the Big Bend country, they do not migrate at all.

Usually pronghorns go to water once a day—either about sundown or very early in the morning. They approach their watering place heading into the wind, in order to scent any enemies which might be around. The old bucks teach the young animals to be very cautious as they near the waterhole, and when the frisky, impatient fawns break ahead, running to the water, they usually are driven back and made to line up with the rest of the herd to survey conditions. In the cacti-covered areas of the Big Bend country, antelope sometimes go for days without drinking, apparently getting all the moisture they require from the water-storing varieties of cacti which they eat.

During courtship, the bucks gamble with their very lives for large harems, winner take all. They begin courting does in September, scattering their attentions as widely as possible. The bucks collect their harems and then fight to a finish to protect them from the advances of other males. If an ardent young buck manages to lure one or two does away from an old buck's harem, he tries to hide them before he is discovered and whipped. The battles between the bucks during breeding season may last two or three hours if the opponents are well-matched in size and strength. On the other hand, a battle might be over in five minutes if one of the bucks can get in a well-placed blow with the sharp recurved point of his horn. Ray Williams witnessed and photographed two bucks battling for the control of a harem. They approached each other with lowered heads, their noses almost on the ground, fencing for an opening. Then they clashed. While they fought they paid no attention to Williams, being instinctively aware of the fatality of being caught off guard. After the first clash, one of the bucks tried to call it quits but was forced to fight. Five minutes later his neck was broken.

After the breeding season is over the fighting stops; and, in November, the bucks begin to shed their horns. In late April, the does leave the herds to have their young, about 70 percent bearing twins. The gestation period is approximately eight months, so that the fawns usually are born in May or early June. For the first few days the mothers guard their young constantly, leaving them just long enough to go for water. Fawns are born with no scent and are so nearly the color of the ground that even the clever coyote has difficulty finding them. Despite the mother's vigilance and nature's protective coloring, the greatest losses occur during the first two weeks before they begin to follow the mothers. Then coyotes and golden eagles take their toll.

A doe can defend her young from a single coyote and can whip him in a fight, but she sometimes is confounded by two of the crafty animals working together. A doe will fight an eagle with her front hoofs, and can defend her fawn if she sees the eagle in time. But the eagle can drop on its prey like a bullet and, when the fawn is very young, can carry it off the ground before the mother can attack. In the Big Bend, golden eagles are the pronghorns' worst enemies.

By the time the fawns are ten days old they can outrun a dog, and when they are three weeks old they follow their mothers everywhere. Then the does begin gathering in herds for mutual protection. Fawns begin nibbling grass by the time they are a month old, and are weaned when they are about four months old. In July and August, the does and their fawns are joined by the bucks and, for about a month, the herd lives together as one big happy family. During this time, the old bucks teach the new fawns all the tricks they know, racing with them, leaping, and kicking up their heels like lambs at play.

When it comes to defending themselves against their natural enemies, pronghorns are masters at cooperative effort, using their hoofs and horns for weapons. Watching them kill a rattlesnake is a rare sight, giving the observer the feeling that he is watching a game of follow-the-leader. One pronghorn will run toward the snake, leap high in the air, coming down on it with all four feet held stiffly together, then bound quickly to one side. Every one in the herd will follow suit, then all line up to survey the effects of their work. After a few moments they will approach the rattler cautiously, satisfying themselves that it is dead and trot off with their heads held high. Their sharp hoofs have cut the rattlesnake into tiny bits.

A few years ago, a rancher watched twelve pronghorns chasing a coyote.

Finally one of the bucks caught the coyote and threw it with his horns. The rest of the herd jumped in and out, follow-the-leader fashion, pawing the coyote to death.

One would expect the pronghorn to be able to protect himself because he can run faster than any other four-footed animal in this country not excepting the greyhound and the racehorse. True, some racehorses might outrun some pronghorns, but match the best specimen of each and the horse is likely to be the loser. A further protective characteristic is the pronghorn's vision, which is so keen that, according to an old prairie scout, "What a live antelope don't see between dawn and dark, isn't visible." But the animal's curiosity offsets his celerity and telescopic vision. If the wildlife conservationists had not come to his rescue with protective game laws, predatory animal control, and refuge ranges, he would be extinct by now. In that 700,000-acre playground, the Big Bend National Park, the pronghorn finds a new refuge where vacationists can observe his interesting habits during every season of the year, and he can indulge his curiosity to the limit without fear of serious consequences [except predation from golden eagles]. . . .[1]

Of all the birds of prey, the golden eagle is one of the greatest hunters. He spends most of his time searching for food and is constantly foraging when there are young ones in the nest. He is not all bad, for he does destroy many pernicious rodents, plus an occasional rattlesnake.

A full-grown golden eagle measures three feet from his bluish hooked beak to his black-tipped tail and has a wing spread of nearly eight feet. His long, death-dealing talons are black. His plumage is dark brown, with golden-brown-tipped feathers on the back of his head and on the nape and sides of his neck. His legs are feathered to the toes, a feature distinguishing him from the bald eagle, which has bare shanks. Until the bald eagle is three years old, he does not have white feathers on his head and often is mistaken for the golden eagle.

The marauding golden hunter sits on a mountain scanning the valleys below or glides high in the air searching out his prey with telescopic vision. When he sees what he wants he folds his wings against his sides and comes down in a dive, with bullet-like swiftness, making a sound like air being forced through a pipe. If his prey is a ground squirrel or a rabbit he usually swoops up with it in his talons, hardly breaking his speed. When attacking birds on the wing he dives under them, turns over, and fastens his talons on their breasts. Many observers have marveled at the eagle's catch games while he is building his nest. He repeatedly drops sticks and dives for them, apparently testing the accuracy of his aim.

Eagles usually prefer mountain cliffs for their nests, but they build also in low trees on greasewood flats, in Spanish daggers, and on old windmill towers. In some regions, they build in high trees. If their nest isn't destroyed by man or storm, they use it year after year, making repairs each spring and adding to it until it sometimes becomes four or five feet across and about that deep. They lay their eggs, ordinarily two, in March. The eggs are white with sienna and purplish markings. The incubation period is thirty days.

The eaglets, for the first few weeks, are covered with soft white down which extends to their toes, and when they begin waddling about the nest on their shanks they toe in, reminding one of a cowboy wearing goat-skin chaps with the hair on the outside. When they are four weeks old, their dark-brown feathers begin to appear, and by the time they are three months old they are fully feathered. One of the oddities of the eagle's development is that from the time it is in full plumage until it is about a year old, it is larger than its parents.

The young eagles have gluttonous appetites and eat great quantities in relation to body weight. One observer found that a single pair of young golden eagles had "polished off" twenty-five antelope fawn carcasses besides numbers of rabbits, ground squirrels, and prairie dogs during their three-months' nesting period. They have disgusting manners, fighting each other in the nest and gulping each feeding as if almost starved. The parents are very considerate of their young, at first tearing the meat into tiny bits and putting it into the babies' yawning mouths. Before many weeks, the young ones are tearing the meat off the carcasses of their prey for themselves.

Young eagles' preflight training is a serious course in calisthenics. They stand on the edge of the nest and flap their wings until they almost knock themselves out. Sometimes vigorous flapping carries them several feet in the air and, apparently, becoming frightened they flop back into the nest. When, finally, they make the trial flight they are a bit wobbly in the air but soon develop the maneuverability and grace of their species.

It is believed that eagles mate for life, but if one is killed the other finds another mate. Somehow they manage to maintain a balance of sexes, for they are nearly always in pairs. Golden eagles normally live to be eighteen to twenty years old. However, some claim that their ages have ranged above the three-score-and-ten mark.

The bizarre stories of eagles stealing children or full grown sheep and flying away with them are untrue, for an eagle can carry only about eight pounds for any distance. But tales of eagles killing full-grown pronghorns, sheep, and even calves are entirely true. When food is scarce, eagles will gang up on a calf and slash at its loins until they rip it open or fly low over a defenseless animal and sink their talons into the muscles of its back and pull it down. Gene Benson, cattleman in the Big Bend, asserts that, in one season, eagles killed twenty-six of his calves. That was before the sheep and goat raisers moved into the section, supplying eagles with easier prey.

Worth Evans, who ranches in Jeff Davis and Presidio counties, says, "Knots as large as a man's fist come where the talons sink into the muscles of a calf's back, infection sets in, and the calf usually dies if he is not killed on the spot. During lambing season, I have seen twenty to thirty eagles hanging around lambing camps, and every morning they fly in and steal lambs." Unfortunately, lambing season and eagle-hatching time in the Big Bend country coincide, and little lambs sleeping in the sun make easy picking for these rapacious birds, hard-pressed by new family responsibilities.

In some sections, the golden eagle does much good and should be protected; but, because of his hunter's instinct and voracious appetite, he will always have to be controlled where his hunting habits conflict with the property rights of ranchmen and violate the game laws of the state. Ranchmen in the Big Bend country agree that they cannot afford to feed the feathered outlaws several hundred lambs a season. Because he is considered an outlaw west of the Pecos, most people find him fascinating and are interested in his life and habits and means of defense.

NOTE

1. Antelope are not found today in Big Bend National Park.

 ## A LETTER FROM THE CHISOS MOUNTAINS
Louis Agassiz Fuertes
1901

CHISOS MTS., TEXAS, JUNE 9, 1901 — THERE IS A BIG FLAT-TOPPED mountain about six miles back of our ridge, with a lot of splendid timber on it, and [Vernon Bailey] was very anxious to explore it to see if it had any chipmunks in it—for it would nach'ely haf' to be a new form. So we got aboard our ships of the desert at about 10:30—a pretty late start, to go around the range of the big mountain. It is also one of the highest points in the range, going up about 8,600 feet, and a pretty stiff one to go up.

We expected to get back for late supper, so only took a couple of biscuits with bacon and peach stew in them, and my little quart canteen of

H_2O. After a long hot ride up and down over stony hills and ridges, and a good part of the way leading the horses to save them, we got to the mouth of the gulch leading from the great basin of the mountain, which reared its forested sides up a good 5,500 feet above where we entered. We found a good little open place with grass, picketed our horses, ate our grub and started up.

It was just 1:30 then, and soon after we had entered the great boulder-jammed forest B. stopped short on a fresh trail, which I could also plainly see, of a big bear and one or two little ones. So we shut up and went as still as possible to get a clip at her if we could. We continued the silent habit all the rest of the way, which though adding to the great impressiveness of the mountain, grew very tiresome—especially as we got up into the thinner air where we got tired and stumbly quicker. It was a very steep climb; the first half was up a boulder-clogged wash or stream bed, with a good many stiff climbs to get up. It was as dry as a bone, except for a little stained pool in a rock bed at the very foot, and as the sun was cooking hot we soon got pretty dry as we left our canteen half full at the horse camp against our dry return.

But at its hottest, when we were nearly up the stream bed, it headed up rapidly and began to hail, thunder and rain. We went into a cave, rested on an old bear's bed, and pretty soon each found a nice little trickle that we could sit under—thus we got a nice cold clean drink just at the moment we wanted it most. After that we struck splendid spring pools all along, and every concave rock held a nice little drink whenever we wanted one. Pretty soon it began to clear again, and it was fine and cool, the hail having worked wonders, and we continued our silent climb, ever on the look-out for bear or deer. Bailey wants specimens very much, and the one he got the other day gave us plenty of delicious fresh venison for a week—which was a true godsend, after our supply of bum Texas bacon had been a week 'all.'

Well, to get back to the trail: we kep' a-gettin' upper and upper, into the junipers and pines, and even spruces—(the same noble Douglas spruce that comes in Alaska!) And finally, at 7,000 feet, left the bed and took to the hillsides and made for the 'high grass'—through half a mile or more of 45 degree smooth grass slope, sprinkled with tall-stalked agaves here and there, and all sheltered under a lovely orchard-like growth of gnarled old liveoaks and nut-pines, as still as a church on week-days. At the foot of the comb-ridge, which all these mountains have, B. and I parted to work both sides, and met again in the stunted growth on top—8,600 feet above sea level, the highest I have ever been on my own pins.

After quietly enjoying the wonderful view we got, for a few minutes, B. looked at his watch, and to our complete dumfoundation it was 7:15!!

and the sun was about to set. So, though we had left our coats below with the horses, and our clothes were still a little damp from the soaking we had gotten (for we had decided to disregard the storm and push up and on) there was nothing for it but to camp, as it was a good three or four hours' climb down to the horses in the daytime, and probably six or eight very dangerous hours' work at night, and then we could have had to wait for the moon before the horses could start out, and it would be daylight before we got to camp. So we found a little cave under the comb-rock, and while B. rustled branches and grass for a bed I humped fire-wood, and by dark we had as nice a lair as ever bear or panther stretched out on. We built a little fire under a live oak log which we placed across the open side of our hole, and by moving the sticks about once an hour (which I got so I could do without waking up) we kept our little cushion of air so warm that we both got a very refreshing night's rest, as we were both pretty weary. We tried hard to find a rabbit, pigeon, or something, but the biggest bird we could get was a chewink, and the biggest mammal nothing at all, though deer were all about us and we even heard one old buck stamp as he got up and out. But the brush was so thick that we couldn't see to shoot anything more than a rod or two away. So we went to bed hungry. We got up at daylight and separated to hunt again, with no better result, so, at 8 o'clock this A.M. we sucked the water out of the little dips in the rock near 'camp' and started down. It took us until 11:30 to get to the horses, which were still there, plus a fine old hound dog which we 'allowed' to follow us back to camp, where we arrived at about 2 this P.M. about as hungry and weary as they grow, I should say. We lapped up a few mouthfuls of food, to get in trim for 'chuck' tonight[1] which is just now ready, so 'YOU MUST EXCUSE ME, MAGGIE'—I eat.

biscuits——* bacon—*—* biscuits—*—* applesauce etc., repeat *ad lib.*

There, I feel better. We are truly lucky in our camp man, who replaces Kelly who broke his foot. He can cook to beat the band, and when the baking-powder gave out he quietly set to work and made up some sour dough, and we have those now, just as good as his b.p. ones.

I think the hound-dog is an old camper, for in the few hours he has been with us he has gone systematically all over the camp—beginning at the camp-tree and spiraling, cleaning up all the burned crusts, bones, etc., till it is really quite a model camp. And he doesn't come to the 'table' (i.e. that part of the ground on which our 'chuck' is spread on its yard of oil-cloth) but lies patiently about six feet off and waits till we throw him potato peelings or other delicate morsels.

We are still at the same camp we came to that first day—June 1—and will probably stay here for several days yet. We have got representatives of nearly all the birds, though there are two or three bully good ones that are yet to grace my little tray-full of Chisos birds. I have written my two hundred and seventh label, and while we have been here we have added about six species to the Texas list and two to the U.S. Yesterday I made a lay for hummers at a big agave flower-stalk and got a male and female of one of the most beautiful of all the N. American hummers, the 'lucifer.' The male is small (also the female) and on the back like a ruby-throat, but the throat, including the ear feathers, is the most resplendent amethyst purple, showing green and rich blue in other lights than *the* light, and the whole patch is spread out like a great star that covers his whole breast, comme ça.

Another hummer, much like our ruby-throat but belonging to the little Alaskan 'rufous' group, and the curiously painted Massena quail remain to be got by me, though the others have shot them. I guess I'll make a special try for them tomorrow, and I *must* get them. There is a fine large hummer with a sky-blue throat gorget that lives in the big forest of the gulch above camp. I have three of him, one a beauty. He sits on his perch and peeps like a little sparrow or warbler, and to-day coming down the big mountain I found a little green and yellow flycatcher with almost the identical note, so that I didn't bother with it until I happened to see it.

The other day I was coming out of the gulch after an unsuccessful day, when I saw what seemed at first to be a dry oak leaf, walking down a little leafy place between some loose stones and it proved, on being l–l–l–l–looked at under the k–k–k–kitchen l–l–lamp to be the biggest tarantula that any of us ever saw. I don't honestly think he would go on my extended hand, all stretched out—I chucked him in formalin and will send him on as a token of my slight esteem some day.

It is just getting to the time of year when the gnats and mosquitoes are getting in their fine work. Especially in the afternoons when our hands are deep in tender birds and arsenic, they delight to crawl way into our ears and buzzzzz, or get far up into the interesting labyrinths of our noses, or perhaps fly bang into our open eyes, and it is certainly an awful exasperation to feel one's ear swell 'visibly' when he can't possibly spare a hand to stop it with, and to hear, for a whole afternoon, the social buzwuzing of the same old fly just out of focus of the flapping hand. But we have been mighty lucky so far at the hands of the bugs, and these are really no worse than those I have struck in lots of places.

NOTE

1. Here Fuertes is referring to being so hungry that he looked for and found a discarded piece of bacon from a previous meal, dusted off the ants, and ate it!

BIRDING AT BOOT SPRING
Herbert Brandt
1940

AFTER EXPLORING RATHER THOROUGHLY THE SOUTHEASTERN reaches of the upper Chisos plateau in the vicinity of our camp, we developed a desire to visit Boot Spring and learn what that spot, so noted in ornithological literature, had to offer in bird life. On May twelfth we made our way down the stream-bed of Boot Canyon, which skirts the sharply inclined base of Mount Emory. The canyon drops rapidly away from the site of our camp, and its granite gorge is often strewn with large boulders, or it finds its course between narrow, towering cliffs. Lower down we found that the canyon broadens, trees of considerable size tower alongside the stream-bed, and within a half-mile of Boot Spring we found the Arizona cypress growing up to sixty feet in height, and more than four feet through. There are also large sycamores and deciduous oaks, besides several other trees, among them a small maple, all of which make the canyon a leafy, well-shaded dell, and we were delighted with this aspect of sylvan scenery that our Ghost Mountains afford.

Before we reached the lower canyon I made my way up on the mountain side where there is a sloping meadow of open grassland which, for some strange reason, is free of trees. I had about crossed it when from under my feet jumped two reddish sparrows which flew into a small bush. This time I aimed with more thoughtfulness, and collected the bird that proved to be the objective of our trip. It was a male and was accompanied by its supposed mate which disappeared at once. From the indications, our bird was either breeding or nearly so.

It is surprising how much beauty and charm is to be found in a plain-colored sparrow when viewed in the hand; the coloration is not vivid or striking, yet there is a soft interblending of the rich, deeper hues that give to its plumage the mellowness of an old painting. Each silky feather seems to fall into its proper place to form a harmonious pattern of coloration, so well fitted to protect the wearer from rapacious eyes in its ground-loving habitat.

The back of our little sparrow was a study in reds and soft grays, and, with its pale chin and clouded under parts, it was a most unprepossessing creature to unobservant eyes; but to us, here was beauty and captivation, born of long-studied anticipation. We did not know, however, at the time, that our bird was not what we hoped it to be—a specimen of a Mexican race; it proved to be the well-known Rock Sparrow of Texas, which, for some peculiar reason, Nature had placed in these high mountains, rather than bringing up one of the highland dwellers of the adjacent Mexican state across the Rio Grande.

The excitement of this capture gave us added zest, and we searched over a considerable area in the vicinity, but without further success. Thus, were we to measure our long motor ramble by our original objective it would have proved naught but a wild goose chase; however, one of the lures of bird study is that Nature can seldom be anticipated, yet she invariably pays rich dividends to the prying student, even though he be one of her unsophisticated worshipers.

As we returned to the forested gorge below, a new bird voice awoke the echoes with a loud, clear song which resembled, to my ear, that of the Eastern Redstart. The owner's actions were deliberate and unafraid as it fed about, crawling slowly among the leafy boughs, more like a vireo than a warbler, and ranging close to the ground among the lower vegetation. It proved to be the Colima Warbler, noted among "the faith" as one of the rarest species of this alluring group that are to be found within our borders. It is a medium-sized warbler of rather dull-greenish coloration strikingly relieved by a bright yellow rump and under tail-coverts which, as it moves about, it seems to display purposely. There is an additional concealed, bright reddish crown-patch which can be detected only by parting the head feathers. For what purpose the bird uses this hidden charm is difficult to observe, but no doubt his lady knows the answer. The mandibles are rather heavy for a warbler, adding to its vireo-like aspect.

We concluded from its actions that it was a canyon-bottom feeder and dweller, and the indications from the male showed that it was just about nesting time; but we were so occupied with the many bird events that were occurring that we did not spend the time we should have spent in searching for its dwelling. The male Colima Warbler in its native sylvan haunts has undoubtedly had but little experience with man, and in consequence was unafraid of us; in fact, he was so confiding that he allowed our closest inspection. While this bird could not be termed common, we did note a number of singing males along the mile of gorge that seemed so much to its liking.

Where a tributary stream broadened the canyon floor, a small group of wide-leafed sycamores had prospered, their pale, silvery trunks adding beauty to the new verdure. Here a number of Ant-eating Woodpeckers caused the rock echoes to resound when they scolded us intruders severely, and when I called they approached inquisitively rather close.

Above, on the canyon side, in a large nut pine, I heard a familiar lisping call, and to my surprise there loomed in my binoculars the silken form of the aristocratic Cedar Waxwing. The pinyon in which it rested seemed

to be decorated unnaturally with odd, reddish cones; on further inspection, the mellow morning sun reflected a well-mannered congregation of
some forty similar birds which had spaced themselves artfully about all
the exposed portions of the tree.

Another migrant was the Rocky Mountain Audubon Warbler which,
this day, was numerous, although confining its busy activities largely to
the upper parts of the taller canyon trees. Here too, the Texas Canyon
Wren whistled its wild, far-reaching, descending carol that made the rocks
resound. The less conspicuous song of the Rock Wren was heard also, and
an adult was seen feeding a begging young nearly as large as the parent.
One noisy Ash-throated Flycatcher was present, bursting forth every now
and then with turbulent notes; while right before me a Chisos Nuthatch
ran up and down a smooth sycamore bole like a big blue fly.

Taking a deep-trodden trail that crossed the canyon, we soon came to
a level open glade on an even terrace some forty feet above the gorge,
and, from the campfire remains, concluded that this beautiful open park
was none other than Boot Spring—the camp of several noted bird-men,
first of whom were those of the famous party of Oberholser, Fuertes, and
Bailey, who here initiated Chisos Mountains bird study in the summer of
1901. We loitered and lunched at this historic spot, around the borders of
which towered perfect pinyons of commanding size, and voted that there
should be no finer enjoyment than to spend a bird season there.

Towering just above us, we saw Mount Emory with its peculiar sculpture of angular brows and faces. As we stood admiring this mountain, we
were suddenly startled by a rush of powerful wings, and looking just overhead, we beheld a Duck Hawk sweeping straight upward as if it had just
attacked a great Golden Eagle which was soaring low in the canyon. The
latter did not seem alarmed, but sailed on, ranging higher and higher, in
growing circles, without moving a wing, its long, pointed feathers reaching out like expanded fingers. As it wheeled it plainly displayed the characteristic pale basal half of its broad, fan-like tail.

Of all the bird ships that sail the great expanse of our sky, none has
the superb poise, the latent power, the reserve speed, and the consum-
mate grace of this great eagle. The Turkey Vulture is a true airmaster, but,
like a light skiff in a troubled sea, it does not seem to dominate its ele-
ment, but often moves along uncertainly. Some hawks and kites, while
they may be the personification of aerial grace and light, buoyant flight,
lack the deliberate stability and wing power of the eagle. His noble form,
from below, has that trim, balanced outline which marks him as the most
perfectly designed ship that sails the free sky—the mainliner of the grand
raptorial fleet.

Over our heads the great eagle climbed, with such power and beauty of movement that I, in my admiration, had forgotten all about the falcon, when suddenly into my binocular field it came, diving headlong at the eagle with rapid, powerful strokes of rakish wings. It rushed along like a meteor, flying furiously with all its energy. Just as it was about to strike, the eagle made three quick, rippling flaps of those powerful wings and in a trice rolled over on its back, offering to the thunderbolt attacker its wickedly upreaching talons. At this the smaller bird shot skyward and left the field; but the eagle glided deliberately for some moments on its back, before rolling gracefully into a soaring position to resume his effortless sailing. The smooth maneuverability of this great bird was marvelous to behold as it reversed its position with wings partly folded. Exactly what happened when impact seemed inevitable was difficult even to surmise, since the wing is quicker than the eye; but it was evident that each bird respected the deadly talons of the other.

Evidence that such respect is warranted is furnished by an incident witnessed by me in a small rocky amphitheatre in southern California. I was standing near the foot of a cliff in which was located the aerie of a pair of Duck Hawks, while overhead both birds were circling and cackling in wild anger. An unobserved Horned Owl suddenly departed from its nesting hole in a cliff face nearby and darted hurriedly away. The hawk was after it instantly, and before the large night-bird had gone more than a short distance the peregrine made its stoop. The owl folded up in midair and fell to earth like a stone; I picked it up but a few seconds later, a limp mass of flesh and feathers without a visible mark. Dissection, however, revealed at the base of the skull a tiny rip, where one dragging claw of the falcon's foot had done its work.

MEXICAN BIGHORN

Vernon Bailey

1905

TWO 5-YEAR-OLD RAMS AND ONE 4-YEAR-OLD FROM THE SOUTHERN end of the Guadalupe Mountains, Texas, and one 7-year-old ram from the mountains north of Van Horn agree in almost every detail of character with the type of topotypes of *Ovis mexicanus* from Santa María, Chihuahua. They are older and a little larger than the type and serve to accentuate some of the characters of the species.

Mountain sheep inhabit the Upper Sonoran and Transition zones of the desert ranges of extreme western Texas. They are found in the Guadalupe Mountains. A few have been killed in the Eagle and Corazones Mountains and on the northwest side of the Chisos Mountains. They come into the Grand Canyon of the Rio Grande mainly from the Mexican side. Mr. R. T. Hill reports specimens killed in the Diablo Mountains, 25 miles north of Van Horn. The sheep are by no means confined to isolated mountain ranges. In several valleys I saw tracks where they had crossed from one range to another through open Lower Sonoran country. In this way they easily wander from range to range over a wide expanse of country in western Texas, and might be considered to have an almost or quite continuous distribution between the Guadalupe Mountains and the desert ranges of Chihuahua. Most of the ranges are steep, extremely rugged, and barren, with deep canyons and high cliffs. Here the sheep find ideal homes on the open slopes of terraced lime rock or jagged crests of old lava dikes, and, thanks to the arid and inaccessible nature of the country, they have held their own against the few hunters of the region. An old resident of one of the canyons, who has supplied his table with wild mutton for many years, considers them fully as numerous now as fifteen years ago. He has seen as many as 30 in a herd, but says they usually go in small bunches of 3 to 10, sometimes all rams and sometimes all ewes and lambs, but usually in mixed bunches. They come down the sides of the canyon in sight of the ranch, and are shot only when needed.

While sweeping the slopes with the glass one evening near our camp in one of the big canyons opening into the Guadalupe Mountains, I located three sheep halfway up the face of the rocky slope, 1,000 feet above me. To the unaided eye they were invisible among the ledges and broken rocks, whose colors they matched to perfection, but through the glass they were conspicuous as they moved about feeding and climbing over the rocks. There were an old ram, a young ram, and a ewe. It was too near dark to make the long round-about climb necessary to reach them, so I returned to camp and early the following morning started my camp man up the slope to the spot, while I went back up the canyon to get beyond them if they should run up the ridge. As I swept the slopes with the glass I heard a shot up where the sheep had been the evening before, and soon locating the hunter, watched him shoot two of them, while three others which were above climbed the cliff and finally disappeared over the crest of the canyon wall. The three that escaped were not much alarmed by the shooting. They jumped from rock to rock, pausing to look and listen, and turned back in one place to find a better way of retreat. They made some long leaps to reach the ledges above, but made no mistakes in their footing. Their motions were deliberate, and there was a moment's pause before each bound. I was amazed at the strength of the old ram, as, slowly lifting his massive horns, he flung himself with apparent ease to the rock above. The two lighter animals followed more nimbly, but with less show of power and without the splendid bearing of their leader, who often paused with head high in the air to watch the hunter below or to plan his way up the next cliff. While from below they seemed to be mounting the face of a steep cliff, I found later that it was not difficult to follow where they had gone.

It was interesting to note that these sheep had remained almost exactly where they were seen the night before. The two others may have joined them during the night, but more likely were all the time somewhere near, either lying down or hidden by the rocks.

The stomachs of the two sheep killed were full of freshly eaten and half-chewed vegetation, and most of the plants composing the contents were easily recognized by the stems, leaves, and fruit. The leaves, twigs, and carpels of *Cercocarpus parvifolius* [mountain mahogany] formed a large part of the contents, while the leaves, twigs, and seed pods of *Philadelphus microphyllus* [mock-orange] were present in less abundance. The seeds, stems, and leaves of the common wild onion of the mountain slopes were abundant and conspicuous in the mass, giving it a strong odor, while the black onion seeds, still unbroken and often in the capsules, were especially noticeable. A few bits of stems and leaves of grass were found in each of the stomachs, but they formed probably not over 2 per cent of the total mass.

Both of these sheep were in good condition, and the meat was tender, juicy, and delicious, with no strong or unpleasant taste. While it lacked the peculiar gamy flavor of venison, it came as near equaling it in quality as the meat of any game I know.

On August 22, in another range in which the bighorns were reported, I left the ranch accompanied by an old resident hunter. Riding hard up one gulch and down another, we were soon 10 miles back in the mountains in a canyon with steep terraced walls rising from 1,000 to 2,000 feet above the open bottom. As we crossed the bottom a band of 12 to 15 mountain sheep bounded from the farther edge and started up the rocky slope in a long line of conspicuous bobbing white rumps led by three magnificent old rams. They had a quarter of a mile start, but in a very short time our hard-hoofed little horses had covered the stony gulch bottom and landed us at the base of the rocky slope within 250 yards of the sheep, which, having gained a point of sharp rocks above and feeling more secure, stopped to look down. As the king of the bunch suddenly paused and turned to face us, my little 32–20 sounded weak and ineffective and only served to make him seek a higher ledge. But at the more spirited crack of the old ranchman's .30-.30, the next in line, a buck with almost as heavy horns, rolled off the cliff with a broken neck and came sliding and tumbling to the base of the rocks a hundred feet below. The rest had scampered around the point of rocks, and as they came out again farther up and climbed cliff after cliff that from our base level seemed smooth and sheer, a few more shots were wasted at long range. The herd divided and passed around both sides of the high peak. Following both trails for a mile or so to see if any of the sheep had been wounded, I found that I could go wherever they had gone. The cliffs were not so steep or so smooth as they had looked from below. In one place the animals had followed a narrow shelf above a sheer drop of 300 feet. Although they had jumped from point to point, striking their feet within an inch of the edge, I could not resist the impulse to lean close to the wall and keep my feet as far from the edge as the narrow shelf, which in places was not a foot wide, would allow. But some of the rocks crossed sloped at a steep angle, and the sheep had made daring jumps from rocky point to sloping surface, where their lives depended on their sure-footedness. The farther I followed the more I admired their skill and nerve. I asked my companion if he had ever known sheep to go where a man could not. He said he thought that they would sometimes make longer leaps down a sheer ledge than a man could attempt with safety, but that otherwise a man could go where they could.

I was especially interested in examining the feet of the old ram we had secured, and was struck first of all by the difference between the front and the hind feet—the front being fully twice as large as the hind, much squarer in form, with deeper, heavier cushioned heels, and lighter and less worn dewclaws. As the hind quarters of the sheep are light and fully two-thirds of the animal's weight comes over the front feet, this difference in size is not surprising. The greater wear of the hind dewclaws is easily accounted for by their constant use in holding back as the sheep goes downhill. While the points and edges of the hoofs are of the hardest horn, the deep, rounded heels are soft and elastic—veritable rubber heels—with a semihorny covering over a copious mass of tough, elastic, almost bloodless and nerveless tissue. While fresh, before the specimen is dried, these cushioned heels may be indented slightly with the thumb. It is easy to see how they would fit and cling to the smooth surface of a sloping rock where wholly hard hoofs like those of a horse would slip, just as you can turn your back to a steep slope of glacier-polished granite and walk up it on the palms of your hands where you cannot take one step with the roughest hobnailed shoes. The dewclaws are also heavily cushioned beneath, but have fairly hard, horny points—mere movable, boneless knots.

Among other peculiarities noticed in the fresh specimen were the pads of the breast and the knee, where the skin had developed to an almost cartilaginous shield over a quarter of an inch thick and so hard that it was not easily cut through with a sharp knife. The whole sternum and front of the knees were thus protected, and for very evident reasons. The beds where the sheep had been lying were found on rocky or stony shelves, usually above a sharp cliff and below a high wall of rocks, sometimes on a bare surface of rock and almost always with at least a foundation of rough stones. If possible the sheep paw out a slight hollow, but they do this apparently more to make an approximately level bed than for the sake of the softness of the little loose dust they can scrape up among the stones. The hair is worn short over the knee and the breast pads, but the skin is unscratched either by rocks or thorns.

The legs of the sheep secured were filled, especially below the knee, with cactus and agave thorns that had gone through the skin and broken off in spikes half an inch to an inch long and lodged against the bone or the inner surface of the skin. A large share of these thorns were terminal spikes from the leaf blades of *Agave lechuguilla,* which grows in great abundance over the hot slopes of the mountains and which the horses avoid with even greater care than they do the numerous species of cactus.

The glandular disks under the eyes of this ram were more conspicuous than in any other specimen I have ever examined, probably on account of his mature age, which his horns showed to be 6 or 7 years. The gland is an elevated rim of thickened, black, scantily haired skin with a depressed center, and measures about an inch across. It stands out prominently on the surface, and appears from the flesh side of the skin as well as from the front as a round thick pad. It has an oily or waxy secretion and a rank, sheepy odor.

In color the old rams were decidedly darker than the ewes and younger members of the herd, but all blended with astonishing harmony into the browned, rusty, old, weathered limestone of their chosen hillsides. Even the soiled white rump patches were just the color of freshly broken faces on the rocks seen here and there over the slopes. As the band of sheep sprang away up the slope, the white rump patches were so conspicuous that I could not believe at first that the animals were not antelope; but higher up, as they stopped among the rocks to face us, they could easily have been mistaken for a group of rocks. As they appeared again and farther away on the ridge beyond the gulch, the bobbing, white rump patches were conspicuous signal marks so long as the animals were running away from us, but when they turned, their forms were completely lost in the background.

These sheep did not appear to run very fast, but probably few animals save the panther can catch them in a race over the rocks. A few days later, while hunting panther in these same hills, it was demonstrated that deerhounds cannot catch nor tire out the sheep over their own trails, although my companion claimed that they were not very swift runners on open ground.

The meat of our 7-year-old ram was rather tough and dry, but without any bad flavor. The people at the ranch where I was staying, who had eaten young sheep, considered the meat superior to venison. Although shot at 4 P.M., our sheep had a full stomach and must have been feeding for an hour or two. His teeth were imperfect. One or two molars were missing in the lower jaw, and, as a result, the contents of his stomach were rather coarse, and many of the plants were easily recognized. Over half of the contents was composed of the green stems of *Ephedra triburcata* [jointfir], which I at first mistook for grass, but which could not be mistaken on careful examination. The stems, leaves and flowers of *Tecoma stans* [yellow trumpetflower or esperanza], a beautiful yellow-flowered bush, were conspicuous, as also were the leaves, stems, and berries of *Garrya wrighti* [Wright silk-tassel]. A few twigs with leaves and fruit pods of *Pentstemon* were found, and a quantity of ripe fruit of *Opuntia englemanni* [Engleman prickly-pear], including the chewed-up pulp and seeds of at least half a dozen of the large pear-shaped berries. Some other leaves and stems were found that I could not recognize, but a careful search failed to reveal a trace of grass in the stomach. Part of these plants are Lower and part Upper Sonoran species, and the sheep seem to inhabit the two zones freely. The cold slopes and upper benches of the mountains are Upper Sonoran, however, and probably are to be considered the animals' real home. Transition zone does not occur in this range.

It is with some hesitation that I make public these facts as to the abundance, distribution, and habits of mountain sheep in western Texas, and only in the hope that a full knowledge of the conditions and the importance of protective measures may result in the salvation instead of extermination of the species. It would not be difficult for a single persistent hunter to kill every mountain sheep in western Texas if unrestrained. Not only should the animals be protected by law, but the law should be made effective by an appreciation on the part of the residents of the country of the importance of preserving for all time these splendid animals.

LIVERMORE JOURNAL
Mary S. Young
1914

AUGUST 5: THE GRASS IS WONDERFULLY GOOD THIS SUMMER AND ALL the hills are green. In the valleys the pasture is excellent and all the cattle are slick, fat, and happy. We seemed to awake much interest, for they followed us and came as close as they dared, looking at us, but at the slightest alarm kicked up their heels and ran a little way, then turned again to look.

August 6: We had passed six fat rascally horses a few miles back that seemed much interested in us. In the middle of the night, I was aroused by hearing a horse trotting along whinnying. Soon I heard more. They stopped near our buggy, and pretty soon I heard some pans rattle. I got up then and started back to bed, but the impudent rascals came right back. I chased them away several times and went back to bed again. Still the rascals rattled things around. That time I stoned them clear over the next hill, took everything loose out of the buggy, covered the rest with a canvas and went back to my downy couch. They did not disturb me again, but when we had breakfast the next morning, we could not find our bread and butter. There was a knife on the ground with which we supposed they must have spread the bread, and I found what was left of the butter on the ground. There is nothing like the hospitality that one meets with on these ranches, and we suppose that horses were presuming upon it. They took our hospitality for granted. They did not grudge us their grass for our burros, so they thought we would be glad to offer them a lunch of bread and butter. . . .

The canyon is beautiful. I have never stayed in a more beautiful place (except the Alps and Glacier Park). There are only two things that I do not like about these mountains. Now and then there are outcrops of white rock which look at a distance like a group of white houses. All the time you know they are not houses. Through the gleaming, clean air they give the impression of a mirage, and the feeling they give one is an uncanny one of intense loneliness. The yuccas have the same effect in a rather less degree. They stand up stiff and straight like men, on the hills against the sky. The sight of cattle affects me sometimes the same way. It is the suggestion of human life with the conviction of its absence. . . . We had a campfire and sat by it until about ten o'clock . . . a lot of *Aloysia liguistrina* [whitebrush] in full bloom and very fragrant.

August 8: It is not easy to keep track of the days of the week here and we are afraid of losing the time of day too. If we should both forget the same night to wind our watches, it would be a long time before we got the time again. This morning I marked . . . where a shadow fell at eight o'clock, and tonight at about five. Soon we shall have a complete sundial to set our watches by. It is about five o'clock now. The "lonely" time is beginning. The air is very transparent and very still and everything glistens. There is something of that uncanny feeling of the consciousness of inanimate things.

August 11: I started up the canyon to collect, but, managing to shoot two rabbits, had to come back with them.

August 14: This was the day that we went to Livermore. We started up the gully . . . around nine A.M. carrying two canteens, two knapsacks, two guns, and a botany can. For lunch we had a can of baked beans, four teacakes, and two cakes of chocolate.

The other canyon is wide and it was easy going after we struck the road. There is a tank some distance up and considerably further along a cement trough with the water from a spring piped into it. We might have left our canteens at home if we had known how much water we should find everywhere, but it is not usually safe to be without a canteen in this country.

We finally lost the trail and, as we had no idea which was Mt. Livermore, aimed for the most attractive-looking mountain. We certainly did some climbing, and Carey[1] with the two canteens must have had a hard time. We went up a very steep long slope, then around the top of that small mountain, only to find ourselves cut off from the next mountain, the one with high rock bluffs topping it, by deep ravines. We made our way partly around the canyons, then crossed them where they were not so very deep.

Of course, there are no trails in these mountains, but what makes them so hard to climb is the fact that long grass and shrubby plants cover the rocks and loose stones in many places, so that one is very much impeded and besides cannot tell where he is going to put his foot. The tales one hears of rattlesnakes on rocky slopes are a little disturbing too. We were tired enough to rest several times. Really we could not have finished the climb without. We reached the base of the first rock bluff and found ourselves quite able to walk about on the level. We climbed a little more, reached another bluff, to discover that we could go no further. Back of us was a cliff several hundred feet high, almost if not quite perpendicular, below, which continued into the bald rock top of the mountain. This bluff is broken more or less in places that look easy to climb. Botanically, it was quite different from anything else I have seen. It was beautifully painted with orange, yellow, and gray lichens, and decorated in every crevice with very many plants—ferns, solaginellas, liverworts, beside more hardy crevice plants. Pine trees appear in some of the more broken portions as apparent crevice plants. The talus slope at the base was a tangle of grapevines, wild tobacco (?) *Mentzelia*, composites of various kinds that concealed the rocks and made passage difficult. We found the best place we could and sat down on a narrow ledge, our backs to the bluff, and ate our dinner. The view before us was certainly magnificent—the foothills in the foreground, with our canyons winding out through rolling green hills to the plains beyond. *There* was space; wide, brown, hazy, spotted with the shadows of the clouds, the plain lay before us, stretching out miles and miles to the mountains, which like gray clouds skirted the horizon.

After lunch, Carey found a place under a clump of *Quercus hypoleuca* [silverleaf oak] and began to do math problems. I started collecting. As I passed around the clump of trees climbing from rock to rock, there was a commotion among the weeds and a black animal ran into Carey's shrubbery. He had a hairy back, and by the color I knew he was not the skunk we had known was somewhere about. I called to Carey, and just then the beast, seeing another enemy ahead, snorted like a hog and rushed out of the bushes. It was a young black bear. I might have shot him if I had had time to get out my gun, but he made tracks around the mountainside at the rate of about twelve miles an hour. He was too far to shoot by the time Carey got around the bushes. We regretted deeply that we could not have bear meat to eat and a bear rug to take home with us, but are glad to have seen a real live wild bear in his native haunts. (Those in Glacier park are almost tame.) There must be a lot of wild animals in these mountains, they are so hard to climb that probably very few people come. . . .

There is a beautiful gorge in our mountain with a small stream of water running down it in a broken waterfall. After you climb the first flight of stairs it opens up with a much more beautiful cut than it looks from below. It is in vegetation, like streams of the northern Rockies. I found several old acquaintances. It looked possible to climb higher, but I came to one place where my courage was not quite enough. More trips in that region would pay, but those places are so inaccessible!

We started back at 3:45. We decided that it would be much easier to come by way of Goat Canyon [actually Pine Canyon], so started down the mountain toward the southwest. The canyon proved to be very beautiful. We went down a branch first. It went down, down, and down, over waterfalls, and more waterfalls.[2] When we reached the larger canyon, we found it an almost impenetrable thicket, largely of *Quercus hypoleuca,* with much *Arbutus,* an occasional willow, walnut, *Ptelea,* and what looks like ash. We found a single leafless, red-purple orchid in the moist soil of one thicket. When we were tired of stooping to go under trees, we would try the bed of the stream for a while, stepping from stone to stone and slipping once in a while. The canyon continued for an unreasonably long time just as bad. Then it grew a little wider and kept on endlessly like that. Finally the bluff began to show signs of widening and I was sure that the next opening would bring us to the forks of the canyon. But it didn't. After another unreasonably long time, I found we were coming to the forks and told Carey it was only about a mile home. But it wasn't the forks. On and on went the endless canyon, and the trouble of it was it kept looking less and less the way it ought near the forks. Another thing that troubled me was the position of the sun. I thought it ought to be in our faces, and instead it was decidedly to the right. We went on and on, and still no signs of the rocks. I was considerably worried; it did not seem possible that we could be in the wrong canyon, and yet what was the matter with it that it kept on so long, and what was the matter with the sun? It is such lonely country and the ranches are so far apart and so hidden in hollows that it would be next to impossible to find one if we were lost. The idea of going without supper or breakfast and sleeping in the open without a blanket was not attractive. We discussed climbing the ridge, but I saw an opening and kept on a little longer. We came to the opening. There was a branch canyon—but extending in the wrong direction, and there was no north branch. Up the big branch was something white, two windmills, that looked like ours, but they were against a background of great mountains not like ours at all. Windmills usually suggest a house in settled countries, but not here. It was the lonely time of the evening and up the other valley was an outcrop of that uncanny white rock.

We were sure we were lost then. The sun was not more than an hour high, and we never could make our way ten miles over the hills home, even if we could see where home was. We started up a ridge as fast as we could go. I felt rather weak. All of a sudden I noticed that the valley with the white rock looked remarkably like the south branch of Goat Canyon, and it flashed over me that perhaps instead of the main canyon, we had been in the north branch. Then over the ridge ahead of us loomed up a familiar and most welcome sight, a pyramidal top of a mountain, our mountain, the one just across the canyon and downstream a little way from our home.

August 15: Neither one of us cared to climb any mountains just for the exercise next day. It took me all the morning to take care of my specimens and all the afternoon to write up notes and go in the creek. . . . I took a careful inventory and decided we had nine meals left.

August 16: Another Sunday. We finished our last bit of bacon this morning, and our hominy. Carey brought up a lot of ripe and unripe peaches, and it would not look well to write down how many we ate. So many, however, that we got along with nothing else for dinner but beans. This sounds like the diary of someone on an Arctic expedition. The interesting item each day is how much food there is left. . . . We hoped for a squirrel for supper, but our hopes were dashed to the ground. Carey tried one and shot it up the hollow of a tree. After chopping for a considerable length of time and finding an empty hole, we gave up.

August 17: Carey shot a big squirrel. . . . We decided to pack the burros and start up the canyon for Livermore; camp as near it as we could and walk the rest of the way the next day. We had dinner first, however. The squirrel was a tough old grandmother. . . . We went up beyond those windmills about a mile before it was too dark to go farther. Our burros did fairly well, though most of the time they were "powerful" slow. I tired myself out pulling Nebuchadnezzar. I might have spared myself, for it did not have any effect. . . . The road got so dim that I was afraid to go farther and really it was all we could do to see to untie the ropes. We camped on a hillside wooded with *Quercus grisea* [gray oak] just above the stream. There was plenty of driftwood that made a good campfire after it got started once, but was hard to light. We had a few beans that were left from dinner and what was left of the squirrel, and coffee mixed with Postum. It had been a very long time since we slept under the stars. They were very bright that night.

August 18: It was a fine morning and we started on our trip about nine o'clock, with one canteen, two knapsacks, and the botany can. . . . The mountains are pretty well wooded—oak on the summits and pretty well down. A sprinkling of cedar [juniper] and pine beginning on the high slopes and increasing toward the bottoms of the canyons where, in the high, moist valleys, they form the dominant part of the tree vegetation. The alligator cedars [junipers] can be recognized at a distance by their silvery blue color. The trail is cut out of the side of the mountain, so one gets a good view. In places it zigzags back and forth, once or twice goes down for some distance, then up, but most of the time it was a pretty steady climb. . . . We tried to keep going northwest, so as to be able to find our way back. . . . Finally, coming to the top of the ridge, however, we saw Livermore before us, and recognized the rocky bluffs we had seen the last time.

The vegetation here is most interesting—a pine tree with cones the length of this page, with the other pine. *Campanulas* [bluebells], *Menarda,*[3] and an entirely different, moist undergrowth. We did not think we were going to reach the top of Livermore, but we ate our beans and chocolate and peaches and felt better.

Down the slope and up the next one gave a complete change from the pine vegetation of the north-facing to the thicket of oak brush of the south-facing mountainside. Whenever we thought we had reached the top there was always another climb ahead of us, and when we really did reach the top there was Livermore peak itself farther off, connected to our peak by a ridge. There was a trail, however, which was comforting, and we followed it, always finding we had farther to go than we thought . . . there is a sort of a rock pinnacle that stands up sharply and I suppose is the very highest point. We made our way over loose, broken rock to it, and started to climb it—almost straight up—but the black clouds and the thunder scared us back. We thought we were in for a soaking and wanted to find our tank with the plain trail home before we got lost in a fog.

August 21: Friday I started shortly after eight o'clock for another tramp to Livermore. The only available lunch was one huge pancake and some bacon. It was not an attractive lunch and I did not in the least enjoy eating it. Cold pancake is not, at best, very appetizing, nor cold bacon either. Oh, for one grocery store!

I went over the ridge between Merrill and Goat Canyons, but probably lost time by so doing, for I had to leave the ridge below the flat-topped rock bluffs. I went up the canyon by way of the bed of the stream and found it much better than our first climb. There are many rockfalls that help one out, like staircases. . . . There was water in the canyon part of the way, but I forgot to put any in the canteen, and the little pink oxalis on the bluff was the only relief from thirst. It did very well, too.

August 26: That afternoon I collected a few things in the canyon down below along the flood plain. It is more like Limpia Canyon down there. The desert willow and the other flood plain weeds appear in abundance, and I found the little silky-leafed willow too. The oaks disappear and there is more walnut.

August 29: I ought to have gone to Livermore Friday, but was too lazy. If I had gone today I should have come back half-drowned. This morning was clear, and the sun hot enough to dry dryers and clothes. Just after dinner, drops of rain began suddenly to fall, and before we could gather up the dryers, some eighty of them, it was raining hard. Later it poured and hailed.

NOTES

1. Carey Tharp was the seventeen-year-old brother of Dr. B. C. Tharp, a colleague of Miss Young's. Carey was her assistant on the trip.

2. Young is describing an unusually wet year. Waterfalls and even water holes are seldom found in the Davis Mountains during years of normal rainfall.

3. *Menodora?*

RIO BRAVO DEL NORTE
Mary E. Humphrey
1981

ONE OF THE MANY ODDITIES OF THE TEXAS RIO GRANDE IS THAT ITS water is not that of the northern river. By the time the Rio Grande reaches El Paso, it is just a muddy trickle, robbed of its grandeur and power by first irrigation canals in Colorado and then irrigation pumps in New Mexico. From El Paso almost to Presidio, Texas, the streambed is rarely more than a mud puddle that is frequently choked with stands of salt cedar, or tamarisk, a prolific ornamental of Mediterranean origin that has been introduced into the area.

A few miles upstream of Presidio, however, the river gains new life. The Río Conchos, with headwaters high in the Sierra Madre of Mexico, flows into the nearly empty riverbed and the Rio Grande once again becomes a viable waterway. Perhaps the Rio Grande of the Big Bend would be more aptly called by its Spanish name: Río Bravo del Norte. Not only is its water of Mexican origin, but most of the valley's inhabitants live on the southern side.

The geological history of the Big Bend area goes back millions of years. Human history, according to archeological findings, began there at least 10,000 years ago. Paleoarcheologists have found many sites that offer evidence that Native American peoples used this rugged land eons ago. The spectrum of identified cultures ranges from the Jumano farmers, cousins of the Puebloan culture, to raiding groups such as the Comanches. The Spanish were the first whites in the region. Entering the area as early as the sixteenth century, they controlled it for 300 years and their influence remains one of the strongest. Anglo culture did not approach the region until the nineteenth century.

All of these peoples found a land harsh in its extremes, one unforgiving of the disrespectful. Not surprisingly, many remnants of their cultures are found along the river, which has been a green ribbon of life in an otherwise parched and apparently barren wilderness. (Of course, all desert rats know that life abounds in the desert; one need only know the secrets of the desert to enjoy its special qualities.)

Today the "Rio Bravo del Norte" is a shadow of its former self, almost a caricature of the river that carved the sheer rock walls of Santa Elena and Mariscal canyons. Since 1966 the flow of the Rio Conchos has been controlled by dam release in Mexico. As a result there is usually the minimum of water needed to float the river. In unusually dry years, however, the river can drop to less than desirable levels; and while there are international treaties prescribing the amount of Mexican water to be released into Lake Amistad, future water shortages in Mexico could lead to reductions in water release.

But at times, during certain seasons of the year, the river will run high as snowmelt or seasonal rains fill impoundments to capacity. And occasionally, local downpours will produce flash floods and the river will rage wildly for a couple of days. And rarely, so rarely, the dams of New Mexico will be tested by a phenomenal snowmelt, and the Big Bend will again taste Colorado. . . .

Like all rivers, and most people, the Big Bend Rio Grande has characteristics peculiar to its region and the region's topography. Many of these are at once obvious.

In the long, open stretches between canyons the river is generally broad, shallow, and slow. Where the river is straight, it has dropped tons of silt that form sandbars smack in the middle of the streambed; in such places the deepest water and swiftest current will be right alongside the cane growth that overhangs the water on either side of the river. Wherever there are bends, the deepest water will shift from one side of the river to the other. At lower water levels, intrepid canoeists looking for the deepest current often founder trying to find it. In the open country most of the swift spots are riffles over shallow gravel bars and around islands; the exceptions are some genuine rapids—complete with steeper gradients and rocks or boulders—at the mouths of a few of the larger arroyos.

In the canyons the river usually runs narrow, fast, and deep. Since rock walls contain the river's flow, bends are usually more pronounced than in the open desert, with obvious deep channels on the outside and shallows on the inside. Riffles are replaced by rapids, which are found at the outwash from side canyons or where sections of wall have tumbled into the river, glutting the channel with rocks and boulders that exercise boaters' skills.

In most places thick growths of carrizo cane line the river. The cane often extends out over and into the water, creating a very underrated hazard. At low water the deepest channel, especially around bends (in desert and canyon alike), frequently runs directly under and through the cane. More than a few unsuspecting canoeists and kayakers have dumped their boats trying to avoid its scratches. At the end of a December day this can be quite unpleasant, not to mention unhealthy.

Other hazards are obvious. Upcoming rapids can be heard in the distance, which gives boaters enough time to stop and scout ahead. There is nearly always someplace to pull over to see what's coming up. Although they are not always easy, there are portage and lining routes around the rapids.

Since the water level of the Big Bend Rio Grande is controlled by dam release, there is nearly always at least the minimum depth of water needed to float the river. The gauge readings at Lajitas, Rio Grande Village, and Dryden provide good guidelines. (The Presidio reading is often higher than the readings at the stations named, and it may be misleading: great quantities of irrigation water are pumped out of the river before it reaches Lajitas.) A Rio Grande Village reading of 0.6 meters (about 2 feet) means that there is just enough water to float, although the open stretches may be painfully slow and heavily laden boats may bottom out frequently. The ideal level is between 0.9 and 1.6 meters (between 3 and 5 feet). When readings are above 1.6 meters, the river takes on many of the characteristics of "heavy water," with areas of turbulence, extremely large standing waves, and strong eddies. The National Park Service strongly recommends against floating the canyons when the river is that high.

Water conditions are usually good in the spring, when snowmelt fills impoundments to capacity and forces the release of water. They may also be good in the early fall when seasonal rains raise the water level in the river. The rains, however, also increase the possibility of flash floods.

Water level information may be obtained by calling the National Park headquarters, (915) 477–2251, which provides the readings, in meters, at the various gauges. The National Weather Service can also supply data on the river's level, but the information is based on computer projections and at times can be quite wrong. The National Weather Service readings are given in cubic feet per second (cfs): 1,400 cfs equals 1.0 meter at the Lajitas gauge. . . .

Santa Elena Canyon is the most popular canyon in the Big Bend. The river has created the canyon, boring a crack through the limestone mass of the Mesa de Anguila, leaving sheer rock walls that tower as much as 1,500 feet above the water. The only major obstacle in the canyon is the Rock-slide, but it is impressive indeed. Allow at least two hours to get through, around, or over it. The National Park Service strongly recommends that only inflatables be used in Santa Elena (as well as all along the river) and that rigid craft be left at home. Of course, canoeists and kayakers will be canoeists and kayakers and will continue to paddle right through the canyon.

The entrance to Santa Elena is a dramatic sight, with a series of riffles right at the opening. Here, and at other points in the canyon, the stratification of the limestone creates an optical illusion that exaggerates the drop in the river. Two side canyons enter: one from Texas and one from Mexico.

Two large boulders seem to block the entire river. A large jumble of boulders lean against the Mexican wall, where the current is slack. Be forewarned: beyond these rocks lies the infamous Rockslide.

If you are adventurous and are practiced in the eddy turn, it is possible on the left to run past the initial boulders and then turn in the eddy behind them and paddle over to the sandy beach on the Mexican side. The current to the left of the boulders is swift, however, and missing the eddy may mean being swept down into the maze that follows.

If you don't trust guides that talk about eddys you can't see, you may want to scout before going on. In that case, pull over into the safety of the slack water on the Mexican side, secure your craft, and climb over and around to survey the situation. Just downstream from the first boulders is a sandy beach on the Mexican side and a small gravel bar on the Texas side. The current is swift along the gravel bar. Further downstream the river is glutted with immense boulders. Further investigation is desirable.

Scouting the Rockslide is possible only from the top of the hill on the Mexican side. Even there only the middle and left-hand side of the river can be surveyed adequately. It is possible to run the Rockslide after scouting if you are an expert paddler with an excellent memory and considerable experience in fast and heavy water. The trick is remembering where you want to go; the boulders are trailer-truck size and impossible to see around. One mistake can easily end in disaster, as can testify the many canoes and kayaks that have been left there in pieces. (Comparatively few open canoes have negotiated the Rockslide perfectly.) It is advisable for most paddlers either to portage along the Mexican side or to line and portage along the Texas side. Neither is easy, but the Mexican portage is safer.

The Mexican portage has been called "strenuous" and "a mankiller." Neither description adequately conveys the pain and hard work involved in carrying craft and gear over a hill 300 feet high and a quarter of a mile long. The trail is over rocks and is barely two feet wide. And watch your step: this is a great spot for spraining knees and ankles and wrenching backs.

At first glance the alternative—to line and portage along the Texas side—may seem unlikely, as much of the Texas wall is sheer. The first trick is ferrying from the Mexican side, where you have been scouting, over to the gravel bar. Once on the gravel bar, you can line to its downstream end and then paddle along the Texas wall to the next pile of boulders. Portage over this mess, get back in your boat, and paddle along the wall to the next, even larger pile of rocks. Climb to the top of this, being careful not to lodge your boat between two boulders when passing it over the rocks. Catch your breath a minute, and then shoot between the two rocks ahead of you (with your boat, of course) and paddle downstream carefully.

If you line your boat through on the Texas side, it is advisable to portage your gear on the Mexican side first. Then, after you've brought your boat through, paddle across to the Mexican shore, land, and reload. If you're an inexperienced or novice paddler, however, portage your gear and boat; just take along some extra sugar and allow time for this less than pleasant task.

The *vega* just downstream from the Rockslide is an excellent campsite. Unfortunately, it's all too often littered with piles of garbage that other boaters have left behind.

Downstream from The Rockslide, Santa Elena Canyon offers nothing more hazardous than a few riffles. Just sit back and enjoy gliding through them.

FIREARMS, EXPLODING ROCKS, AND A CENTIPEDE IN BED

Dudley Dobie

1952

HANK IS A LOVER OF SPRINGS FOR THE GOOD DRINKING WATER THEY yield, but in this instance he was also counting on taking advantage of one of nature's finest bathing "resorts." These springs are one of the "high spots" of the canyon country in that section of the Rio Grande. When we passed them and saw water pouring over the rocks to join the river, it was natural for us to be a trifle jealous of those Mexicans [who had arrived first and claimed the hot springs campground] and Hank's face registered keen disappointment.

We drifted downstream about a mile and compromised with the first campground that we felt we could put up with for the night. As the day died out, the sun went down in a blaze of glory. Naturally its setting came earlier for us in the canyon. The western sky seemed aflame while the gilded crests of the mountains were wrapped in a lovely haze.

Some of us scurried about in search of wood along rocky stairs, while others removed articles from boats to the bank. Considerable effort brought only blackbrush wood, but it served its purpose well. I have a feeling that Guy holds a bit of contempt for the rest of us while on a river trip, because usually we scatter or become greatly occupied with other chores while he is engaged in preparing a meal. The truth of the matter is that so far I have found but one camp mate who approaches being a match for him. He is Syril Wilks, but Syril has not made a river trip with Guy. Neither of those fellows has to be taught how to prepare good food.

So Guy turned to the campfire and the evening meal. The aroma of that burning blackbrush which was very pleasant to my nostrils still lingers with me. By the time night came down, our bedrolls were spread out. Some time before darkness had gathered in the folds of the mountains some owls had spoken to each other, but now they had reached the gossip stage. We could have listened to them for hours had we not been greatly spent from a full day of events and labor. Hank was aware of our weariness, so he rose to the occasion by turning to the "snake medicine" cabinet and making us one of his Rio Grande cocktails. That fellow has become famous with us in the concoction of such a refreshing eye-opener. He did not have to twist our arms to persuade us to turn to the "fountain" for a second helping. In due time our strength was so renewed that we felt equal to removing a fair portion of the mountain.

We supped royally. Before we turned to our bedrolls, Guy entertained us with his "six-shooter." I do not care for the report of a firearm in such fine solitude, but Guy used some tracer bullets, and as they sped across the river they cast a brilliant glow which lighted the mountainside and reflected on the water.

We slept soundly. That is, until some of us heard a report equal to that given out by a firearm. Guy rose early and built a fire in the depression of a rock shelf. Since the shelf was several feet above the river, he did not expect it to contain moisture. However, once the fire was well under way, the heat brought on an explosion which scattered fragments of hot rock over the camp kitchen and Guy's bedroll nearby. This occurred before daybreak, so we dozed fitfully for a little while, too lazy to arise and greet the dawn.

There was further movement on the part of Jack, who had placed his bedroll on a rock buffet a few feet above the rest of us. It seems the presence of a centipede between covers that later moved across Jack's body brought him back to this world and threw him into action. Jack related that he waited a moment for the centipede to quit surveying him, then he bolted from the bed and flung it about to get rid of his visitor.

Things settled down once more. The eastern sky was heralding dawn through its lovely crimson shade. I lay there drinking in its penetrating beauty. Then I heard a very familiar song. Yes, there it was, given out by that music box of the rocks, the Canyon Wren. That little sprite commissions himself to wake the hills. Doubtless he is the first tenant up and the last to retire. His song, with its descending scale, is one of the sprightliest, most musical and resonant to be heard in the western hills. The rock walls make a splendid sounding board. Heard along rock corridors, or in the cool depths of a ravine, or even across wastes of the desert, the "dropping song" of the Canyon Wren, to me, is the most soul-stirring and the most delightful thing the canyon country has to offer. Furthermore, that discerning soul lends much to the imagination as one watches his movements in such a sanctuary. Not only is he choirmaster — he is the presiding genius of this rock tabernacle. Fearless, inquisitive, we see him flitting from rock to rock, inspecting hidey-holes, poking into crevices, probing for spiders, nibbling larvae, scaling sheer heights, or just hopping and bobbing about. There is nothing subdued or melancholy about his bearing. He always seems to be happy. So his habits and his bugling are a benediction to me.

Then came the sonorous call of the White-winged Doves. The vocal offerings of these amorous birds added greatly to the morning chorus. Though I am devoted to the tender, impassioned notes of the Mourning Dove, which could also be heard on the morning air, I am less familiar with the soulful lyrics given by the Whitewings, and on this occasion I was struck with their pronounced calls. Their singing through the nose is charming enough for me.

The redbird was next on the musical program. So brilliant in color, he is a challenge to attention anywhere, but there in the green carrizo his presence was not only marked by his vivid costume but through his singing as well. His is a voice of dignity, a voice of the heart and the spirit, and so expressive. Perched on the tallest stalk of cane to observe and be observed, he seemed to be a vision of ravishing redness, yet the presentation of his recital in the morning symphony bore out that he is one of God's gentlest creatures.

Turning from the morning concert I gave my attention to the mountain silhouettes. For that matter, I had been studying the profiles while the birds declaimed. While patches of darkness lingered, the figures of the landscape took on various definitions. Some of the rocks along the canyon walls resembled human faces. High on a cliff a stalk of bear grass appeared as a cross, while numerous sotol stalks stood as sentinels guarding the streets of the mountains. An ocotillo standing on the rim of the mountain wall seemed far away. Then, when light spread over the land, all things assumed a different aspect. It was a scene of enchantment while it lasted and it gave one something to appreciate and think about.

One by one we crawled from our resting places and huddled about the fire and kitchen. Making the most of a good breakfast, we were soon on our way downstream. That was Saturday, the 17th. We had a strong south wind to push us along. We saw numbers of last season's Mexican Swallow nests on the cliffs.

I studied the talus slopes for an assortment of vegetation and found lechuguilla, bear grass, sotol, cenizo, mountain laurel, mesquite, blackbrush, leatherweed, Spanish dagger, fishhook and rainbow cacti. Then there were a number of bushes I was unacquainted with. The candelilla plants decorated the flanks of the mountains profusely.

The blackbrush was blooming. So was the Spanish dagger. Other yuccas were rushing their stalks for spring blooms and soon would stand like lighted candles. Ash trees dotted the margins of the river. Their bright green foliage proved restful to our eyes. Their loveliness made me want to worship them. My thoughts turned back to the recollection of large cottonwood and ash trees distributed along the river, where they stood out against a semidesert stretching for miles away from the stream.

Round-shaped plants, doubtless members of the fern family, clung to rock walls high over the river. Apparently they obtained moisture sucked from crevices in the rocks. Still other plants seemed to hang precariously. Ocotillo plants standing on the rims of high cliffs appeared to be watching us, and they reminded me of shy Mexicans who barely greeted us as we came into their midst. Tall brown grass was prominent whenever the soil was reasonably good on the slopes. Broken rocks occupied much of the land.

Bright green Bermuda grass carpeted sandbars, mounds and benches and invited us to pause and rest. The carrizo lining the river's banks was very thick and usually formed an impenetrable barrier. Much of it was last season's old stalks and still partly green. It was supplemented with this spring's shoots. Most of it was very disputatious and jabbed some part of our bodies when we endeavored to thread it. It serves as a refuge for the king of beasts in those parts, the panther, and is a wonderful bird haven. When it becomes dry, that is, after cold weather has "cured" the leaves on the stalks, thickets of carrizo may be ravished quickly by fire. As we moved along, we observed long stretches of the carrizo bordering the river that appeared to have been scorched. We concluded that it was a victim of the late freeze.

I have said before that there was always something to draw and hold our attention. Moving downstream is an advantage in seeing much new country, but movement also suffers a disadvantage, especially rapid movement. There is so much to seek out and study. Since it was springtime, one could devote many hours to the lovely flowers blushing unseen on the benches and bars. Likewise for a variety of grasses and plants. Or the beautiful scenery arresting one's attention—such as the splintered peaks and cathedrals of the mountains. It did not seem right to move out of their presence. Perhaps the river was glistening in the morning sunshine. The scene was framed in green borders, the shoulders of the stream. Perhaps a blue sky matched the setting. So one would enjoy lingering in such lovely places. After all, why should we languish between walls of stone and cement while many corners of the world are still full of sunshine? . . .

Guy, Jack and I placed our bedrolls on a sward of Bermuda grass above the main camp. Before the moon rose, the light from the flickering campfire played on the mountainside. The canyon walls loomed as a black curtain, a dark outline against a great vault with stars for diamonds, and later the moon rose to serve as a chandelier. The oar-tailed beaver engaged in the festivities of the night by sliding down sandy banks and plunging into the water with a boom. A gentle wind moved through the trees and bushes, rustling their leaves as it passed. Then the sedative of sleep rocked us away from things moving about us. Later in the night we were disturbed by a group of donkeys grazing a few feet away. Doubtless they needed to graze the grass, but I think they must have been lonely, because they would not shoo away easily. As we departed next morning, they reminded me of children's antics when they staged a mock fight among themselves.

The Monday morning blue sky was one of the loveliest I have ever seen. It seemed to magnify the new types of rock sculpture and scenery which we were passing. Buzzards, those scavengers of the rural air, were patrolling the area. They had taken themselves to the upper air where they seemed to hang motionless, but I was thinking of their convention among the crags at the scene of our storm camp. Late that evening while we fumbled about camp, I observed the buzzards assembling on the rafters of a peak descending to the night's roost. It is possible there were vultures among them, but if there were I failed to observe the white patches under their wings. They realized that they were beyond our reach and exhibited no concern over our presence.

Everyone knows that buzzards smell to heaven. Despite their offensiveness they have a stately flight, and I usually envy their ability to sail through the air with such ease. They are quite sociable among themselves, and generally they tend to their own business. Call a buzzard a bandit of the air if you must, but please bear in mind that he was designed for a special purpose here on earth—the removal of offal and carrion.

Speaking of wings of the air reminds me that on several occasions we observed the American Raven. His croak is the authentic voice of the wilderness and it is the most natural thing for that handsome fellow to deign to dwell among the crags. Being the most highly developed of birds, it is also natural that he is a satanic ruler of this part of the bird world. As an outlaw confined now to the wilderness and the waste places of the earth, he probably is the most dominant bird of the canyon and desert country. At least few birds dispute his sway.

We worked down the river until we arrived at Panther Draw. There we paused to examine one of the largest Indian camp grounds in the Reagan country. Shelters are numerous and should afford the archaeologist a host of artifacts, once time and careful excavation are devoted to them. Our time was limited so we moved away.

We enjoyed riding several small rapids in that vicinity. Each time that we rode one, the rough waves spilled into our boats to form puddles. Also, one usually was soaked with the spray. The past day had seen the river on a slight rise and muddy, but it soon receded and cleared. Occasionally one of our rafts would be delayed a few minutes by becoming lodged on a rock that did not reveal itself in time to be missed. Generally, this ridiculous position drew laughter from the rest of the party.

We passed what now remains of Cooper's Pump, a landmark to rivermen. I believe that Colonel M. L. Crimmins and Claude Young put into the river here the time they met with disaster at Lozier Canyon and nearly lost their lives. The country was still exceedingly rough, but we could see that the walls were breaking down. We descried several goats feeding on high shelves that appeared utterly inaccessible to us. Presently we passed a pair of Mexican goat herders. They stood motionless and when we hailed them their sole gesture of recognition was the slight raising of a hand. Shy "children" of the desert, they manifested no emotion over our presence. With their simple, solitary lives on the semisterile plains bordering the river, I can imagine how curious they could become about us, our equipment, and our boats.

It was along the lower reaches of Reagan Canyon, between Panther Draw and Cooper's Pump, that we observed several colonies of Blue Herons. We also found them established at other points along the river but none that compared with their stations in this vicinity. Their immense nests, frequently as big as a washtub, were bulky platforms of sticks carried from afar and deposited among the slender branches of the vase-shaped ocotillo decorating the rock terraces overlooking the river. Here and there a nest would be constructed on a rock on the crown of a cliff or in a niche of the rock wall. In a few instances some nests were placed barely above the flood line, but a majority of them were erected a safe distance up, bearing testimony that most of the birds were good architects. It is interesting to note how these nests, in spite of their bulkiness, blend with the landscape and are not conspicuous until one draws close to them.

The Blues themselves were exceedingly wary and through their bluish cast were hardly discernible when they stood motionless. I am certain that in their minds we were dreaded humans now invading their sacred precincts and solitudes, because they exhibited considerable nervousness when we moved into their presence. They demonstrated how annoyed they were by taking to the air, muttering protests as they retired to outposts beyond camera as well as rifle range. When one or two remained as sentinels or flew only a short distance away, we were permitted to observe them reasonably well. Of large size and elongate proportions and with bills elevated, they formed picturesque features of the landscape and waterscape. Standing motionless as statues save the trembling of their throats, they appeared stately in their heavenly redoubt. May the Rio Grande always serve them as a good fishing ground is my wish.

We continued to breast the stream until we gained that point where San Francisco Creek, a large canyon draining Bud Roark's country, unites with the river. While we were pausing to determine the strength of the rapids, I espied the lovely Painted Redstart skipping about on a bank of sand at the mouth of the creek. Although he graces the canyon country with his presence, this was the first time I was favored to see his kind, and I have been wandering through that most interesting region for twenty years. I will always associate a beautiful bird with San Francisco Creek where it meets the Rio Grande.

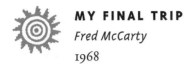

MY FINAL TRIP
Fred McCarty
1968

EARLY THE SECOND MORNING, A PARK RANGER CAME BY OUR CAMP with a large life raft tied on the top of his panel truck. He visited with us, sharing our coffee, and told us many things about the park. He was on his way to Castolon, where he was to meet a party of three others who were to make the life raft trip down the river through Mariscal Canyon. Later in the day, they floated down the river and beached the raft near our camp. We helped them carry it to the panel truck where it was tied on the roof.

This gave me the idea for the later trip through Santa Elena Canyon. . . .

I am not a superstitious person, yet I am almost willing to concede that my efforts to visit and photograph all areas of Big Bend National Park have been providentially hindered. Something always made it impossible for me to follow through on plans for complete coverage of the park.

The park ranger, as explained previously, had given me the idea of floating through Santa Elena Canyon on a life raft.

I sought, from among my friends, companions for this venture. During the late spring of 1966, arrangements were made with those who were to accompany me on the trip. They were: Loren Denton, superintendent of schools, Turkey, Texas; Andy Gardenhire, superintendent of schools, Hart, Texas; and finally my old companion of the second trip over the Chihuahua al Pacífico Railroad, John Slavik, superintendent of schools, Nazareth, Texas.

I had a six-place life raft ordered by a firm in Amarillo. I had no fishing tackle, but Loren Denton and Andy Gardenhire—both being ardent anglers—did. I proposed to furnish the station wagon, and my three friends gathered up all the paraphernalia we would need to make the float trip through the canyon. This included life preservers and sleeping bags, for we expected to spend one night fishing while we were in the gorge. . . .

When we arrived at Park Headquarters and told them of our plans for a trip through Santa Elena Canyon, we were told that the river was high, and it would be their advice that we not make the trip. We arranged for rooms in the Chisos Basin, and went picture taking and sightseeing in Boquillas.

We did this because I knew that we could see the condition of the river in the Boquillas area. We were undecided whether to attempt the raft trip or not. The river's flood stage would influence our decision. We had planned it for a long time and had come a long way. We were not willing to forgo it if there was a possibility of our doing it. Yet, we hesitated to ignore the advice of the ranger who had advised against it.

We found the river not excessively high when we reached it. . . .

Then we slowly made our way to Lajitas, where we spent considerable time visiting with the proprietor of the store and asking his advice about fishing in the river and of the hazards of the passage through the canyon. He did not think the river dangerous.

We examined the river again and thought it was lower than on the previous day. We decided to take a test run on it, so went about five miles upstream and launched the raft. Slavik had decided that he would not make the trip with us, for someone had to drive the station wagon to the mouth of Santa Elena Canyon to meet us when we emerged from it.

The test run indicated no difficulty at all. So when we reached Lajitas, we decided to make the trip.

We loaded the raft with sleeping bags, food, a refrigerator box of styrene, with ice and perishable food. My camera and film were sealed in plastic, as was my telephoto lens.

Andy sat in the bow and rowed. Loren worked the stern oar, while Andy steered from his forward position. I sat in the center. Only two paddles were used.

It was several miles before we entered the canyon. Fishing began almost immediately, but no strikes were had until we got into the gorge, when Loren pulled in a nice channel catfish. It was necessary to cut off its fins for fear they would puncture the boat. It was, of course, put on a stringer and floated behind the raft.

Beautiful cumulus clouds began to form, adding much to the beauty of the scenes when I put the camera into play.

The river was bordered by tall cane, making it impossible to see beyond the edges. We passed near some Mexicans who, on their side of the river, were engaged in cutting the candelilla plants, from which wax is extracted. This is one of the few marketable crops or native plants which provide income for the people of that region.

Finally, we entered the canyon. The walls grew higher and higher until they were fifteen hundred feet. Often they were almost perpendicular. The rock was a grayish, slatelike formation.

We began to hear the dull roar ahead, for we were approaching the rapids. I suggested to Andy that we tie the boat up and walk down the canyon to inspect the water conditions ahead. He did not accept the suggestion.

The current became swifter, as the channel narrowed. Again I urged Andy to steer toward the Mexican, or south, side of the river so we could see around the curve to the northeast, but we continued in the middle of the channel.

The rapids were caused by a landslide that had partially blocked the channel of the stream. In times of low water this was portaged, but when the stream was in flood it could be run.

Suddenly we swept around a curve and saw ahead of us white water with huge rocks dotting the stream. It appeared that we were going to be all right, but suddenly the boat was swept between huge boulders, with the passage between much narrower than the life raft.

We were stopped, and the water began to pile over the raft, sweeping out everything loose, like the sleeping bags and the styrene ice box. I had my camera around my neck, so I kept it, but all film and the telephoto lens were washed out of the raft.

The rocks were too steep and slippery for us to climb to safety. Andy had brought a parachute cord, of nylon, about thirty feet long. This had been tied to the eyelets of the boat on both sides. I, being in the center of the boat, saw that this cord had been washed from the raft and entangled in the rock, and was acting as an anchor. I pointed this out to Andy, thinking he would cut it with his knife. The roar of the current made conversation impossible. He leaped overboard to attempt to untie the cord. He disappeared for what seemed like minutes, only to finally climb back to the raft by means of the cord. He had swallowed considerable of the muddy water and was sick and completely exhausted. He had lost his life preserver.

Loren, seeing that Andy had not released the cord, also leaped overboard. I thought for sure he had drowned, but his head bobbed up several hundred feet downstream. That was the last I saw of him.

Finally, the power of the current tore the eyelets out of the boat. We were free. Andy was clinging to the side of the boat. About one hundred yards downstream was a large rock. We seized it and held the raft, which was full of water, for it had been punctured by the rocks. I managed to climb onto the rock with the rope in my hand and held it until Andy could recover strength enough to join me there.

Sometime later, he regained enough strength to permit us to tow the raft to the downstream side of the rock that was not so steep. We gradually pulled it onto the rock, letting the water drain over the stern, and through the holes in the bottom of the center of the raft.

We discovered that our worldly possessions consisted of three cans of soft drinks, a quart canteen of water, a small hand axe, a steel fishing tackle box, and the pump for inflating the raft. Everything else had been lost in the stream. I still had my camera, but the muddy waters had ruined it.

Loren had managed to swim to the south, or Mexican, side, but had not the strength left to climb onto the bank. He continued for hours, it seemed, to lie in the water with his head and shoulders on the bank.

The roar of the rapids made conversation with him impossible.

We struck the rapids about 5:00 P.M. By the time we had the boat, or raft, on the rocks and had pulled off our wet clothes and wrung them out, it was beginning to get dark in the gorge, whose perpendicular walls rose about fifteen hundred feet.

We, of course, had no food, but I drank some of the river water that had collected in potholes in the rock. It was fairly clear. We shared one of the canned soft drinks but kept the others for future need, as we did the canteen of water.

Finally, Loren regained his strength and climbed onto the bank, but, being very sick from the muddy water he had swallowed, he immediately stretched out in the rank Bermuda grass and we lost sight of him.

Two of the air pillows that had not been inflated we found when we drained the boat. They were to prove invaluable, later.

We had no idea how far we were from the mouth of the canyon. Neither did we have any way of communicating with anyone on the outside. We hoped that John Slavik would see some of the materials from the raft come down the river. Surely, something would be spotted and this would indicate that we were in trouble.

Apparently the raft was useless. Large holes in the bottom permitted water to enter the boat part of it, though the air chambers were intact.

Andy and I talked over the possibilities of rescue. We hoped that a helicopter would be used.

Andy said he would not consider trying to patch the boat, for he would not enter the river under any circumstances again without his life preserver, which had been lost.

We were badly worried about Loren, for he could not be seen because of the tall grass in which he was lying.

Expecting the night to be very cold, we emptied all water from the raft and arranged it on the flat rock, hoping it would give some protection.

Neither slept any, though we tried. The rock was uneven and not conducive to comfort.

When we discussed how we might be rescued, we doubted that any effort would be made for many hours, for we had planned to spend the night fishing, and John Slavik knew that.

Fortunately, the cold we had feared never came.

It was a bright moonlight night. The roar of the river made conversation difficult. The sheer, almost perpendicular, walls mocked us. We wondered what would happen if a cloudburst or heavy rain caused the river to come down in flood!

The floor of the gorge was fairly wide on both sides, and we felt sure we could climb high enough to be out of the path of anything but an unusually high headrise, if we could know it was coming in time to take action.

It was a long night. When light began to enter the gorge, I got up and went up the river, in hopes that I could recover an oar I had seen lodged on one of the rocks in the stream. I could not reach it.

Andy still refused to make any effort to repair the boat. We found a large roll of adhesive tape in the fishing tackle box, and I suggested that it be used to patch the raft. He reiterated that he would not think of getting into the river again without a life preserver.

Finally, I told him that he could take mine and I would rig up something with one of the air pillows. He agreed to this arrangement, and we started work with the adhesive tape patching the holes in the raft. By placing the tape on the inside and outside both, we were able to seal up the holes. We were uncertain how long it would hold, but we just had to take that chance.

We took the pillow and inflated it, and put it in my leather jacket and taped handholds on it. I was to use this in lieu of a life jacket.

We then cut forked mesquite limbs, about three feet long. We cut the second air pillow in half and placed the fork in each of these halves and taped them to the limb to form a paddle, much like a bird's webbed foot. These made serviceable paddles.

With the pump, we increased the air pressure in the compartment. We put the raft into the water to test it. It floated high and dry and it appeared the patching of the bottom of the boat was going to keep the water out.

About 10:00 A.M., a plane came over, apparently looking for us. It circled over us several times, then disappeared. We felt relieved, for we knew that something in the way of debris had been spotted. We put off making the attempt to reach Loren on the south side, hoping that the plane would return. We waited an hour. Finally, we gave up and decided to try to cross the river. We soon saw that it was hopeless, the stream was too swift, Andy stood up and threw one of the canned soft drinks to Loren. It hit a rock and burst. He threw the canteen. It fell on the river and was lost. I was rowing frantically in the stern of the boat. Loren had followed us as far as the riverbank would permit. We were swept downstream. We were able to use the oars to fend off contact with the sharp rocks. We soon moved out of the rapids and found the river fairly safe.

Two hours later, we floated out of the mouth of the canyon. John Slavik was watching for us. We managed to beach the boat on the north side and pulled it up on the sandy shore.

We met some people soon after that who had a thermos bottle of ice water. I have never enjoyed a drink so much in my life.

We learned that Slavik had seen Andy's life preserver float by, and that alerted him to the possibility that we had been in trouble. He called the park authorities, and they had a Coast Guard plane make the search for us. The pilot, seeing the raft floating in the water, assumed we were fishing and radioed back that everything was all right.

As soon as we could do so, we reported to the park rangers that Loren Denton was still stranded on the Mexican side. We learned that the barricade was some six miles from the mouth of the canyon.

The rangers offered to send a canoe, with three paddlers, up the river to try to rescue him, but since it was Sunday of a holiday weekend, it was difficult for them to get under way. About three o'clock they started up the river in the canoe.

John, Andy and I spent much of the long afternoon at the store in Castolon. It was hot and unpleasant, and the hours seemed to drag by much slower than their normal pace.

Late in the afternoon, we drove to the campground near the river, where we prepared some food, for there was no cafe nearer than the Chisos Basin, almost forty miles away.

About sunset, we moved to the mouth of the canyon to await the return of the rangers—we hoped—with Loren.

About 8:00 o'clock, the canoe came down the stream and it pulled to a landing. There were only three Rangers in it! They had been unable to reach the barricade where Loren was stranded. Darkness and the swift river current had prevented their going further upstream. They lacked only a mile, however, of reaching their objective.

The leader of the group promised us that they would have a large life raft, with four paddlers, launched at Lajitas at 5:00 A.M. the next day. They would float down the stream and take our stranded companion off.

They invited us to place sleeping bags in the Ranger Station at Castolon. We accepted their offer.

We were, of course, terribly worried, but we could only hope for the best—that Loren would be rescued without further delay.

The next morning, we arranged the station wagon for his return. A bed was made for him behind the front seat. Food, ice water and everything possible was provided to take care of him when he returned.

It was a long, long morning. It seemed it would never end.

At 1:00 P.M. we heard the sound of paddles around the bend of the river, and soon it came in view—the life raft with five occupants.

Loren was bearded, and very weary. We hurried him into the station wagon and drove to Castolon, where he was given an opportunity to wash and shave and put on clean clothes. He had been given food and water.

He seemed in fairly good condition, in spite of the forty-eight hours he had been in the river. We placed him in the bed and drove hurriedly to park headquarters, where I called my son in San Angelo, asking him to meet us in McCamey, with my wife, for the trip back to Amarillo. We had planned to return by way of San Angelo.

We then drove rapidly toward Marathon, some 69 miles away. The dips slowed our speed somewhat, but Andy drove at a speed of eighty miles per hour.

Before reaching Marathon, Loren complained of shortness of breath and pain in his chest. We feared he might have suffered a heart attack.

I instructed Andy, who was driving, to stop at a filling station and have the tank filled with gas and have the oil checked. I rushed to a telephone and called the hospital in Fort Stockton asking for a doctor. None was available, but they assured me one would be on hand when we reached the hospital 58 miles away.

I hurried to the car, only to learn that they had not checked or added oil. This, of course, delayed us another few minutes while it was being taken care of by the service station attendant.

We drove the distance in less than one hour.

They were ready for us at the emergency entrance to the hospital when we arrived. After a brief examination, the doctor ordered him to bed for at least 24 hours.

Andy, John and I took the station wagon and hurried toward McCamey to keep our appointment with my son. However, we met him some distance west of that town. I got in his car, and John and Andy took the station wagon back to Fort Stockton. I went on to San Angelo.

The next morning, we learned by telephone that Loren could not be released from the hospital. We arranged to meet in Midland at noon.

Loren's wife and son came from Turkey to be with him, and we returned to Hart, Nazareth and Amarillo.

Two days later, Loren was released and returned to his home in Turkey. He later entered the hospital in Memphis for a while, but finally seemed to have recovered completely from his harrowing experience.

That was my last visit to Big Bend National Park.

SIX

A Big Bend Sense of Place

WHEN JOHN C. VAN DYKE WROTE HIS BOOK *THE DESERT* in 1901, he described the desert as a starkly beautiful art gallery full of color and light where nothing lived.[1] Two years later, perhaps in direct argument, Mary Austin published *The Land of Little Rain* and described the desert as a home teeming with plants, animals and people. Her desert was a maze of trails, all eventually leading to water.[2] The "pathless wilderness," she said, never existed except in the white "pathfinder's" imagination. Instead, the desert, like all places, had always been home to thousands of men, women, and children who knew its every wrinkle. No one knew who made the first trails, but she believed they had originally been made by animals.

Collected herein, Will F. Evans attributes at least a few of the trails in the Davis Mountains to wild cattle. Much of his sense of place rests on his personal knowledge of local history and immersion in the area's culture. As a rancher, born in a tent and descended from pioneer stock, he knows where the trails begin and end, what the views are like from the tops of the mountains, and how much water the springs produce from year to year.[3]

John Klingemann's sense of place also comes partly from the fact that he was born and raised in the Big Bend. With a Mexican mother and a gringo father, he is completely bilingual, has dual citizenship, and believes people and cultures come together and blend at the Rio Grande, rather than separate there. In the story collected herein, he and a "damn Yankee" friend, as immortal teenagers, explore some dangerous paths together in order to find the sublime. When their descent into the bowels of the desert reaches its most dangerous climax, the white boy wants the Mexican to go first—and the rooster in John would have it no other way.

A sense of place is accumulative and subconscious—a sixth sense, and quite subtle. It is the way a person unconsciously tilts their head into a strong West Texas wind in order to keep a hat in place. It is knowing where to look for something lost or something needed: dig for wood, climb for water. It is sensing a change or an intensity in the weather, choosing appropriate clothing, resting during the heat of the day. A sense of place has nothing to do with positive or negative feelings toward a place, but rather with adaptation and survival. How does one feel safe miles and days from the closest doctor, without air conditioning, without money?

A sense of place can accumulate through trial and error or through observation of native creatures. Did we learn to make adobe by watching mud-dauber wasps, as Carl V. Jarrell describes, or by watching Mexican swallows? Did we learn to flash messages by watching antelope and desert bighorn? Did we learn when to work and when to rest by watching burros?

Sense of place is currently being touted as the answer to America's troubles. Apathy, competition, restlessness, prejudice, and greed—all the evils of modern society—are believed to be rooted in our placelessness. Television, malls, subdivisions, chain stores, and imported food give us the impression that anywhere is just like everywhere else. The vernacular, on the other hand, represents those land uses, buildings, occupations, and forms of communication that grow out of the native climate, resources, and landforms found in a particular place. Desert plants and animals show up as vernacular food choices, as drugs and liquor. A form of vernacular message sending might be inspired by intense sunlight.

Homes in the northern forests are often built of logs, but in the Chihuahuan Desert logs are scarce. In this chapter authors describe living in cool caves or homes built from native materials. Some homes, like Alsate's cave, described by Ross A. Maxwell, are free for the taking.[4] Homesteader J. O. Langford's 12 ft. × 14 ft. adobe, native rock, river cane, and yucca fiber house cost only $10 to build. In symbolic contrast, Henry David Thoreau's 10 ft. × 15 ft. board, brick, and shingle house cost a whopping $28.12 and one-half cent. Thoreau's economy is even less impressive when one takes into consideration almost a hundred years of inflation and the fact that Thoreau did not share his house with a wife and children—nor were the Langfords or the Alsates able to walk home to their mothers' houses for supper every evening as Thoreau did. Alice Jack Shipman describes place-based sources of foods, fibers, salt, water, and recreational or spiritual chemicals.

Eden and "wilderness" are both imagined as places where no one works but people somehow exist in a state of leisure and pleasure. However, in this place that calls itself the last frontier, everyone works hard, even the wind. Place-based work often gives the worker a sense of pride and accomplishment: how long can one go without water or shade, how hot, how far, how often? Before the days of modern water supplies, it was said that young Terlingua girls began hauling water as toddlers. By the time they were half-grown, they were able to carry two ten-gallon pails on each end of a pole balanced across their shoulders, balance another ten-gallon pail on their heads, and still do fancy needlework as they walked along barefooted over rocks and thorns.

How creative can one be when completing a task where supplies must either be found, invented, or conjured? A sense of place is always indicated by the ability to improvise, make do, to know what might solve a problem and where to go to find the materials. I've read that candelilla wax makers, running short of acid for rendering wax, once sneaked into the Boquillas campground and stole the battery water from tourists' cars. Thirty cars mysteriously failed to start the next morning.[5]

Several kinds of natural work are included in this chapter: Joe Graham's candelilla wax makers,[6] Sam Richardson's river guides,[7] and Ted Gray's cowboys.[8] With only hats and slickers for shelter, Gray's crew is caught in a severe rain and hailstorm while out doctoring "worms." Anyone who understands what he means by "worms" already has a little of a Texas sense of place. Gray means screwworms: the maggots of a fly who lays her eggs in living rather than dead flesh. Prior to the USDA's eradication program in the 1970s which air-dropped sterile male flies (females mate only once), screwworms wreaked havoc on all desert animals. The maggots would eat into the living flesh, their bloody wound drawing more and more flies, until the animal either died or was roped and doctored. Any tiny wound (thorns, fighting, birth, mating) in any animal (lions, deer, bighorns, cattle) soon bloomed with voracious screwworm maggots. Today the screwworm has been pushed back to the Panama Canal, and even the most antigovernment militant will give a grudging concession of thanks to the program—except maybe the cowboys who liked to rope.

Children also sometimes seem to develop fast and close ties to nature as they explore their surroundings: swimming into submerged caves or hunting lizards. As W. D. Smithers knew, if one wants to photograph rare bird nests, one should ask the local children for help. Smithers was an early Big Bend photographer who traveled with a chuckbox and shovel. When he wanted to develop the fragile glass negatives produced with his homemade cameras, he would dig a darkroom in the ground. His processing techniques did not require water, and he often cheerfully shared these underground tombs with scorpions, centipedes, and spiders. When he wanted to print the actual photographs, he simply removed some of the thatched desert plant roofing material and created vents to let in sunlight in order to expose his paper. Although all photographers worship the sun to some degree, perhaps Smithers carried it to extremes. This book ends, fittingly, with his essay about sun messages flashed across the desert mountains by avisadores or message senders. It is my hope that some of the messages flashed in these pages will also catch the attention of the reader.

NOTES

1. John C. Van Dyke, *The Desert.* 1901. Reprint, Tucson: Arizona Historical Society, 1976.

2. Mary Austin, *The Land of Little Rain.* 1903. Reprint (with an introduction by Edward Abbey), New York: Penguin, 1988.

3. Will Evans' father first settled in a tent in the Davis Mountains in 1884. The family eventually became prominent West Texas ranchers.

4. Dr. Maxwell was a National Park Service geologist in the Southwest and the first superintendent of Big Bend National Park. He served in the latter position from 1944 to 1952.

5. Richard Phelan, "The Trans Pecos," in *Texas Wild: The Land, Plants, and Animals of the Lone Star State* (New York: Excalibur Books, 1976), 32.

6. Graham became a well-known Texas folklorist who wrote many books and articles about border life, among them *Hecho in Tejas: Texas-Mexican Folk Arts and Crafts* (Denton: North Texas Press, 1991); *The Jacal in the Big Bend: Its Origin and Evolution* (Chihuahuan Desert Research Institute monograph, 1986); and *El Rancho in South Texas: Continuity and Change from 1750* (Denton: North Texas Press, 1994). In 1917 one of his ancestors, also named Joe Graham, accumulated over 110 sections of land surrounding the Rosillos Mountains and gathered his horses from wild herds that roamed there at the time.

7. Richardson has been living in Terlingua since 1987, writing weekly columns called "SAM.U.L." for local newspapers. He also guides, lectures, and edits the *Lajitas Sun.*

8. Gray came to Brewster County in 1938 and worked for the Kokernot O6 Ranch for over twenty-three years, later leasing part of it for five years.

DAVIS MOUNTAIN STORIES
Will F. Evans
1940

STEEPED IN ROMANCE ARE THE OLD TRAILS THROUGH THE DAVIS Mountains. Hundreds of years before the first cowmen drove their herds through these rocky passes, old Spanish adventurers led their pack-trains along the rugged paths in quest of the Seven Cities and untold treasures. Mute evidence of Indians' use of the wild thoroughfares of nature's engineering still stand today; the tough, unshod hoofs of ponies perhaps first cut the path, later to be worn smooth by the moccasined tread of the squaws as they followed their braves.

The Old Spanish Trail skirts these mountains so closely that many who traveled its desert course in the distant past must have cut through their wilds, seeking the old Rio Grande, which they knew lay to the southward.

Since the early '80s, the pioneers and their children have been naming these trails and making new ones, which lead from pass to pass, and from canyon to canyon. Many of these trails had their inception when the old long-horned cattle themselves chose the best course from out a canyon. Just as the old cow never looks, unless she has something at which to take a look, one of them will never start up the side of a rough mountain, unless she knows she will be able to make her way out.

If any man would possess the engineering instinct of a cow, he could build roads at which the world would marvel. Unerringly, she picks the path of least resistance, where the eye of a mere man would not be able to see it at all; it would appear as only a solid wall of rocks and trees and gulleys and rim-rock to him.

One of these old trails is known as Indian Trail; it leads from the mesa east of the head of Brown Canyon, off the steep mountain and winds around the bluffs until it reaches the bottom in Limpia Canyon. A wagon road was worked by the early-day cowmen down this old trail, which lies farther up the canyon than the present McDonald Observatory road.

Joe Marley, while riding around in the wilds of the mountains, chanced into a thicket of oak brush in a little delta on a mountain bench, on the east side of Cherry Canyon. There he found a gushing spring, whose limpid waters formed a small creek as it splashed off down the mountainside. On his telling of his find, on returning to an old tent up in the canyon, where he was living at the time with his wife, she named the fountain Bonanza Spring.

By that name it has been known ever since, but it is located in such a terribly rough spot—the junglelike brush makes any attempt to approach it so formidable a task—that, even today, it remains in the primordial state in which Joe Marley made his find. The only cattle that water there are those that have become outlaws of the brush.

Directly to the east of this spring, on the high wall that is the west side of Madera Canyon, an old trail zigzags off into the canyon far below; this pathway is known as Bonanza Trail. It was up this trail that W. L. Kingston made his way with his wife and family of small children to attend a big barbeque and celebration by the Evans family, just after they bought the Nunn Ranch.

Anyone doubting the roughness of this route and its difficulty even for a sure-footed horse should just try to make the ride. Start in at the Kingston Headquarters Ranch at the mouth of Madera Canyon, go on up by Lewis Phillips' Ranch in the canyon, and, if one's luck is right, he may find where Bonanza Trail leaves the canyon and starts its spectacular climb to the top, two or three miles away. If the rider is not used to riding in the roughs but does manage to reach the Nunn Ranch, Tim Woods, that wild old cowboy who runs the outfit for C. M. Caldwell, more than likely will welcome the arrival with, "Well, how in hell did you ever get through?"

On up above Bonanza Trail, a distance of a few miles and where the canyon seems to get rougher and rougher, Buck Knob Trail leads out; it is the steepest path in all the Davis Mountains to be known as a regular cattle trail and be in actual use. As a matter of fact, it is a safe bet to wager that no old cow made this trail; she would have picked a better way.

There are hundreds of these old trails in the fastness of the Davis Mountains proper; wild cattle have been driven up and down them, and the blood of many bears and panthers have dripped upon their surfaces in being carried on the backs of horses out to the habitats of man.

To the west, the Rim Rock is cut by Biejo Trail, Nine-six Gap, Candelario, and other trails leading down to the Rio Grande that have been traveled by men of all races and characters through the years.

In attempting any description of nature's marvels, always there is the regrettable inadequacy of words. These Davis Mountains constitute one of the most imposingly beautiful ranges on the continent and Limpia, Madera and other canyons through their majestic contours are noted for their attractions. The Davis Mountain Park has been developed as a CCC project; Mount Livermore (Baldy) in the Davis range is the second-highest peak in Texas.

Once when a man was buying a suit of clothes from a Jewish merchant, he asked, "Is it broadcloth?" Unhesitatingly came the reply, "Vy sure it iss; it is both broad and it iss long, and it iss damn gud stuff."

And so it is with the Davis Mountains; they are both broad and long, and they are "good stuff." That is, they are the best place in the world, according to men of that region, for the running of cattle, and for everything that pertains to the cattle business.

Then, there was the Irishman who worked on a skyscraper which towered over the streets of New York City. When asked how high was the building on which he was working, he replied, "Bedad, it's so high that I have to lay flat on my back to let the moon pass over."

Of course, there is still a little room above a cowboy's hat for the moon to pass over when he is on top of some of the Davis Mountain peaks, but they are high enough, for the most part, to make a man's head swim when he is up there and looking down.

It was an old cowboy, who after visiting his first sizable town and being asked for his impressions, said frankly, "Hell, I couldn't see the town for the houses, when I got in the middle of 'em."

That is the situation, literally, when one finds himself in the interior of these mountains. His vision of the great mountain range surrounding him is cut off, entirely, by the walls of the canyons, or by the tall peaks that ascend so abruptly and so close at hand.

Thus, only partially and inadequately can a conception be given of the length, breadth and height of the rugged multitude of mesas, high "back-bones," "saddle-gaps," peaks, canyons, draws and valleys, coves and deltas that characterize this marvelous achievement of nature.

From the distant Bankhead Highway, these formidable mountains appear like a small row of hills within rifle shot; they are judged the same way by those who travel Highway 90, to the south of this range, and pass around on the western side as they journey on toward Van Horn. From Highway 67, which passes along the eastern side, they do not impress travelers with an idea of their actual magnitude. Those who travel Highway 17, from Toyahvale to Fort Davis, cut right through the middle of the eastern part of this range, but still it is a case of "You ain't seen nuthin' yet."

One has to climb Gomez Peak, that high, razorlike pinnacle which lies directly south of the Davis Mountains Filling Station, at the junction of the Old Spanish Trail with Highway 80, to realize actually its impressive elevation.

Mrs. M. W. Tatum, whose husband once owned the Joe Stocks Ranch east of Kent, used to climb this summit with her brothers, the Leatherman boys, as they escorted sightseers up to its lofty top. She explains, "They were just spellbound by the view that met their eyes: a whole world seemed to stretch out below them and to extend far, far away. I never before heard such exclamations of rapture as burst from their lips."

Only by climbing them can there be gained a real conception of what mountains actually are; even the lowly Boracho Peak, which from Highway 80 would seem to be something similar to an anthill, will give a startling idea of its height to one who stands upon its summit and gains a bird's-eye view of the valleys, hills and distant mountains disclosed to the vision; there is afforded the impression of far horizons, lying beyond an intermediate and delightful medley of vivid hues—of whites, blacks, browns, greys, purples and pale blues mingling and blending into a variety of scenic landscapes.

To one quitting the Old Spanish Trail a half-mile west of Phantom Lake Camp and headed south, the mountains seem to stand up like a great timbered wall; as approached, the cliffs stand out against the sky-line in bold relief, their rugged sides cut with many gashes and festooned with moss-covered boulders. Fantastic patterns seem hewn in the sides of the towering cliffs, which encompass and dwarf the man, who tops out at Madera Springs Lodge, right up in "the middle of things."

The full glory of the view from the Look-off Seat beggars description; there one is afforded a "close-up" of the mountains that but serves to enhance the impression of majestic splendor. In front and to the left, the gigantic wall of rock is riven by Madera Canyon, which wags its tail back against the base of Mount Livermore, far to the south. Just below this wide gash lies the ranch home of W. L. Kingston, where Duncan Kingston and his wife are in charge. The house is a big two-story affair, in reality, but from this great height, it would seem to be of a size fitted only for a doll.

On climbing the high "backbone" of Timber Mountain, which arises straight up into the air just to the south, one is afforded a view that doubtless is unsurpassed anywhere, unless by those from the high peaks in Colorado and other far-western states. For the Davis Mountains are truly "the Rockies of Texas"; in height and immensity, in grandeur and natural beauty, they rival any scenic attraction on the continent. And anyone who ever tried to ride a horse from one of the peaks to another has realized their broad expanse; an attempt to negotiate some of the interior regions in the mountains would give a conception of their immensity. Their height can only be appreciated in their being scaled.

These mountains lie in between the Texas and Pacific Railroad to the north and the Southern Pacific Railroad to the south, being penned in by the triangle which is formed by Highway 80 and Highway 90, where they converge at Van Horn to make the western point. The Hovey cut-off, which forms the eastern side of the triangle, connects with the Old Spanish Trail just east of Limpia Creek, many miles below the mouth of Limpia Canyon. From this junction, the Old Spanish Trail goes on westward to join Highway 80 and helps to form the north side of the triangle.

Phantom Lake ever has been a mystery; the first old-timers to gaze upon this stream wondered whence it came and to where it went. For untold centuries, its great volume of water emerged from the limestone underground reservoirs and then returned, almost at once, to some undetermined retreat in the bosom of the earth.

It was not until 1888 that W. L. Kingston and a few other men in the Madera Valley thought of a scheme to utilize this bountiful supply of water, in a region where irrigation is an essential for any growing of crops, and make it flow off down the valley. They succeeded; so, the Phantom Lake of today is not what Ed and Zack Neville and Jack and Tip Franklin saw in 1884.

These daredevil boys determined to find the hidden source of the stream, which in those days emerged from a cave some 450 feet in length. By swimming, they succeeded in reaching a point where they found that the ceiling of the cave came to the surface of the water, but diving in under this edge, they were unable to find the back of the cave. Having candles with them, tied on the ends of long poles, they were able to determine that the ceiling of the cave was lined with bats' nests. In fact, there were many bats in the cave, and that was to bring about a near tragedy before the adventure should end.

Following the river for a few feet back from the mouth of the cave, the boys found where it forked, one stream coming in on their right and the other on their left. From the stream to their right, there jutted up out of the water a little prong of rock.

Finally, tiring of just swimming around in the bottomless pool and in inky darkness, they returned to the open air outside. All, then, wrote their names on a piece of paper. This, Ed Neville took in his teeth and, swimming back in the cave and to the right branch of the stream, tied the paper on the jutting rock point. This done, he rejoined his comrades outside.

They related their experience, but for a long time could never persuade any grown man to be foolhardy enough to swim into the cave with them, although they wished to be able to prove that they had been telling the truth. Finally, however, they persuaded their schoolteacher, Ed Brady, to join them in another swimming trip into the cave.

There occurred nothing untoward in this second venture, until the teacher and the boys had succeeded in reaching a point in the cave where the ceiling was very near to the water. Thinking to scare the man, the youths began to throw water up against the low ceiling and on the bats' nests. As a result, the bats came down in swarms; Ed Brady in trying to keep the bats off of him, began to fight them and to kick so violently in his efforts that, inadvertently, he kicked Zack Neville in the stomach. This knocked the breath out of the boy, who went under, and it was only by the efforts of his brother that he was rescued from death in the underground stream.

After this near tragedy and the boys and the teacher had emerged from the Phantom Lake cavern, no one else has tried to decide whence this stream of water originates. The water has been raised above the cave's mouth.

This was done by stopping up the great crevices in the bottom with sacks of dirt, which were loaded on rafts that were made with poles. Men would guide a raft until it was just over a crevice; the water was very clear and the bottom could be seen, although at a great depth. Then the sacks would be dumped off into the crevices until they were filled. As a result, the water rose several feet and ran off down the Madera Valley, which it still irrigates today, the volume never having varied.

SUBLIME
John Klingemann
2001

AS KIRBY AND I EASED OUR MOTORCYCLES DOWN THE DIRT ROAD, missing the ruts created from last month's rain, we came upon a locked gate. "Shit. Oh well, never stopped us before," I say. We did our usual ride around the minor inconveniences and headed up to the opening of our next adventure.

That morning Kirby had woken me up in the usual manner, playing "Guns and Roses" as loud as he could on his stereo. I jumped up as soon as the music started and cursed at him while he laughed at me. "Get up," he said. "We're going to the Mariposa Mines to look for that place that old Mexican told us about." I got up and staggered to the breakfast table and sat down to eat a bowl of cereal. On the table was his mother's usual note detailing the day's chores for us. I threw it away as usual.

The day before we had been down at the Trading Post playing pool. An old man had been sitting on one of the benches drinking Lone Star out of a can. He had a rugged face with many dark ridges that said he had seen his fair share of hard work. He was wearing an old white button-down shirt with roosters on the front of each shoulder. Sandals protected his feet and the Wranglers he wore were faded from many years of use. His crusty old hat had become a part of his head. You couldn't tell where one started and the other ended. He had been listening to us talk about the mines we had been in and how we had not found anything worth talking about.

"I work in a mine called La Mariposa," he said in broken English. "And there was a cuarto we used to visit when we had a chance."

"¿De qué habla, señor?" He seemed surprised to find out I could speak Spanish and began to tell us his story in his native tongue.

According to the old man, one mine at La Mariposa contained a special room.

"What's he sayin'? What's he sayin'?" Kirby kept asking me as the old man talked.

"Shut up, goddamnit, I'm trying to find out." I did my usual translating for Kirby. Deep in one of the mine shafts lay a special room. You had to go down hundreds of feet to find it. It was dangerous. That immediately attracted us and we thanked the old man.

"You need to learn Spanish, stupid Yankee," I told Kirby. To which he nonchalantly raised his middle finger.

Kirby was from Minnesota and had recently been transplanted to the Big Bend. His parents had lived and worked in the north all of their lives. The first time they came to the Big Bend they had decided to come for the winters. They called themselves natives. We called them snowbirds. They were now living here full-time, and Kirby was learning everything about the local culture. I had introduced him to my beautiful Mexican culture, and he tried to ram his stupid northern culture down my throat.

After we had eaten, we gathered our supplies of water in canteens, sandwiches, flashlights, more water, and extra batteries. As we stepped outside the condo door we were hit with the familiar blast of hot desert air. It was 9:30 in the morning and already the chicharras were striking up their music. "We better get on the road and get down into that cool mine shaft before we melt," I joked.

Across the river in Mexico you could see storm clouds gathering as we headed down the road. We passed Comanche Creek and then we were on the flats across from the Lone Star Mine. About ten miles from Lajitas we came to the dirt road that led to the Mariposa Mines. To our right you could see, off in the distance, Santa Elena Canyon and Needle Peak. At the first fork in the road we took a left, as the old man had directed.

Parts of the road had been washed out and you could tell where people had tried to cross in vehicles and had probably gotten stuck. A roadrunner ran across the road about twenty feet in front of us. It reminded me of a story told by older women in the region. A roadrunner near you always meant good luck because it would protect you from snakes.

"I wonder if we could take him down in the mine with us?" I asked Kirby.

"Why?"

"Nothing, never mind," I said.

Pretty soon we came to a couple of old buildings without any roofs. We pulled out some maps that Kirby's father had given us for our adventures and proceeded to find out where we were. I did not like the way things were starting to shape up. Instead of having a side entrance, it looked more like there was a deep shaft next to the mountain without any ladders or nearby objects to use for securing our ropes. We parked our motorcycles and walked up to the deep pit.

"Shit, not even a ladder for us to climb down, and I don't feel like going down a rope today," I grunted as I spat down the 150-foot shaft.

Many times we had gone down rotting old ladders that would collapse if you stepped in the middle of the rung. To avoid this we stepped directly above the nails that fastened the rung to the ladder. Sometimes it made for a nerve-racking adventure, especially if you thought about what your parents would be thinking if they knew.

We walked around to one side and were overjoyed to find that there indeed was a tunnel that could lead us down. We had gotten directions from the old man, but nevertheless it would still be hard to find the special room of the cave. At the opening of the tunnel we prepared our flash-lights, drank some water, and headed down the cool tunnel. The tunnel was about seven feet high and about five feet across. A cool breeze hit us as we entered and our world went from a bright sunshine to a moldy, black, sulphuric-smelling earth. "I think we're supposed to go down this tunnel for a while until we come into a shaft with a sturdy ladder," Kirby said.

The tunnel wound its way into the mountain and every so often would pass a deep shaft that with a slight slip would send you down into a lower level from which you would never emerge. The rocks on the walls were crumbling and several cave-ins had occurred. Luckily, we had never had the pleasure of being a part of a cave-in. Every ten feet, old wooden beams held the tunnel from collapsing. But you could still see where the cracks had formed, threatening to unlodge tons of material on top of you.

Finally we came to a shaft with a ladder. "Oh man, that ladder looks like it goes all the way to the top," I said. But upon further inspection, we noticed that no sunlight shone from the top, leading us to believe that it probably just went to another level.

"Well, here it is," Kirby said as he grabbed the ladder and shook it a little. The old wood creaked, as years of dust and rusty nails had eroded much of its sturdiness. As dust was falling through the air, my good friend told me, "Okay, you're up, Stud. Down the ladder you go."

"What? Bullshit! I thought you were going first," I barked.

"We'll flip for it," he said.

The ladder wasn't too bad as I went down. Every now and then it would feel as if it were about to give, but sure enough it stayed true. "How far down am I supposed to go?" I yelled.

"I don't know, just keep going."

Pretty soon I came to a horizontal tunnel, and I stepped off the ladder and onto the dirt. Sweat was dripping down my face, collecting the dust and forming dark lines.

"I think I found it, come on down." We had been told by the old man that we would know we were on the right path because there would be a hand-written sign on the wall that said "Cueva," and I was looking at an old sign that said "Cueva."

By the time Kirby had gotten down to my location, I was already looking at the modern rock art found along the walls of the tunnel. Some were dates with names such as "José Domínguez, 1923." Others were intricate drawings of females with oversized breasts and long legs. We took some time to take in the surroundings and then proceeded down the tunnel. We had been underground for about an hour and a half now, close to lunchtime. We discussed whether or not to eat and finally decided to wait until after we found the cave. As we proceeded down the tunnel, we noticed the structures were getting worse and worse. Old cave-ins became more frequent, and at one point we thought we would have to turn around.

We finally came to a large room where the tunnel ended. On the other side was nothing but the deposit of another large cave-in. "Damn, we came all this way for that?" I asked.

"Man, this can't be the end of the line," Kirby said.

"I'm going to go back and kick that old man's ass for telling us to come down here."

Our flashlights looked like light-sabers in the dark room as we shined them from one corner to the other. "Hey, what's that?" Kirby asked. At the bottom of one of the walls was a small opening about two feet high and three feet wide. I scrambled over to take a look. As I shone my light down the opening I could tell that it went for about five feet and then opened into a larger room.

It reminded me of another cave on another adventure. We had been looking for this particular cave for about three days. After we finally found the one we thought we were looking for, to our dismay the cave was only about thirty feet deep. But for some reason the walls seemed to be alive. Further inspection revealed what seemed to be thousands of daddy long-leg spiders crawling all around the entrance. Kirby had let out a scream, and we ran out. After gathering ourselves, we went back in and noticed that the spiders were all over the walls for only about the first ten feet. So we walked to the end of the tunnel and confirmed that the cave ended there. As we were standing a few feet away from the end, we noticed markings on the wall, but at the level of our knees: dates and names left by previous explorers. Some were drawn with charcoal, while others were carved.

While we discussed the strangeness of the level that the names had been placed, we noticed a small opening at the very bottom of the tunnel's end. I lay stomach-down in the cool dirt and shined my flashlight through the opening that was only about two feet wide by about a foot and a half tall.

"What do you see?" Kirby asked.

"I can't tell, but I'm going to crawl through." I could barely fit my torso through the entrance, and as I crawled through, I started feeling like a hot dog. After about ten feet, I spilled into a room that had a thirty-foot ceiling. I yelled back for my friend to come through and meanwhile stared in amazement at what lay before me. Stalagmites grew out of the floor, reaching up like serpents out of a sea of dust.

Now, here we were again, in another cave, again looking at a small opening with the promise of something beyond. I got down on my belly and crawled in. As I neared the edge, my light seemed to bounce off the walls.

I pulled myself out of the small hole. When I stood up I was amazed at the beauty that mother nature had created. "Kirby! You have got to come take a look at this!"

"What is it? What is it?"

"Just get your ass in here!"

In front of me were walls of nothing but crystal. A fine dust covered all of the walls, making the crystals brown. There wasn't any loose dirt anywhere. Kirby came out of the hole and stood next to me. We both shined our lights in different directions. It was amazing; we were in a geode. It was as if we had been shrunk to the size of ants and placed in a geode.

In the corner we found another small entrance and crawled into it. We quickly found out that it led into a yet smaller room. As we crawled into the tiny space no bigger than the front seats of a small car, we found a notebook—a sign-in guest book.

Someone had been there recently, for the book looked to be only two to three years old, and left it there for anyone who dared to enter looking for the cave. In the binder was a pencil for names and remarks. It was as if we were signing in to gaze at one of mother nature's desert museums. We each took our turn with the pencil and didn't bother to tell the other what we had written.

Just for kicks we turned the flashlights off and sat for about five minutes in the darkest of darkness I had ever seen. I could see absolutely nothing, not even my hand in front of my face. I could hear my friend's breathing, and that was it.

"Man, this is creepy," I said. No answer. "Kirby?" I said in an inquiring voice. "Man, cut that shit out." I finally said, "I hate it when you do that." We both started laughing. We were both notorious for bringing friends down into these mines and scaring them. One time we even had one of our friends start crying because he thought he was going to die.

After the five minutes were over, we crawled out and returned to the larger room. From there we went back out the small opening and up the ladder.

"I'm going to bring my girlfriend down here," Kirby said.

"You do that. I'd like to see how far down you get her before she freaks out on you."

A WASP CALLED THE MUD-DAUBER
Carl V. Jarrell
1936

IT WAS A BALMY JULY MORNING. I WAS SEATED ALONE AT MY DESK. Softly out of the din of the street there entered a visitor. She was of an old and respected family. Her ancestors date back to a period long before the Caesars. Her progenitors, perhaps, were present when the world was young—when the evening stars first lighted the heavens.

My caller was a near relative of the family *Polopaeus coeruleus,* a female of the solitary variety, a builder extraordinary of homes, a Wasp called the Mud-dauber. She was arrayed in all the pristine beauty of her race. Her faceted eyes sparkled with a confident gleam as she began the duties of her appointed rounds. I welcomed my visitor as one of the world's most gifted insects, as one of Nature's most ingenious craftsmen.

Back in childhood days I had known her family, and as a boy I had whiled away many summer hours in the company of her kin. I was intrigued then, as I have been since, with the arts and sciences that are peculiar to the wasp.

There are many varieties of mud-dauber wasps. Some families build one-cell homes; others ten cells or more. I have in my possession now a clay home of twenty-two separate rooms. These domiciles and group nurseries are always found in protected places, usually within doors of barns, corn cribs, covered sheds, and in garages.

While the chief food provided for young wasps is spiders, some species store caterpillars and crickets. Wasps vary in size, and in shape of body, according to Nature's plan. They are colored in beautiful tints and hues of brown, green and black. Also they differ in methods and mannerisms, each individual remaining true to the inherited type.

Now this new acquaintance had flown in through an open window to afford me an opportunity to observe her operations in a more leisurely manner, and in a more methodical fashion. She was very prim and precise. Very cautiously she inspected the premises, and as I had suspected, she was surveying the site for her home.

This adventurous female first had seen the light of day from the portals of a modest clay home which her mother had built the season before. The time now had come when this representative of a later generation must do likewise, in answer to the eternal urge that was throbbing in her breast.

She selected a location for her home upon the wall, just above my desk, and presently began to build exactly as had countless others of her kind before her. For seven weeks she was to be my daily guest. As she began the construction of her domicile, I said to myself: "Business or no business, I will observe your operations carefully as you go along, and watch you intently to the end of your life's journey. I will ask you many questions as you proceed, and speculate as to your part in the great plan of Life."

Perhaps, I thought, the secrets of the universe are wrapped up in your tiny head. I may catch a gleam of the intelligence that inspires and animates your life, or I may glean a hint of the Master's wisdom Who in the long ago laid out upon the trestle-board of life the plans and specifications that were to guide the insect dynasty throughout all the countless centuries of time.

This brown streak of animation loses no time in getting started, once she has selected her building site. She chooses some moist earth that is suited to her needs and adds a liquid cement which she exudes from her body as required. This mortar mixture is then fashioned into a ball about the size of a pea, which she carefully molds into place in the construction of a room or cell as an individual nursery, or habitat, for her offspring.

The diminutive architect, engineer and builder finishes one room at a time. The room is slightly more than one inch long, and one-fourth inch in diameter. About twenty-five loads of mortar are required to finish the room completely. The actual building time is three hours, and the job is completed at high noon each day. After the room is finished, the wasp inspects her work very carefully, inside and out, going over the surfaces with her antennae to locate any defects that might appear. These she corrects with fresh mortar as she thinks necessary.

One end of the room is left open for drying purposes and for seasoning until the evening shades appear; then, just before sundown, the industrious worker returns, and with a few balls of mud very deftly closes the aperture for the night, as much as to say: "This is necessary to guard against the enemies or parasites who might intrude during the night to steal away my secrets or mar my handiwork, and thus menace the young life for which I build."

Three evenings the cell or room was closed. Three mornings the cell was opened, until the afternoon of the third day, when the cell was some three and one-half days old, when the wasp returned for what proved a final inspection. A little later she flew in with a black spider bearing a gray stripe down its back. The spider was almost as large as herself, and was being provided as food for her young. She placed the victim in the cell and carefully arranged the corpse in such a position as suited her, folding the spider's legs neatly beside the body. With the spider in the proper position, the wasp deposited her egg in the spider's back. Then she backed out of the cell to seal it, this time permanently, to await the birth of her child.

Thus, in similar manner and in exact sequence, the individual cells are constructed, and the spider provisions are stored, until ten cells are completed, all joined together into a symmetrical whole.

The spider victim, while entombed and oblivious to the world about, is not dead in the usual sense. The sting of the wasp has only suspended animation and halted its body functions to await the coming of the little white grub that will feed readily from its body. The wasp is equipped with a small hypodermic needle with which she paralyzes the nerve centers of the spider, rendering it, as it were, embalmed or refrigerated, with the sirloins and porterhouse steaks fresh for her young, as needed, and with the vitamins intact and unimpaired.

The species of wasp represented by the visitor store only one spider to each room. The young wasps devour the body, legs and all. Wasps of some other families store three or more spiders to each room, with the young feeding only from the tender meat, leaving the shells as mute reminders of the feast.

After the spider is treated and safely stored away by the mother wasp, the egg in due course hatches into the larva, which begins to feed almost immediately upon the spider. Another life is now on its predestined way.

Little is known concerning Papa, or the husband wasp, except that he never once showed up while the work of building was under way. He, like many other males of the insect world, doubtless reckoned that his duty to society was performed when he had mated with the female of his choice. This marital embrace, perhaps, carried with it the penalty of death; so we see him no more.

As I watched the skilled artisan and patient builder, my first thought was: Who taught you to use so expertly the little mason's trowel with which you are equipped? Who told you about the trip-hammer you have, which serves you in rounding the walls of your home and pressing them into such perfect symmetry? What instructions have you had in the use of the poisoned dagger with which you so successfully paralyze your spider victims? How did you find out where their nerve centers were located? Since you never saw your parents, or listened to a mother's lullaby, what light of inspiration has gleamed so steadily out of the past to point the way to your life's high aim? Since you will never see your offspring and hold them to your breast, what light of faith has burned so intensely along the way to assure you a springtime for your progeny?

But this radiant bit of femininity only seemed to give me a sly wink as she moved serenely on. I was amazed at her incredible patience, intrigued with her amazing skill, and thrilled by her dexterity in the use of the tools of her profession. . . .

One afternoon, when my fascinating guest had completed her task, she sat on the edge of my desk preening herself. She seemed to look at me earnestly and to say: "Brother, we have finished; the job is done; I go hence." Yet she hovered around for a while, seemingly happy over her handiwork. She appeared to realize that the promptings of Life and the demands of destiny had been attained, and she was content that others should gather the fruits of her toil and her passion.

And now the observer must watch intently, and listen, for the shadows are beginning to gather around the little mother. Soon she will go away with the flowers, and lie down with the autumn leaves. . . .

What power, Mother Wasp, is given your offspring to attain maturity unaided; then to plan and build and live to destiny's end, without instruction; whereas other children of earth are nurtured to growth, and then, in the main, seldom plan and rarely build except when directed?

She was disappearing as I aroused from my musing, and something told me she would never return; that I would finish this narrative by the light of the inspiration she had left behind. . . .

Little Wasp, it is interesting to speculate upon the inscrutable forces that control your destiny—forces which appear as fixed and as constant as the pole star that gleams and glistens in the northern sky to guide the lone mariner through the night. In comparison, man seems a weak and vacillating thing, buffeted about by all the winds that blow. His infirmity of character, and his lack of faith in the eternal verities of life, establishes his stability of about the comparative strength of the tiny candle flame that is blown out with a breath.

You see, Man, in the main, is still pretty badly mixed up about Life. One day in college, perhaps, he was told that once upon a time, away back in the dim and shadowy past, there was a thing called a protoplasm, and he has been worrying his insignificant self ever since about where man came from.

Added to that scientific theory, he read that men were created free and equal, being endowed with inalienable rights. Thereupon he declared that he was just as good as anyone else—if not a little better. But after all these thousands of years, the fact remains that man is largely a creature of environment and suggestion, subject to the whims and caprices of chance, and to the miscellaneous interference of society; mistaking shadows for substance, accepting means as ends, and treating effects as causes. . . .

Socialized man has developed almost a mania for meddling with nature, and interfering with the rights of each other. He has misinterpreted "Go ye into all the world and preach the gospel," and has substituted, "Go ye into all the world and spread propaganda, that ye may steal the lands and substances of all races." His specialty is taking away that which you have and replacing it with something that you are not naturally fitted to use, the result to the individual being a false and tragic philosophy that destroys his faith in God and that undermines his confidence in himself.

For instance, you, little insect, had you been under man's dominion, might have found yourself assembled into a class composed of dragon-flies, bumblebees, yellowjackets, grasshoppers, tumblebugs, and other nondescripts. Your teachers, in all probability, would have told you that your mud houses were "all wet"; that your architecture was "old stuff" and not being done anymore; that the latest approved building material was lichen, like the hornets use. After they had influenced you to doubt the wisdom of Him who gave you craftsmanship, and had left you uncertain, they and their henchmen probably would have been taught that you and your kin, including the hornets, were all wrong; that your forefathers were old fogies, and that building houses by hand was antiquated drudgery; that modern methods provided that homes be built by machinery; that you needed more time for recreation, leisure, self-expression and cultural development.

Having perpetrated these physical and mental upheavals, the ultra-modernized social system would have begun to tamper with your personal life—with what you must eat, and what you must not drink; in all probability would have suggested that you were not getting a balanced diet; that you should sip more of the nectar of the flowers—and eat more carrots and spinach. . . .

To carry the analogy further, Man might even have begun meddling with your family life—yapping about birth control; perhaps, in his stupidity, attempting regulation. The cohorts of social uplifters might have decreed that ten children were too many; that you should reduce your output, for the benefit of society, "the fuller life," and the ultimate perfection of the species.

Yes, little architect, were it not that you are protected by your Creator, and guided by divine Providence, Man would have made you so scientifically standardized that you would have been of little, if any, use to yourself, and no good at all to the world. He would have made you so super-sanitary that instead of you paralyzing the spider at the first contact, the spider might have paralyzed you. . . .

Though a season has passed since you went away with the flowers, we recall the excellence of your handiwork, and upon memory's film remains engraved the record of your cares and vigils; and as other spring-times come, with their multitudinous life, and after Nature has assigned her tasks, perhaps none will fill their niche with such fidelity or inspire to greater intrepidity than you did, little Wasp.

We have kept your clay home, though the family has moved away. It is here before me as I write. Like other old homesteads, it is mute and inanimate, perhaps, except to those who have known the lives that have passed over the thresholds and who have heard the lullabies that were sung around the hearthstones.

CUEVA DE ALSATE AND NATIVE HOMES
Ross A. Maxwell
1968

NEAR THE MOUTH OF GREEN GULCH THE ROAD PASSES THE EASTERN end of Pulliam Peak intrusion. Here erosion has sculptured the intrusion; from certain places, in the proper light, the mountain profile takes the shape of a man's face that is looking skyward. The mountain profile is locally known as Alsate's Face.

Alsate was an Apache chief who was a brave warrior and one of the great Apache leaders of his time. One story relates that Alsate and his band were hard pressed by the Comanches and took refuge in the Chisos Mountains. The fighting continued and Alsate was finally killed. According to the legend, when Alsate fell, the earth shook, rumbled, and moaned, and the mountains rose. When all was quiet again, the Comanches saw the profile of Alsate's face on the mountaintop. The enemy warriors left immediately and in great haste, for they believed that the mountain stronghold was still in the custody of Alsate's ghost, and so long as his face remained on the mountaintop, the Chisos Mountains were the happy hunting grounds for the spirits of Alsate and his braves.

Another story of Alsate's last days goes back to 1880 when a band of Apaches was making its last stand in the Chisos Mountains. The tribe was "sort of hemmed up" in the Chisos Mountains by the Comanche Indians to the north and by the Mexicans, whose ranches and villages Alsate and his tribe raided at every opportunity, on the south. Finally, a spokesman for the Mexican garrison at San Carlos, Chihuahua, Mexico, came to Alsate and invited the entire tribe to a fiesta. Now a fiesta in the Big Bend country used to mean everything to eat and drink and dancing for days. Alsate and his tribe, intrigued by the promise of food (for they were hungry), went to San Carlos. On the first night of the fiesta, Alsate's band wined, dined, and got gloriously drunk. The next morning they awakened to find themselves in chains. The Mexicans rejoiced and had their own fiestas because Alsate had been captured. They planned to march the Indians into the interior of Mexico to be sold into slavery so that Alsate would trouble them no more.

Alsate, his squaw, and a few followers, however, managed to escape their Mexican captors. The chief dropped out of sight, and for years most people believed him dead. After a time, however, sinister rumors began to creep over the countryside about Indians in the Chisos Mountains. Some persons claimed to have seen Alsate. Others, on awakening in the morning, found moccasin prints in their camps. Some were large, others small, as if made by a man and a woman. Most persons believed the prints were made by Alsate and his squaw, and the makers became known as "Big Foot" and "Little Foot." The campers never saw or heard anyone during the night and only food was taken.

Finally, the San Carlos authorities sent customs guards to search for the track makers. In searching about the mountains where the "ghosts" and tracks were reported to have been seen, the guards found a cave with signs of recent occupancy, but they did not find the inhabitants. The users had been able to carry in grass for a bed, to kill and eat birds, rabbits, and other small animals, and to build a fire for cooking. As the Indian "ghost" was often seen in the vicinity, the cave became known by the name "Cueva de Alsate" (Alsate's Cave), but as Alsate's ghost harmed no one, the official pursuit was stopped. In later years, some of the more venturesome people entered the cave. In an obscure corner lay the mummified remains of Alsate, the Apache chief. Nearby were the charcoal remains of a fire and a small bed. The squaw was not found, and it was supposed that she had previously returned to her people in San Carlos.

Ocotillo is a spiny shrub, with few or many unbranched stems, 5 to 20 feet tall, that is leafless except during or immediately after the rainy season. Repeated rains bring forth a succession of leaves throughout the growing season. The showy flowers normally appear in March to early April and are a brilliant scarlet cluster, 4 to 10 inches long, borne at the terminal end of the stem. Because of the heavy spines, the plant is often mistaken for a cactus, but it is not related to the cacti. It grows on the lower slopes of the Chisos Mountains and at many places on the surrounding desert but is most abundant in gravel deposits derived from igneous rocks.

Ocotillo, which is used to build small corrals, various enclosures, and fences, has the ability to grow when only the stem is placed in the ground. Consequently, it is not uncommon to see portions of a fence growing and blooming in the proper season. Occasionally, two rows of the stalks are placed in the ground about six inches apart and the space between the stalks filled with bundles of candelilla or chino grass to form the walls of a house. With canvas hanging over the door and a small fire inside, such houses are comfortably warm even in extremely cold weather. Ocotillo stalks were commonly laid across the *vigas* (rafters) in the ceiling of a house or placed on a frame and thatched to form an arbor. Occasionally during a wet season, when there is enough sap in the ocotillo stalks, they will bloom.

Carrizo cane, sometimes called giant cane, grows in many thickets along the flood plain of the Rio Grande and at a few well-watered places in the desert. The plant has a straight, unbranched jointed stalk that grows up to a height of 15 feet, and a broomcorn-like brush at the top of the stalk appears in early summer. The mature plants are dry, coarse, and hard, and only a few of the leaves are suitable for forage, but when the cane is young and fresh, livestock and game thrive in these lush patches of vegetation. It is a common practice for the Mexican ranchers to burn the cane thickets during the winter, so that the fresh tender growth is available for spring forage. The mature *carrizo* stalks, when stripped of their leaves, are also used as a covering on top of the *vigas* before a thatched or dirt roof is placed on a house or arbor. The old Straw House near the mouth of Boquillas Canyon was constructed of upright *carrizo* cane stalks, chinked with bundles of candelilla and chino grass.

PRIMITIVE MAN'S FOOD
Alice Jack Shipman[1]
1933

THE LAND WEST OF THE PECOS IS MOSTLY SEMI-DESERT AND THE principal vegetation is the cactus. However, this vegetation served primitive man in many ways. Some of the species produced palatable fruits, especially the Prickly Pear (Nopal) and the Pitahaya.

Most prominent among the spiky family of the West is the Maguey, the generic name for many species which thrive along the Rio Grande. In Mexico this plant is a great source of wealth. In Texas the plant matures but once in a century. Lechuguilla and sotol of this family grow in the greatest profusion along the Rio Grande and were used extensively by the primitive people. They were roasted in pit ovens and became sweet and nutritious food.

Mescal pits are very plentiful in this section. They are usually circular depressions in the ground, varying in circumference, sloping evenly to the center, a foot to three in depth, and lined with small stones. A fire was built in the pit, raked out after the stones became hot, and the roots of the plants put in and covered with grass. After two days' steaming, the pile was opened and the mescal was ready for consumption. Mescal was a valuable food source among the Indians. So far as is known, the mescal was not fermented by the Indians until after the coming of the Spaniards.

Peyote, a species of small cacti, found in the arid hills along the Rio Grande and southward in Mexico, was formerly and still is much used for ceremonial and medicinal purposes by the Indians from the Rocky Mountains to the Gulf of Mexico. Among different tribes it is known under different names, as *seni* (Kiowa), *wokowi* (Comanche), and *kikori* or *kikuli* (Tarahumara). In appearance the peyote plant resembles a radish in size and shape, the top only appearing above the ground. From the center springs a beautiful white blossom, which is later displaced by a tuft of white fuzz, which contains the potent "button." North of the Rio Grande this "button" only is used. In Mexico the whole plant is cut into slices, dried, and used in decoction, while the ceremonial also is essentially different from that of the northern tribes.

Salt played an important part in the lives of the first inhabitants of our country, as it does in our affairs today. Of the many persons who daily lift the lowly saltshaker, few have any conception of the important part which common salt has had in the history and the development of West Texas. It caused the making of the first trail across the Big Bend.

Salt is to most people but a simple condiment. Yet wars have been waged for the possession of salt deposits, and the trend of great trails have been bent for easy access to the regions of salt.

There are two large deposits in this section; one north of Van Horn, west of the famous Guadalupe Peak, and another east of the Pecos River, northeast of Castle Gap in the Castle Mountains. The Indians had well-worn trails leading to these lakes when the first civilized men arrived west of the Pecos four centuries ago. Just as the mighty Rio Grande rises among those lofty peaks of Colorado, and is augmented by rills, brooks, springs, creeks, riverlets, and rivers, and fights its way downward through the rocks and rapids, through gorges and stupendous canyons to the peaceful plains, and finally mingles its dusky flood with the waters of the Gulf, so the human stream comes from some misty mountains of the past.

First as individual hunters and herders, then as tribes, clans, families, and finally nations, this human stream came roaring down the ages, fighting the elements, fighting each other. On they came through the great canyons of doubt and hope. Just as the rivers are made of drops of water, so is this human stream made of people.

Hidden in the caves on the mountain sides in the lonely canyons of the Big Bend, many feet beneath age-old layers of ashes and earth, lies a record of a people who lived in this country long before the time of those Indians, who were here when the first white men arrived. These aborigines brought the fiber of the native cacti, ocotillo, sotol, lechuguilla, maguey, and Spanish dagger into caves for bedding, baskets, strings, and many other uses. They also brought quantities of cooked sotol and lechuguilla, which they chewed and spat fiber upon the floors of the caves. These cuds are to be found to this day.

Roman soldiers were paid in salt, hence the derivation of our word *salary.* Scientists say that we would quickly starve to death on food that contains no salt, even if it were otherwise 100 percent nutritious. Salt is essential to the formation of gastric juices, without which there can be no digestion. In addition to being an aid or factor in digestion, salt is a purifier of the blood and a preventative of disease.

The primitive people had great trails leading from Mexico across the Rio Grande at the San Carlos Ford, and another at the San Vicente. From this point the trail led directly north between Tornillo Creek and the Sierra Rosillas to the Santiago Mountain Range, where it went through a natural pass in the mountains leading northwest between the Maravillas Creek and the Santiago Range to Peña Colorado where there was plenty of water. Here the trail turned north, passing east of the Comanch (Glass Mountains) to Comanche Springs (Fort Stockton). From Comanche Springs the trail went to the Horse Head Crossing on the Pecos, on through Castle Gap in the Castle Mountains, to the salt lakes in what is now Crane County.

From the junction of the Rio Grande and the Conchos, the Indians had a trail leading to Alamito Creek, up this creek to a warm spring, then to San Estaben, Antelope Springs through Paisano Pass, on to Kokernot Springs, then Leoncito, Leon Water Holes, to Comanche Springs where it joined the Comanche Trail. Then it passed on to the salt lakes east of the Pecos, and this was also buffalo land. We will call this trail the Jumano Indian Trail. When the first Spaniards arrived at the junction of the Conchos and the Rio Grande, they found a trail leading from this vicinity to the Paso del Norte section. However, it was only passable during dry season when the Rio Grande was low.

NOTE

   1. Shipman was the editor-publisher for *The Voice of the Mexican Border,* from which this excerpt comes. No author was listed for this article, so I am assuming she was the author.

HOMESTEADER'S BEDROOM
J. O. Langford
1952

BY MID-AFTERNOON OF THAT FIRST DAY, WE HAD TRAVELED ONLY about ten miles when the burros came to a halt. I looked up in surprise. We had been winding between hills listing sharply on either side. And now the rimrocks glowed with an opalescent light under the slanting rays of the afternoon sun. It couldn't possibly be past four o'clock.

But the indications were obvious. Juan was leisurely climbing down from the freight wagon and slowly unharnessing the burros. Apparently, we were already pitching camp for the night.

I protested vigorously. I pointed out to Juan that we had at least three more hours of daylight. I told him that it was a long way to our claim on the Rio Grande, that we were anxious to get there, and that if we stopped this early every day, it would take us at least a week to make the trip.

To all of this, Juan, who could not understand a word of English, bowed and smiled politely and continued to unharness the burros.

Enrique slid from the back of the belled mare and stooped to put rawhide hobbles on her forelegs. He stripped her of saddle and bridle, then slapped her on the rump. Finally, he turned stiffly and explained in his sketchy English, with obvious contempt at my ignorance. It was the burros, he said; they had pulled the wagons as far as they would go today. Enrique didn't bother to enlarge on the subject, and I still didn't understand.

I was to become much better acquainted with burros before I left this country. In fact, I was to own one myself before I caught onto the curious fact that man's enslavement of the typical Mexican burro can go only so far and no farther. The burro reserves certain personal rights of his own.

For instance, he will pull and carry monstrous loads for man; but always on his own terms. Those terms being that he travel his own pace, that he carry or pull not one pound more than what he considers his full load, and that when he is ready to stop for the day, he stops. Man, with his superior intellect, can devise all sorts of ingenious methods of torture in an effort to get more work out of the little animal, but it's all wasted. When a burro's mind is made up, man may as well accept that fact gracefully. Man may kill the burro, but he'll not change the animal's mind.

My protests coming to nothing, I helped Bessie and Lovie down from the buckboard. We stood and watched till the harness was removed from the last burro and he was free to trail after his teammates. They all followed devotedly after the mare as she grazed toward a grass-filled box canyon that fronted on the camp site.

I wondered some at releasing the burros in such a manner. What was to keep them from straying away, leaving us and our wagons stranded out here in the foothills? But I didn't worry about it. The banker in Alpine who'd recommended Juan Salas to me had pointed out that Juan was a regular freighter between Terlingua and Alpine; I supposed Juan must know his business.

As the clanging of the mare's bell moved away from camp, I was struck by the death-like stillness of this new world. There were sounds, of course. There was the sound of the mare's bell. There was the scream of an eagle soaring high in the blue overhead. And near at hand were the peculiar noises of disturbed blue quail, flushed by the browsing burros. Yet, somehow, these were only surface sounds, each one separate, so that they in no way affected the vast, impenetrable silence that hung over the country. . . .

We had stopped at an old camp site and there was no wood in sight; no wood of any size, that is. Just bits of algerita bush and the dead bloom stalks of the sotol plant. And here and there the ocotillo, a strange desert plant that lifted its thorny branches like the groping arms of an octopus. When I examined the plant closer, I found a fresh scarlet bloom in the top of each branch, although the main branches looked dead enough to burn.

I returned to camp, carrying a skimpy load of dead brush that I felt sure would flare up, burn fiercely for a moment, then die away before the heat could possibly cook anything.

Juan and Enrique looked up from helping Bessie clean the quail, caught sight of my firewood, and grinned. Juan rose, dragged a grubbing hoe from his wagon, and strode out to the edge of camp, where he started digging around a dead mesquite shrub whose base was hardly bigger than my wrist. In a moment, he was working away from his starting point, as if intent on digging a crooked trench in the ground.

I moved closer and found this to be the case; he was digging a trench. But down in the trench was the root of the dead mesquite shrub, much larger and heavier than I would have believed.

Following the root out till it became too small to be of any use, Juan reversed his grubbing hoe and used the bit to chop the root free at both ends. Stooping, he dragged from its earthen bed a long stick of wood worthy of being carried to any camper's fire.

That was my first experience in having to grub for wood.

We ate as the sun dropped behind the hills, setting fire to the ragged peaks at first, then dying out to leave an afterglow of vivid coloring.

The silent night closed in. Bessie and I kicked aside a few loose rocks on the level ground near the wagon and made down our bed—a mattress thrown down onto a spread-out wagon sheet, with sheets over the mattress. We didn't bother with quilts; the night was too warm.

The Mexicans each lifted a tattered and dirty blanket from the wagon and moved out into the darkness beyond the firelight.

Lovie, silent at last, slept between Bessie and me; and Tex curled up on the ground as close as she could get to the mattress. Tex slept fitfully between periods of rising with a low growl to go investigate some strange scent that might mark the approach of an imagined danger.

Along about midnight, a spatter of rain aroused us. We got up to move our bed in under the wagon. After that, I lay awake for a time, listening to the weird singing of the coyotes among the hills, thinking of the venture ahead of us.

Bessie stirred in the darkness and I wondered again if I'd done the right thing. Was I risking her life when I made the decision to come out here? Back in Midland, I had gone by and had a long talk with Dr. W. W. Lynch; he had given me full instructions of taking care of Bessie, should the baby come before we could get a doctor. Still, I was no doctor; I wouldn't be able to help Bessie if there were any complications with the birth.

She stirred again, and I knew she was awake. "Bessie," I called softly. "Did I do the right thing? Do you think we'll make a go of it, or have I just made a mess of everything?"

Bessie answered quietly, but with confidence in her voice: "Oscar, I think we're all going to love this country. And I just have a feeling you're going to get well out here."

That was Bessie. If she ever had a doubt about my ability to take care of her and the children, she never let me know it.

I turned over and went back to sleep.

As my health improved, I began to take more interest in the matter of building us a house. The new baby was expected in November and, although the winters here were said to be exceedingly mild, we still thought it best to have our house ready to receive the baby.

Our first thoughts went to the building of a pine plank cabin; but after we'd considered the cost of lumber and the even greater expense of getting it hauled to us, we gave up the idea and looked about us for new ones. The homes of most of our neighbors were built of materials that existed right here on the land—native stone, adobe bricks, and cottonwood poles for rafters. And, after studying such dwellings awhile, we found that we were better pleased with them than we'd be with any sort of lumber house that we could afford to build with our limited means.

At last, we decided on adobe blocks. I didn't know how to make them, but my "renter" Cleofas Natividad did. And this might prove a way to collect my rent.

I went to talk with Cleofas. He couldn't understand English and I couldn't understand Spanish; but with lots of gesturing and pointing and explaining, we finally got together on the trade. For ten dollars in labor, Cleofas agreed to make me one thousand adobe bricks twelve by four by eighteen inches. For ten dollars more, he was to transport them from where he made them at his well to the house site Bessie and I had chosen.

Cleofas, with the help of his many children, set to work. He made the bricks out of a mixture of mud, grass, and goat manure. The children did the mixing with their bare feet, trampling the ingredients as Cleofas put them into a hole he'd dug into the ground.

Once the mud was of the proper consistency, it was scooped out, put into wooden molds, then laid out on the bare ground to dry. When the bricks were finally "cured," Cleofas caught up his six burros, loaded six bricks to each burro, then drove them over the rough hills to unload and stack the bricks on a high point above the hot spring.

Bessie and I had chosen this spot with care. It was high, with everything open to the south, so that we had a wonderful view of the Rio Grande canyon below, and would catch every breeze that came across the mountains in Mexico during the summer. Yet we were still far enough down the slope so that in the wintertime we'd be protected from any wild winds that came from the north.

Since working on our new house would require several trips a day, up and down the steep, half-mile slope from our camp to the house site, we decided to move camp to the new site before starting work. We got Cleofas and his burros to help us again.

But after we'd erected our tents and thought we had everything set for going to work, it finally came to us that we'd made one rather serious miscalculation. Our hot spring was close now, just under the hill, in fact; but packing water for mortar-making up a slope that was almost a sheer drop for about one hundred and fifty feet was going to require a stupendous amount of back-breaking labor.

This set me to thinking. There just had to be some easier way to get water up that slope.

At first, the only thing I could think of was to improve the zigzag trail leading down to water. This I did by picking out rocks and building shelves to hold dirt, and exaggerating the zigs and zags to make the climb gentler. But that incline stood at something like a seventy-five to eighty degree angle, so that, no matter what I did to the trail, it was still a breath-taking struggle for a man to climb it with a couple of buckets of water.

Finally, I came up with a solution and a good one. I stretched a heavy steel wire from a steel pin wedged into a rock fissure at camp down to another at the spring. Once pulled tight, the wire stood at something like a forty-five degree angle and was clear of all protruding ledges. Then, at the top, I built a windlass, around which I wrapped a strong fishing cord. The loose end of the line was tied to a window-sash pulley on the wire, and to this a harness snap was fastened to hold a bucket bail. The weight of the empty bucket, descending on my wire, was sufficient to turn the windlass; and down at the bottom, I erected a bumper to stop the bucket where it would fill. Once the bucket was full of water, I could draw it back up the wire cable by winding the windlass. By testing and making a few adjustments, I soon had our "slow-drawlic" water system operating so easily that a five-year-old child could have drawn water from the spring.

Now, with everything ready, Cleofas and I began actual construction of the house. That was in September. Cleofas was a faithful worker, and he took pride in helping us. Together, we worked from early morning each day till sunset, mixing mortar and laying bricks.

For door sills, I used long flat stones that Cleofas dragged from the surrounding hills with his ever-faithful burros. Such stones were also used for headers above the doors and windows and to frame the fireplace. We wrecked an abandoned hut a mile up the valley and dragged off such timbers as we could use. One long straight log we used as a center pole. There were some smaller poles, too, which we used as rafters. We cut cane from along the river with which to roof the rafters, tying the cane down hard and fast with strings of split yucca blades. Then over the cane we heaped a six-inch layer of damp clay, which dried and hardened to make a good water-proof roof and later did much to keep our house cool in the summer.

By using all we could of available material, we cut down on material I had to order from Marathon. All in all, the nails, hinges, small amount of lumber, and one window I did have to order came to only around ten dollars. And since Cleofas' work was credited toward the lease money he owed me, that ten dollars was my total cash outlay for a good, weather-proof, one-room cabin, twelve by fourteen feet and nine feet high.

CANDELILLA WAX
Joe S. Graham
1975

THE CANDELILLA WAX INDUSTRY, LIKE THE GUAYULE RUBBER INDUS-try, is almost unknown in the United States, outside the trans-Pecos region of West Texas. Few visitors to the area are exposed to what has been an industry of considerable consequence in the past, and is certainly one of the most fascinating in the area. Most of the residents of the Big Bend region know something about the candelilla wax industry because of the many articles about it which appeared in local newspapers during the period from 1930 to 1950. Since that time, however, one does not read or hear much about it because it has declined greatly in importance, another casualty to modern technology.

The first wax production in West Texas began sometime during the second decade of this century and blossomed into a multi-million dol-lar industry during the 1920s, 1930s, and 1940s. With the drop in price in the early fifties the industry fell on hard times and has never recov-ered, though production still goes on in the area—mostly in Mexico at present. Another factor in the decline of the industry is that technology has produced a synthetic substitute for about one-fourth the cost of can-delilla wax. So where once there were hundreds of wax camps scattered up and down the Rio Grande, in the 1930s and 1940s, now there are no more than a few dozen, and at times there are none producing wax on the Texas side. As a result of the activity in the past, however, one fre-quently encounters those who have worked in wax camps—both Anglo and Mexican-American.

For the uninitiated, candelilla wax is a natural wax taken from the plants of the Euphorbiaceae family, principally *Euphorbia antisyphilitica* (so named because of the folk belief that the acidic, milky juice of the plant was a cure for syphilis), *Euphorbia ceriform,* and *Pedilanthus pavonis.* Candelilla means "little candle," and the name indicates one of its uses—making candles. Centuries ago this wax was used to waterproof leather; during World War II it was used extensively to waterproof army tents. The natives of Mexico have used it for hundreds of years in making amulets and figurines. It now has well over a hundred uses, among them waxes and polishes for shoes, cars, and floors, and even as a base for chewing gum. It is used in tanning leather, in cosmetics, and in phonograph records. Two of the largest consumers of candelilla wax in the United States reportedly are the Johnson Wax Company and Wrigley's (gum) Inc.

In 1954, 95 percent of the world's supply of this wax was produced in five of Mexico's hottest, driest states: Coahuila, Nuevo León, Chihuahua, Durango, and Zacatecas. Most of the rest was produced in West Texas, in four of the state's hottest and driest counties: Presidio, Brewster, Terrell, and Val Verde. It is ironic that this harsh region, which ranges in altitude from 3,000 to 6,000 feet above sea level, whose temperature varies from more than 110 degrees F on summer afternoons down to nearly 0 degrees F on early winter mornings, and whose annual rainfall is less than two inches in places, produces plants which give the highest wax yield. In areas with more favorable climate the plant may grow to gigantic proportions—as high as nine feet in the Dallas area—but it produces almost no wax and consequently is commercially unexploited. In order to produce wax, the plant must grow in the hot, dry climate found in north-central Mexico and in West Texas because the plant, in order to survive in this environment, forms a heavy wax coating along its stems to prevent moisture loss and to protect it from the cold. The hottest, driest summers and coldest winters produce plants with the most abundant wax.

At present, almost all of the wax shipped from West Texas is brought over from Mexico because it is easier to import than to produce on this side. "Import" is the proper word because it is not illegal to bring the wax into this country (indeed, there is not even an import duty). It is, however, illegal to export the wax from Mexico without channeling it through the Banco de México so that the export tax can be collected. Thus, for the American it is importing; for the Mexican wax maker it is smuggling.

There are two ways that the wax gets to the border. Smugglers bring burro pack trains loaded with raw wax from the interior of Mexico, sometimes as far as 150 miles. Most of this wax finds its way into Lajitas, Texas, a few miles upriver from the Big Bend National Park. Here the smugglers sell their wax, buy badly needed supplies, and disappear back into Mexico. These men are full-time smugglers, clandestinely buying the wax in Mexico and selling it in Texas at a good profit. As long as the *mordida* (or bribe, part of the Mexican way of life, particularly along the border) is paid, these men go unmolested.

The other source of wax is the small producer who lives in camps along the Rio Grande. These wax camps usually are made up of from two to six men who produce the wax and bring it across the river on burros or in small boats. Each man, either by himself or with a partner, is an entrepreneur who works for himself and receives no wages. It is this group that is of interest in this paper.

Perhaps I should explain briefly how I came to know about candelilla wax making. My father was a river rider from 1947 to 1954. A river rider was one who patrolled the Rio Grande on horseback for the federal government to keep animals from crossing into the United States during the hoof-and-mouth epidemic in Mexico. During that period of time our family lived in camp with my father (I say camp because few river riders had houses to live in, and army tents were more common) during the summer months after school had ended. For three of these summers our camp was located a stone's throw from a large wax camp on the Texas side, and my younger brother and I spent most of every day with the Mexican wax makers. Eighteen years later, after I joined the faculty at Sul Ross, I had the opportunity to renew my acquaintance with the wax camps while making a documentary film (funded by a Sul Ross research grant) of the industry. This time I was able to observe through the eyes of a folklorist.

By any standard or definition these candelilla wax makers comprise a distinct folk group, in this case an occupational group. Much of the folklore of this group is unique only in that it deals with the occupation and hazards (primarily getting arrested by the *federales* when the *mordida* is not paid). Anyone who has read Oscar Lewis' *Tepoztlán* knows the cultural background of these men. They are neither ambitious nor inventive, as we normally think of the terms; they are neither lazy nor stupid. They possess an esoteric knowledge pertaining to their occupation, which helps to form them into a fluid though cohesive group, isolated from other members of society for long periods of time.

They learn to make wax through apprenticeship, often beginning as early as twelve years old on one of the ranches in the interior of Mexico. By the time they come to the border they usually have all the knowledge required to gather and process the plant. They do not work for wages here as they did in the interior; they are businessmen—they gather, process and sell the wax, and their wages are their profits. The harder they work, the more they make. Most of these men earn almost twice the average wage for a laborer in this area, averaging about $4.00 per day. To see how this business is operated, we shall observe one man, Antonio Avila, as he produces candelilla wax.

Like many of his compadres, Antonio is functionally illiterate; having no formal education, he writes his name with effort. And like the rest of the local population, Antonio relies on the same folk cures and remedies that his ancestors relied upon. He uses a tea made of the *cenizo* plant for a chronic stomach ailment; he is not sure what the problem is, for it has been years since he has seen a *médico*. At forty-two Antonio is married and has three children, but they live over a hundred miles away in Durango. This summer he has a fourteen-year-old nephew, Juan Valencia, helping him. Juan thinks that making wax may be fine as a summer job, but he is convinced that an education offers him a better future. Antonio and Juan share the camp with Gregorio Martínez, a taciturn man who works by himself. Gregorio's right leg was severed in an auto accident ten or eleven years ago and he has a peg leg from the knee down. He would like a job on one of the large ranches in Texas because, as he explains, "es más fácil," it is easier. Making candelilla wax helps provide for both of his wives, one in Boquillas and one in Juárez.

The other resident in the camp is Philippe Madrid, whose wife died three years ago and left him with seven boys. The three youngest, ages six, eight and eleven, live in camp with him. The eleven-year-old helps with the wax processing, but the two younger boys spend their time hunting lizards, June bugs, and an occasional bird with their slingshots.

Antonio lives a life of such simplicity that Thoreau's Walden is a Statler-Hilton by comparison; one significant difference, however, is that Thoreau could leave anytime he wanted to—Antonio cannot. He cooks over a campfire with the barest of utensils: one tin skillet and the top cut from a fifty-five-gallon steel drum placed over hot coals to cook his flour tortillas on. He hauls his drinking water from the river in a five-gallon bucket with a Fina oil products label on it. If the river is muddy, he lets the water settle for a few minutes before drinking it. His diet consists of flour tortillas, beans, coffee, sugar, onions, chilis, and vermicelli. He could have fish, but he usually doesn't take the time to catch them. He has little or no shelter from the elements because he really doesn't need it. All of his belongings fit easily into one cardboard box.

Antonio rises from his bed (usually located in one of the stacks of un-processed candelilla plant, or *yerba*) shortly after sunrise and gets about the day's affairs. He makes strong coffee on the open fire and sips this from a tin cup as he prepares breakfast, usually beans in some form with hot chile and flour tortillas. He mixes enough dough to make enough tortillas for the whole day, then patiently rolls them out on a piece of board and cooks them on his makeshift grill. When breakfast is over, he wipes his utensils clean and begins his day's work—we could say a week's work, or a month's work, or even a year's work, because there is little variation. He must take his burro out into the rugged mountains along the river in search of the candelilla plant. When he finds enough of the *yerba,* he must pull it by hand, tie it into bundles, bring it into camp on burros, stack it, and then process it. Once the wax is processed, he must then smuggle it across into Texas and sell it to a local refiner. After selling his wax, he buys the necessary staples from the small store near the refinery and goes back to camp to repeat the cycle.

Antonio's life is not run by the clock, and he seems the happier for it. The whole time I have been among these men I don't recall having seen a watch or clock. Only if he works for an Anglo must Antonio concern himself with the time of day. Looking through his ethnocentric bias, the Anglo sees Antonio as lazy and indolent. Antonio simply marches to another drum. His concept of time differs from that of the Anglo, upon whom he looks with disdain through his own ethnocentric bias. For him, time, like any good Mexican clock, walks; it doesn't run. When he feels that it is time to arise, he does so, without relying on a clock to tell him when; when it is time to work, he works; and when it is time to rest, he rests.

Antonio's first task after eating is to locate his four burros, which is no great problem even though they are not in a corral, because he has hobbled them the night before. He removes the hobbles and drives the animals into camp and saddles them. He uses no bridles and the blankets he uses to protect the burros' backs from the pack saddles are nothing but worn-out gunny sacks. His saddles may either be handmade or bought from one of the small stores along the river.

After saddling his burros, Antonio places one of the modern technological miracles onto one of his saddles—a half-gallon plastic Clorox bottle filled with river water. He then jumps astride one of the burros, behind the saddle of course, since the human posterior is not designed to be draped over a pack saddle. He leaves camp in search of candelilla. He may have to travel as far as five miles, depending on how long the camp has been operating. The older the camp, the farther he has to go to get the weed.

When he locates sufficient candelilla, Antonio stops his burros and hobbles them, leaving them free to search for what food is available in the area nearby. He learned many years ago how to turn a two-foot piece of grass rope into an effective hobble. The center of the rope is placed above the hoof of the foot opposite where Antonio is squatting. He pulls the rope around the leg and twists it eight or nine times. The two short ends then are placed around the burro's other leg, just above the hoof, and the large knot on one end is pushed through the braid of the other end.

Once the burros are hobbled, Antonio takes the ropes used to tie the *yerba* into bundles and gives half of them to his fourteen-year-old nephew. These ropes are about twelve feet long, with a loop at one end which is either lined with leather or made of wood. The wooden loop consists of a short U-shaped piece of wood fastened to the rope. It is simple, effective, and durable. There are four ropes to each burro.

Then the real work begins. Antonio stretches the rope out along the ground near several large clumps of the candelilla plant. He then proceeds to pull the weed, which grows to a height of about eighteen inches. The only technique thus far developed for pulling the weed is the grunt and heave method. Antonio learned long ago that he could not cut the weed, because the roots would bleed to death. If pulled up by the roots, however, the plant will grow back in even greater abundance in five or six years, ready for another harvest. He has also learned that the plants, after pulling, must be stacked properly or the bundles will not last until he gets to camp. When he has gathered enough *yerba* for one bundle—about forty to fifty pounds—he then ties it. There must be a hundred different ways to tie a bundle of candelilla, but of the many men I have observed working with candelilla, all have used the exact same steps and have tied the exact same knot.

My experience teaching college freshmen to write process papers convinces me to avoid attempting to describe in detail the mechanics of tying this particular knot. Suffice it to say that the process of tying the bundle and the knot used are masterpieces of efficiency. Certainly it is as complex as throwing a diamond hitch, which is almost a lost art. The rope passes twice around the bundle to hold it secure. The knot is so tied that it can be suspended on the pack saddle and not slip, yet when the bundle is placed into the stack at camp, a single pull unties the knot and removes the rope from the bundle. None of the men could tell me who invented the knot; they could tell me only where they learned to use it. Though some among us, through trial and error, might develop an equally successful way to tie the candelilla into bundles, we doubtfully could invent one more effective or efficient. For Antonio, who is not particularly inventive by our standards, it is a simple process—use the technique tried and tested by generations of wax makers.

Once the bundles are tied, four for each burro, they are loaded and hauled into camp and stacked. Once Antonio has one hundred *cargas* (bundles) of the candelilla plant, he may take his turn at the vat. Since the vat does not belong to these men (it belongs to the purchaser and refiner of the wax), they have worked out this system for sharing it.

The equipment used in boiling the plant is minimal—enough but just barely. The one piece of equipment especially made for wax producers is the *paila,* a steel vat which is about eight feet long, four feet wide, and four feet deep (the size of the vat differs from one camp to another). The *paila* is covered with a heavy removable grate. It is set into the riverbank with a space for the fire beneath it. Besides the vat, Antonio's equipment consists of two pitchforks, two fifty-five-gallon barrels, two or three five-gallon buckets, an *espumador* (a shallow, sieve-like scoop), an urn or glass jar containing sulfuric acid and a *bote para el ácido* (a can or jar attached to a stick used to pour the acid into the vat). Sometimes there is a *chivo* (literally, a goat, but in this case a stick about four feet long with a small fork on the end which resembles a billy goat's horns), which is used to push protruding ends of the candelilla below the surface of the water after the grate has been fastened into place. The *espumador, bote para el ácido,* and *chivo* are handmade. *Espumadores* differ only in size: they are made of a round or oval, dish-shaped piece of sheet metal with many fairly large nail holes punched through it making it resemble a sieve. A round wooden handle, usually a piece of a tree limb, is attached to the metal. Making *espumadores* is like tying bundles of candelilla—it is simple if someone has shown you how. The *espumador* is used to skim the molten wax which rises to the surface of the water during the boiling process, and the holes allow most of the water to escape back into the vat. It would be hard to conceive of a simpler but more effective tool. Again, Antonio does not have to invent this or to depend upon a store to furnish this piece of equipment. Somewhere he has learned to make *espumadores* and is the more self-sufficient for it.

Anyone who has had even elementary chemistry knows that when one pours concentrated sulfuric acid into water there is a violent, boiling action. Antonio uses the handmade *bote para el ácido* to pour the acid into the vat of water without being splattered by the acid. Like the *espumador,* this implement resembles almost every other one. It consists of a small "tin" can or glass jar fastened to a stick with a piece of bailing wire; this is done in one of two ways: Either the container is placed in the fork of a stick or it is simply wired onto the side of a straight stick.

Cooking the wax is the most tedious and difficult of Antonio's tasks, for he will spend several hours a day working in the hot sun, which brings the temperature above 100 degrees F in the shade on hot afternoons. This heat is compounded by the heat of the boiling vat of water. Since handling the vat is a two-man job, Antonio needs assistance. His nephew helps him now, but when the nephew leaves to attend school, Antonio works out an agreement with one of the other men: You help me process my *yerba,* and when you are ready, I'll help you. This kind of working agreement is very common in wax camps.

The men begin their day's work at the vat by building a fire under it, using the dried, processed candelilla plant as fuel. Using a pitchfork, one of them must stoke the fire every five or ten minutes because the dried weed burns like tinder, though it produces a tremendous heat which will bring the vat of water to a boil in about thirty minutes. While one man is tending the fire, the other adds what water is necessary to bring the level to within six inches of the top of the vat. He must also fill up a barrel with water to be used as needed throughout the day. All of this water is hauled in five-gallon buckets from the river. When the vat is filled with water, about a quart of sulfuric acid is added. This acid serves as a catalyst to help remove the wax from the outside of the plant. Antonio is no chemist and he doesn't understand how the acid works, but he knows that he gets more wax when he uses acid than when he doesn't.

Once the fire is started and the acid has been added, the two men fill the vat with the raw candelilla plant. Each bundle of *yerba* weighs about fifty pounds and the vat will hold about two bundles. In a good year when the plant yields much wax, the vat full of weed will produce about three or four pounds of wax.

When the vat is full of candelilla and tramped down by foot, the metal gate is placed on top of the vat and the weed is forced below the water level. As the water boils, the wax is melted from the weed and floats to the top as foam. Using the *espumador*, Antonio scoops the foam into a barrel placed at the end of the vat. Experience tells Antonio when it is no longer profitable to boil the weed further, since it is impossible to remove all the wax from the plant. If an Anglo were processing the wax, he would probably let his watch tell him how long to boil the weed, but Antonio lets experience guide him.

When this point is reached, water is added to the vat to cool the contents and the fire is allowed to die down. The grate is removed and the weed is taken from the vat with pitchforks and stacked to dry, later to be used as fuel. The vat is again filled with raw candelilla plant, the fire is again stoked, and the process is repeated again and again until either there is no more plant to work with or Antonio feels that it is time to quit work for the day.

As the wax in the barrel cools and hardens, the water goes to the bottom and is drained away. The wax is broken into small pieces and placed into a gunnysack. When Antonio finishes cooking all of his *yerba,* he takes his wax across the river and sells it. He can expect around seventy-seven cents a pound for it, but the market fluctuates. When he gets his money he returns to camp and repeats the cycle of gathering, processing and selling his wax.

When I first returned to a wax camp to study and observe, I had to squelch the urge to "improve" the modus operandi of the wax makers. In my infinite *gringo* superiority I thought that I could improve their methods. In the end, however, it was I who learned and they who taught.

Through tradition passed on by apprenticeship these Mexican wax makers have developed a system which is as effective as it will ever be. Normally we find that technology can increase output. But the candelilla wax processing along the border has not changed since the introduction of the steel vat in the 1920s or 1930s. There is simply not a more efficient way to gather the candelilla plant, transport it and process it. Attempts to modernize have ended in dismal failure. A machine was designed by some enterprising *gringo* to harvest the plant by cutting and baling it. It worked in relatively flat areas but was useless in the mountains where most of the weed grows. Besides, cutting the plant killed it, and replanting became necessary. Attempts were made, again by enterprising *gringos* looking for a better way, to cultivate the plant by irrigating fields of candelilla. This failed because the plants would form little or no wax to protect the plant from moisture loss.

Burros are the most useful means of transportation in this mountainous region. They are cheap, they don't break down like a truck does, and if treated with care at all they require no maintenance. In some areas trucks might be useful, but not in this rough terrain. Besides, machines tend to complicate matters for those who are not handy with machinery.

Various attempts have been made to improve the processing procedures to enable the Mexicans to recover more wax by making the vat a one-man job. Antonio has learned to be comfortable with traditional ways. He is not inventive by Anglo standards; he does not attempt to build a better mousetrap, to devise a better way to extract the wax. He is willing to learn from tradition, to let it be his inventor. In some occupations the willingness to continue in the traditional methods has proved detrimental to progress, but among the candelilla wax makers along the Rio Grande, this dependence upon tradition has vindicated itself.

RIVER GUIDES AND BIG WATER, GOOD WATER
Sam Richardson
1997

RIVER GUIDES ARE AN INSCRUTABLE LOT. AS A GROUP THEY DEFY DEscription and resist classification. The average river company is like Ellis Island: a gathering place for people from all walks of life and from everywhere. Bring us your artists, gamblers, salesmen, computer programmers, guitar pickers, potters, poets, housepainters, environmentalists, rednecks, successful and unsuccessful dropouts; bring them to an area remote and put them to work in the blue-collar work of rowing boats, where the common denominator is the river and the love of the wilderness.

Of an evening you can always find a group of them on the porch at the Terlingua Trading Company going over the day's events in great detail. Each run through the Rock Slide is examined and cross-examined, graded and put away for future discussions. Probably no quarter mile of the planet has been chewed on as much as that stretch of river in Santa Elena Canyon. It's the Big Bend's best known rapid, no question, and is, among other things, a proving ground for guides in this part of the Rio Grande. To really break into the rotation and become a professional, you've got to be "SE Qualified," and that means running the Rock Slide.

Now that the river is back up, the runs through the Slide are becoming more interesting, not to mention challenging. And one of guiding's rituals is to come at the end of the day, sit on the porch, crack open a cold one and repeat the liturgy of boating so many have recited before.

The role of romantic hero once occupied by the American cowboy has been assumed by the river guide. They've traded boots and spurs for waterproof sandals, Levis and chaps for shorts, lariats for oars. They roam the country looking for whitewater and adventure, enough of a paycheck to get to the next river, a good campfire and the camaraderie of other boatmen. They live the free life, and this time of year they'll be drifting back to Terlingua—back from New Mexico, Colorado, Idaho and Arizona—with war stories of runs and adventures on the Box, the Arkansas, the Middle Fork and the Salt.

Ed Bruce could well have written his famous song about river guides instead of cowboys:

> Mamas, don't let yore babies grow up to be river guides,
> Don't let 'em pick guitars and row them ol' boats,
> Make 'em buy houses, get real jobs and vote. . . .

Good to be back on the river again. Big rise came through last week and cleaned everything out. Estimates were that it got as high as 12 feet, running as much as 10,000 cubic feet per second: Big water, good water.

We boarded Gray Dog, a sixteen-foot, oar-powered rubber raft, at Lajitas. We were bound for Santa Elena Canyon, Mike and Danielle and I. No hurry—didn't get on the river until elevenish. At high water levels, you can make the twenty-mile run in three, maybe four hours. Normally, it's an all-day trip.

Water was running a rich brown, the color and almost the consistency of a chocolate milkshake. Lots of debris floating around. The Rio takes care of its own housekeeping at these levels and flushes its banks, leaving them clean and slightly—sometimes greatly—rearranged.

I love the anticipation of a river trip when the water level changes. It's like visiting a place I've never been before. There's a sense of renewal.

Half hour after put-in, we hit the first rapid—Matadero. Bam, we ran it. Not much of a splash. It was actually a little washed out, but there was enough of a hole to get us wet. At some levels, Matadero has a boat munching hole that can invert one's rubber chariot. I know. They don't call it Samadero for nothing. Ancient history. Thursday, we rolled over it, no problem.

Around noon we arrived at San Carlos Creek, just outside Santa Elena Canyon. It was cranking and spewing dark water the color of a Hershey bar, water even darker than the Rio. There were noisy boils and waves where the creek coiled into the river. Take one river, add one creek at flood stage: Big water.

Last year, a vaquero tried to ford this spot during a rise like this and drowned—both he and his horse. It's no toy, the Rio Grande.

A few minutes later, we entered the canyon. The sense of awe one feels in that great chasm is indescribable. We were transported, both figuratively and literally. Not only were we inspired, we were picking up speed. The same amount of water that we'd been riding on the Rio had been juiced up by the flow from San Carlos—then all that water was compressed into a much narrower space between walls of the canyon. Same amount of water, half the space—we were truckin'. And just around the first bend was the Rock Slide, the Big Bend's biggest rapid: Apprehension.

The Rock Slide: a maze, a boulder field of house-sized rocks that fell into the river in some bygone era. It's an ever changing puzzle, different with each change in the water level. We eddied out and climbed Scout Rock to see what we were dealing with. What we saw that Thursday were boils, eddies, standing waves and holes, cooked up to a gnarly chocolate froth that culminated with two big pouroffs at the bottom. Just a few feet to the left of the pouroff on the Mexican side—where we needed to go—a big log had lodged itself on top of Clamshell Rock; one jagged end stuck out like a dagger, intruding on our intended route—a little extra challenge to add excitement to our run: Adrenaline.

We decided to go right (Mexican side) anyway, log or no log. Center pouroff (Texas side) looked flippy. No point in going swimming at that point if we didn't have to.

Mike's turn on the oars—smooth run, no problems. Danielle and I high-sided in the front of the boat. Somewhere under us, under all that roaring brown water, were the Mexican Gate, Center Slot, Dog Nose,

Space Capsule and Pillow Rock. We pushed over them pretty fast. Part of the Dog Nose was showing, so we went to the right of it, cut back to the left, then hard to the right to avoid getting sucked into the Slide's angry, churning center. Then, there was another move to the right, and the nose of the boat kissed the boiling water above Pillow Rock before we pulled into an eddy (go to the left of Pillow Rock, and you're in the belly of the beast). Then, we punched the pouroff on the Mexican side, being careful to stay away from the log on top of Clamshell Rock.

A pouroff is like a little waterfall that ends in a violent hole. Everything that goes into it comes back out and takes a slap at you. The boat must have disappeared for a minute when we hit the bottom. The wave at the end of the hole came up over our heads, stopped the raft with a deafening, tidal crash, and we side-surfed for a second. Seems like forever when you're in there and it's got you. It's like hitting a brick wall, bouncing to one side, then resuming speed—a split second unraveling in slow motion, a small forever. Then, we were through it and rubbing our eyes. Felt like a handful of sand had been thrown in our faces—lot of silt flushed from the banks in that new water.

Afterward, we pushed downstream, and from there on out the water was steady. Fast but no more rapids. The 1,500-foot walls of Santa Elena towered above us like a cathedral, and as the boats turned each bend of the river, more surreal limestone shapes appeared ahead. Far above, hawks and vultures rode the thermals, and just overhead dozens of smaller birds darted back and forth, going about their business. Some things are eternal.

The Rio Grande took thousands of years to cut its way through this wilderness. It's given life, and it's taken it away. It's been the main landmark in an isolated territory claimed by the Spanish, the Apaches, the Comanches, the United States, Mexico, bandits, bootleggers and businessmen from all walks. Now we're here. Someday, someone may write a little chapter about us, then file us away with all those who were here before: History.

Count us lucky.

 **YELLOW SLICKER**
Ted Gray
1984

ONE TIME WE WERE WORKING IN THAT LOWER COUNTRY AND IT WAS in April, April 11. It generally doesn't rain in this country that early. We'd finished branding and stopped by some traps to doctor worms. I kept watching this cloud and told the men, "We'd better whip it up, or we're going to get caught." The farther we went, the bigger the cloud got. We finally struck a long lope and got into camp just as the rain hit.

We didn't have anything to get under except two wagons, and we had eighteen men. Old Jesús Terrazas didn't know it was going to rain a flood. He put his bed up on a cot, sat on it, and spread his slicker out over it like a hen would over her eggs. Well, it rained and it rained and it hailed and the water ran. Over a foot of water ran through camp at one time. It washed away the cook's fire, dishpans, washpans, everything that would float. It nearly washed the woodpile away.

It rained all over the country. That was the only general rain I ever saw in April, and that's been about fifty years ago. It hailed the roof off the buildings at headquarters, which were fifteen miles from us. Chunks of ice knocked holes in the ground you could stick your hat in. I never did find a dead calf, but it killed some rabbits.

About sundown, it quit raining. Old Jesús sat on his bed all this time. When the wind would change, he'd turn a little, and the cot would sink in that wet ground a little more. After a while his bed was sitting right on the ground with water a foot deep, but he was still on top when it quit raining.

We got out from under those wagons, and the water was running in the creek nearby in Hatch Canyon a quarter of a mile wide. We were under those bluffs to the north and west, and you could see ten miles of it. That water was coming off there pouring great spouts, a beautiful sight.

We had everything in camp wet and no possible way to have anything to eat. But old Gabino generally managed to improvise and figure out some way to cook. We all started helping him. We took a shovel and built a levee around the wagon to turn the water to either side of camp. With a bucket we dipped water out of the hole where he'd had the fire and got some wood and kerosene. After a long time with that wet wood, we finally built a fire and made some coffee. Under normal conditions, even if it was raining, Gabino could put his skillets under the chuck box lid to keep them dry. I've seen him cook bread and beef under that lid where the rain wouldn't hit his skillets. If rain hits those hot skillet lids, they break, cracking that cast iron. He knew how to do those things and was a great old fellow. He cut up some beef and got some bread cooked. It was sometime after dark, but we managed to eat.

SUN MESSAGES
W. D. Smithers
1976

THE NOTION THAT AVISO COMMUNICATION WAS DEVELOPED FROM observing animal behavior has some followers. The animal in question is the pronghorn antelope, *Antilocapra americana*. The shape of the antlers gives this group its name. These horns are about seventeen inches high on the mature male, a bit smaller on the female. Both bucks and does are tan in color and have two white bands on the throat and an oblong white spot on the lower side that blends into a white underbelly.

Two white spots on the buttocks have given rise to the *aviso* speculation. The spots are a series of hairs arranged in a concentric pattern—short hairs in the center, longer ones radiating outward, filling a ten-inch circle. When the animal is startled, flanks tighten and all the white hairs in these spots can spread and stand out. In the sunlight, this creates a "flash" that can be seen for several hundred yards. Antelopes graze in groups of ten or twelve—does, yearlings, fawns, and a single buck. The buck is keenly sensitive to danger, but it often is the doe that "flashes" the first warning. The flashing is observed by the others, and soon the whole herd is blinking out an *aviso con tiempo* among themselves and to other antelope herds. It is interesting to note that frontier soldiers and surveyors called the antelope a heliograph because of the similarity between their flashed warning signals and man's messages sent by reflecting the sun's rays from a mirror.

If man got the idea of avisos from observing animals, he has developed it considerably. The principle has been used for centuries, by message senders in many parts of the world. Probably the most outstanding features of avisadores are their secrecy and their wide distribution. While surveyors and the military in this county have employed the Morse code in heliograph communications, the avisadores' codes are assumed to have been arranged among the members of various families or clans. I never learned any of their codes, although I was told that they did send avisos that included words not ordinarily used in normal conversations. An aviso "dialect," then, seems a possibility. I recall an incident in which this construction of phrases and translation proved avisos as effective as speaking. . . .

In 1930, I asked Alejandro Garcia to send an aviso announcing that I would buy fifty or more deer antlers of the three species found in the Big Bend area—the mule, whitetail, and flagtail. I told Alejandro to explain that I wanted no horns that had been shed. The aviso had no distance limits and, in the following weeks, antlers were brought in from as far as sixty miles away. All were according to my specifications.

Alejandro sent another aviso for me in the spring of 1932, this time with a much more intricate message. It was delivered to boys between ten and fourteen years old living within three or four miles of the river. The project behind the aviso was wildlife photography, made possible by my having worked a year in St. Louis, Missouri, saving enough money to buy twelve lenses and shutters and a supply of film and flash powder. I also had devised a system whereby night-feeding animals, such as deer and antelope, would trip the shutter of a camera while nibbling food I had put out for them. The other subjects of my wildlife photography were birds, and I was having trouble finding enough variety. Thus, my avisos to the Mexican boys were calls for research assistance.

The aviso was specific: many nests were needed, and none was to be disturbed. Rather, I asked that each boy who found a nest take me to it. For each nest, I gave the boys a Boy Scout knife and, if the nest was rare, a coin or two. Such rewards were really appreciated by the boys, and the response from them was strong. So strong, in fact, that several days after the project began, I asked Alejandro to send another aviso telling my researchers not to include the nests of roadrunners, white-winged doves, and several others of which I had more than enough specimens. I also had Alejandro reiterate the three-mile boundary stipulation, for I could cover only so much ground. It was clear to me that much could be said in aviso communication—its two-way signaling a simulation of spoken dialogue, with messages that could be corrected and amended. Even reprimands could be given.

Several amusing and educational incidents occurred during the bird project, like the time a boy ran up to me with the news that he had found a nighthawk's, or bullbat's, nest. When he tried to relocate it, there was no trace of the bird's eggs, since nighthawks do not build nests but move their eggs from place to place. Once we found the eggs, I tied a strip of cloth to a nearby bush, but the hen moved her eggs by the very next day.

One eight-year-old youngster, for whom the avisos had not been intended, knew that his older brothers were getting pocketknives and wanted to get in on the action. Discovering a hummingbird nest with two babies in it, he proceeded to break off the branch that cradled the nest and bring it to me. He wasn't aware of my stipulation that nests were not to be disturbed, so I did not scold him harshly. But those young hummers had to be cared for. I took the nest to Ada Johnson, who was happy to feed them a sugar solution through a medicine dropper. From their nest in one of the Johnsons' patio ferns, the young birds soon began to fly—around the yard and garden, and in and out of the house. They stayed around the Johnsons' until their first migration, from which they did not return. I never secured proof that hummingbirds return to their hatching place, like swallows and some other birds.

By marking swallows' legs with a bit of aluminum paint, I discovered that even after lengthy migratory flights the birds returned to their former nesting sites at the Johnson ranch.

It was amazing to watch a swallow build its nest of mud, requiring of the male at least a thousand trips to and from the riverbank, and of the female many hours of padding the damp mud with fluffy blossoms of cottonwood trees. . . .

Despite my close relationships with Juan Hinojosa, Maria [Garcia], Alejandro García, and many other Mexicans on both sides of the river, they would never divulge to me the secrets of the avisadores. The one fact they would admit was that avisos did indeed exist as an established, secret communication system. But this was acknowledged only after I discovered that they had uses for mirrors other than as looking glasses.

A U.S. Cavalry outpost from 1916 to 1920, Castolon was one of the few such stations with buildings intact. In 1921, Wayne Cartledge bought the buildings to establish the largest trading post in the Big Bend. He also ran a huge cotton farm and a cattle ranch near Castolon. It was there in 1928 that I saw one of his ranch hands flash an aviso.

I was on one of my monthly two-week trips to the lower end of the Big Bend district. Castolon was one of my regular stops, as were the homes of most Mexicans and the Americans who lived in lower Brewster County—Mr. and Mrs. Woodson and Det Walker. The Woodsons had a small farm about three miles above Walker's and both homes were on the bank of the Rio Grande. A man named Derrick operated the trading post at Castolon for Wayne Cartledge.

Standing near my Dodge roadster, talking with Mr. Derrick, I was about to leave Castolon when we heard a car coming up the hill. A Border Patrol vehicle topped the rise and stopped, and Shelly Barnes and Oscar Stetson got out. Paying little heed, I was facing the opposite direction still talking with Derrick when I saw a sudden flash of light from a rocky hill at the foot of Castolon Peak—less than a mile away.

It was an aviso, warning all Mexicans in the area of the Border Patrol's presence. You can bet that numerous other avisos were sent during the next few days, while the patrolmen were en route from Castolon to Glenn Springs.

About a minute after I saw the flash, I drove away but stopped at the edge of the hill where the road started down and got out of the car. With my binoculars I could see the Mexican ranch hand standing where I had seen the flash, but he was no longer flashing. I figured that he was waiting for the patrolman to leave, and perhaps me as well. That would require two avisos—one of warning, regarding the Border Patrol, and another of "friendly gossip," about my whereabouts. . . .

Perhaps the most mysterious and inexplicable aspect of this aviso business is how avisadores know when an aviso is being sent their way. Avisos gave no audio warning of their arrival, but I have seen many avisadores look up, change directions, and drop whatever they were doing to read them. Many times these messages were sudden warnings, so their receipt could not have been prearranged. Some uncanny sixth sense seemed to tell avisadores when avisos were on the way, and they would then turn to receive and relay them. Even during work that required constant vigil, such as irrigation, avisadores knew precisely when they should look up to catch a message. Mental telepathy? Supersensitivity? Whatever, this special sense rarely failed the avisadores. . . .

I managed to conduct a bit of research while on assignment, talking to avisadores and curanderos and studying plant life. I found it interesting that the avisadores' techniques, ethics, and hardware differed little from Texas to California. Chief among my contacts were the Papago, Yaqui, and Apache Indians along the Arizona border, and other Yaqui in the state of Sonora, Mexico.

Not everyone knew as much about avisadores as I. In New Mexico and Arizona, in fact, I educated patrolmen who were baffled as to how the Mexicans knew so much so soon about intruders into their areas. But avisadores were not new on the scene. I'm sure that most Indians of North America at one time had some sort of aviso system. Only some of them, because of necessity, topography, or tradition, have retained this marvelous mode of communication longer than others.

Sources

I would like to acknowledge that copyright holders have given me permission to reprint material by the following authors:

Edward Abbey, "Disorder and Early Sorrow" from *The Journey Home* (23–27), copyright © 1977 by Edward Abbey. Used by permission of Dutton, a division of Penguin Putnam, Inc.

Edward Abbey, "Sierra Madre" from *Abbey's Road* (81–97), copyright © 1972, 1975, 1976, 1977, 1978, 1979 by Edward Abbey. Used by permission of Dutton, a division of Penguin Putnam, Inc.

David Alloway, "Where Rainbows Wait for Rain." Unpublished manuscript. Courtesy of David Alloway.

Charles L. Baker, "Geologist's Heaven," excerpted from "Marathon Country" in *The Magnificent Marathon Basin: A History of Marathon, Texas; Its People and Events,* ed. by AnneJo P. Wedin (Austin: Nortex Press, a division of Eakin, 1989): 541–543. Courtesy of John Wedin.

Lisa Beaumont, "Autumn." Unpublished manuscript. Courtesy of Lisa Beaumont.

Roy Bedicheck, "The Wing of the Swallow" from *Adventures with a Texas Naturalist* (40–51), copyright © 1947, 1961, renewed 1989. Courtesy of the University of Texas Press.

Ludwig Bemelmans, "Tinkling Spurs" from "The Texas Legend," *McCall's,* August 1956, 24–27. Used with permission of Madeline and Barbara Bemelmans.

J. P. S. Brown, "The Brown-and-White Spotted Aristocratic *Corriente*" from *Jim Kane* (NY: Dial Press, 1970): 254–263. Courtesy of J. P. S. Brown.

Bob Burleson and David H. Riskind, "Rural Housing," excerpted from *Backcountry Mexico: A Traveler's Guide and Phrase Book* (93–100), copyright © 1986. Courtesy of the University of Texas Press.

Dudley Dobie, "Firearms, Exploding Rocks, and a Centipede in Bed," excerpted from *Adventures in the Canyon, Mountain, and Desert Country of the Big Bend of Texas and Mexico* (San Marcos: Private Printing, 1952): 11–17. Courtesy of Dudley R. Dobie, Jr.

Martin Dreyer, "A Mountain for Suzy and for You," reprinted from the *Hous-*

ton Chronicle, May 2, 1965. Copyright © 1965 Houston Chronicle Publishing Company. Reprinted with permission. All rights reserved.

John C. Duval, "Mr. Cooper Was a Humbug," excerpted from *The Adventures of Big Foot Wallace* (Lincoln: University of Nebraska Press, 1936): 64–70, 123–129, 136–146. Courtesy of D. Tom Nomand.

Antonio de Espejo, "Exploring the Rios," excerpted from "Spanish Exploration along the Conchos and Rio Grande" (1583), translated by John Klingemann and Rubén Osorio Juniga (unpublished manuscript). Courtesy of John Klingemann and Rubén Osorio Juniga.

Will F. Evans, "Davis Mountain Stories" excerpted from "Winding Trails," "The Davis Mountains," and "Phantom Lake" in *Border Skylines: Fifty Years of "Tallying Out" on the Bloys Round-Up Ground* (Dallas: Cecil Baugh, 1940, 425–444; private edition reprinted by Grace Evans Cowden in 1982). Courtesy of William Cowden.

Louis Agassiz Fuertes, "A Letter from the Chisos Mountains" from *Louis Agassiz Fuertes: His Life Briefly Told and His Correspondence* (59–63), edited by Mary Fuertes Boynton, copyright © 1956 by Mary Fuertes Boynton. Used by permission of Oxford University Press, Inc.

Frederick R. Gehlbach, "Poison, Poison" from *Mountain Islands and Desert Seas: A Natural History of the U.S.–Mexico Borderlands* (College Station: Texas A&M University Press, 1981): 43–48. Used with permission.

Joe S. Graham, "Candelilla Wax," excerpted from "Tradition and the Candelilla Wax Industry" in *Some Still Do: Essays on Texas Customs* (a publication of the Texas Folklore Society, No. 39, 1975): 39–48. Courtesy of the Texas Folklore Society.

Ted Gray, "Yellow Slicker," excerpted from *The Last Campfire: The Life Story of Ted Gray, a West Texas Rancher* by Barney Nelson (College Station: Texas A&M University Press, 1984): 71–72. Courtesy of Barney Nelson, Ted Gray, and Mike Hardy of Iron Mountain Press.

Michael Jenkinson, "River of Ghosts," excerpted from "River of Ghosts: The Rio Grande" in *Wild Rivers of North America* (NY: E. P. Dutton, 1981): 284–292. Used with permission.

John Klingemann, "Sublime." Unpublished manuscript. Courtesy of John Klingemann.

William Langewiesche, "The River Is Not a Ditch," excerpted from *Cutting for Sign,* 23–28, copyright © 1993 by William Langewiesche. Used by permission of Pantheon Books, a division of Random House, Inc.

J. O. Langford, "Homesteader's Bedroom," excerpted from *Big Bend: A Homesteader's Story* by J. O. Langford with Fred Gipson (12–16, 62–65), copyright © 1952, renewed 1980. Courtesy of the University of Texas Press.

Mary Lasswell, "Coloraturas in the Canyon," excerpted from *I'll Take Texas* (Boston: Houghton, 1958): 119–129. Courtesy of the Authors Guild Foundation, Inc., New York.

Aldo Leopold, "Guacamaja" from *A Sand County Almanac: And Sketches Here and There* by Aldo Leopold (137–141); copyright © 1949, 1977 by Oxford University Press, Inc. Used by permission of Oxford University Press, Inc.

Fred McCarty, "My Final Trip," excerpted from "My Final Trip to Big Bend Park" in *Big Bend Country: A Guide to Big Bend Country* (Amarillo: Pelican Publishing Co., 1968): 32–48. Used with permission of Pelican Publishing Co.

Ross A. Maxwell, "Cueva de Alsate and Native Homes," excerpted from *The Big Bend of the Rio Grande* by Ross A. Maxwell (Austin: The University of Texas at Austin, Bureau of Economic Geology, Guidebook 7, 1968): 69–72. Courtesy of the University of Texas at Austin, Bureau of Economic Geology.

Richard Meade (Ben Haas), "Den of Thieves," excerpted from *Big Bend* (Garden City, NY: Doubleday, 1968): 14–15. Courtesy of Doubleday, a division of Random House, Inc.

Evelyn Mellard, "They Live Here Too—Our Quail" from *Spur Ranch—and Other Circles of Time* (Salado, TX: Anson Jones Press, 1977): 102–113. Courtesy of the Mellard family (Weldon Vaughn Cockran, executor).

Horace W. Morelock, "Kokernot Springs," excerpted from *Mountains of the Mind* (San Antonio: Naylor Co., 1956): 117–121. Courtesy of Billy Washington.

Richard Phelan, "God's Country," excerpted from "The Trans Pecos," in *Texas Wild: The Land, Plants, and Animals of the Lone Star State* (Amarillo: Excalibur Books, 1976): 15–36. Courtesy of Richard Phelan.

Kenneth Baxter Ragsdale, "Cinnabar," excerpted from *Quicksilver: Terlingua and the Chisos Mining Company* (College Station: Texas A&M University, 1976): 3–21. Used by permission of Texas A&M University.

Sam Richardson, "River Guides and Big Water, Good Water," in *Bites, Stings, Scratches: A Desert Journal* (self-published). Courtesy of Sam Richardson.

Shipman, Alice "Jack," "Primitive Man's Food" and "Savage and Successful," both excerpted from "Savage and Successful" in *Voice of the Mexican Border* (Vol. 1, No. 1, 1933, pp. 10–12; self-published). Courtesy of Pat Bramblett.

W. D. Smithers, "Sun Messages," excerpted from "Mexican Grapevine" in *Chronicles of the Big Bend: A Photographic Memoir of Life on the Border* (Austin: Texas State Historical Association, 1999): 83–95. Courtesy Texas State Historical Association, Austin. All rights reserved.

Kathryn Williams Walker, "Tarantula" excerpted from "Flora, Fauna, and Fickle Weather" (Alpine, TX: Archives of the Big Bend, Sul Ross State University, 1967): 40. Courtesy of Harriet Walker Herns.

Barton H. Warnock, "Capote Falls," excerpted from "The Big Bend of Texas," *Naturalist*, no. 2 (Summer 1961): 9–13. Courtesy of Kirby F. Warnock, executor.

Kirby F. Warnock, "Ghost Lights." Unpublished manuscript. Used with permission.

Roland H. Wauer, "Maderas del Carmen" from *Naturalist's Mexico* by Roland

H. Wauer (College Station: Texas A&M University Press, 1992): 43–54. Used by permission of the Texas A&M University Press.

O. W. Williams, "The Honca Accursed," excerpted from *The Romance of the Davis Mountains and Big Bend Country,* edited by Carlyle Graham Raht (El Paso: Rahtbooks Co., 1919): 286–295. "The Lobo" from *Historic Review of Animal Life in Pecos County* (Fort Stockton, TX: Fort Stockton Pioneer, 1908): 47–51. Courtesy of Janet Williams Pollard.

Mary S. Young, "Livermore Journal," excerpted from "Mary S. Young's Journal of Botanical Explorations in Trans-Pecos Texas, August–September, 1914," edited by B. C. Tharp and Chester V. Keilman, in *Southwestern Historical Quarterly* 65 (January 1962: 366–393; April 1962: 512–538). Courtesy Texas State Historical Association, Austin. All rights reserved.

The following authors' works originally appeared in these sources:

Mary Austin, "Jornada del Muerto," excerpted from "Down on the Rio Grande" in *The Land of Journey's Ending* (NY: Century Co., 1924): 198–202.

Vernon Bailey, "Mexican Bighorn," excerpted from *Biological Survey of Texas,* 70–75; North American Fauna, No. 25 (Washington, D.C.: Government Printing Office, 1905): 70–75.

John R. Bartlett, "Horse-Head Crossing to Delaware Creek," excerpted from "Travel in West Texas 84 Years Ago," 1850; reprint, *Voice of the Mexican Border* (February-March 1933): 236–250.

Herbert Brandt, "Birding at Boot Spring," excerpted from "Boot Spring" in *Texas Bird Adventures in the Chisos Mountains and on the Northern Plains* (Cleveland, OH: Bird Research Foundation, 1940).

William H. Echols, "The Camel March," excerpted from Index to the 1860–61 Special Session Executive Documents, 36–50; Senate of the United States, Second Session of the Thirty-Sixth Congress.

Keith Elliott, "The Marvelous Maligned Mesquite," from *The Nature of Texas: A Feast of Native Beauty,* edited by Howard Peacock (College Station: Texas A&M University Press, 1990): 102–106.

Robert T. Hill, "Running the Cañons of the Rio Grande," in *Century Magazine* (January 1901): 371–387.

Mary E. Humphrey, "Rio Bravo del Norte," excerpted from *Running the Rio Grande: A Floater's Guide to the Big Bend* (Austin, TX: AAR/Tantalus, 1981): 3–5, 5–7, 41–43.

Carl V. Jarrell, "A Wasp Called the Mud-Dauber," in *Outdoor Texas No. 2,* edited by Ralph Selle; Outdoor Nature Series, no. 12 (Houston: Carroll Printing Co., 1936): 5–27.

Roy T. McBride, "Las Margaritas," excerpted from *The Mexican Wolf (Canis lupus baileyi): A Historical Review and Observations on Its Status and Distri-*

bution, A Progress Report (Endangered Species Report 8, 29–33; Albuquerque: U.S. Fish and Wildlife Service, 1980).

Virginia Madison, "Pronghorn," excerpted from "Fur, Feather, and Fang" in *The Big Bend Country of Texas* (Albuquerque: University of New Mexico Press, 1955): 200–210.

Frederick Olmsted, "The Mustangs," excerpted from *A Journey through Texas, or, A Saddle Trip on the Southwestern Frontier* (NY: Dix Edwards Co., 1857): 443–445.

Eugene Manlove Rhodes, "Crossing to Safety," excerpted from *Bransford in Arcadia; or, The Little Eohippus* (1914; reprint, Norman: University of Oklahoma Press, 1975): 190.

Ralph A. Selle, "Opal Fields of Shimmering Blue," excerpted from *Texas Bluebonnets* (Houston: Carroll Printing Co., 1932): 18–30.

Walter Prescott Webb, "Wrecked Earth," excerpted from "The Big Bend of Texas" in *Panhandle Plains Historical Review* 10 (1937): 7–20.

A. Ray Williams, "The Golden Eagle" from *Monthly Bulletin of the Texas Game, Fish, and Oyster Commission* 5, no. 6 (1942).